The
Dreams *of*
Interpretation

The
Dreams *of*
Interpretation

A Century down
the Royal Road

Catherine Liu, John Mowitt,
Thomas Pepper, and Jakki Spicer, Editors

University of Minnesota Press
Minneapolis
London

CULTURAL CRITIQUE BOOKS
An occasional series of publications in association with the journal *Cultural Critique*,
edited by Keya Ganguly, John Mowitt, and Jochen Schulte-Sasse.
www.upress.umn.edu/journals/culturalcritique

Chapter 4 is a slightly revised version of pages 155–69 in Patricia Gherovici, *Hysteria in
the Barrio: Freud, Lacan, and the Puerto Rican Syndrome* (New York: Other Press, 2003);
reprinted with permission of Other Press. An earlier version of chapter 5 was published
as "On the Relatedness of Ethics to Masochism," in Avital Ronell, *Stupidity* (Champaign:
University of Illinois Press, 2001); copyright 2001 by Board of Trustees of the University of
Illinois; reprinted with permission of the University of Illinois Press. Chapter 18 was
previously published as Jonathan Kahana, "Cinema and the Ethics of Listening: Isaac
Julien's 'Frantz Fanon,'" *Film Quarterly* 59, no. 2 (2006): 19–31; copyright 2006 Regents of
the University of California; all rights reserved; reprinted by permission.

Published by the University of Minnesota Press
111 Third Avenue South, Suite 290
Minneapolis, MN 55401-2520
http://www.upress.umn.edu

Library of Congress Cataloging-in-Publication Data

The dreams of interpretation : a century down the royal road /
Catherine Liu . . . [et al.], editors.
    p. ; cm. — (Cultural Critique Books)
  Includes bibliographical references and index.
  ISBN: 978-0-8166-4799-6 (hc : alk. paper)
  ISBN-10: 0-8166-4799-2 (hc : alk. paper)
  ISBN: 978-0-8166-4800-9 (pb : alk. paper)
  ISBN-10: 0-8166-4800-X (pb : alk. paper)
    1. Freud, Sigmund, 1856–1939. Traumdeutung. 2. Dreams.
3. Psychoanalysis. I. Liu, Catherine. II. Series.
  [DNLM: 1. Freud, Sigmund, 1856–1939. Traumdeutung.
2. Dreams—ethics—Essays. 3. Dreams—psychology—Essays.
4. Freudian Theory—Essays. 5. Psychoanalysis—Essays. WM 460.5.D8
D77193 2007]
  BF1078.D75 2007
  154.6'3—dc22

                                    2007027908

We dedicate this book
to the memory of Mary Lydon, to whom
we wish to give the final word.

Contents

Editors' Note

References to James Strachey et al., eds., *The Standard Edition of the Complete Psychological Works of Sigmund Freud* (London: Hogarth Press, 1940–68), are given in the text by SE, followed by the volume (in Roman numerals) and the page (in Arabic numerals).

References to Sigmund Freud, *Gesammelte Werke,* edited by Marie Bonaparte et al. (London: Imago, 1941–53), and to its *Gesamtregister* (volume XVIII) and *Nachtragsband* (Frankfurt am Main: Fischer, 1968 and 1987), are given in the text by GW, followed by the volume (in Roman numerals) and page (in Arabic numerals).

Acknowledgments

For generous support of the conference from which this book stems, we extend our warmest thanks to the Frederick R. Weisman Art Museum, the Walker Art Center, Other Press, and Mohawk Paper Mills, Inc., as well as to the following University of Minnesota colleagues, departments, and programs: Tom Trow and the College of Liberal Arts Scholarly Events Fund; Jeanine Ferguson and the Office of Research and Development of the College of Liberal Arts, and Steven Rosenstone, its dean; Daniel Brewer and the Humanities Institute; Gerhard Weiss and the Center for Austrian Studies; Jack Zipes and the Center for German and European Studies; the Institute for Global Studies; Kate Porter, Richard Leppert, and the Department of Cultural Studies and Comparative Literature; and the departments of English, French and Italian, and Spanish and Portuguese.

Douglas Armato, director of the University of Minnesota Press, was the midwife of this book, working overtime.

To all those who attended the conference and made contributions, we give our warmest thanks. And to those whose contributions we are fortunate to have between these covers, our thanks are augmented by our gratitude for your patience.

Finally, we thank George Hoagland and Thomas Stubblefield, both of whom worked with great care in the preparation of this manuscript.

INTRODUCTION

"What Are You Doing Tonight?"

Catherine Liu, John Mowitt,
Thomas Pepper, and Jakki Spicer

Elephants and scholarly volumes with multiple editors are creatures of long gestation. In the case of the elephant, birth remembers what is hoped was a joyful moment of conception. In the case of this book, another joyful event is marked, also a birthday celebration: most of the contributions here were originally delivered at a conference, "The Dreams of Interpretation/*The Interpretation of Dreams,*" held at the Weisman Art Museum on the Twin Cities campus of the University of Minnesota in early October 2000 to commemorate the centennial of the date on the title page of Sigmund Freud's Dream Book. At the conference (as was the case with the bimillennial celebration, then in progress, of the birth of Christ, which marks one of the first milestones of an ever more imperious globalization), everyone present knew perfectly well that the party was a year off (this time late rather than early). In fact Freud had published his book in 1899, but had deliberately dated it with the following year to make it the inaugural volume of the new century.

Indeed, it is hard—because such a painful anamnesis—to remember the time before the millennial party of accurate date, marked as it is by other events of the months and years following our conference on Freud, itself an event conceived from the outset as an open, nondogmatic, international, and truly cosmopolitan encounter. We hope the essays presented here shall be received both as a rich archival document and as a theoretical intervention. The intellectual ferment of the conference belongs to the integrity and originality of its participants, and we hope that a good portion of the excitement of those few days in Minneapolis will be preserved here.

But by the work of afterwardsness, those of us who tried, with a different faith, to bring this event about (we ourselves started work on our own project for a new

Freudian century in July 1998) now see it as having come just before a different Fall. And thus it is even more important to remember the hopes around the preparations for a joyful event, which was not (to be) only a commemoration of Freud's Dream Book, but turned out, even more importantly, to be a congress at which different aspects of psychoanalytic experience and theory—some of them marginalized and occulted both in analytic practice, with its own institutional isolations, as well as in the symptomatic and often stereotyped receptions of psychoanalysis within the academy—instead were freely spoken of and debated. When both clinicians and academicians (as well as hybrids) began to accept our invitation to revisit an enriched Freudian adventure, we realized there was so much important work being done in so many different ways, fields, and places that there could and should be a forum in which people from all of these disciplines could come and work together.

Even more urgently we now know that Freud's less bloody head-birth has never been more necessary for the purpose of understanding, and with hope, working through the uncanny horrors of the psychopathology of our current globalized daily life and death, with its incessant skirmishes—and this despite so many proclamations of the death of psychoanalysis at the pregame show of this new millenium. Such proclamations, aiming as they do at a kind of magical wish fulfillment, are hardly accidental, nor are they the products of conspiracy—that complementary, ever-available American alternative. Rather what is at stake is the possibility of systemic and systematic causal thinking for the purpose of trying to understand the phenomena of mass destruction we are witnessing at what seems like an ever accelerated pace and with ever greater intensity. That the mainstream American press was, at the time of the celebration of the millenium, the venue for a vastly disproportionate number of obituaries of psychoanalysis is no accident.[1] Likewise, it is no accident that these same organs served gleefully (as the Paper of Record itself has acknowledged) as the emergency broadcasting system for the cries of *Terror!* heard from the hallucinated voices being relayed as though from everywhere, via the channels of projective identification—the mass-destruction media—and telling of the risks lurking out there, on the dark continents and archipelagos of the non-Christian world.[2] The ideology involved in both sets of proclamations—psychoanalysis's death, Terror!—is sutured of the same phantasm, and hangs together (returns to the same place) with an overwhelming structural necessity.

As the religions of Abraham fight it out in nationalisms and racisms competing for the distinction of descending to apparently unsoundable atavistic depths, in which the non(-Judeo-)Christian is evil and can be disposed of as naked life—Giorgio Agamben: that which can be merely killed without being sacrificed—who can(not) fail to see that it is Freud who warned us that it is not so easy to whitewash the Father, thus to make him all Good? That we and our civilization suffer from the idealization of the Father? Who else has tried to speak this unwelcome truth apparently still so difficult for those who would like so much to believe in their own impunity with regard to the Other and others? Each of the contributions brought together here attests, in its own manner, to the fact that psychoanalysis is essentially bound up with the problems of maintaining an ethical relationship to the work of interpretation and other action. This ethical stance is manifest in an attentiveness to alterity that would refrain from what Lacan calls "Samaritanism."

When, at the beginning of the end of the last (seventh, of course) chapter of Freud's book, the whole of which is so one-pointedly devoted to the prosecution of the thesis that the dream is the fulfillment of a wish, the author erects the riddling, hieroglyphic stele of the Dream of the Burning Child, it is, from a historical moment so deeply invested in whitening the Father, difficult not to read the wish of this Father's dream, in which his dead child comes (back) to him and says with reproach, "Father, don't you see that I'm burning?" as the Father's very own wish that the child burn, as the Father's desire to kill his reproachful child.

And while Freud himself does not advance this interpretation thematically, in any direct fashion, he has left the overdetermined traces there for us, his as yet undead children, to gather—that is: read—even by way of the interpretation he gives of the wish expressed in the dream at issue, namely, that the Father here wishes, once again, to see his child alive, and burning with the Father's desire.

Thus the assertion that the proclamations of terror and of the death of psychoanalysis are of the same piece has to do with what, in psychoanalysis, is called a structural regression, and an angry one at that: for what can now be seen is that the hallucinations of terror, and of a terror characterized by the unwelcome realization of *other monotheisms*, of other claims to worship another one-and-only god, are rooted in fantasies in which the need to believe in the All Good Father, and to have him at one's side, is so strong that it must reject any claim (1) that any other one-and-only Good Father might exist; (2) that he might exist by the side of someone else and somewhere else, far from me; and, (3) most important for us here, that there be any claim to a critical practice that might reveal the price we pay in clinging to all of the above, and that might work toward authentic liberations, ones leading to declarations of independence imposed neither by occupying forces, nor by violent and coercive conversions. Such emancipatory critique could be made on the grounds of having alternative mechanisms with which to deal with such violent, paranoid, aggressive projections by means other than religious, but rather mundane. This practice and these means are called by the name Psychoanalysis.

And isn't it even more of an insult to the captives and purveyors of the deadly fantasies presiding over the new world order that analysis, as though it were answering Kierkegaard's desperate attempt to speak to that single individual, not only takes place person by person, case by case, but even dares to denounce the dangerous pleasures of mass identifications, and, on top of this, demands much hard and painful work and—like the churches—tithing.

If, in the century in which Freud's own life began, it was still necessary to secure a stronghold in the divine, and Pascal's Wager thus had to be transformed, honed into the sharpest superegoic injunction imaginable—"believe!"—as the only apparent means to this end; if thus it was still apparently necessary to submit unconditionally to the Father *at every instant,* to remain standing awake all night to assure one's salvation—if this is the way the post-Copernican theologians would have it,[3] Freud, nonetheless, and luckily for us, offers a new turn, something quite different, in the necessity of thought and practice.

Taking the dream as the messenger of sleep, of the unconscious, Freud teaches: Put two people into a new and highly structured situation (at a regular time, and in a regular place, over a long period, since what they have to deal with knows no time, and dealing with it takes some time therefore), and let one who has him- or herself undergone a certain period of training in what thus has some roots in the Stoic, ascetic practice of listening Freud thus instaurated and made new (by having listened to others and to the other in himself for a long time) listen patiently to the other, to the one who comes so as to be heard, patiently, and then remark, at certain intervals, what is being said. What will come out of the secret of this encounter will be truth, overseen by the regulation of this new kind of relationship that Freud bequeathed to us, which is psychoanalysis.

As its motor this practice has no transcendent leap—no "believe!"—but something we can see all around us, entirely immanent, and which, in its properly channeled form, under the conditions already described, is called transference—really a name for a bold new conception of love and all its ruses. Resituated in the analytic chamber, transference, which exists everywhere in relations among subjects, but which Freud isolated and named for the first time, can be used to help live—to love and to work—better. And all of this works by virtue of its practice and its structure, and not by any belief in or intervention of the transcendent.

If one does this—if people do this, they will profit from a hard-won discovery of technique gleaned from years of experience and insight: the royal road to what is being said is to go over what comes not *when one is awake, but asleep.* And it is through this laborious process that one will come to the knowledge of one's desires, not only so as to live better oneself, but, if possible, to go unto the other and do more good than harm through the cultivation of this practice, in which that which is timeless touches upon, and is treated in, time. So grind your lenses well, so as to see into the night. What is offered here is the continuation of an unending education into human life and nothing miraculous. And like other parts of education, it should not be a rite, something rote, but rather a right, a human right: the right to psychoanalysis. A new, and fitting, *human right:* a fitting light for this night.

Happily, the contributions to this volume are heterogeneous in orientation, concern, style, tone, and subject. Far from any supermarket or consumerist imaginary desire for the inclusion of all positions, the lack of pretense to totality here manifests, rather, the robustness of thought concerning psychoanalysis in many domains and in and at their intersections. Rather than organizing the richness of these offerings according to any prefab schema of intellectual identities—psychoanalysis and politics, psychoanalysis and literature, psychoanalysis and philosophy, psychoanalysis and culture, psychoanalysis as practice, psychoanalysis and theory, psychoanalysis and psychoanalysis, etc.—instead we have made every effort to allow open constellations to emerge from the texts we present here. No doubt these essays could have been ordered differently. Our hope is that the way we present them, which was not preconceived prior to our rereading all the texts in view of the present publication, should enable both contributors and readers to see established problems in new constellations and to open new paths for further work.

RELATIONS WITH NEIGHBORS: ETHICS

If we begin the presentation with a remarkable set of contributions focusing on the ethical sphere, it has, perhaps, something to do with the fatigue—and untruth—of limiting the imagination and interpretive power of psychoanalysis to the family drama and to the atomized household, as well as with the urgency of thought about matters of globalization, neoliberalism, imperialism, colonialism, and violence that emerge (though not uniquely so, even within these covers) in these essays.

Gérard Pommier's "The Ethics of the Dreamer" is a polemical intervention in debates about ethics. Pommier proposes that ethics emerges from the unconscious, not from the social sphere. It is our capacity to dream, and our capacity to recognize that opaque space in the Other that corresponds to this capacity that allows us to establish our relationship with our fellow beings. Violence or aggressivity constitutes the traumatic encounter with the Other. Pommier argues that the place of violence has to be taken into account if we are to arrive at a full theoretical articulation of the difficulties of "being-together." This reevaluation of "Mitsein" allows for a radical reconsideration of basic elements of psychoanalytic theory, but also raises important issues in current debates around conceptions of community and collectivity.

Jean-Michel Rabaté's "In dreams begin responsibilities: Toward Dream Ethics" is an exploration of the radical disruption in intersubjectivity engendered by a confrontation with the unconscious. Dreaming is what we all share, yet dreams are almost impossible to exchange or transact. This essay makes explicit the ethical questions raised by both Jacques Lacan and Gérard Pommier with regard to "das Ding," and also underlines what is symptomatically omitted from Lacan's account of the Freudian concept of radical helplessness. In dreams, that helplessness and extreme egotism are activated by the lifting of censorship. In his surprising conclusion, Rabaté reads Ayn Rand's philosophy of radical selfishness as a hysterical demand for a pure capitalism that actually reveals the failure of the Master's discourse. Rabaté suggests that a properly psychoanalytic ethics would entail an overturning of Platonism, especially in the image of the "good" that is supposed to govern our idealized relations with the unbearableness of the neighbor.

Situating his wide-ranging essay within the concerns of clinical practice, Willy Apollon coaxes his reading of *The Interpretation of Dreams* toward the provocative formulation, "the dream is interpretation," thus capturing in one stroke the broad theoretical and practical concerns of the texts assembled here. Arguing that the dream, as understood by Freud, though accessible to philosophy, religion, and neuroscience in fact designates an object that radically eludes the paradigms that prevail within these fields, in "The Dream in the Wake of the Freudian Rupture," Apollon tries to render palpable the clinical challenge posed by the dream. Implicitly recognizing the rhetorical link forged by Freud between transference and the dream-work, Apollon uses the former to think the specific space occupied by the radical hermeneutical object of the dream. In doing so, he offers us a new way to think about the utopian character of clinical practice, now situated in a world in which the human itself hangs in the balance.

Patricia Gherovici's "Freud's Dream of America" is powerfully original in its approach to two distinct theoretical operations: first in its reinterpretation of one of Freud's dreams in the context of the Spanish-American War, and second in forging a relationship between *The Interpretation of Dreams* and symptomatic traces of Freud's highly mediated encounter with the imperial ambitions of the United States. In so doing, Gherovici prompts us to reconsider the relationship between the individual and the social, and political conditions that overdetermine subjectivity's fantasies. Gherovici amplifies the background noise of Spanish-Austrian affinities marking Freud's "Breakfast Ship Dream." Here Freud's dream appears resituated in the context of the confused coverage in the Austrian newspapers of the explosion and sinking of the *USS Maine* in the harbor of La Habana in 1898. Gherovici's rigorous reading of both Freud's writing and Freud's self-analysis draws upon a Lacanian theorization of "knot" and "thing" that allows for a revitalization of interpretation along the lines of linguistic materializations.

Avital Ronell's "Literature and Pathology: Masochism Takes the Upper Hand" centers its discussion of ethics in the encounter between Freud's own text and that of the novelist Fyodor Dostoevsky, whose life and works provide Freud and Ronell with an intricate network within which to situate not only the relations between the thinking of ethics in its relation to that of masochism in Freud's own theorizations, but also with an original and sustained meditation on the relations between these and the fraught matters of literary indebtedness and intertextuality as these manifest themselves in Dostoevsky's appropriations of Gogol and Flaubert. Unbound by the pieties of the psychodynamics of a national canon and its purportedly linear unfurling of anxieties of influence, Ronell, through her comparative account, also de-aestheticizes the discussion of literature by showing how characters and their authors function in an elaborate economy of symptoms, nosographic and nosological pictures, family romances, and aesthetic ideals, and thus she sets the stage for a sophisticated theorization of the relations of life and art.

FAMILY, FRIENDS, AND OTHER RELATIONS

In Laurence Rickels's "Sounds of Satan," the Demonic in Freudian psychoanalysis is analyzed as having something to do with the Father in his various guises. But more specifically, it turns out that in the dream-work the presence of the Devil is often associated with both philosophy and music. Rickels points out that the Devil's indestructibility lines up neatly with the ego's sense of its own immortality, and that the freedom of the Devil's "conscience-free" condition resembles the sociopathy of dream representations. Taking us through readings of *Faust, Don Juan,* and Arthur C. Clarke's science fiction to the autobiography of Aleister Crowley, Rickels demonstrates that the Devil works overtime—within psychoanalysis as a representation of the paternal function, and in resistance to psychoanalysis as that which lies on the borderline between neurosis and psychosis. In short, the Devil is evoked as an insurance policy against both death and lack.

Silke-Maria Weineck's "Heteros Autos: Freud's Fatherhood" is merciless in its unwillingness to cede to the apparently overwhelming desire, not only within psychoanalysis but in its reception and in culture and cultural studies at large, to tell the story of the father-son relationship solely from the point of view of the son. Moving beyond unreflective and prepackaged clichés according to which the son is always cast into the starring role of the Oedipal drama, Weineck not only reexamines the implications of her reconsiderations for the classical theory of tragedy, inasmuch as Aristotle, in his *Poetics,* is one of Sophocles' first readers, but, more important for her work here, of how Aristotle's own considerations of the family drama extend into both his *Nichomachean Ethics* and into his lesser-read *Eudemian Ethics.*

Elke Siegel's "'Non Vixit': Friends Survived" is a detailed revisiting of the Freud-Fliess relationship. Siegel's analysis is based on the question of this tortured friendship, which served in many ways as the midwife to Freud's *Interpretation of Dreams.* The symptomatic interest following upon the publication of Jeffrey Masson's edition of the complete Freud-Fliess correspondence, as well as Masson's later broadside, *The Assault on Truth,* has further spurred theorists, historians, and clinicians of psychoanalysis to contemplate the relationship between Freud and Fliess, as it is played out in their letters, as Siegel does, with greater rigor and neutrality. Siegel offers a constellation of concepts by which we can understand Freud's "friend": encrypted in this figure is the radical Other, the Brother, the Cousin, as well as the specter or "revenant."

OTHER DESIRES

Paul Verhaeghe's "The Dream between Drive and Desire: A Question of Representability" argues, based on the author's clinical experience, that we can no longer take literally or uncritically the statement that all dreams are deformed or distorted expressions of "wish fulfillment." The conditions of repression have changed, and Verhaeghe challenges us to rethink the dream in relationship to drive, desire, and representation. According to Verhaeghe, the dream-work must be interpreted with the Other in mind, that is with the fantasy of the Other's desire as a linchpin on which the transferential relation depends. Our dream life is a product of a demand for representation: in fact, Verhaeghe argues, desire and representation are synonymous. Interpretation is a process by which the drive's demand is rearticulated or analyzed. Verhaeghe emphasizes the nonphenomenal character of the unconscious and of fantasy in relationship to the idea of the network of signifiers as advanced by Jacques Lacan in the light of Saussurean linguistics. The easing of repression and/or the strengthening of the ego are not the therapeutic ends of analysis.

Through her clinical experience, Judith Feher-Gurewich considers differences between "French" and "American" psychoanalysis—not as walls that cannot be breached, but as symptomatically rich sites for further analysis. (French) Lacanians tend to treat borderline symptoms in patients as masks for the classical structures of desire: hysteric, phobic, obsessional or perverse; and American psychoanalyists often assert that social change produces these new psychic positions, thus requiring revision of the Oedipus complex. Feher-Gurewich claims that these "new maladies of the ego" actually shed light on the clinical relevance of Lacan's extraordinary statement that woman is "not-all." Considering one of her own cases, Feher-Gurewich realizes that the "not-all" can neither sustain the Oedipal fantasy that produces desire, nor the fantasy that masks the absurdity of the social order. This patient has learned too early that the Father/Law does not possess the phallus, and that the Other is ultimately powerless, and, in fact, does not exist. However, the "not-all" turns this revelation in on herself, believing that it is she who does not exist, and that it is not that the social order is absurd, but simply that she does not have access to an understanding of it. Through this analysis, Feher-Gurewich reaches a new insight regarding borderline symptomatology that a strict adherence to either Lacan's theories or to ego psychology will elide. Such symptoms tell the truth of psychoanalysis: The other does not exist. The task of the clinician, then, is to show the "not-all" that this is the condition of the Other—not of herself.

A practicing analyst, Claire Nahon asks us to return to Freud's insistence on the *Bild* of dreams—the image in its relation to condensation, regression, autoeroticism—indeed, to the unconscious itself. The ever more common failure to attend to this aspect of psychic life, exacerbated by ego psychology, has led to diagnoses of narcissism or borderline personalities in patients who cannot be reduced to these categories. Nahon insists on returning to the complexities of the image, and of the imaginary, as sites of the ego's emergence; only by doing so can the analyst hope to see the unconscious meaning of sexuality and its images. This is particularly apparent in the transsexual, who, in casting out the unconscious from the enclosed space of the psyche, and embodying it in the flesh itself, unsettles an understanding of sexual difference in terms of polarity. Sexuality should, instead, be understood through the unlimited plasticity of the unconscious. By returning our attention to the image, we can understand the transsexual's uncanniness as containing the potential for "the emancipatory and transgressive potentialities of unconscious sexuality."

FOCUSES ON THE APPARATUS

In "Closing and Opening of the Dream: Must Chapter VII Be Rewritten?" Jean Laplanche, one of the foremost thinkers and writers in the history of psychoanalysis to date, opens our eyes to the importance of a footnote added to a later edition of *The Interpretation of Dreams*, in which Freud forces this most attentive reader of the Freudian text to a major "aha" experience concerning the famous and persistent model of the psychic apparatus, the apparatus of the soul that punctuates Freud's writing (as well as that of many of his most important commentators, from Walter Benjamin to Jacques Lacan and Jacques Derrida) at least from the 1895 *Project for Scientific Psychology* to the 1925 "Note on the 'Mystic Writing Pad.'" In his added note to the Dream Book in 1919 (SE V, 541), Freud tells us that his famous linear or optical diagram presents his model of a series of plates as unfurled or *unrolled.* Pursuing this major clue as no one has before, Laplanche explores its implications for the—only apparently—separate matters of what the dream communicates, on the one hand, and the matter of the origins of sexual desire, on the other.

In "Dreaming and Cinematographic Consciousness," Laura Marcus notes that, despite employing metaphors of other visual apparatuses, such as photography, in illustrating psychoanalytic principles, Freud's writings are virtually silent on the topic of cinema. She suggests that this indicates not psychoanalysis's indifference to film, but rather the fundamental connection between the two. Indeed, this connection is foundational not only in the similarities in their apparatus—projection, the screen, and so forth—but also in that both psychoanalysis and the cinema attend to the transitional stages of the psyche—the borderlines between waking and dreaming, past and present, absence and presence.

In "A Knock Made for the Eye: Image and Awakening in Deleuze and Freud," Yün Peng takes an important step in redrawing the intellectual-historical map of the allegiances and alignments of the last century. Whereas many French and American intellectuals have inherited the superegoic shibboleths of a split between Gilles Deleuze on the one hand and Freud and Lacan on the other, Peng's nonpolemical, patient, and lucid articulation of the concept of the crystal image in Deleuze's cinema books (among his last) and of the account of the dream image that Freud offers in *The Interpretation of Dreams* is exemplary in its return to what these authors actually said, as opposed to the obeisance to the *Verbot* according to which these authors (and, by Peng's extension, Foucault as well) are not to be mentioned together. Peng's essay reveals such splits to have been constructed in the imaginary representations on the part of these thinkers' followers. As a model of attention to what has been said rather than what has been imagined to have been said, this essay should serve as a model for thoughtful intellectual endeavor and as a testimony to the important difference between the student of thought and the disciple of a master.

MATTERS OF INTENSITY

In his lapidary "Insomnia," Pablo Kovalovsky delves into the processes at that most labile site of thought, the boundary between wakefulness and sleep. Drawing on the post-Freudian developments of Otto Isakower and the moment of "subjective destitution" experienced when *falling* into sleep, as well as on Bertram Lewin's later meditations on the dream-screen in relation to the infant at the mother's breast, Kovalovsky's night thoughts reveal the work of an original thinker, one capable of taking what is most useful and important from many strands—Freud, Isakower, Klein, Lacan, Lewin—in the fabric of psychoanalytic thought in order to further weave a subtle and profound dialectic shuttling between Freud's formulation of the dream as the guardian of sleep on the one hand and the way in which the dream can also serve as a protection *from* sleep.

In "Strange Intelligibility: Clarity and Vivacity in Dream Language," Rei Terada departs from a probing consideration of the troubled distinction drawn between vivacity (*Lebhaftigkeit*) and clarity in *The Interpretation of Dreams*, thus reopening the question of language in psychoanalysis. Through a reexamination of several of the germinal dreams in Freud's text (the Irma Dream, the *non vixit* Dream, and others), Terada shows that the instability of the hermeneutical status of vivacity indeed underscores or displaces meaning, prompting us to become more attentive to some of Freud's more speculative formulations concerning the relation between language and thought. This deft essay culminates in a vivid discussion of the consequences for the theory of interpretation (whether analytic or not) of the notion that thought selects and combines "concentrates" of unthinking stored in language. Thus this contribution is a remarkable examination of what is at stake in the dream of interpretation in the wake of the Freudian breakthrough.

INTERPRETATIVE ARTS

Probably best known for his resourceful complications of the encounter between psychoanalysis and the cinema written during the 1970s, Raymond Bellour here presents "The *Marnie* Color," a pointedly focused reading of Hitchcock's film, in which the appearances of red are tracked down on screen. Typically associated with the staging of the return of the repressed—Marnie's frigidity inducing the killing of one of her mother's tricks—this red here is read by Bellour as involving something more formal, more figurative. Specifically, by comparing this film to *Spellbound*—where the psychoanalytic relation itself is put on display in an almost parodic mode—Bellour shows that the Marnie color bleeds over and into another repressed, that of the film work itself. Here again psychoanalysis encounters the cinema—not at the site of the symbol, but at the point where sight itself is overcome by that which focuses its attention.

Jonathan Kahana's "'Other Languages': Testimony, Transference, and Translation in Documentary Film" rethinks the use of psychoanalytic theory in film theory through an attention to aurality, specifically in reference to the analytic scene itself, the documentary interview, and utterances coerced under torture. Kahana examines instances of the interruption of documentary cinema's "magical" or "faith-based" relation to reality. Focusing primarily on Isaac Julien's film, *Fanon,* Kahana demonstrates that documentary cinema can, through such interruptions and interventions, recall us to the difficulty and importance of listening.

Andrew McNamara's "Wondrous Objectivity: Art History, Freud, and Detection" is a theoretical archaeology of art-historical methodology. Here McNamara offers an account of the struggle between art history's allegiance to empiricism and the ambivalence of its investments in critical inquiry and theory. In his compelling theorization of apprehension and singularity, McNamara "interprets" art history's symptomatic relationship to the detail. Citing Yves-Alain Bois's imperative to reconstitute as densely as possible the material conditions of the artwork's production, McNamara argues that Freud's reconceptualization of interpretation sheds light on various and often contradictory art-historical attempts to apprehend the artwork. It is in this context that McNamara, following upon Carlo Ginzburg's seminal essay on Freud and Morelli, turns to a reading of the detective novel and suggests provocatively that the apprehension of an art object and the fictional solving of a crime perform the work of framing fantasy.

Thoughtful Articulations

Just when you thought it was safe to forget the dream of a Marxo-Freudian synthesis, along comes A. Kiarina Kordela's "Marx, Condensed and Displaced." Her articulation of the power of surplus reveals it to be the notion upon which the logics of capital, sign, and subject themselves must be thought. In each case, Kordela triumphantly shows how the tendency of the binary oppositions—use and exchange value, metaphor and metonymy, etc.—organizing these discourses is the effect of an enabling surplus that, in exceeding such binaries, grounds them in the real of capital. Like Žižek, who discovers resources for Marxism in Lacan, Kordela reads the latter's mediations on surplus enjoyment in Seminar XVII as the means by which to radicalize psychoanalytic hermeneutics.

Karyn Ball's "The Substance of Psychic Life" freights its short title with much portent. Specifically Ball broaches a thorough reconsideration of what substance might mean in the psychic register, while also tracking Freud's rhetorical investment in substance as the means by which to think the psychoanalytical concept of the psyche itself. Following the first reception of Jean Laplanche's reinvigoration of the concept of sexuality, or more specifically the instinct supporting the *Geschlectstriebe*, Ball shows how substance provides Freud with a way to ground distinctions fundamental to psychoanalysis—distinctions such as life and death, inside and outside, space and time, and even memory and perception. Reluctant to simply "textualize" substance, Ball draws out the way this concept is converted into place names where biology and chemistry refuse to tread—for example, the mnemic traces that sustain and reiterate trauma. Perhaps most provocatively of all, Ball's engagement with both Kant and the Freud of *Beyond the Pleasure Principle* establishes the vexing way in which death and substance converge to radically scandalize all vitalisms.

Klaus Theweleit's "Young Mr. Freud; or, On the Becoming of an Artist: Freud's Various Paths to the Dream Book 1882–99" is an unorthodox montage and commentary on the trials and errors along the way to the birth of psychoanalysis. Mobilizing Freud's relationships (and the correspondences in which they were furthered) with Breuer, Martha Bernays, and Fliess, as well as alliances and conflicts (Charcot, Meynert, and so on), Theweleit tracks the vicissitudes of Freud's search for a monument and the inscription thereupon, a search coextensive with the very invention of psychoanalysis itself as a new mode of human relationship. In a powerfully suggestive turn, this essay moves from the marble tablet upon which Freud, writing to Fliess in 1895, imagines the memorial to his discovery of the secret of dreams, to the inscription upon the compact disc and bodies dancing to its music as not merely a figure by which to interpret the transference and the memories reactivated within it. Thus Theweleit himself invents and names the *third body* as that in which analysands and analysts, dancers, correspondents, and lovers share in their different enactments of transference.

The text that concludes the volume, Mary Lydon's "Such Stuff as Dreams Are Made Of: Life and Literature," is preceded by an introduction in which its location and status are addressed at some length. Professor Lydon died months after delivering this paper at the University of Minnesota at the Dreams of Interpretation conference. We felt that its function as an inaugurating discourse was best preserved by making it the closing piece of the edited volume. This article is exemplary of her expansive intellect, and of her unique ability to encompass the ethics and poetics of the dream in her thinking. Professor Lydon, through a consideration of the enigma posed by Beckett's dreamless character in *Waiting for Godot*, confronted the problem posed by the almost impossible communication of dreams. Mary Lydon sought to inaugurate the event of the conference by recalling for us the challenge placed before both literature and psychoanalysis by the "French Freud." We pay tribute to her here in our attempt to meet that challenge as she so beautifully articulated it.

NOTES

1. See the first section of Michel Foucault's essay on Maurice Blanchot, "La Pensée du dehors," now in Foucault, *Dits et Ecrits* I (Paris: Gallimard, 1996).

2. One remembers a millenial issue of *Newsweek* here (although, since we are talking about chatter, *fama,* what everybody says and knows, it really doesn't matter, since the voice is the voice of no one in particular) in which Freud was actually killed twice.

3. At least ever since Pascal's "Mystery of Jesus," a text so dear to him he had it sewn into his cloak over his heart, and part of which reads: "Jesus will be in agony until the end of the world. One must not sleep during that time."

RELATIONS *with* NEIGHBORS: ETHICS

1. The Ethics of the Dreamer

Gérard Pommier

Initially it may seem strange to suggest that dreams contain ethical standards, as they often stage violence, murder, and perverse situations. To move beyond this apparent contradiction it is necessary to make the distinction between ethics and morals. Samurai warriors, gangsters, and politicians all possess ethical ideals dictating their codes of conduct. Both the gangster and the Samurai have codes of conduct based on the ethical standards of the groups with which these figures are affiliated. (In the case of politicians, this affirmation is less certain.) For example, a Samurai who chooses to commit *Hara Kiri* does so in accordance with the standards and in the established tradition of the Samurai (*haga kuré*). Prostitutes also have ethical standards: for example, no money, no sex. Thus ethics implies only acting in accordance with the underlying identifications of a chosen group.

As can be inferred from the examples I have chosen, the goals held by any given group are not necessarily moral. I do not wish, however, to set the solitary nature of ethics against the collective nature of morals. What interests me more is to show that the ethics of unconscious desire imposes moral consequences, ones to which the ethics of such desire is not opposed. The ethical subject stems from what is impossible in his desire, namely all the monstrous things that appear in its dreams.

Here I shall attempt to demonstrate the manner in which dreams, as essential manifestations of the unconscious, are the only ethical foundation for subjectivity. In Spinoza's treatise, somewhat ironically entitled *Ethics*, the author sees no foundation for ethics other than the threat of the police, since, for Spinoza, each subject is guided by the search for what is pleasurable. And this search for what is pleasurable is limited only by society's higher interests, which curb the respective appetites of all individuals—hence the necessity of the police. Common interest has a coercive function in respect to each person's individual(istic) desires.

The theoretical position I advance here is, to some extent, diametrically opposed to the vision proposed by Spinoza, since the point I shall develop is that ethics is based solely on the unconscious and is independent of all external coercion. I shall assert that the unconscious is the only ethical foundation of all human activity. First I must point out an interesting problem of translation from French into English: in French there is a major distinction between "bon" and "bien," both of which can be translated in English as "good." "Good" can mean at once "good enough to eat" or "good," "right," in the ethical sense. Therefore I shall translate "bien"—in the ethical sense—as "right." Thus we may distinguish between "Right and Evil," on the one hand, and "good and bad" on the other. What I want to emphasize here is that from the point of view of the good—the fulfillment of needs, or the satisfaction of pleasure—man cannot be distinguished from animals, which have no sense of right or evil. Spinoza, too, knows this. Animals do not have an unconscious, and therefore they have no ethical conduct.

Is there any other criterion of Ethics? Science, for example? Science, or general knowledge, does not generate any sort of ethical criterion. The only criterion for science is to distinguish between precision and inaccuracy—and this has no relation whatsoever to the notions of right and evil. Furthermore, science does not even take into consideration the evil it can generate itself! By this I mean simply the evil of bad consequences, such as weapons, atomic bombs, ecological disasters, and so on. Rather I point to the evil of the destruction of ethics itself. For if everything is determined, then there is no more question of being able to choose between right and evil. What tyranny could be more stifling than that of a universal knowledge, which would prescribe conduct in all circumstances?! One can calculate the velocity with which an object falls, the temperature of the sun, or the movement of the planets. But if I consider myself, am I, too, an astral body, the trajectory of which can thus be predicted? At any rate, for myself I am not such an object. I am incapable of precise foresight regarding what I shall do next. It is possible to predict the ever-changing course of winds and clouds, but no one can predict what I shall dream tonight. Even considered in the light of all the dreams that have been created since the origins of sleep, my next dream will still be the first of its kind.

The meanings of "right" and "evil" stem from a common root: Oedipal guilt, which has conveyed a sense of fault. In consequence, for every subject repression and the unconscious have set the foundations for ethical standards. In showing us the "evil" of desire, our dreams teach us the ethics of what is considered right. Thus, to support this postulate or hypothesis of the ethics of the dreamer, I wish to put forth two arguments. The first is that it is upon the foundations of unconscious feelings of guilt that the notions of "right" and "evil" are built. The second is that it is the overdetermined nature of causality, such as it is manifested in dreams—and which must be distinguished from the sufficient reason of scientifico-mathematic reasoning and of physical-material determination—which is the guarantee of the individual's freedom, as well as his ethical standards.

There is an essential difference between what can be determined scientifically according to mathematical or physical-material reasoning on the one hand, and that which is overdetermined on the other. Determination objectifies, while overdetermination—while it does not deny determination—takes account of subjectivity.

To criticize science is a well-trodden path for religious, philosophical, literary, and even psychoanalytic thinkers. Musil, for example, in chapter 72 of *The Man without Qualities*, writes: "[T]he science that smiles into its beard, or first full-dressed encounter with evil."[1] Musil goes on to say that the scientist's ideology resembles that of "merchants, highwaymen, and warriors." Science would have no other goal than to disparage what people value most, for example in "Regarding goodness as only a form of egoism . . . asserting that man is eight or nine tenths water; explaining the characters' celebrated moral freedom as an automatically evolved philosophical appendix of free trade" (361).

How can we understand what Musil calls the inclination for evil? The very example he provides shows that evil diminishes mankind by reducing humans to being the products of a determinism that can only diminish them. That man consists of 90 percent water, or that love is a matter of hormonal or endocrine reactions, and so on—this is the attempt to reduce oneself to a series of causally determined phenomena. This inclination toward evil, here attributed to science, is in fact an inclination for incest: to be the object of the other, that is what makes for the pleasure of science.

Yet, what the dreamer encounters in his sleep are not the products of such determinism, but the products of overdetermination. Overdetermination is what is to be found in the condensations of any dream figure; as such, images refer to a portion of diurnal events added to childhood memories, readings, theoretical knowledge, and so on. Overdetermination is the end result of a super-addition of causal chains contained in any dream image. Nevertheless, this overdetermination, which thus goes against the determinisms of the Other and of science, cannot be understood as merely an accumulation of possible causes all leading to a similar outcome. On the contrary, overdetermination must be taken as the juncture of contradictory determinants. For example, consider a subject who simultaneously loves and hates his father. At the same time, he both desires and has the fantasy of having been raped. The psychoanalytic meaning of overdetermination could be said to consist in the contradictions among determinants. And it is this inevitable situation of such contradictions that demands of each individual that he or she make his or her own choices. Consequently, the subject is thus confronted with its own freedom to choose, regardless of whether it likes this freedom (or not), and this leads the subject to determine the ethical standpoint it wishes to endorse.

Presently I shall attempt to describe how such an ethics is to be realized, thanks to the powerful link that exists between the capacity for dreaming and the ability to recognize the other as distinct from oneself. This hypothesis can be tied together with neurophysiological conclusions about the importance of dream activity, and with the fact that newborns spend a third of their time dreaming.

Whence comes the need to dream? In his *Project for a Scientific Psychology*, Freud describes the moment at which the infant, in distress, is confronted with the complex of the fellow person, with the presence of the nearest person—the *Nebenmensch*—in its alterity, which is both comforting and a source of anxiety. This closest person is divided into a comprehensible part on the one hand, and an incomprehensible one on the other: "Thus the complex of the *Nebenmensch* divides itself into two segments, one of which is imposed by a constant apparatus, which remains together as a cohesive entity as Thing [*als Ding*]" (SE I, 331). The mother is this Other, but in the *Project* Freud elevates this other to the title of *Nebenmensch:* a divisible fellow being, both a familiar one and a complete stranger. The unknown—the Thing—reappears each time someone meets someone else. When speaking or listening, one is divided between oneself and the Thing, between the Thing considered as familiar and as what remains unknown and provokes anxiety. The subject itself becomes divided at the very moment this division of the Thing occurs: the formation of the subject is simultaneously the instant at which the subject is exiled from the loved object, which remains unknown. *Das Ding*—the Thing—is divided as a result of its own disarrayed existence, and is unveiled by the presence of the other. The birth of the subject is also its exile from what it loves and does not understand.

The subject and its fellow being come into existence at the same moment. But the relationship with the other is determined by what is thus an absolutely impossible love.

As narcissism is inevitable, this is a love that is always already there, and always already lost. It is a love invested at all times by the death drive, and it is the division of the *Nebenmensch*, which is itself enacted by this love limited by its opposite. This division concerns no one in particular, and every individual at once in his or her relationship with the Thing. And this relationship with the Thing is the relationship of every subject—to the extent that every subject is divided between itself and the Thing—with what remains known and what remains unknown about the Thing. It is this unknown aspect and its insistence that forces us to dream. And this means there is a constant link between our fellow beings and the formation of dreams. We always dream for someone or about someone, because our fellow human being has always been the source of our dreams. Thus children dream intensely so as to perceive, through hallucination, the solution to the problem represented by their fellow beings, *Nebenmenschen*.

Dreaming is necessary because the unknown is pushing, and the unfathomable must be conjured in a dream. But dreaming, then, becomes an aspect of the unfathomable. This is what Freud calls "the navel of the dream." In *The Interpretation of Dreams* he refers to it on two occasions: first in the course of the analysis of the Dream of Irma's Injection, where he points out, in a footnote, that there exists a point in the dream where interpretation can go no further, that the thoughts in the dream express everything there is to be said and to which there is nothing to be added. The dream is incapable of further solution. It comes to a standstill, Freud adds, at a point that is "impossible to recognize [*unerkannt*]." The term appears a second time in chapter 7, in the section on "Forgetting in Dreams":

> There is often a passage in even the most thoroughly interpreted dream which has to be left obscure; this is because we become aware during the work of interpretation that at that point there is a tangle of dream-thoughts which cannot be unraveled and which moreover adds nothing to our knowledge of the content of the dream. This is the dream's navel, the spot where it reaches down into the unknown. (SE V, 525)

First the divergence occurs between the thoughts that run in all directions into the net-like entanglement of our intellectual world, and then second is the unfathomable representation. And in this "navel of the dream" we encounter exactly the same invariants as in the division we saw in the case of the Thing: thus what we find here is the division between, on the one hand, the opaque and incomprehensible body as a source of pleasure, and, on the other, signifiers. It is clear that the unknowable, the *unerkannt*, is by no means a representation evading perception. On the contrary, it is entirely perceived as real while simultaneously being completely recalcitrant to thought. This resistance itself thus creates thought, which in turn seeks to interpret this unknown, impossible thought.

Nightmares provide the best example of this division revealed by the navel of the dream. Usually it is said that nightmares constitute an objection to Freud, who would explain dreams as the realization of a wish. But in fact, the nightmare poses no objection, because any desire, taken to its ultimate conclusion, realizes the desire of the Other, and thus every dream is a latent nightmare. Realized desire becomes a nightmare, and this is the only explanation for the disguise adopted by dream images. Indeed, why does representation exist within the dream itself? It is precisely because the dream already disguises the realization of desire—and this despite the fact that it is pushing for the realization of that same desire. It is because all dreams move toward the realization of a destructive desire that they are repressed. All dreams are repressed, and the representations of the dream contain within themselves a duality that renders them incomprehensible. The most opaque moment of the presentation of this duality is the navel of the dream. Every dream is thus the realization of desire, and, simultaneously, the repression of that desire.

When the dreamer begins to dream, perhaps he wanted to sleep, to be reduced to nothing: he wanted to disappear in his sleep. But this "nothing" is, in fact, something. This nothing is his link with the Thing. And so, when he is sleeping, he is obliged to dream that he is sleeping. His desire is to fall into himself as grounded in the Thing (according to the ambivalence of the latin *res*, which gives both "nothing" and "something" in the French *rien*).

Dreams dissimulate: they seek not to understand that point at which, if desire were to realize itself, the subject would disappear. This is the first trauma, which every subject seeks to conceal by means of creating a story. The dream's primary hallucination is a negative machine, which the subject uses to invent stories and to experience them in order to create his own history. The story is written so as to create dreams, which themselves are a form of concealing the dissimulation of this hallucination.

Now it is possible to see the train of thought I have tried to sketch: we are obliged to dream because of the difficulty raised by our encounter with a fellow being. Each fellow being we encounter reproduces the division of the Thing, and this encounter is equivalent to the navel of the dream, at which point the dream thoughts are divided off from the unknown. Each fellow being first occupies the place of the unknown at precisely this point of divergence of the Thing between the known and the unknown, which is itself analogous to the navel of the dream. The first encounter between the individual and language—in other words, a traumatic demand—constitutes the primary trauma, whence there emerges something hallucinatory, which dreams attempt to conceal.

The encounter with the unknown is the first representation of the trauma, which corresponds to the primordial fantasy: "a child is being beaten." "A child is being beaten" may be linked to the original trauma, and behind this fantasy can be heard the scream of the primary experience of disarray during the first encounter with the fellow person. The primordial or fundamental fantasies cover over the first trauma— that between the subject and language—which puts all other traumas (sexual trauma, the primal experience, seduction) into perspective. The subject's existence develops in stages according to the series of traumas that cover this primary trauma, which itself, however, is timeless and is repeated whenever one person addresses another.

In a sense, there exists a continuity between the first shout of the newborn and, if you will, the cry of orgasm. In a sense, this cry is itself the underlying stratum of life, a silent cry that accompanies the individual and is repressed at all times.

I hope I have been clear regarding the position of the navel, which is first occupied by one's fellow being, and which itself exists at a point identical to that of the navel of the dream as presented by Freud. This corresponds to the division of the *Nebenmensch* in the *Project for a Scientific Psychology,* between that part that depends on the signifier—the formations of the unconscious—and the unfathomable part represented by the presence of the fellow person. I have shown this path leading from the presence of the fellow man to the need to dream. But I would still like to demonstrate that the link existing between the dream and the fellow person leads to ethical injunctions.

We have seen that the division of the *Nebenmensch* in return divides the individual himself. In a sense, this is a kind of mutual recognition, but in this very act of recognition, the unknown part is violently rejected. It is rejected not only because it is not understood, but because it is threatening. There is a violence that goes hand in hand with the recognition of one's fellow being, a violence that inhabits our relationship with him, and that implies an aggressiveness toward him—indeed toward his very elimination—as soon as he is recognized as such. And this is the source from which ethics comes to emerge.

This is clear if we recall the development of the super-ego. Freud seeks to explain this development at the end of *Civilization and Its Discontents*. He begins by showing that the super-ego emerges as a consequence of aggressiveness, from an urge to destroy one's fellow being. In the previous chapter he criticizes the biblical injunction to love one's neighbor as oneself. He wonders how this commandment came into being when the narcissistic relationship with our fellow being urges us, on the contrary, toward destroying him, exploiting him, or abusing him sexually. And it is easy to understand that "love thy neighbor as thyself" results from an inversion, from the will to destruction, after the repression of the drive. According to an ordinary process of repression, the ideology of our culture reveals this relationship at the level of the drive in the relationship with our fellow person.

But as the other is also a fellow human being, we now understand how the super-ego develops to prevent the realization of this urge. If the subject were to give way to his narcissistic aggressiveness, he himself would disappear along with what he attacks—given that his fellow man is, in fact, himself! This is why he invents the authority that forbids this aggression. Regarding this Freud writes:

> A considerable amount of aggressiveness must be developed in the child against the authority which prevents him from having his first, but none the less his most important satisfactions, whatever the kind of instinctual deprivation that is demanded of him may be; but he is obliged to renounce the satisfaction of this revengeful aggressiveness. He finds his way out of this economically difficult situation with the help of familiar mechanisms. By means of identification he takes the unattackable authority into himself. The authority now turns into his super-ego and enters into possession of all the aggressiveness which a child would have liked to exercise against it. (SE XXI, 129)

Thus the situation has been reversed, stood on its head, to the extent that the super-ego now plays an aggressive role toward the ego: "The relationship between the super-ego and the ego is a return, distorted by a wish, of the real relationships between the ego, as yet undivided, and an external object" (SE XXI, 129).

But we are now faced with a new problem, a contradiction even: Freud had already considered another genesis for the super-ego as deriving from the Oedipus complex following an introjection of the father's characteristics. It is easy to understand that incorporation can follow aggression against the father. Indeed, identification will follow the thought of murder, since the underlying motive is to take the father's place at the mother's side. The patricidal son identifies himself in the very act of killing, since he fantasizes for this very purpose! He internalizes the persona, but at the same time he internalizes the taboo he himself has just overstepped. This is not a very economical process! Desire is structured by the taboo with this strange yet efficient characteristic of human sexuality. Thus the "inheritance" of this identification with the father obtains the contrary of the wish: it prolongs the harshness of the desire and ensures the sustainability of the super-ego.

The death drive is the common denominator of these two super-egos, and it can move from the fellow being, the brother (the first super-ego, as I have elaborated it above) to the father (the second): when violence against the fellow being is translated into aggression toward the father, this represents a considerable economy, since the fantasy of "killing the father" has never resulted in anyone's death (it only obliges one to arduous religious rituals). And the symbolic father suffers even less, since he is always already dead. The first super-ego is solitary, ethical, while the second is moral and social.

In the progressive series of transformations beginning with the birth of the dream in the subject's relation to the *Nebenmensch,* the division of the two super-egos is equivalent to the division of the Thing between the known and the unknown. As ethical consciousness, this division explains the contradictions of the dream. Thus the relationship with the *Nebenmensch,* with the fellow being, shows how ethics emerges from the unconscious. In its relation with fellow beings, the super-ego represses the death drive. In our relationship with our fellows, there is first of all this violence, this outlaw role, which is primarily that of the subject. But with the development of the super-ego, the individual enters into the realm of transgression: he is already a potential criminal who must pay for a crime he has merely imagined. In this sense he is a martyr to a guilt that itself was only a fantasy, as long as the other aspect of the outlaw is that of the one who pays: a Christ-like figure. As I said in my introduction, the outlaw creates the law in the same way that all dreams of perverse realization ultimately lead to moral laws. We learn ethics by dreaming.

NOTES

1. Robert Musil, *The Man without Qualities,* trans. Eithne Wilkins and Ernst Kaiser (London: Secker and Warburg, 1961).

2. "In dreams begin responsibilities"

Toward Dream Ethics

Jean-Michel Rabaté

In a dense passage of *Nadja*, André Breton puzzles out a complex sequence of factors that account for his inexplicable fascination with a terrible play. Admitting that a bad melodrama entitled *Les Détraquées* had made a powerful impression on him, he narrates a disturbing dream he had at the time. The dream's climax came when a moss-colored insect about twenty inches long slipped down into his throat until it was pulled out of his mouth by its huge hairy legs. Meditating on the nausea this still triggers in him, Breton tries to generalize, reflecting on the links between dreams and waking life. Here is what he writes at the end of a long parenthetical digression within his story:

> Since the production of dream images always depends upon at least this *double play of mirrors*, there is, here, the indication of the highly special, supremely revealing, "super-determinant"—in the Freudian sense of the word—role certain powerful impressions are made to play, in no way contaminable by morality, actually experienced "beyond good and evil" in the dream, and, subsequently, in what we quite arbitrarily oppose to dream under the name of reality.[1]

Here Breton introduces his own version of the Freudian concept of overdetermination, namely the idea that each element of a dream means several things at the same time, often with contradictory meanings. Overdetermination leads directly to positing an extra-moral site for dreams: because of their plurality of meanings, these images are beyond good and evil; they clash and rebound in a complex polyphony, which does not preclude, however, the possibility of a different sense of ethics.

Breton's *Nadja* argues forcibly that life demands a confusion of the domains of dream and reality, discovering in dreams a new mode of attitude, a new relationship to desire as a true foundation of ethics. Dream and reality have too much in common to be separated, or worse, made to represent each other, as if one side was the "real" body followed by its shadow. The idea is taken up and developed in a passage of the first "Manifesto of Surrealism":

> The mind of the man who dreams is fully satisfied by what happens to him. The agonizing question of possibility is no longer pertinent. Kill, fly faster, love to your heart's content. And if you should die, are you not certain of waking up from the dead? Let yourself be carried along, events will not tolerate your interference. You are name-less. The ease of everything is priceless.[2]

The strangeness of dreams entails that one has to acknowledge that they belong to a different realm, in which moral issues have no relevance. This does not mean that dreams are worthless fantasies—on the contrary—or that one should not attempt to think the world of dreams and reality together. Breton adds in "Manifesto": "And yet I can believe my eyes, my ears: this great day has arrived, this beast has spoken. If man's awaking is harder, if it breaks the spell too abruptly, it is because he has been led to make for himself too impoverished a notion of atonement" (13).

Like André Breton, but in less ringing tones, Gérard Pommier makes a vibrant plea for the foundation of ethics in the domain of dreams, while suggesting their being similarly situated "beyond good and evil." It seems at first sight that this ethical foun-dation beyond common morality would be more consistent with a program defined by a revolutionary or aesthetic "avant-garde" than in conformity with Freud's prudent conservatism. According to Freud's view, isn't man asleep often slipping back into a "regressive" moment, moving closer to unbridled drives, becoming the prey of all sorts of murderous or destructive urges? How can one found an ethics on a state that, according to Freud himself, barely bridges the gap between the normal and the pathological?

And, indeed, if a measure of freedom (a small measure to be true) is granted in dreams by their very overdetermined nature ("granted" is not the right term, since after all *Überdeterminierung* postulates or demands a certain type of interpretive free-dom that may not translate as freedom to act), dreams, in turn, in their layered and confusing essence, open onto a domain in which I cannot arrange or predict anything according to my intentions. I will never manage to force myself to dream this or that; no one can decide to have a happy or sad dream in advance; no one can dream in order to solve a philosophical problem—even if it happens for some subjects—for such a notion, put forward by Herbert Silberer under the name of the "functional phenome-non," met with Freud's nuanced but firm rebuttal. Freud's intense discussion with the neo-Jungian Silberer should serve as a warning to anyone who might be tempted to found the ethics of the dreamer on higher ideals, on an almost rational thinking con-tained in dreams—in short, on secondary elaboration. No: if there is an ethics of the dream, if dreams provide the only foundation for an ethics, the foundation will have to be found in primary processes and in the dream's intimate connection with drives.

But what of the role of censorship? We may remember that when Freud revisited *The Interpretation of Dreams* in the last decade of his life, he compared the world of dreams to "a modern State in which a mob, eager for enjoyment and destruction, has to be held down forcibly by a prudent superior class" (SE XXII, 221). A lot could be said about the cautious politics implied by this image, but the least one can deduce from it is that if there is, at first sight, any "ethical" issue, it would have to be filtered by the various agencies of censorship. The danger, as Pommier reminds us, is to confuse issues of ethics with morality, or to think that when we are in doubt about ethics, the best answer will turn out to be the police.

If dreams provide a foundation for an ethics of desire and the unconscious, however, how can we avoid the dead-end of a situation in which everyone would be assured of an ethical position, provided he or she remains true to a particular dream? In this sense, Creon would be as "ethical" as Antigone, since both are true to their personal dreams of justice (which is not far from being Hegel's interpretation of the play, but was not Lacan's), and the conflict that makes the play's dilemma so universal would have no sense. For according to that view, one might just as well say that they disagree and then collide—that's all.

Is this the problem Yeats had in mind when he wrote "In dreams begins responsibility"? The self-made epigraph to *Responsibilities* (1914) alludes no doubt to the dreams of national liberation that were then rife in Dublin, and were similar to those that would soon lead to the sacrifice of a few Irish heroes in the doomed anti-British insurrection of Easter 1916.[3] We are far from a "mob" eager for destruction and enjoyment here, since the main problem of the leaders of the coup was that the crowd failed to join them. Yeats's "dreams" keep their Romantic aura, which is derived from a mythical past. The archaic origin is always invoked as a paradigm of lost unity and perfection, especially in the case of a failed nationalist uprising that knew itself to be doomed from the start. But beautiful failure in a generous enterprise and the subsequent blood of the martyrs will more often than not reinforce the appeal of such dreams, the added ethical power of which will then strengthen the "cause." This is not exactly the case with Freud's dreams, although indeed they appear much more political than he himself would like to admit.

To advance I quote a passage from an essay by Pommier recently published in *Lacan in America,* and which should be quite relevant here. Pommier, who wishes to account for usual resistances to psychoanalysis, takes the canonical example of *Antigone:*

> We all love Antigone, don't we, this magnificent heroine who braves the laws of the city in the name of higher laws that appear to be placed even higher than our modern humanitarian human rights. But we should ask ourselves a question: would Antigone have reacted so bravely if she had been in analysis? Would she have acted in the same way knowing that her desire to bury her brother with her own hands was the other

side of her desire to kill him, or the result of her ambivalent incestuous love for him? You see then how psychoanalytic discourse can be hated and how there are perhaps good reasons to resist it! And if Antigone had said: "I realize that my passion to bury my brother is as great as my passion to kill him with my own hands, but nevertheless, I will not give up on my desire and keep obeying the higher laws"—then this would probably not have made a very good drama.[4]

As this commentary shows quite pointedly, we would be wrong to mix ethics up with the election of "higher" ideals.

It is also clear that one of the reasons Antigone remains so powerful as a character is that she seems to be acting all the time as in a dream: she crosses the stage and the city as a sleepwalker who obeys less the injunctions of her conscience than of her deepest unconscious. It is as a sleepwalker that she goes to the end of a dream of justice, only to wake up when it is too late. Here, rather than go back to Musil's witty accusations of the evil ideology of a value-free Science, I would be tempted to quote a friend of his, a fellow Austrian and one similarly obsessed with the issue of ethics, Hermann Broch. In his polyphonic trilogy, *The Sleepwalkers*, we meet one character, Esch, who is defined as the "Anarchist," and who sets out to enact a dream of justice and denunciation. Esch begins a journey through Germany in a sort of trance; he has lost sleep, which means he cannot return to his previous values:

> Great is the fear of him who awakens. He returns with less certainty to his waking life, and he fears the power of his dream, which, though it may not have borne fruit in action, has yet grown into a new knowledge. An exile from dream, he wanders in dream.[5]

For Broch, "sleepwalking" characterizes an intermediary state enacted by all the characters of the novel at one point or another. In their goings on (they murder each other once in a while) they share the same dreamlike precision, the hallucinatory acuity of perception that characterizes the last anti-hero's actions. Hugenau acts with a sense of security; he remains suspended in a dream that began when he decided to desert the army in time of war. Everything that followed was given gratuitously, as if he were rediscovering a child's vision and beginning a period of vacation. I shall return to the Nietzschean echoes of this conception of freedom and ethics and, to go faster, I cite from the ending of the last section of *The Sleepwalkers*:

> Whatever the individual man's attitude to the course of the revolution, whether he turns reactionary and clings to outworn forms, mistaking the aesthetic for the ethical as all conservatives do, or whether he holds himself aloof in the passivity of egoistic knowledge, or whether he gives himself up to his irrational impulses and applies himself to the destructive work of the revolution: he remains unethical in his destiny, an outcast from his epoch, an outcast from Time, yet nowhere and never is the spirit of the epoch so strong, so truly ethical and historical as in that last and first flare-up which is revolution . . . the last and greatest ethical achievement of the old disintegrating

system and the first achievement of the new, the moment when time is annulled and history radically formed in the pathos of absolute zero! (646–47)

Without falling into such apocalyptic rhetoric, it looks at times as if *The Interpretation of Dreams* was willing to allow for an identical moment of ethical destruction and a rebirth of values. This is probably why Nietzsche is quoted several times by Freud. In a first sketch of what later in the book will be defined as "overdetermination," he compares the intensity of the dream images to the intensity of the impressions from the day—the "material" that has given rise to them—and writes: "The intensity of the elements in the one has no relation to the intensity of the elements in the other: the fact is that a complete 'transvaluation of all psychical values' takes place between the material of the dream-thoughts and the dream" (SE IV, 330). The *Standard Edition* translation misses the recurrent tag in the section devoted to the Forgetting of Dreams: "As we already know, however, a complete reversal [*sic*] of all psychical values takes place between the dream-thoughts and the dream" (SE V, 516). Joyce Crick translates more accurately: "a total transvaluation of all psychical values has taken place."[6] Freud's German is *eine völlige Umwertung aller psychischen Werte*,[7] which suggests a direct equivalence between what dreams accomplish and what Nietzsche planned to do in the book he announced as early as the *Genealogy of Morals,* a book often described as Nietzsche's major work on ethics.[8]

It was Nietzsche's unfinished and posthumous *Will to Power*—quite a different text as we know—that was eventually subtitled "Attempt at a Revaluation of All Values" (*Versuch einer Umwertung aller Werte*). Let us note the curious coincidence of dates: Nietzsche died in 1900, but his book was published in 1901, a year after Freud's *Traumdeutung.* Without reopening the debate on the extent to which Nietzsche's influence on Freud is significant, or referring to Freud's own awareness that he was often merely rephrasing Nietzschean themes, let me just state here that Freud's reference indicates his strong perception of the ethical function of dreams.[9] Moreover, this ethical function is perceptible not in the explicit moral (or immoral) content of dreams, but in the metamorphic process of their formation—that is, fundamentally, in their production of images "beyond good and evil."

To grasp better the somewhat paradoxical nature of these statements, let us go back to the beginning. Freud begins his *Traumdeutung* with a survey of the available literature on dreams, and one subchapter in this summary is devoted to what has been translated either as "the moral sense in dreams" (SE IV, 66–74) or, more literally, as "ethical feelings in dreams" (*The Interpretation of Dreams,* 55–62). When Freud recapitulates current theories about the links between ethics and dreams, he wisely concludes that points of view differ and that no agreement has ever been reached on the links between dreams and morality: "The certainty with which one writer asserts that the dream knows nothing of moral demands is matched by the assurance with which another affirms that mankind's moral nature also holds good in our dream-life." (*The Interpretation of Dreams,* 55). He does suggest, however, that his own theory about the real nature of dreams will eventually solve the riddle, for when he criticizes the "remarkable inconsistencies and evasions" of most writers, he makes fun of the embarrassing difficulties they meet:

> Strictly speaking, for all those who believe that the moral personality of man disintegrates in dreams, any interest in immoral dreams would come to an end with this statement. They could reject the attempt to make the dreamer responsible for his dreams, and from the wickedness of his dreams conclude the existence of an evil tendency in his nature with as much composure as they would the apparently equivalent attempt to demonstrate from the absurdity of his dreams the worthlessness of his intellectual attainments when awake. The others, for whom the "categorical imperative" extends even into dreams, would have to assume responsibility for immoral dreams without reservation: it is only to be hoped that if they themselves have dreams of a reprehensible kind this does not oblige them to lose faith in the soundness of their own morals. (57)

The last dig at Kant is a recurrent theme in Freud (and will be taken up by Lacan in a more perverse fashion). Freud has indeed found a solution to all these aporias, to what might be described in a Kantian way as the "dialectics of dream morality," when he shows how the dream is fundamentally a "dream-work," the complex machinery of which taps the energy of desire. But does this theoretical displacement entail that all such ethical considerations are idle? Lacan and Pommier would disagree, though I shall attempt to point out difficulties that remain in their versions of dream ethics. Following Lacan's lead in his *Seminar on The Ethics of Psychoanalysis,* Pommier moves back from the *Traumdeutung* to the *Entwurf,* and returns to Freud's momentous introduction of the term of *das Ding* at the core of the subject's psychic structure. Let us recall how Freud links the issue of the "fellow-creature," the *Nebenmensch,* with the problematic of *das Ding:*

> Thus the complex of a fellow-creature falls into two portions. One of these gives the impression of being a constant structure and remains as a coherent "thing"; while the other can be understood by the activity of memory—that is, can be traced back to information about the subject's body. (SE I, 331)

Lacan is, of course, entirely right to see in this *Thing* a center of exteriority within the subject, an inner exterior as it were, or a trace of "the prehistoric Other that it is impossible to forget—the Other whose primacy of position Freud affirms in the form of something *entfremdet,* something strange to me, although it is at the heart of me, something that, at the level of the unconscious, only a representation can represent."[10] Later I shall pay more attention to the curiously tautological last part of the sentence, because first I wish to pose a basic question: why does Lacan never pay attention to the very explicit mention of ethics in the *Project* while he is apparently investigating "the ethics of psychoanalysis" in his seminar? Is it because he is so eager to connect Freud's *Ding* with a Heideggerian meditation on the "Thing that things," or to launch into a heady discussion of the Thing=X of Kantian metaphysics, revisited by Lacan via Sade?

Nonetheless, no reader of the *Project* can fail to be struck by the very powerful description provided by Freud of the small child's helplessness—a *Hilflosigkeit* that requires attention and help and then leads to a fundamental sociability defined by an "understanding" with other people, a *Verständingung* in which one sees the source of all morality: "This path of discharge thus acquires an extremely important secondary function—viz., of bringing about an understanding with other people; and the original helplessness of human beings is thus the primal source of all moral motives" (SE I, 318). Why does Lacan remain blind to this tantalizing suggestion? Is it because when he encountered it, in 1959, it may indeed have smacked more of a humanism or a personalism that he wished to avoid at any cost?

Is not the dream, essentially, an oxymoron, a paradoxical state in which we experience both this basic helplessness and also a totally imaginary delusion of power and control over everything? As Pommier states, when Freud follows the dream core to its darkest center, to its unanalyzable umbilicus, are we not on the very same path that leads to the discovery of the *Thing* in us, as the trace of an irreducible otherness, arguably first met when encountering some "fellow-beings"? The sense of power and impotence I can discover every night through my dreams should introduce another lesson to be gained from overdetermination: my ability to represent this otherness through dream images—be they delusions, harbingers, or truth—at least fundamentally as fragments of a narrative. But, as Lacan wrote with an exact insight, the "something strange in me" is indeed "something that on the level of the unconscious only a representation can represent." Thus, to discuss Freud's central insights on what I have called "dream ethics," I shall take a slightly different point of departure, negotiating between Freud's concept of egoistic dreams and the theory of egoism deployed in representations and fictions, notably in Ayn Rand's novels.

I guess most of us would agree that an egoist is not a very ethical person, since it seems that it is only his or her private values that count. Yet for Freud, one essential characteristic of dreams is that the dreamer, by the effect of the structure of the dream, is totally egoistical. As we know, Freud first demonstrates that every dream represents the fulfillment of a wish. Then, taking the example of a "dream of convenience" (a dream in which he tries to satisfy his thirst by imagining that his wife offers him an Etruscan urn), he concludes that one could see how beautifully and efficiently everything was arranged: "Since its only purpose was to fulfill a wish, it could be completely egoistical" (SE IV, 124). The thesis is reiterated several times in the following sections, as in the section on "typical dreams": "This would not contradict my assertion that dreams are wish-fulfillments, but my other assertion, too, that they are accessible only to egoistic impulses" (SE IV, 269). When Freud suggests that the dreamer becomes a child again, one cannot forget that for him, "[c]hildren are completely egoistic" (SE V, 250). An almost humorous footnote was added in 1911, with a reference to a lecture given in the

United States by Ernest Jones on "the egoism of dreams." Jones met with strong resistance when an American lady declared that the Freudian hypothesis was valid for Austrians, but not for Americans: she was sure that all her dreams were strictly altruistic![11]

The leitmotif of egoism in dreams recurs throughout *The Interpretation of Dreams* until it acquires the character of a dogmatic thesis in the structural account of the "Dream-Work." Typically Freud retains the moralistic overtones of "egoism" in his description of a structural function deriving from the position of the "subject of enunciation" or the unconscious Cartesian cogito present in the dream:

> Dreams are completely egoistic. Whenever my own ego does not appear in the content of the dream, but only some extraneous person, I may safely assume that my own ego lies concealed, by identification, behind the other person; I can insert my ego into the context. . . . Thus my ego may be represented in a dream several times over, now directly and now through identification with extraneous persons. By means of a number of such identifications it becomes possible to condense an extraordinary amount of thought material. The fact that the dreamer's own ego appears several times, or in several forms, in a dream is at bottom no more remarkable than the ego should be contained in a conscious thought several times or in different places or connections— e.g., in the sentence "when *I* think what a healthy child *I* was." (SE IV, 322–33)

What Freud offers us, in other words, could be called the "grammar of egoistic overdetermination," in which the active and passive voices keep revolving around a mobile subjective center—much as he was to propose later about fantasy in "A Child Is Being Beaten."[12] According to Pommier's logic, this grammar also paves the way for a new grammar of ethics.

Freud's analysis of egoistic dreams paves the way for a later development on the writer as a person gifted with the paradoxical power of at once releasing and sharing this egoism. In "Creative Writers and Day-Dreaming" (1907), he points out the links between children seriously engaged in playing, dreamers deeply ensconced in their private images, and writers of popular fiction ("the less pretentious authors of novels, romances and short stories, who nevertheless have the widest and most eager circle of readers of both sexes" [SE IX, 150]), who know how to create heroes with whom we immediately identify. We identify with the recurrent figure of the hero to whom, despite all the dangers braved, "nothing can happen": "this revealing characteristic of invulnerability we can immediately recognize—His Majesty the Ego, the hero alike of every daydream and of every story" (SE IX, 150). Popular fiction functions at the level of daydreaming and panders to our childish fantasies: if all the women fall in love with the hero in a totally unrealistic manner, we are nevertheless as flattered as if this might happen to us. The difference between day- or night-dreamers, on the one hand, and novelists, on the other, lies in a sense of participation.

We are bored or repulsed by the telling of intimate images or fantasies, whereas we are kept interested by narratives that provide such great pleasure: "How the writer accomplishes this is his innermost secret; the essential *ars poetica* lies in the technique of overcoming the feeling of repulsion in us which is undoubtedly connected with the barriers that rise between each single ego and the others" (SE IX, 153). Freud answers his own question by disclosing the two most common techniques: "The writer softens the character of this egoistic day-dream by altering and disguising it, and he bribes us by the purely formal—that is, aesthetic—yield of pleasure which he offers us in the presentation of his phantasies" (SE IX, 153). Thus Freud's view of literature is power-fully simple: the function of art is a mere means to an end, which consists in the over-coming of the barriers that separate one *ego* from other *egos* with the ultimate aim of releasing the deeper egoism of a dream or a fantasy that can be shared by all. Art is clearly reduced to a little bribe that will then release even greater pleasure—an "incite-ment premium" or a "fore-pleasure" before a quasi-orgasmic ego-trip can be unleashed. These ideas correspond with surprising exactitude to the argumentation put forward by a very popular novelist who also happened to be have invented a whole philosophy of egoism, Ayn Rand.

Ayn Rand was a professed Romantic, a writer attached to portraying ideal figures and clinging to hero-worship. Her deliberate idealization provides a basis for a whole vision of life in which raising one's self-esteem implies understanding the rules of radical egoism. Her earliest note for *The Fountainhead*, her first best-selling novel, stresses this concept of egoism: "The first purpose of this book is *a defense of egoism in its real meaning*."[13] Indeed, the rather contrived plot culminates when the "genius" architect Howard Roark is led to dynamiting cheap buildings just erected for the poor because his original design had been tampered with, and then he has to defend his "egoistic" conception of art and life in court.

One idea put forward by Ayn Rand is that the egoist's indifference to others frees him from his petty delusions, restoring his self-esteem by bringing him in closer contact with the Drive (the Freudian *Trieb*) hidden beneath his limited desires. This constitutes a sort of inverse pornography, in a contagion of separateness affirming the solipsistic structure of the drives. The Lacanian Master posits his absolute Ego by considering only his relationship to drives, which then compels others to move into a hysterical position of recrimination and theatrical negation until they themselves overcome their limitations and turn into Masters. The narratological issue in these novels boils down to an interaction between the intolerable demands arising from the subjective entanglements of sexual desire and a truth to be sought on the side of the solipsist drive underpinning creativity.

In Ayn Rand's later developments of her philosophy, "Selfishness" comes to mean "pure devotion to an ideal," while "altruism" means a perverted spirit of sacrifice for the masses instilled by any religion of God or humanity. These terms clearly evoke more or less the opposite of what they mean in everyday discourse. And the main rea-son one can find for her choice of "Objectivism" as the name for her system is that she wishes to avoid any reproach of subjectivism or solipsism: for the only "objective" value we have here is, in fact, the Freudian *Trieb*, posited as the single locus of truth.

Since one should not take Rand's philosophy too seriously, I would like simply to point out that the weakness of her thinking is compensated for by a way of writing that has managed to captivate her audiences. Tapping into the same logic that underpins our dreams, she knows how to produce "page-turners" despite the general incoherence of plot and the weakness of the writing. The explanation is to be sought in the way Rand blends the allegorical vision of pulp fiction, in which everything is good or evil, with a pretense of rationalization, which itself hides a fascination for the drive hidden in desire. Her "philosophical novels" are simply extended versions of the Harlequin genre, in which the trick is always to produce a figure of "love at first sight" and then to multiply obstacles until the desired reunion is achieved. In Rand's fictions it is always the woman who fears the absolutist character of love so that she will want to destroy the object of her passion by killing it. We haven't left the domain of daydreaming, but we are also addressing the heart of the problem of ethics in its intricate connection with politics.

As Slavoj Žižek has remarked, in a subtle reading of Rand's "hysterical lesbianism," this novelist "falls into the line of over-conformist authors who undermine the ruling ideological edifice by their very excessive identification with it."[14] Her overenthusiastic endorsing of capitalism (which might also remind us of Freud's curious insistence on the idea that the dream plays the role of the capitalist with respect to the unconscious) retains its hysterical force, so that somehow the Master's discourse is forced to confront his failure. Capitalism is never pure enough for Rand; it constantly falls prey to the recurrent danger of collectivism or religiosity. "A pure system of capitalism had never yet existed, not even in America; various degrees of government control had been undercutting and destroying it from the start."[15] One of the ironies besetting Objectivism in the domain of economics is that one of its most gifted and famous disciples is none other than Alan Greenspan.

Since all her strong heroes, her "Prime Movers," are embodiments of the Freudian Drive in its autotelic affirmation, Rand's position comes curiously close to a certain feminism in her showing how her fascination for the masculine Will leads her to a position of hysteria, but a hysteria that can be overcome, surmounted, and transcended. The main fantasy is that the creative Ego can live and produce just for himself, independent of the gaze of the big Other—which is not tantamount to asserting that the self makes up reality. What this can teach, finally, is that solipsism and relativism can be avoided if and only if the subject destroys his narcissistic ego in the name of a transcending Egoism that contains the dialectical means by which it can be superseded (be it through an almost impossible gift or through an even more paradoxical hospitality toward the other). Above all, dreams may yield the key to a more rigorous sense of ethics by reminding us of the proximity between the Other and the other, hinted at by a deeper echo, a submerged rhyme linking the darkest "navel" of dreams to an openness to what I may have to call, in spite of all, "my neighbor." The *Neben-Mensch* is also a *Nabel-Mensch*, and this German pun is strengthened by the fact that it was with the famously personal and revealing Dream of Irma's Injection that Freud for the first time puts forth the notion of the "navel" [*Nabel*] of dreams.[16]

This abysmal site seems a strange place to secure a foundation for ethics, but it is precisely because it can function as a nonplace or a "not-all" that ethics can keep its radically dialogic nature, a nature put forward by Buber and Levinas, among others. It is also the site at which ethics and aesthetics meet, as Lacan indicated by his startling decision to read *Antigone* not as a play articulating a traditional ethical dilemma, but as a drama staging the impact of feminine beauty on a collective audience. Thus we are strongly reminded of the fact that dreams also stress the need to take into consideration "the means of representation" and the "considerations of representability," to refer once more to chapter 6 of the *Traumdeutung*. It is in this scene of an "other" presentation that my *rebus* language as well as our common language, shot through by a shared Otherness, constantly touch their jagged borders: again and again they encounter their limits, showing us quite simply, as Wittgenstein had it, the site of ethics.

NOTES

1. André Breton, *Nadja,* trans. Richard Howard (New York: Grove Press, 1960), 51.

2. André Breton, "Manifesto of Surrealism," in *Manifestoes of Surrealism,* trans. Richard Seaver and Helen R. Lane (Ann Arbor: University of Michigan Press, 1972), 13. I have slightly modified the translation.

3. William Butler Yeats, *Collected Poems* (London: Macmillan, 1965), 112. Yeats gives as his source an "Old Play."

4. Gérard Pommier, "New Resistances to Psychoanalysis," in *Lacan in America,* ed. Jean-Michel Rabaté (New York: The Other Press, 2000), 81.

5. Hermann Broch, *The Sleepwalkers,* trans. E. and W. Muir (New York: Universal Library, 1964), 303.

6. I quote Joyce Crick's translation of the first edition of *The Interpretation of Dreams* (Oxford: Oxford University Press, 1999), 250, 335.

7. The *Traumdeutung* has the phrase in italics with quotation marks the first time only (327) and repeats it in the text on 494. Sigmund Freud, *Studienausgabe II, Die Traumdeutung* (Frankfurt: Fischer, 1972); all subsequent references will be to this edition.

8. See Friedrich Nietzsche, *On the Genealogy of Morals* (1887), in *On the Genealogy of Morals and Ecce Homo,* trans. Walter Kaufmann (New York: Vintage, 1967), 160, and editor's note 1.

9. See the copious book put together by Reinhard Gasser, *Nietzsche und Freud* (Berlin: Walter de Gruyter, 1997). Like most commentators linking the two authors, Gasser does not mention the ominous presence of a Nietzschean "transvaluation of values" in the *Traumdeutung.*

10. Jacques Lacan, *The Ethics of Psychoanalysis,* trans. D. Porter (New York: Norton, 1992), 71.

11. See SE IV, 270, n. 2. Ernest Jones, who is quoted here, concludes a paper on "A Forgotten Dream" with the remark: "Most of the individual features of Freud's dream theory are

also illustrated in the analysis, the almost grotesque egocentricity of the dream-thoughts." See Ernest Jones, "A Forgotten Dream," in *Papers on Psycho-Analysis* (Boston: Beacon, 1967), 241.

12. See SE XVII, 175–79. Symptomatically, Joyce Crick's translation of the first edition of *The Intrpretation of Dreams* downplays the theme of egoism. When Freud writes explicitly, *Träume sind absolut egoistisch,* Crick translates, "Dreams are absolutely self-centred" (246), as if such Freudian "egoism" were in bad taste. For the German original, see Sigmund Freud, *Die Traumdeutung* (Frankfurt am Main: Fischer, 1972), 320.

13. Quoted by Barbara Branden, *The Passion of Ayn Rand* (New York: Doubleday, 1986), 133.

14. Slavoj Žižek, "The Lesbian Session," 1997; *Lacanian Ink* 12 (1997), 59.

15. Ayn Rand, *The Virtue of Selfishness* (New York: Signet, 1964), 37.

16. For the word *Nabel,* see *Die Traumdeutung,* 130 and 503.

3. The Dream in the Wake of the Freudian Rupture

Willy Apollon

Translated by Steven Miller and
John Mowitt

THE FREUDIAN RUPTURE TODAY

Even as he maintains remarkable rigor in his search for the validation of his clinical practice, Freud does not entirely subscribe to a certain conception of science—in particular, to the conception of experimental science. Nevertheless the knowledge (*le savoir,* thus translated passim) of psychoanalysis Freud invents only presents itself in experience. With dreams Freud claims that a space other than the one defined by neuronal, synaptic, electrical, or chemical interconnections, and other than the imaginary, traverses, in both man and animal, the psychical apparatus regulating them. This is a space where, among other activities he will attempt to define, the dream produces thoughts. On the other hand, these dream thoughts reveal the constitution of a knowledge, that is, intellectual work, intellectual intuition, memory, logical reasoning, etc., to which consciousness cannot gain access by its own means. And thus in inventing psychoanalysis, Freud revolutionizes the very notion of experimentation as a mode of access to rational and scientific knowledge. What he proposes—once he abandons hypnosis—is not to submit the dream to a critical examination of the sort an experimenter would have carried out. Instead he proposes that one trust in the dream as the bearer of another thought and another logic, ones other than those animating the consciousness of both the dreamer and the experimenter. Experimentation only gives access to what takes place in consciousness, whether that consciousness belongs to the experimenter or to the subject submitted to the experiment. Freud needed something else. He had to create the possibility of gaining access to this knowledge revealed by dream thoughts, access to a mental object situated in a place other than the one to which consciousness has access.

Freud effectively subverts the notion of experimentation by grasping the dream as an experience of the subject outside the fundamental conditions of consciousness—

conditions that are the basis of all experimentation with claims to be scientific. To this end he distinguishes the narration of the dream from the experience of the dream that the narration reconstructs. The very mode of his analysis of the dream is what operates this distinction—an insight we do not often take into account. The excellent work that today's biological sciences have been doing on the dream tends to distract us from this fundamental distinction. At the very least, when faced with this work and this research, we should ask ourselves Freud's question: What is a dream outside the narration that evokes its experience only in reconstructing it? This question does not concern the cat or the monkey, but it has to do with any one of our dreams. If it is not taken seriously, the significance of the Freudian rupture with respect to this question will escape us. When he analyzes the narration of the dream, what Freud in fact seeks is precisely the experience of the dreamer; but what he attains is what he will call the "dream thoughts." On the one hand, the experience of the dreamer brings him up against a real (*un réel,* passim) that will not yield to consciousness and its instruments of analysis. On the other hand, the dreamer, upon awakening, remembers scraps of this experience and attempts to reconstruct it in the signifiers through which his or her consciousness grasps everyday life. Freud calls this passage—for a real consciousness cannot assimilate to the signifiers through which consciousness grasps reality—both a reconstruction and a transformation. Its product is the very loss of experience. Only traces of experience remain, and these are what Freud interrogates. He thus sets up his research on the experimental content of the dream as an inquiry. He puts himself in the position of those researchers and scientists who seek traces of the dawn of humanity and the great stages of its history in order to reconstruct the movement and the episodes of its evolution. He examines the smallest detail of the dreamer's narration in search of an organization that would account for this intimate experience. What he finds are strange remains, pieces of spaces and times, of a lost history, that of the being's confrontation with something it cannot assimilate. Every day, whenever we decide to remain faithful to the Freudian discovery, we recreate this frustrating but insistent experience with each of our patients. Everything happens as if the experience of the dream were right there, always within reach, ever so close to being grasped by consciousness, by intuition, and intelligence. But it remains ceaselessly out of their reach—leaving us only scraps, these dream thoughts that, along with Lacan, we analyze under the heading of the signifier. We are left with this vortex, this hole where even signifiers fail to articulate themselves and make sense, much less to deliver to an intuitive or reasoning intelligence the long-awaited revelation.

DREAM THOUGHT AND THE KNOWLEDGE OF THE OTHER SCENE

The difficulty begins when we start to wonder why Freud decided to follow the dream rather than to submit it, as any other scientist would have done, to a critical examination.

In effect, what we are dealing with when we deal with the psychoanalytic dream is a narration (*un récit*, passim). The neurophysiologist considers the dream a product of the brain, and his or her task is to analyze the verifiable manifestations of the brain activities according to neurophysiological methods. He or she may identify its neurological and physiological components; he or she may attempt to scan a representation of the activities of the brain in a dream state, and to make hypotheses about the links between these activities and REMs during sleep. Doing all these things and doing whatever else such a scientist can do, nonetheless this person does not thus have access to what Freud calls a dream. The dream the biologist studies is definitively not the one that Freud analyzes. The neurophysiologist does teach us many interesting things about the function of the dream, about the way the dream functions as a mechanism allowing the living being to try multiple associations between the facts of memory and those of current perceptions in order to adjust the individual's behavior to changes in the environment and in the social group. The neurophysiologist also has very instructive things to teach us about the function of the dream for the newborn child, about the way it engages more and more complex explorations of the information coming from various sensations, explorations that assure the child's adaptation and its early acquisition of survival skills. Basically the neurophysiologist always leads us back to the idea of the utility of the dream in managing memories necessary to the articulation between the individual and its group or environment, on the one hand, and to the neuronal, synaptic, electrical, and chemical connections that, on the other hand, assure the dream's use in daily life. In so doing, this scientist comes close to the idea, presumed to be Freudian, that the dream takes part in the management of hypotheses, experiments, and solutions to which the individual has recourse, whether conscious or not, in order to resolve the problems of everyday life. This is all quite interesting. But it is fundamentally foreign to what Freud discovers through the dream and what prompts him to revise his therapeutic techniques in order to adjust his clinical practice to what he learns from the dream.

Indeed, the activities of the dream as considered by neurophysiology operate in the space of perception, of sensations, and of memories, all of which consciousness uses as tools in its analysis of situations, environmental modifications, and in its efforts to solve problems of adaptation and survival. This is all certainly vital, but it is limited to the dream's function in survival. In contrast, the mental objects that Freud calls dream thoughts operate in a space that is entirely other. It is not a space of language, in which certain memories support in consciousness the relation of the living being to its social group, the activities of its coexistence, and its survival. Let us take as an example the phenomena of so-called culture that anthropologists have taught us to recognize in chimpanzees, those primates genetically closest to Homo sapiens. Following the lead of certain psychologists, psychoanalysts try in vain to split language into verbal language and nonverbal language when confronted with the discovery of the function of language in the evolution of some species. Today it is necessary to take account of the rupture of speech through which Homo sapiens transcends language in order to have access to a space other than the psychical apparatus—for the apparatus is precisely what Homo sapiens has in common with the other species sharing the territory on which all must provide for their survival. Beyond the consciousness that traverses the psychical apparatus, this rupture reveals the insistence of a knowledge or this scene, where death is at work in the *jouissance* causing the subject of speech.

THE DEATH DRIVE

The subversion of language by the upsurge of speech in Homo sapiens opens this being onto a specific space determined by the structure of an address, in which a non-programmed death is at work, a death not linked to the development and growing old of the individual. In species for which the organization of social life is overdetermined by the concern for survival, the structure and field of language regulates the activities of communication both between individuals and the group, and between individuals and the memories necessary for the analysis of new and dangerous situations. Language thus becomes a dimension of consciousness and of collective memories and their role in adaptation, survival, and reproduction. This is a concept of language according to which the complete retention of the data passed between sender and receiver is as essential to consciousness and its functions as it is to the dream as a neurophysiological activity in the service of such functions. With speech, another dimension intervenes within a specific field.

Beginning with Homo sapiens, the fact of speech introduces into language a structure of address in which the hypothesis of the Other is central. The space structured by communication as the fundamental manifestation of a collective consciousness that perceives, remembers, anticipates, and decides—such a space is subverted by the structure of address to the Other introduced by speech, which presupposes a subjective event, an event that is decisive and determinant for survival. Collective consciousness does not have access to it. The point is that the space structured by an address to the Other is the place of a work *jouissance*—the work of death imputed to this Other. Indeed, humanity has never been able to speak except to address an intimate experience to the group, an experience of which the group as such has neither perception nor consciousness. Therein lies the ground and status of the notion of the Freudian subject. Subjective speech constructs a space where mental objects translate a singular intimate experience and to which no perception and no intellectual intuition correspond. This experience with which the individual is confronted separates it from the group and subjects it to something other than the concern for survival, adaptation, and reproduction. The individual discovers a radical autonomy and break from the rest of a collectivity, a break that progressively constitutes him or her in his or her subjective solitude as the object of an anxiety that signals the proximity of his or her own death.

In this experience, man claims to see and to hear beings who do not fall within the bounds of common perception. One's nights are not the only things haunted by these "voices" and these "visions." Some people claim to see a lost ancestor and to receive revelations from this figure about their origins. Others conceive of the dream as a voyage to another place, one more true than the space of collective life. Thus what progressively emerges for humanity outside access to collective or individual consciousness reveals itself to be more important than life itself—to the point of becoming the axis of all collective life and all rules of coexistence. At the same time, Homo sapiens becomes the only species the objective of which seems to be to destroy itself, going beyond even the irrational tendency to destroy the environment in order to procure its subsistence. The concomitant upsurge in humanity of a space that transcends the psychical apparatus and of the auto-destructive drive was never lost on the author of *Beyond the Pleasure Principle, Totem and Taboo,* and *Civilization and Its Discontents.* Toward the end of *Beyond the Pleasure Principle* Freud notes that the goal of all life is death. Thus for him the opening of this space that subverts the psychical apparatus opens into the dream as the subversion of consciousness. That which is constructed in the dream carries into biological life the logic of an antinomy. From this scene, other than the one that governs consciousness, the work of a death inhabits the human being, a death Freud calls the second death in that it is not governed by the same rules. According to Freud, what the dream evokes on this scene other than consciousness is the work of the second death, which leads the human being down paths unmarked by the norms, the rules, and the ideals of culture. Confronted by an experience rendered incommunicable by that which traverses consciousness and driving it to both its limit and its disappearance, doubtless humanity was compelled to create speech.

Accordingly, speech communicates nothing. It evokes. It creates a space where constructions accessible to consciousness are possible. The Freudian dream is a construction of this order. In the same way that mathematical constructions make the relations underlying numbers and algebraic operations accessible to intelligence relative to a space with definable and calculable limits, the narration of the dream, in effect speech without a subject and inspired from an other place, constructs mental objects and relations that make accessible to consciousness the phantasmatic logic whereby death regulates the smallest details of our everyday life. The space of the Freudian dream is this space, constructed by the rupture that subjective speech institutes in the field of linguistic communication. For us—as for the first humans and for children—what is elaborated in such a space is only calculable and constructed through a subjective speech given over to a liberty defying the logic and rules of communication. Freud evokes this speech liberated from language and its means of communication with the concept of "free association." In the narration of the dream, the dreamer reappropriates the experience that traversed him or her during sleep, and where the dream thoughts have constructed a solution with regard to what will have been unassimilable for consciousness during its waking hours.

The Question of Transference

From *The Project* to *The Interpretation of Dreams*, what Freud discovers and puts to work is a space that transcends the psychical apparatus by introducing into the human being a relation to "thoughts," mental objects, the logic of which themselves subverts the powers and limits of consciousness. Freud has not yet elaborated his concept of the second death as sustained by the death drive, but he already knows there must be a particular instance to account for this space where dream thoughts fracture psychic space. As we reread Freud today in the wake of Lacan, we know that already a *jouissance* in which a death not programmed into our DNA is at work, structuring this space, calculating, and deciding for us through the activity of the dream. To the very extent that what, for Freud, is elaborated in the dream cannot be reached by means, such as contemporary neuroscience posits them today, that consciousness has at its disposal, regardless of whether these are understood as perception, intuition, intelligence, or collective memories, or for that matter, even the will or the domain of the sensible itself—to this extent it becomes a question for Freud of knowing by what means or by what constructions such objects or dream thoughts can be made accessible to consciousness or intelligence, thus becoming either the object or the cause of knowledge. To respond to this question, Freud will set to work examining what is at work in the narration of the dream. Since the dream is, for the moment, the only experience through which he can gain access to what plays itself out on this other scene and which introduces a rupture in the powers of consciousness, he will create a strategy to enact this subversion of consciousness and the psychical apparatus and to analyze its effects.

Such are going to be the stakes of the transference for Freud: it is a strategy for enacting what happens on this other scene so as to grasp its stakes, its logic, its means, and its objects. And what if one were to object that the dream is already inadequate to this task? In effect, the activity of the dream, to which the dreamer's narration refers, is precisely what confronts him or her with the work of the unconscious. The dream is going to be the model upon which Freud will construct his strategy for gaining access to what thus escapes consciousness and its powers of intuition, analysis, and intervention. But what then is involved in positing transference as a strategy, modeled on the dream, for gaining access to the knowledge of the unconscious? Couldn't one read *The Interpretation of Dreams* simply as a text sufficient unto itself? Why bring in the question of transference? At stake here is a difficulty specific to psychoanalysis as a practice and as a strategy of treatment. The great texts of Freud, such as *The Interpretation of Dreams*, bear witness to Freud's concern to take into account what happens in the analytic experience as rigorously as possible. They are not primarily theoretical texts developing a new conception of humanity within the field of the human sciences. Only secondarily do they have such a dimension. They are first and foremost writings meant to account for the clinical practice of psychoanalysis.

The basic strategy of this practice is transference. Furthermore, the success of clinical practice rests upon its ethical dimension, so much so that Freud will not hesitate to recommend that Tausk give up working with this or that patient, arguing that the patient seemed to lack ethics. It is within the framework of the strategy of transference that the ethical dimension assumes all of its importance and significance. Accordingly it seems that the explication of a dream as an opaque text or rebus, and the operation of interpreting the same dream by referring certain dream thoughts to certain elements from the life of the dreamer, are two activities of a very different nature. It is a question of two perspectives on the dream entailing two different readings of *The Interpretation of Dreams.*

Here it becomes necessary to measure the importance of the concept of work such as it operates in *The Interpretation of Dreams.* Freud literally says that the dream works. But what is it, in fact, that matters about this dream-work? In fact it is only somewhat later, with the analysis of the Rat Man, that we will be given a better idea about what was already at stake in *The Interpretation of Dreams* when Freud refers to the dream-work. Freud needs this concept to support his conception of the dream as an experience in which the unconscious goes into action unbeknownst to the dreamer. What does this concept represent in the scientific universe in which Freud's thought is immersed? The steam engine, electricity, and the telephone have barely been in existence for twenty to twenty-five years. The concepts of force and inertia in mechanics and in physics are in the midst of their development, and they are transforming the concept of work. In physics, the closely related notions of energy, transformation, and the magnetic field, along with, in mathematics, the notions of construction, and the displacement and the conservation of the properties of a set in the course of a displacement—all these combine to make possible an entirely other approach to phenomena, objects, and activities of spirit that, until then, had been inaccessible to consciousness and its ways of knowing. When I say an entirely other approach, I mean an approach that is as independent and autonomous from philosophy and metaphysics as it is from theology and other religious discourses. It was Freud's ambition to give his depth psychology the scientific means to have access to the so-called activities of the spirit, in order to found the clinical practice he calls psychoanalysis. From that early point on, Freud already possessed a field of concepts that allowed him completely original hypotheses about the possible construction of a model for the field of the unconscious, of the forces at work there, and of eventual action upon such a field. *The Interpretation of Dreams* is impregnated with these concepts, which articulate an epochal *epistémè* for Freud.

For the analyst who adopts Freud's position and his work, it is the clinical perspective that is determinant because of the ethical strategy of the transference. Thus the analyst's reading of *The Interpretation of Dreams* risks differing rather profoundly from that of an academic intellectual or a scientific researcher. From the perspective of the intellectual, *The Interpretation of Dreams* seeks the meaning of the dream in analyzing the elements of the narration constituted by the givens of the dream. Intellectual work contents itself with seeking the dream's meaning in the givens of the dream's narration and with establishing on this basis a conception of the human or the dream. This perspective is congruent with all the efforts to deepen our knowledge about myth, even fantasy—considered from the point of view of its origins—and of their respective functions. The scientific researcher, for his or her part, finds him- or herself obliged to question the relation between the narration of the dream and the experience of the dream as such. His or her technical means lead to concentrating research on the nature of this experience and to reducing it to what is accessible to what such research is capable of accounting for—in particular, to neurology.

From the perspective of the analyst it is the ethics involved in the transference that will give the dream its function and its scope. For us analysts the transference creates a field on which it is possible to enact and to interact with this other scene that traverses the psychical apparatus; and it is within this framework that the dream becomes the royal road to the unconscious. Indeed in the analytic session, what is put in play is the narration of the dream. This narration can be the seventh or the ninth version the analysand tells him or herself, as he or she tries to get as close as possible, or to distance him- or herself as far as possible, from what constitutes the kernel of this experience of the dream. This experience is itself rather curious, since nothing the dreamer claims to have seen or heard has in fact been perceived. Still, we cannot conclude this to be a hallucinatory phenomenon, particularly if we take into account its frequency and universality in the human species. The narration of the dream presents itself as a construction, in the mathematical sense of the term, one that gives consciousness access to an experience that took place on a scene to which consciousness itself does not have access. This construction as such is not a spontaneous activity of the spirit, in the sense that it would have no orientation or predetermination. At the moment that the mathematicians are asking themselves about a place where the mere existence of numbers would allow the validation of their operation so as to respond to the even more radical and decisive question of whether one can trust in the results of these operations, two positions and two methods will confront one another. The logicians will put their trust in the rules and principles that insure the rigor of the demonstration, while the intuitionists will prefer to invoke the necessary construction of the very place of such a demonstration. This is exactly the problem Freud was confronting, and he responds to it in the same way as his contemporaries in mathematics. In psychoanalysis, as in mathematics, construction is a rigorously oriented activity. It is overdetermined by the assumption of a position that is only unveiled once the work of construction concludes. Thus, the different versions of the narration of the dream the analysand tries out, before choosing one to tell to the analyst, are transformations of an initial construction that has defined the basic elements of the narration. It is this work that we see Freud ceaselessly taking up in order to reach the initial construction that has yielded the dream thoughts.

Across a sequence of texts that runs from *The Project for a Scientific Psychology,* *The Interpretation of Dreams,* and the case history of the Rat Man to "The Uncanny," *Beyond the Pleasure Principle,* and *Civilization and Its Discontents,* Freud establishes a place, inaccessible to consciousness, where the destiny of the human being is decided. He undertakes a construction that makes this place and its operations accessible to consciousness in order to allow humanity to take a position with respect to what plays itself out in this place. With such an undertaking Freud not only aims to complete what Darwin and the evolutionists brought to the conception of humanity—the scope of his work goes beyond that. He claims to allow humanity to participate in its own place, subjectivity, to participate in what happens to it and passes beyond it, rather than simply undergoing it. Such is the perspective within which, today, we should belatedly situate *The Interpretation of Dreams.* The dream is that construction that offers us a symbolic representation of what traverses us and carries us beyond the axis of what we want and what we hope for. It is therefore the model for those constructions by which we might come to assume and participate in what exiles us from the places of our biological, social, historical, and cultural entanglements.

THE CLINICAL CONSEQUENCES OF THE
FREUDIAN RUPTURE REGARDING THE DREAM

It is in the clinical practice of psychoanalysis that this operation of the dream, inseparable from the rupture that Freud introduces within our conceptions of humanity, has its full impact. Today this practice—more specifically, the practice defined by the action of transference—allows us to discern *four* dimensions in *The Interpretation of Dreams,* and thus to recenter clinical work around Freud's own objective: an ethics that includes rather than represses, negates, or hopes to cure humanity of the dark forces and unconscious thoughts that subvert human life. Indeed, transference counts on a modification of the ethical position of the analysand with respect to the death drive and the absence of the Other. In one way or another, depending on the particularity of the clinical case, what the construction of the dream makes accessible to the subject in analysis is a defect or discrepancy in the analysand's ethical position with respect to the work of the death drive within. In relation to this action of death drive, his appeal to the Other, through which the analysand seeks to escape both his solitude and his responsibility, remains futile. The dream thus confronts the dreamer with something that, in a certain sense, cannot be logically assimilated. Freud invents the transference, or the introduction of a third party, thus allowing for the construction of a fictive address for the dream. Thus, Freud produces the transference as an intervention within the construction produced by the Other, or the unconscious, in the dream, even before this construction of the Other has undergone the analysand's manipulations and transformations. It is thus necessary for us to grasp the status of the fictive address Freud introduces for the dream, insofar as the dream is a construction of the Other meant to signify something. This fictive address is a position introduced into the construction that the Other makes of the dream, in order to overturn its strategy. In effect, the introduction of this fictive address transforms the construction that the dream is into a message addressed to the analyst by the unconscious of the analysand. This reversal, operated within the construction of the dream by the invention of transference, becomes fundamental in that it finally makes psychoanalysis possible as a science of ethics, a science of the possibility of the subject's intervention and participation in what affects it beyond and out of reach of its consciousness.

The Bad Encounter—A Real Consciousness Cannot Assimilate

In his model of the dream Freud thus shows us how the dream as an experience is a construction produced on another scene, that of the unconscious, to make what plays itself out on that scene accessible to the scene of consciousness. In more technical terms, let us say that Freud makes the dream, as experience, into a construction of the Other to represent what causes the subject on the scene of the unconscious. The invention of transference introduces the element of fiction, or the hypothesis of an address corresponding to the analyst or, more precisely, to his desire to know. And this invention aims to steer the dynamic specific to this construction of the unconscious toward a certain transformation. From there the analytic apparatus is ready to require— through the dream—both the interpretation of the Other that is addressed to the analyst and, within the same strategic field, the response of the subject in terms of a change in its ethical position.

Within the framework of the transference defined as the condition of possibility for the clinical practice of psychoanalysis, the subjective experience of the encounter with the unconscious in the dream, or, of the *jouissance* in which the second death does its work, as well as of the absence of the Other to the request of the subject—this experience is submitted to a specific constraint. The dream thereby enters fully into its own dimension as a discourse without a subject to which the constraint of transference proposes an address. One could underestimate, in effect, this fundamental dimension of the dream, which presents itself in the narration of the dreamer, as a discourse the enunciation of which cannot be attributed to the subject of consciousness. In its construction of a space in which the inaccessible and the nonlocalizable take on a symbolic consistency, making them susceptible to evocation, this discourse of the dream—like all discourse—presupposes a subject of enunciation the place of which cannot be determined within the utterance itself. In other words, the dream does not give us the Other who constructs the dream, but it does presuppose its position. The status of this Other is calculable in the construction of the dream. But the ethical position of this Other remains a problem. In other words: why does the Other construct the dream? This problem brings us back to Freud's formulation: what does the Other want of me?

Freud tells us that at the heart of the construction the dream is, that something occurs as a vortex, something that can be treated as a black hole within the space created by this construction. This is the navel of the dream. It is the point in the dream where the signifier fails. In a way it is the internal limit of the dream as a construction. At this limit point, the dream escapes all signification. Today, clinical practice establishes that this internal limit on construction nullifies in advance all interpretations of the dream. Everything happens as if the dream were in fact the construction of this internal limit, the calculation by the Other of a point that resists assimilation. This translates perfectly the encounter of the subject with a real, with something that remains fundamentally foreign to all the powers of consciousness, from perception and intuition to the domain of the sensible and of the will. This encounter with the real, which is at the heart of the clinical practice of psychoanalysis, opens the space of the sublime for the subject, in that it realizes the rediscovery of an experience that leaves reason powerless, but not indifferent.

THE DEFECT IN THE SIGNIFIER—
ITS LIMIT AS THE ETHICAL MOMENT OF THE DREAM

This powerlessness of reason there at the place where the signifier fails in calculating a fitting position for the subject in the dream is a decisive logical moment in the strategies of transference. Freud did not underestimate the role of intelligence and reason in the strategies of consciousness with respect to this intrusion of something other, where a death propelled by the unconscious imperils the aims of the ego on the social scene. Certainly he did discern, in the dream-work and in the processes of the dream, that the whole mounting of the construction cannot do without the activities of intelligence and reason—perhaps even to an extent outside the scope of consciousness. But he also left us remarks of stunning insight—in his "Notes on Obsessional Neurosis," in his text on "The Unconscious," and in his "Metapsychological Supplement to the Theory of Dreams"—about intellectualization and rationalization in the distortions of the dream. But this entire work of reason and intelligence encounters a limit that the dream constructs so that it may calculate the position of powerlessness in which the subject finds him or herself with respect to what is decided for him or her (or against, but that amounts to the same) in the field of the Other.

The powerlessness in which the subject finds himself faced with this thing, the work of death, and which the construction of the dream makes into the navel of its narration, can be detailed in two forms. First, it takes the form of something impossible to say with respect to what the subject encounters in the space opened by the dream. This is undoubtedly one of the reasons for the revisions of the narration of the dream—as Freud suggests in chapters 4, 5, 6, and 7 of *The Interpretation of Dreams*. These revisions are not only attempts to obscure what remains unbearable for consciousness in the experience of the dream; they also refer to the defect in the signifier, to the fact that language is powerless to bear the speech of the subject faced with what breaches consciousness. The "difficulty in saying" (*mal à dire*) the subject encounters in its confrontation with the real, and which subtends the navel of the dream, is a metaphor of castration in which the subject is sent back to the horror of its own death, as well as to the solitude of the subject's responsibility. It is not surprising that the revisions of the dream normally slant toward the forgetting of details surrounding the bad encounter.

But even more radically, the moment at which the signifier turns out to be defective in the encounter with the real makes the subject confront the emptiness of the ideologies with which consciousness arms itself so as to bolster the positions of the ego in its relations with the other on the social scene. The knowledge the dream thoughts make accessible to the analysand calls into question the ideological foundations of his or her narcissistic positions. This is important to observe in the clinical practice of dream analysis today. The knowledge of the dream obliges the subject to reconsider its ethical positions, in the sense that such knowledge progressively unveils the way the logic at work in the phantasm radically contradicts the aims and the pretensions of the ego on the social scene. The knowledge of the dream also brings to the light of day not only the mode in which death is at work in the symptom, but also the profound link uniting this work of *jouissance* to the structure of desire, where the scenario of the phantasm offers up an imaginary construction. These effects of the dream-work are not spontaneous. They presuppose, of course, the constraints of the transference by virtue of which an ethical commitment detaches the analyst from the stakes of his or her own narcissism, so that the transference may center on the love of that knowledge produced by the activating of the unconscious in the dream.

Chapters 6 and 7 of *The Interpretation of Dreams* show us evidence that the dream-work triggers the action of the unconscious, from which the analysand derives a new knowledge of what until then consciousness had been unable to assimilate. But this activation of the real of *jouissance* in the unconscious is precisely what both the analysand and the analyst can come to dread. The occurrence of such a shared fear is precisely what Freud cautions us against in transference love, where the process of transference is reduced to a dual relation between the analysand and the analyst. In the case of neurosis, such an approach to transference, in which the narcissism of the analyst takes the place left empty by the absence of the Other of the unconscious, can only become an obstacle to the work of the unconscious. In perversion it can only transform the work of transference into a competition and a fight to the death. In psychosis this approach to transference only makes it swerve into erotomania. Against such impasses, only the ethics of the analyst, which keeps the transference oriented toward the love of the knowledge to be derived from the dream, can sustain the action of the dream that puts the unconscious to work in the production of knowl-edge of *jouissance.*

The knowledge coming from this putting to work of the unconscious in the dream through transference undermines all the certainties and assurances that sup-port the ego in its assumption of positions on the social scene. The analysand is thus constrained to make an ethical choice between, on the one hand, the knowledge that comes from the experience favored by the dream-work and, on the other, the preser-vation of both the ideological and narcissistic positions taken up within the social bond. The analysand comes up against these ethical stakes from the moment the navel of the dream forces him or her to confront the powerlessness of the signifier with respect to the real that surges up on the occasion of the dream-work. This limit to saying and to interpretation, which the process at work in the structure of the dream seems to calculate, leads the analysand into a singular solitude where he or she is faced with the unbearable thing the dream brings into the open. At this limit of the dream-work, the subject is alone faced with the real, and with the unsustainable exigency of that subject's responsibility for its own acts. It is this precise moment that the ethics of the analyst pinpoints in the clinical analysis of the dream. No interpretation—least of all the analyst's—can substitute for the exigency that an ethical position or decision come from the analysand at this strategic moment. The Freudian dream thus assumes its full meaning as a demand coming from the Other that the subject alone should decide about its relation to *jouissance.* The knowledge that supports the dream-work is then the subject's only support with regard to this demand from the Other.

THE RESPONSE TO THE DESIRE FOR THE ANALYST'S KNOWLEDGE

The dream-work, which allows analysis to count on the production of a knowledge that contests the ideological and narcissistic position of the analysand to the point of compelling him or her to take a new ethical position, comes about due to the maneu-ver the analyst performs in establishing the transference. This maneuver is made pos-sible by the conception of the dream that can be deduced from chapters 6 and 7 of *The Interpretation of Dreams.* Here the dream is conceived of as the construction of a space where the dynamic in which unconscious thoughts are put to work culminates in a representation of desire. What is at stake, then, is knowing by what means the ana-lyst can obtain this activation of the unconscious that gives rise to a knowledge about *jouissance* as it is metaphorized in the representation of desire.

Here the conception of the transference as love of the knowledge expected to come from the unconscious assumes its full clinical importance. In effect, the dream is clearly not a matter of passing from interpretation to interpretation. It is a matter of recogniz-ing how the dream calculates the point that limits the reach of interpretation, a point at which the analysand is required to take a position with respect to the knowledge coming from the Other about the real of *jouissance.* The strategy of the analyst thus becomes decisive. In other words, because the Freudian dream entails the specific work of constructing a space for the representation of the activated knowledge of the Other, it presupposes both a psychoanalytic act as well as the ethical position of the analyst at its foundation. Not every dream has the characteristics of the dream Freud speaks of in *The Interpretation of Dreams.* Every dream is not a psychoanalytic dream. The transference as such must be involved in it, as must the analytical act that supports the transference. This is what clinical practice belatedly imposes on us as its conditions, compelling us today to reread *The Interpretation of Dreams* from a new perspective, one that, at least to me, seems closer to what Freud was seeking to do in writing it.

What, then, is thus required of the analyst as the condition of the dream in the analytic experience? What is properly required is that the analyst takes up Freud's position with respect to the dream at the moment that he was writing *The Interpretation of Dreams.* But what is Freud's position at this precise moment, such as it appears in the structure and the global strategy of his writing? It is obvious that Freud was not interested in an eventual dual relation between himself and any of his patients, and even less in what might be repeated between them about the affective block between his patients and one or both of their parents. What interests Freud is only gaining access through the dream to a knowledge elaborated on the scene of the unconscious in the course of the analytic experience, a knowledge that escapes the grasp of the means he has at his disposal as an intellectual, a man of science, and a researcher; it is a knowledge that also escapes the consciousness of his patients—but also a knowledge that Freud expects to come from the organization and the work of the dream itself. One of the most stunning but also notorious revelations to come from the experience of the *passe* and the *contrôle*—by which today we can, in certain cases, verify or even validate Freud's most daring affirmations and intuitions—is that the dream does not spontaneously, nor in the absence of constraints, yield the stakes of what is woven together on the scene of the unconscious. For this to occur several conditions are necessary—though, curiously, they are not sufficient.

Today the repetition and resumption of the analytic experience make it belatedly apparent that Freud's desire to know was fundamental in triggering the process of the dream as it is put to work in *The Interpretation of Dreams.* Also apparent is that the very least one can demand of the analyst in the experience of the treatment is that he or she take on Freud's desire to know—if only because it pertains to what, from the other scene, drags the life of the analysand through the arcana of despair and suffering.

This ethical constraint of analytic practice on the position of the analyst is built into the analyst's experience of his or her own cure to the extent that, in his or her experience as an analysand, the transference was a matter of taking on the desire to know of the analyst in the form of love (if not passion) for the knowledge the analyst expected from his or her own dreams. Like Freud, in effect every true analysand, who has left behind a therapeutic demand for love, the demand for help, or the appeal to the Other so as to take over from the analyst the desire to know, is aware of this passion, which prompts him or her to wait only for the Other, to await across the dream (among other manifestations), this knowledge where his or her unconscious constitutes itself as the discourse. Strengthened by this experience, the analyst then takes distance from every dual relation into which the patient might drag him or her by means of the narration of the patient's sorrows, or exploits, or with any attempt at conversation. The analyst confines him- or herself to the exigency of knowing what, from the place of the unconscious, motivates the avatars of the patient's life. The analyst's concern for knowledge must be cultivated from both his or her silence and interventions, until it becomes something the analysand can share. It is within this ethical problematic that the desire to know of the unconscious joins the analyst and the analysand together in the same work, in which the dream acts as a response of the Other to the desire to know, which binds the analysand and the analyst to the same passion for knowledge.

What functions as knowledge in this response of the Other in the dream is justified in the dream-work itself, as Freud conceived it. This work is at once a matter of constructing a symbolic space, the place of the other scene, and the activation of the drive upon this other scene. But as we have suggested above, the narration of the dream incorporates the experience of this construction and this activation into the dream thoughts as a discourse lacking a subject of enunciation. The analyst's desire to know is articulated around a question that addresses the subject's bad encounter with the real—an encounter that, in the form of day residues, provoked the dream. Of course the analyst wants to know what weaves itself together on the other scene of the unconscious. But he already knows, thanks to his own experience, and to Freud's indications, that the dream questions the ethical position of the subject with regard to what it would recoil from during its waking hours. The dream is interpretation. Within the regime of the signifier and its defect, it deploys a certain relation of the subject with a real that, as a stranger, intrudes upon the subject's everydayness. It is this relation of the subject to the death at stake in the *jouissance* before which it recoils that becomes the object of a desire to know on the part of the analyst. Thus it is not surprising that such a desire constructs the strange body as an object or as a constraint within the work of elaborating the dream, so as to construct the subject's relation to *jouissance.* It is in this sense that we say the desire to know introduces into the discourse without a subject the constraint that it be addressed in such a way that the narration of the dream constructs the interpretation of the Other concerning the ethical position of the subject with regard to *jouissance.*

An Unpleasant Surprise for Reason at This Beginning of the Century

With *The Interpretation of Dreams,* Freud issued us right into a depth psychology— at an initial stage, that was his term—that submits our conceptions of humanity and spirit to a rupture that subverts both the psychical apparatus and consciousness, giving spirit all the room it needs for the revolution undertaken before him by Darwin. In fact, with this text—the profound meaning of which escapes us if we separate it from *The Project for a Scientific Psychology* and from *Beyond the Pleasure Principle*—Freud introduces a decisive point of view that radically changes our approach to the question of spirit. In it he constructs the model for a space that traverses the psychical apparatus, a space inhabited by the forces of death that fundamentally contradict our ideas about life, social coexistence, and even natural evolution. Our concept of life finds itself subverted by this death, which, in accord with a logic that does not obey simply the laws of biology, leads life to death's door. Or rather, in accordance with Freud's wishes, these are the very laws that his conceptual contribution would revolutionize. Our notion of society, guided by a civilization haunted by the idea of enviable progress, is compromised by an internal discontent where the worst is not the enemy of the good. All of our most modern conceptions will be contradicted in advance by this discontent, and will be so to the precise extent to which they are developed in the shadows of a quasi-religious caution and an interdiction upon thought that were initially imposed on Freud's works, within both the field of medicine, with its scientific and naturalist orientation, and the field of politics with the rise of Nazism. The oddest thing that Freud's text announces, at the beginning of the twenty-first century, is that the good news is that the dream thoughts are the worst nightmare of a humanity whose only objective in life is death. These dream thoughts contest constituted knowledges and the pretentions nourished by them. They calculate the limits of such knowledges with regard to an ethic according to which humanity, in total solitude and faced with its future and that of the environment, must take responsibility for its successes, as well as its errors.

4. Freud's Dream of America

Patricia Gherovici

Fully immersed in a book I was writing on hysteria in the Puerto Rican ghetto, I chanced upon historical material about the colonial history of the United States at the end of the nineteenth century. It was in that connection that I reopened the pages of *The Interpretation of Dreams* in which Freud describes one of his most peculiar dreams, a dream of a castle by the sea, a dream of naval war, too, a complex narrative dealing with the Spanish-American War (SE V, 463-64). This was the war that ended with the annexation of Puerto Rico by the United States; it meant the end of four hundred years of Spanish domination over the island, and it inaugurated a new form of colonialism for the United States. You can imagine my surprise and excitement when I discerned a confirmation that this historical incident had left unmistakable traces in Freud's own dreams.

We tend to forget the echoes of colonial struggles that found their way into *The Interpretation of Dreams,* above all because we rarely associate the Austrian context of the turn of the century with overseas imperialism. In this essay I wish not just to test the extent of my own interpretive paranoia, but to reconstruct the circumstances surrounding Freud's momentous discovery of the meaning of dreams. By a curious historical coincidence, one of the most influential findings of the twentieth century took place at the same time that Puerto Rico was passing to U.S. control. In the name of liberty, justice, and humanity, American forces occupied Puerto Rico, beginning a new chapter in the Caribbean island's colonial history. "Our purpose is to grant all those who may come under the control of our military and naval forces the advantages and benefits of civilization," proclaimed Major General Nelson A. Miles upon occupation of Puerto Rico on July 25, 1898. In his invasion speech, Major General Miles announced the "advantages and benefits of civilization" and expressed his desire "to put the conscience of the American people into the island."[1] If the conscience of the American people was going to be put into the island, however, one may wonder about the fate of the Freudian repressed, and most important, of the unconscious, now "under the control of military and naval forces." To start answering, let me quote Freud describing his dream:

> A castle by the sea; later it was no longer immediately on the sea, but on a narrow canal leading to the sea. The governor was a Herr P. I am standing with him in a big three-windowed salon, in front of which rise projections of walls like fortress battlements. I belong to the garrison, perhaps as a volunteer naval officer. We fear the arrival of enemy warships, because we are in a state of war. Herr P. has the intention of going away; he is giving me instructions what to do in case of what we fear. His sick wife is with his children in the besieged castle. When the bombardment begins, the big hall is to be vacated. He breathes heavily and tries to get away; I hold him back and ask him in what manner I should let news reach him in case of need. Then he says something else, but at once his head sinks down dead. I may have overstrained him unnecessarily with questions. After his death, which makes no further impression on me, I wonder whether the widow should remain in the castle, whether I ought to announce the death to the Higher Command, and whether I should take over the control of the castle as next in command. Now I stand at the window and inspect the ships, which are passing by; they are merchant vessels, which rush rapidly past on the dark water, some with several stacks, others with bulging decks. Then my brother is standing beside me, and we both look out the window upon the canal. At one ship we are frightened and cry: "There comes the warship." But it turns out that only the same ships are coming back which we have already seen. Now comes a little ship, comically cut off so that it ends in the middle at its broadest; on a deck there are peculiar cup or box-like things. We cry out as of one mouth: "That is the breakfast ship."[2]

In his analysis of this dream, Freud acknowledges that the dream contains allusions to the maritime war between America and Spain and to anxieties it had created about the fate of his relatives, who had recently moved to New York. He explains that the deceased Herr P. appears as a substitute for himself, from which we may infer that Freud was one of the first casualties of the Spanish-American War. Freud's personal connection with this war could be seen as having wider implications. Perhaps the creator of psychoanalysis was already aware of the ominous consequences of American colonialist aspirations at a time when the United States looked to the Caribbean islands as territory to be conquered. What is even more ominous is that the dream describes an Etruscan urn looking like a boat—quite similar to the Greek urn in which Freud's ashes were to be deposited in 1939.

To understand better the political implications of the day-residues that have elicited this dream, it is indispensable to recapitulate certain events that Freud does not develop in his analysis of the dream, but that quite strikingly reappear in his recollection of it. They arouse our suspicion because they emerge in Freud's dream not just as distorted remnants, but almost as word-for-word transcriptions of what he had read in Austrian newspapers about the Spanish-American War. Although Freud's interpretation of the dream alludes to them in passing, because he seems more interested in idiosyncratic or private associations leading to a distant past (an enjoyable Easter trip to the Adriatic, a trip to Venice, some Etruscan pottery, mourning customs, funeral boats, gloomy thoughts of an unknown future), the material of the dream is brought forth by the curious historical events that took place in the month preceding it. To enhance scientific neutrality, Freud chooses in his narrative to downplay the obvious political content of the dream.

After a careful examination of all the issues in the daily paper, Leslie Adams asserts that this dream must have taken place on the night of May 10–11, 1898.[3] This thesis is confirmed by all the curious details that crop up in it. At this time there were fears that New York might be attacked by the Spanish fleet. Freud's dream recombines elements of the battle of Manila, which was fought on May 1, the news of which reached the media by cable only a week after, on May 7. It is clear that Freud had read the relatively bewildering account of the battle, which was spread over the first three pages of the *Neue Freie Presse* on the morning of May 10, 1898.

Here are the events that preceded the dream. After mounting tension between the Americans and the Spaniards, the USS *Maine*, which had come into the harbor of Havana on a friendly visit, was shattered by an explosion and sank on February 15, 1898. President McKinley was notified in his bedchamber that 266 Americans had been killed. The Hearst press began throwing the American people into fury with a saga involving an endangered, virginal, young, beautiful woman who had been kept unjustly in prison by the Spaniards. War was actually declared two months later, on April 22. By May 2, the world press reported that a strong Spanish squadron under Admiral Cervera had left the Azores and taken to the high seas in a westward direction. Would it attack America or the West Indies? The fear extended along the coast, reaching as far as New York. Lighthouses were dimmed and buoys were placed from Maine to Florida. The whole Atlantic coast was on the lookout for enemy ships. Worried watchfulness was the mood in every newspaper during the following days.[4] Only on May 11 did the *Neue Freie Presse* make it clear that the Spanish fleet had been sighted off Puerto Rico, which implied that it was headed for the Antilles and not New York.

While this international drama developed, a dreamlike series of events had unfolded elsewhere. Admiral Dewey, in charge of part of the American fleet, had been in Hong Kong when the war began; he then sailed into the Pacific and had been lost to view. On the last night of April, Dewey, aboard his flagship *Olympia*, led his fleet into the harbor of Manila. This action should have led to certain destruction according to the principles of warfare because the Spanish fleet was entrenched and supplied in a land-locked harbor, well protected by the guns of fortresses. At five o'clock on Sunday morning, May 1, Dewey's fleet swept in front of the enemy squadron in single file, as if in a parade. The Spanish fleet began to fire, but the American ships swept on, not answering the fire, in exasperating contempt of the poor marksmanship of the enemy. It looks indeed as if the historical event already had the structure of a dream.

"CALL OFF FOR BREAKFAST!"

The most astounding element of this episode was the behavior of Admiral Dewey. According to contemporary press reports, including those in the Viennese papers, which covered the battle in great detail, he stood on his bridge quietly, remarking on the weather and the distant hills, saying that they reminded him of his native Vermont. A half hour went by while his fleet swept back and forth, coming into ever-closer range. He finally uttered, "You may fire when you are ready, Gridley." Sailing in closer ellipses, the American ships all opened fire. At half past seven, after two terrible hours of steady firing, Dewey ordered, "Call off for breakfast!" This was a command that became world famous. Admiral Dewey interrupted the battle at breakfast time, just when conditions for battle were excellent and there was no resistance on the enemy's side. Some men cried out, "For God's sake, Captain, to hell with breakfast; give it to them now," while the Spaniards raised a great shout as they thought the Americans were fleeing. After breakfast the firing resumed and lasted several hours. Finally, when the smoke was gone, the Americans could see that that all the Spanish ships were sinking or on fire. Captain Cadarso, commander of the *Reina María Cristina*, had fallen dead on the bridge and had been replaced by his second in command, who was immediately killed. The rear half of the ship had been blown up, and Admiral Montojo, commander of the fleet, would not quit the other half. The marksmanship of the Spaniards was obviously terrible: during the battle not one shot of theirs hit any target. Half an hour past noon—in time for lunch—the Spanish fortress hoisted the white flag. Even though the scene of destruction was awful, with flaming hulks, shattered fragments of ships, and the water-battery devastated on the Spanish side, this was nonetheless a "clean war" for the Americans, as not one single person on their side had been killed.

During the breakfast cease-fire, however, the Spanish, who controlled the city of Manila, had sent a message of victory to Madrid. Later they sent a second message of defeat, concealed in comforting euphemisms. Although victorious, Dewey was prevented by the Spaniards from using the cable. Exasperated, he fished it from the sea and cut it. As a result, the outcome of the battle was learned only much later, when a ship reached Hong Kong. Thus for a whole week the Americans knew that there had been a battle, but they were not sure whether Dewey had won or whether the Spanish fleet was heading to New York. Finally, the full story was published in Vienna on the morning of May 10. Only a week after the battle did the public realize that the Spaniards had been defeated and that New York was out of danger.

We see many elements of the dream appearing as repetitions of the battle events. Let us review just a few: Freud talks about "the arrival of enemy warships, because we are in a state of war," and says "I hold him [Herr P.] back and ask him in what manner I should let news reach him in case of need. Then he says something else, but at once his head sinks down dead. I may have overstrained him unnecessarily with questions." It is easy to imagine how "overstrained" the international public may have been then, submerged in tense expectation after hearing contradictory accounts, fearing an attack on New York and worried about the uncertain results of the battle. "I wonder whether I ought to announce the death to the Higher Command, and whether I should take over the control of the castle as next in command." During the battle, Captain Cadarso, commander of the *Reina María Cristina*, was killed, and, like Herr P., he was replaced by his second in command. Since the cable had been cut after the battle, neither the general public nor even even the High Command were properly informed. Who was in control "of the castle" remained unknown between May 1 and May 10.

"At one ship we are frightened and cry: 'There comes the warship'... Now comes a little ship, comically cut off so that it ends in the middle at its broadest; on a deck there are peculiar cup or box-like things. We cry out as of one mouth: 'That is the breakfast ship.'" The appearance of the seemingly nonsensical "breakfast ship" is self-explanatory after Dewey's striking, dreamlike breakfast cease-fire and his famous command. As for the strange shape of the "little ship, comically cut off so that it ends in the middle at its broadest," let us recall that the rear half of Captain Cardarso's ship had been blown up, and that Admiral Montojo, commander of the fleet, had refused to quit the other half.

SAFE ON HIS SHIP, THE OLD MAN QUIETLY SAILS INTO PORT

This dream of Freud's provides an excellent example of the function of overdetermination: "[T]wo interpretations are not mutually contradictory, but both cover the same ground; they are a good instance of the fact that dreams, like all other psychopathological structures, regularly have more than one meaning" (SE IV, 149). Let us note that in this dream the day-residues do not seem to undergo many distortions; they are not mere allusions, but reappear almost intact in the dream material. Since, as Freud says, "our dream thoughts are dominated by the same material that has occupied us during the day and we only bother to dream of things which have given us cause for reflection in the daytime" (174), the political implications of the dream are even more relevant.

I shall now concentrate on the striking political and historical relevance of this dream, taking advantage of the positive character of overdetermination. Freud does not see the dream as having only one unique and exhaustive meaning; rather, he sees it as a point of emergence for a series of meanings. Louis Althusser's concept of overdetermination (for something to occur, there must be several conflicts at work) can help in this case, since the Freudian heritage in Althusser's "symptomatic reading" of Marx's *Capital* confirms that we need to cross the gap between the social and the individual.

Each of Freud's dream elements is overdetermined. Even when motivated by very personal and idiosyncratic circumstances, every point is nonetheless traversed by the effects of a wider context, betraying a connection with social structure. Following Lacan's topological model, one can read the dream as a knot tying different meanings, corresponding to various levels, together. From this perspective, the Freudian idea of overdetermination demonstrates that the dream has several causes working together, bringing about a new concept of causality. If, however, the manifest content of the dream seems to be motivated by very identifiable daytime ideas, I do not want to stress only one meaning. Thus, I would also like to speculate on the psychic factors instigating this dream in order to trace back its latent content. In this regard, Freud himself offers a lucid interpretation of the dream. He alludes to a line of Schiller, "Still, auf gerettetem Boot, triebt in den Hafen der Greis" (Safe on his ship, the old man quietly sails into port), allegorizing life and death. He analyzes this dream as expressing fears about his own death.

Interestingly, Freud notes that the Governor's death left him quite indifferent, despite the fact that his analysis showed that Herr P. was a substitute for himself. Freud's fears involve the future of his family after his premature death. The profound impression awakened by the arrival of the warship led him to recall an event that had occurred a year earlier, during a "magically beautiful day at the room on the Riva degli Schiavoni" in Venice. At the sight of a ship, his wife had cried out "gaily as a child: *Here comes the English warship.*" When those words reappear in the dream, they are cause for deep fright.

The "tense and sinister impression" at the end of the dream is produced by the return of the shipwreck (*Schiffbruch*, literally "ship-break")—the cut-off, broken-off ship. Freud analyzes the appearance of the "breakfast-ship" by referring to the word *English*, which is the leftover of his wife's phrase, *Here comes the English warship*, which, in the dream, becomes "*Here comes the warship.*" This missing signifier reappears in the word *breakfast* (literally, breaking fast). "Break" relates to "ship-break," which returns intact, and "fast" becomes "fasting," then connected to mourning dress. Freud notes that the breakfast ship was comically cut off, and that on the deck there were peculiar cup-like or box-like things bearing great resemblance to some objects that had attracted his attention when he had seen them in Etruscan museums. They were rectangular trays of black pottery similar to modern-day breakfast sets. These were, in fact, the toilette objects of an Etruscan lady. The idea of black "toilette" relates also to mourning dress, thus making a direct reference to death. Then Freud attributes the origin of the "breakfast-ship" to the English word *breakfast*, here linked to both ship-breaking and the black mourning dress:

[B]ut it was only the *name* of the breakfast ship that was newly constructed by the dream. The *thing* had existed and reminded me of one of the most enjoyable parts of my last trip. Mistrusting that food would be provided at Aquileia we had brought provisions with us. . . . And while the little mail steamer made its way slowly through the "*Canale delle Mee*" across the empty lagoon to Grado we, who were the only passengers, ate our breakfast on deck in the highest spirits, and we had rarely tasted a better one. This then, was the "breakfast-ship," and it was precisely behind this memory of the most cheerful *joie de vivre* that the dream concealed the gloomiest thoughts of an unknown and uncanny future.[5]

Here life and death converge, as in a pagan wake, in which intense joy and deep fear all get played out in this rich dream. Behind a memory of the happiest joie de vivre, the *jouissance de vivre* emerges. Freud's analysis about what lies behind the coining of the "breakfast ship" includes the phrase, "The *thing* had existed." It is almost impossible not to hear echoes of both Freud's and Lacan's elaborations on *das Ding*, the "unforgettable thing" that ex-ists beyond our attempts at symbolization. The dream stops when the domain of the Real is encountered.

Still Freud chose not to explore the evident parallel between his inner thoughts and the sociopolitical realm. However, the impact of the historical events that may have brought up "the gloomiest thoughts of an unknown and uncanny future" were clearly there.

So the Dream Will Be

In a letter to Fliess written one year after this dream (May 28, 1899), Freud calls the *Traumdeutung* simply *der Traum* (the dream) and writes: "So the dream will be. That this Austria is supposed to perish in the next two weeks made my decision easier. Why should the dream perish with it?"[6] As William McGrath observes, even though Freud's "ironic estimate of Austria's durability was not borne out, Freud's sense of impending political disintegration was well founded":

> The bitter divisions over language, nationality, and class that beset the Habsburg Empire seemed to threaten its existence repeatedly during the closing years of the nineteenth century, when Freud was engaged in what proved to be his most important scientific project.[7]

As McGrath notes, Freud's comment sets the writing of *The Interpretation of Dreams* against its political background, demonstrating Freud's awareness of how profoundly influenced his "dream" had been by the political conditions of his day.

During his analysis of what is called the Castle by the Sea Dream, Freud mentions that the dream-work brings about a *suppression of affects.* Thus, it reduces intense emotions to a level of indifference. Since political issues often raise intense emotions, can we say that the suppression of the political implications of a dream is due to their highly emotional tone? I will contend that political elements not only make their way into the dream, but that the collective is a formation of the unconscious, itself comparable to a dream.

Manila's almost surrealist battle had baffled the principle of noncontradiction, since both sides for a while were uncertain about the issue. If there were political allegiances for Freud, they were mixed. On the one hand, he was worried about his relatives living in New York. Four years earlier, in 1892, the brother of Freud's wife, Eli Bernays (who was married to Freud's sister, Anna), had emigrated to the United States, and in 1889 his relatives were living at 1883 Madison Avenue (between 121st and 122nd Streets). However, Freud's position in the dream, fearing the arrival and attack of the breakfast-ship, may remind us that he was not very fond of America, that he considered it a "gigantic mistake," being the "anti-Paradise" and "useful to nothing else but to supply money."[8] We may assume that Freud regretted the defeat of the Spanish, perhaps in the name of the long-standing Spanish-Austrian alliance, and sided with the former Empire, now weakened and victimized. An earlier event in Freud's life will shed more light on the content of this dream.

Freud had a particular transferential relationship to the Spanish language, which he fondly called "the beautiful Castilian tongue," and which he had learned on his own at a young age. As an adolescent, he founded an exclusive secret society with his intimate friend, Edward Silberstein. This he called the "Spanish Academy."[9] So as not to allow the others to understand, they used Spanish as a secret language. Freud had taught himself Spanish to read *Don Quixote* in the original. Perhaps, in the same way, he had set aside—in fact abandoned—hypnosis to teach himself a new language, psychoanalysis, so as to listen to the unconscious in the original dialect of hysteria.

Let us remember that Freud had this dream in 1898, three years after the publication of *Studies on Hysteria*, thus at a time when he was establishing the foundations of psychoanalysis. When he abandoned hypnosis and created psychoanalysis, Freud abandoned a therapy that was structured like a crowd, according to the demonstration of *Massenpsychologie*. (Freud states that, in hypnosis as in the crowd, the psychic mechanism at work is basically the same.)

Freud's main thesis describes hypnosis as a crowd of two, an idea that is taken not in the metaphorical sense, but quite literally. What is at stake for both hypnosis and for the crowd is group identity. Crowds erase difference because they crave conformity: they need a master to love and to be loved by, without any concern for truth. Whenever we find mass phenomena, we encounter segregation. Segregation is not a secondary consequence, but the condition of a crowd's formation. Segregation is what constitutes the crowd.

Segregation is the disavowal of difference. All group formations erase difference because their constitution is based on a principle of identity. Any attempt to stress differences, no matter how minimal, can be experienced by the crowd as an attack that threatens its very existence. Against the grain of the logic of group formations, psychoanalysis opens up a space of tolerance for difference if analysts are prudent (remaining on their guard against the temptation of playing the prophet or the master), and if they stubbornly refrain from the practice of suggestion, that is, if they abstain from exercising a form of hypnosis (and from producing a therapy that can be called a crowd of two).

THE CROWD, THE DREAM OF DREAMS

Freud renders the meaning of dreams intelligible; he makes the royal path to the unconscious interpretable. Nonetheless, as we have seen, in his analysis of this dream he chooses to disregard any of the obvious political implications of its content. Is this because psychoanalysis is a clinical practice built upon singularity, difference, and particularity? Then how can it stand up to the challenge of history, which entails an engagement with collective formations? How is the psychoanalytic practice affected by the political conditions of its day? How far do the affairs of the city extend? Could it be that psychoanalysis, in spite of its love for knowledge, passionately ignores, in fact actively "resists," the social?

At the very end of the dream, at the sight of a small ship, Freud and his brother cry in one voice, "That is the breakfast ship." Freud tells us about this last scene of his dream: "[T]he rapid movements of the ships, the deep dark blue water and the brown smoke of the funnels—all this combined to create a tense and sinister impression." What rises up at the end of this dream seems clearly to be anxiety. As Freud and Lacan formulate it, anxiety would be the radical way in which the subject sustains, even in an unsustainable way, a relationship with his or her own desire. Freud's dream ends with breakfast, marking the end of the night; satisfying the desire for hunger; waking up from history to the concrete needs of everyday rituals: it is time for breakfast. The war—even the dream—can wait. Admiral Dewey himself had repeated this gesture in going from the collective imperative of the war to the individual need for food, punctually interrupting the battle to have breakfast.

As we have seen, the brothers Freud cry in one voice: "as of one mouth" would be a literal translation of the German. One might think of another mouth, the one and only mouth, the open mouth leading to the throat at the back of which Freud found the secret of dreams. When Lacan, in his second Seminar, discusses the dream of dreams—the dream *princeps*, that of Irma's Injection—he mentions in passing this very dream about the Spanish-American War.[10] There, in fact, Lacan establishes a peculiar connection between language, segregation, and psychoanalysis when he proposes a correlation between the crowd and the dream. His specific topic of discussion is the *ego* seen under the light of his mirror-stage logic. Here Lacan notes that the narcissism we see in dreams is not there for the subject from the start, but rather is a "new psychic act," as Freud calls it: it comes into being in the mirror stage, the *ego* does not exist before a relationship with a *semblable* is started. The borrowed image of one's own body is appropriated in anticipation, and it becomes the principle of every unity the subject may perceive in objects. At the time Lacan was still telling the ego-psychologists that the subject of the unconscious is decentered in respect to the *ego*. Thus, this subject is alienated and in a constant state of tension, perpetually in a state of fictitious unity in a world structured around the wandering shadow of the ego. Lacan even calls this an "egomorphic" world.

In dreams, because of an easing-up of imaginary relations, this constitutive alienation is even more poignant. The very truth of the subject appears exposed in its decomposition, in the real brought by the night, and which usually culminates in anxiety. Referring to the Irma Dream, Lacan adds that there is a moment when something of the real, something at its most unfathomable, is attained. He therefore explains how the quest for signification contains a moment at which the meaning of the Dream of Irma's Injection is revealed to Freud. Strikingly, Lacan names this moment *the crowd*, stating that this crowd is not just any crowd, but a crowd structured "like the Freudian crowd."[11]

What is Lacan doing when he describes the revelation of the secret of dreams as a crowd? Lacan puts this moment in the dream side by side with the Freudian crowd (the type of crowd that Freud analyses in *Massenpsychologie und Ich-Analyse*) because he locates an analogy in their structures: both the dream and the crowd are formations of the unconscious that result from a failed *jouissance* and, as such, are equivalent to other formations of the unconscious, such as parapraxes, slips of the tongue, and symptoms.

Using these sets of equivalences, one could better understand how the ahistoricity of the unconscious is traversed by history; how the political is articulated with the subjective; how the sexual and the group life are intertwined. The crowd illustrates the relationship of each member with its own image. If Lacan compares the dream to the Freudian crowd, it is precisely because this crowd, according to Lacan's reading of Freud, is structured as the image of the body of the subject; indeed, it is structured as a polycephalic subject or even an *acephalic* subject.[12] It is well known that the Irma Dream allowed Freud to discover the royal path to unconscious desire. If dreams and the Freudian crowd share a common structure, a dream or a crowd can be read as an "inmixing of subjects."[13] This corresponds to the dialectics of intersubjectivity, which take place when a subject is constituted in its interacting, "mixing" in with things or with other subjects as counterparts: the genesis of meaning has no other site. According to Lacan, subjects only become subjects of speech (barred subjects) once speech exists, and there is no before. The polycephalic subject of the crowd is made up of the imaginary plurality of the subject, of the multiple identifications of the ego. Lacan notes that this polycephalic subject is almost an acephalic subject, a subject that no longer has an ego, and yet is the subject who speaks and gives to all the characters in the dream their nonsensical lines.

The acephalic subject speaks the nonsense of the dream beyond the ego, revealing a knowledge, for instance, of the arrival of the uncanny breakfast ships of the Spanish-American War—called "a splendid little war" by the U.S. Secretary of State, John Hay. This is the war that included both the famous battle of Manila, which was punctually called off for a breakfast break, and an invasion of Puerto Rico, which was often described in military records as a "picnic."

Identity Is Structured Like a Crowd

Lacan notes that Freud says, about his dream, something Freud himself paraphrases as "I'm not in the dream where one might think. The character who just died, this commandant who is with me, it is he who is I."[14] The fact that Freud was not situated in the dream where one might suppose him to be uncovers the unfathomable, fundamental component of the narcissistic relation upon which identity is based. This is the same type of relation revealed by the crowd as by hypnosis—an identity always constructed in alienation, that is, as other. This dialectic entails a passionate rapture and overjoy: I am the other, the other is me.

In the dream context, the Spanish-American War, to which Freud is alluding, resulted in a new form of colonialism for the United States, and has had lasting consequences that are still changing America's identity today. The rise of the Hispanic "crowd" brings up questions about race, identity, and culture. Indeed the Hispanic could be seen as the repudiated other of the construction of American identity.

If the Hispanic as other is segregated, we could say that this separation occurs precisely because of its role as the leftover other upon which identification has been built. Here the mirror stage appears replayed in racial disarray. As the paradigm of all resemblance, the specular, anticipated image of the body functions as an image alienated in a fictional figure. The Hispanic as marginal would appear as the other under the domination of its American counterpart. However, in this dialectic of Other and other it is not so easy to determine, in these pendular oscillations, who is the one and who is the other. This fascination with the image of the other will bring over into the world of objects a tinge of hostility or transgression, by projecting onto them the manifestation of the narcissistic image. When facing a fellow being, the pleasure derived from meeting oneself in the mirror is transformed into an outlet for the most intimate aggressiveness. This aggressiveness emerges full force in racism, and runs the risk of being resolved through murderous or suicidal aggressiveness.[15] This logic of identification entails that one cannot see oneself, but one can find one's image in the neighbor in the crowd, granted that there is a leader that occupies the place of the ideal.

Freud's dream collapses the individual together with the collective, because these are in fact inseparable. Identity is structured like a crowd. The transference that makes all groups cohere is part of a movement, started by love, that always includes some narcissistic element, and can at times crystallize in a "crowd of two" when the object is placed in the position of ego ideal (*Ichideal*), as in the process of hypnosis.

How could the crowd be the model for subjective identity? One might well assert the contrary: a crowd would abolish the subject, who gives up her individuality to belong to the crowd. But in fact the logical order is reversed: first there is the crowd, second there is the individual; first the dream, afterward the subject. Something quite extreme takes place, both in the crowd and in the dream. A truly dramatic instance may indeed have been lost in translation. Isn't Freud's *Massenpsychologie* mistranslated into English as *Group Psychology?* Why is the signifier "group" replacing that of the crowd? William McDougall makes it clear that a group is not a crowd. Interestingly, in the Spanish version of Freud's complete works, among the illustrations accompanying the text of *Massenpsychologie* there are two pictures taken in the United States around 1920. The captions claim that crowds became part of the American life years before they appeared in European countries.

If there is a discrepancy in translation, the reasons may be both geopolitical and chronological. It seems that the first part of the twentieth century has been rightly called the age of the masses, from Le Bon to Canetti,[16] and that the end of the last century has been variously described as the age of nationalities or of minorities. Could it be that we need to shift our conceptual paradigms to address a different situation, one described by Michel de Certeau as that of "culture in the plural"?[17] Can we overhaul the model of identification, mass hysterization, and mass delusion, of which we formerly have made great use? Has the mass phenomenon been extinguished and replaced by mass-media phenomena? Or is the idle crowd of *Massenpsychologie,* repressed by a linguistic slippage in its mistranslation as "group," returning with a vengeance in the "mass" of the Hispanic minority? If in the present, the "crowd" has been replaced by minority "groups," as collective formations these nonetheless share a common pattern, that of a similar and failed *jouissance.* Perhaps it was also in the name of *jouissance* that since October 1996 in Washington, under waving flags, tens of thousands of Hispanics gather massively. "Gone are the days when people could talk about Latinos as a mob without ideas and without a political program," declared Juan José Gutierrez, director of Coordinadora 96, the group organizing the march. Nonetheless, the event was portrayed in the *New York Times* as "the first mass protest organized by Hispanic people in the nation's capital."[18] This is how the journalist described the event: "[A]s much as the march and rally reflected anger among Hispanic people, it was an attempt by many participants to display pride in their heritage and to remind the larger society of their presence."

FREUD'S DREAM OF AMERIKA

According to Freud's own logic in *Group Psychology and the Analysis of the Ego* (1921), even though his "Spanish Academy" had but two members, it was already a collective formation, a crowd of two, and conceivably a repetition of the mythical primal horde. This myth, often contested because of its weak anthropological foundations, is in fact an ahistorical myth used by Freud because this Darwinian fantasy allows him to explain the function of the father as what guarantees the place of a speaker who may believe that *jouissance* is possible. However, it is at the level of the brothers, who feel guilty afterward, that things start to move for civilization. Back to the dream: Herr P is dead, left behind are his wife and children. Freud and his brother stay alone in charge of the garrison, taking care of the castle and of the wife and children. A replay of the old totemic myth? The immediate historical context traverses this dream, creating a continuum between Freud's private psychic life and the political world. The collective is not opposed to the unconscious. As Freud's dream illustrates, the collective is itself a formation of the unconscious.

Why is Freud dreaming about this war, fought far away in foreign lands? His interest in the war was probably influenced by the political situation of Vienna at the time and by the prevailing sense of looming disintegration. The 1897 government of Count Badeni obtained the anti-Semitic Christian Socials' support, which had a profound emotional significance both for Jews and for Germans nationalists.[19] Freud may have been identified with both groups. We also know of the growing anti-Semitism in Vienna at the time, and of the direct impact it had on Freud's career. His dream of his uncle with the yellow beard (February 1897) shows his concern about his university appointment being blocked by anti-Semitic pressure. Freud was obviously in the position of the segregated other. On the other hand, Peter Gay notes that Freud honestly admits, in *The Interpretation of Dreams*, that in his life he needed an enemy as much as a friend. Therefore, Gay understands Freud's lifetime staunch anti-Americanism as a construction of a gigantic collective manifestation of the enemy he said he couldn't do without.

The Viennese Jew Freud may have seen America as "Amerika," that is to say as a mystic writing pad upon which to project his experience of otherness—as may have been the case for the Czech Jew, Kafka. Neither Kafka, when he wrote *Amerika*, nor Freud at the time of the dream, had visited the United States. America was the most familiar and most strange at the same time, fascinating in and through its otherness.

LIFE IS A DREAM

Freud woke up from his dream of the Spanish-American War, but the United States still dreams this same dream of a Hispanic-versus-American War over and over again. Latinos have become the largest U.S. minority (a crowd!), and, given massive immigration and high birthrates, by 2050 nearly one quarter of the U.S. population, an estimated ninety-six million people, will be Latino. Hispanics overall are younger than the rest of the nation's population. They are also the least educated and the poorest: 40 percent of Latino children in the United States live in poverty, the highest poverty rate in the country's history.

I have suggested elsewhere that the United States constructs itself as an empire with the Spanish Empire as the repressed Other. Therefore, the role of Hispanics, as Spanish-Americans becoming the "first" minority, is crucial. If Martin Luther King were here with us today, he would not say "I have a dream," but exclaim "[W]e are the dream, we are the crowd, we are the Real thing." Or perhaps he would repeat the memorable words of the main character of Pedro Calderón de la Barca's *Life Is a Dream*. In this play, the imprisoned Polish Prince, coincidentally named Segismundo (Sigmund!), had been kept in a tower since birth by the King in order to foil the prediction that his fate was to bring disgrace to the kingdom and his father's downfall. After years of imprisonment the King had a change of heart and the young man was brought to court for a trial while in a drugged sleep. Awakening to the majestic grandeur of the court, he saw his father, the King Basilio, and vengefully tried to attack him. The guards intervened, and Segismundo, asleep, was returned to his prison. Back in his tower, he believed that everything was just a dream. Nonetheless, when a peasant revolt liberated him, Segismundo was magnanimous with the vanquished King and, aware that his new life was but a dream, this time he behaved more prudently. This was what he said:

> I dream that I am here,
> burdened with these prisons,
> and I dreamt that in another,
> I saw myself in a more joyful state,
> What is life? A frenzy,
> What is life? An illusion,
> a shadow, a fiction,
> and the greatest good is small;
> all life is a dream,
> and a dream, is a dream.[20]

If we agree, as the mirror stage teaches us, that the collective is a formation of the unconscious, and that the individual, far from preceding the crowd, is in fact produced by it, then the unconscious is at once singular and yet traversed by the plural. The unconscious makes of the collective a singular question. The subject, however, is lost in the dream, but reappears in the telling of the dream. Freud's originality as a psychoanalyst was in taking the dream in its associations to its forgotten parts. This is to say that Freud takes the dream as the telling of the dream. What is important in clinical practice is that the dream can be told; the dream makes us speak. If the social link materializes oneiric life, then, paraphrasing Gérard Pommier, one may say that the social link allows us to dream while awake.[21]

NOTES

1. Ralph Hancock, *Puerto Rico: A Success Story* (Princeton, N.J.: D. Van Nostrand Co., 1960), 69. Quoted by Roberta Ann Johnson in *Puerto Rico: Commonwealth or Colony?* (New York: Praeger Publisher, 1980), 12.

2. SE V, 463–64; translation slightly modified.

3. Leslie Adams, "A New Look at Freud's Dream 'The Breakfast Ship,'" *American Journal of Psychiatry* 110 (1953): 381–84. I am much indebted for a very careful examination of the *Neue Freie Presse* articles.

4. Ibid.

5. Ibid., 466.

6. Sigmund Freud, *The Complete Letters of Sigmund Freud to Wilhelm Fliess, 1887–1904,* trans. Jeffrey Moussaieff Masson (Cambridge: The Belknap Press of Harvard University Press, 1985), 353.

7. William McGrath, *Freud's Discovery of Psychoanalysis: The Politics of Hysteria* (Ithaca: Cornell University Press, 1986), 15.

8. All quoted in Peter Gay, *Freud: A Life of Our Time* (New York: Doubleday, 1986), 563.

9. Ibid., 22.

10. Jacques Lacan, *The Seminar of Jacques Lacan Book II: The Ego in Freud's Theory and in the Technique of Psychoanalysis 1954–1955,* trans. Sylvana Tomaselli (New York: W. W. Norton & Co., 1988).

11. Ibid., 160.

12. Ibid., 167.

13. Ibid.

14. Ibid. This passage that Lacan mentions is found at SE V, 467, 448, and 464.

15. See Jacques Lacan, *Ecrits: A Selection* (New York: W. W. Norton & Co, 1977), 1–113.

16. Elias Canetti, *Crowds and Power* (1962; New York: Farrar Straus Giroux, 1973).

17. Michel De Certeau, *La cultura en plural* (Buenos Aires: Ediciones Nueva Vision, 1999).

18. Steven Homes, "Hispanic March Draws Crowd to Capital," *New York Times,* October 13, 1996, 26.

19. The language conflict between the Czechs and the Germans was resolved by the government of Badeni, which had the support of Karl Lueger's anti-Semitic Christian Socialists. They assured him of their support or abstention in parliament in return for the confirmation of Lueger as mayor of Vienna. This development offered cause for profound anxiety to all Jews living in Vienna.

20. My translation.

21. Gérard Pommier, *Libido illimité—Freud apolitique?* (Paris: Éditions Point Hors Ligne, 1990).

5. Literature and Pathology

Masochism Takes the Upper Hand

Avital Ronell

Unbearable Examples of Suffering

Ever resisting the temptation to be born again, even today, as we mark the one-hundredth anniversary of its initializing text, psychoanalysis was from the start just about the only one to confront human cruelty, the punishing aspects of the psyche, without a theological alibi—in fact, with no alibi or safety net. Psychoanalysis ventured forth without an alibi—with no excuse, as it were. This is one of Derrida's recent themes: that psychoanalysis met head-on with unbearable examples of suffering, but took no recourse to theology. It may have scanned monotheism, or even served as witness for Dr. Schreber when he took wedding vows to the Almighty, but it rigorously steered clear of cutting a deal with transcendental power brokers.[1] Psychoanalysis took no recourse, had no alibi, but bravely faced the facts of human cruelty. The trajectory of Derrida's argument leads him, via psychoanalytic writings on war—"Warum Krieg?"—to pass severe words on the United States, the only Christian and democratic nation to uphold the death penalty. Why has psychoanalysis as a political body had nothing to say about this state of affairs? Psychoanalysis, which has had so much to say about death drives, paranoid aggressions, annihilating forces, and has itself led a number of historical initiatives that are yet to become comprehensible to us? From the start, psychoanalysis viewed itself as a legitimate transmitter of dissident views and did not hesitate to voice them publicly or privately (as in the correspondence between Freud and Einstein, to name but one example, where the uninterrogated principles of war are at issue). In its own way, according to different idioms, psychoanalysis put out a call for revolution. In fact, it has jammed the switchboard with such calls: a micro-revolution should occur in every analytic session. A lot remains to be done, not the least of which involves responsibility and a fuller understanding of that for which psychoanalysis is held responsible.

We are here because psychoanalysis is mortal. Psychoanalysis is ineffaceable, irreversible, but like every civilization, mortal. It needs our testimony. Psychoanalysis has taken suffering seriously, that is to say, without justifying or transcendentalizing—approving—suffering, without taking recourse to the Christian reappropriation of pain that is always in some measure seen as justifiable. Pain is unjustifiable. As Jean-Luc Nancy has written, it is perhaps unjustifiable that pain be unjustifiable.[2] Still, anyone who tries to present a case for its justification is a stoic or a Christian or worse. One could be a Hegelian, getting by on the "work, patience, and pain of the concept." Nonetheless, there is an area where suffering and distress tend to subsist on themselves or expand their scope by morose delectation or masochistic surplus. And here we enter the area that I would like to tour. It would be more accurate to say, remembering the architectural cues and spatial mappings of the *T-deutung*'s injection of Irma, that we are entering the propylaeum of what I hope to see—if seeing is at issue.

THE QUESTION OF STUPIDITY

I would like to inflect these preliminary notations in such a way as to consider a kind of symptomatology—actually, a parasymptomatology—that flies beneath the radar of psychoanalytical appropriations. Here I am not speaking to those fields or grammars of behavior that were excluded from the purview of psychoanalytic intervention—in the sense that paranoia was acknowledged to exceed the probe of Freud's thought—but with a view to discerning what delimits the field of psychoanalytic responsibility today and engages the aporias of understanding with which it accounts for its insight. To some extent psychoanalysis is a figure for understanding—possibly, indeed, for the irony of understanding, so that the limits of understanding become a crucial concern for those of us engaged with and by analysis. For his part, Freud was scrupulous about naming his hesitations and doubts as he proceeded; he submitted himself and his work to rigorous tests, and he was prepared to retract or revise at a moment's notice. The diction of doubting with which he often approached a problem remains exemplary. Freud's hesitations were rigorous. To this end, he was necessarily on the side of and an exponent of tremendous *Bildung*, capable of mobilizing prodigious erudition to assist in the effort of sense-making.

Let me state my question, then: It is not clear to me what, on this side of class struggle, he would do with the class of *Dummkopfs*—a certain slacker ethos, or the reserve of cultural stupor so widespread today, a class of phenomena that cannot be reduced to the protocols of resistance or transferential stalls with which we are familiar. I am asking about a psychic space beyond—or, more exactly, beneath—that of resistance.

Masochism gets close—but no cigar—in terms of the problem I am trying to approach here: namely, it demarcates, in Freud's various writings on the subject, a psychic slump toward a radical passivity and primary stupor that are susceptible to at least two appropriations. There is good stupor and bad stupor, just as, in another context, there is good and bad memory (the Hegelian split between *Gedächtnis* and *Erinnerung*) or the good *pharmakon* and the bad *pharmakon.* There is, for instance, the philosophical experience of stupor, disclosive of what is "awesome," the sheerly stupefying stupor, what occupies Heidegger in the Freiburg lectures, namely the Greek experience of *thaumazein.*

What of the irrecuperable stupidities? A major phobia in the lexicon of learning, expulsed from any *Wissenschaft* worth its salt and originary wound, stupidity also opens up new unintelligibilities (as F. W. Schlegel might have said), an unexpected range of noncognitive stammers, marking at times a new beginning, repeating the philosophical primal scene of stupor. Stupidity stumps and stunts anyone who tries to approach it critically. It also points to what has been historically inappropriable: the banality *and* stupidity of evil, as Hannah Arendt says of Eichmann.

So let us consider the way psychoanalysis has considered or, in some instances, evaded such cognates of unknowing as puerility, idiocy, ignorance, stupidity—para-concepts that have been evicted equally from philosophical and psychoanalytical premises. Still, philosophy itself, in its empiricist days, had to smuggle in the idiot-child, to invent it, in order to account for the radical experience of stupidity; or rather, in the works of Locke, Hume, Condillac, in order to arrive at an originary type of memory. Psychoanalysis shares with philosophy a refusal to admit the problem of stupidity into its door or onto its couch—but for entirely different reasons that have to do perhaps with deploying another logic, lending support to the blunder, motivating linguistic misfiring, accommodating the uninsurable reference or reading the anasemic stumble. On a more everyday-life kind of level, should such a thing exist, it was rare to have Freud be bored by his patients or remark on the dimwittedness of one in his charge. On the contrary. Rat Man was highly intelligent, we are told on several occasions, and why wouldn't he be? He had read some Freud, as Freud himself tells us, setting the countertransferential machine in motion. There is no question regarding Wolf Man's or Irma's or Dr. Schreber's or Anna's or Dora's or even Little Hans's intelligence. Nonetheless, when Freud gets to Dostoevsky, he begins to write of mental impairment by means of epilepsy and masochism.

In the meantime, between then and now, psychoanalysis changed its tone and began deploying, at some level of rhetorical consciousness, a diction that involved—well, stupidity—as if the affect of discovering stupidity in the other would give it some traction. The tone in a number of essays and seminars of Jacques Lacan would be exemplary in this instance. For here is a thinker who is not shy about outing even his own disciples as imbecilic. Melanie Klein is painfully stupid, but manages (accidentally) to get it right. The Americans are hopelessly stupid (ego psychologists). Lacoue-Labarthe and Nancy have achieved in their book on him what no student of Lacan would be capable of doing, being too dumb to grasp the true stakes of his return to Freud. Nor should we leave out of consideration Lacan's reflections on the idiot king, when he scours the psychic interior of the despotic ruler. There is something unquestionably Nietzschean about treating practically everyone as puerile and stupid (though Nietzsche never did so: he credited stupids with cleverness and, at most, with acting stupid or like Christians, who introduced a substantially new and improved wave of stupidity, revaluating and honoring the stupid idiot: *o sancta simplicitas!*). Be that as it may, when Lacan developed the need for establishing a crowd of ordinary, delusional *Dummkopfs* in his seminar and at his lectures, psychoanalysis began setting up the masochistic imperatives of true learning. The masochist signs on with an educator, enrolls in a kind of oedipedagogy he is bound to flunk or maybe even pass—what is important is that he is *bound* to it.

Freud mentions masochism three times in the *T-deutung*—linking it at one point with "humiliation in thought," and later on, in his article on Dostoevsky, connecting it to a certain kind of ethical behavior. As we ask the question of responsibility, of what it is to and for which we hold psychoanalysis responsible, we want to understand the exhaustion, the depletion of the psychoanalytic subject; we do not want to leave out of the picture what persistently poses a challenge to my sovereignty and autonomy.

THE EPISTEMÉ OF THE AIRHEAD, KNUCKLEHEAD, BIRDBRAIN, SPACE CADET, BIMBO, ETC.

Where politics intersects with ethics, the question emerges of where to draw the line—if there is one—of responsibility. To be what it is, responsibility must always be excessive, beyond bounds, unaccomplished. You are never responsible enough; and it is unclear whether, like Heidegger (whom I discuss at length, but not today), it suffices to say, "I made a stupid mistake" (in 1934 I made the dumbest—untranslatability, blah-blahblah) in order to adjudicate a lapse in responsible thinking. To explore the extreme limit of such responsibility I have appealed to the debilitated subject: the stupid, idiotic, puerile, slow-burn destruction of ethical being that, to my mind, can never be grounded in certitude or lucidity or prescriptive obeisance.

Some of these issues are most compellingly addressed by the troubled writer, Fyodor Dostoevsky, whose acute sense of answering for the other is frequently invoked by Levinas: "We are all responsible for everyone else—but I am more responsible than others."[3] Dostoevsky teaches us about the assumption of ethical liability by placing responsibility close to the extinction of consciousness, at the point where it becomes necessary to ask: what can be assumed by the limited subject? The domain of the human all-too-human, menacing enlightenment with knuckleheadedness, punctually threatens hopes of an original ethicity, which, in the case of *The Idiot*, Dostoevsky also posits.

Freud had a significantly ambivalent relationship with Dostoevsky, one that allowed him to posit a link between masochism and ethicity while deploring the man Dostoevsky himself. To shed some light on this difficult relationship, I have to travel at warp speed, I'm afraid, according to a new algorithm of the *Entstellung* or distortion, which the *T-deutung* teaches. Freud's quarrel with Dostoevsky is over idiocy, or the medical appropriation of idiocy. But this quarrel is secretly allegorized in the text of *The Idiot* itself.

HOLY SIMPLETON!

Within the folds of *The Idiot* a slow burn occurs, a contained rage against the impudence of stupidity, all of this waged in a battle, it would seem, over small narcissistic differences. Dostoevsky seeks to establish a strong boundary between stupidity and idiocy to offer sanctuary to the sacred alien, Prince Myshkin, whose purity is menaced by neighboring narratives of stupidity. (Please bear with me as I fast-forward to Freud's discussion of masochism in conjunction with Dostoevsky.) For theological Reasons, Dostoevsky needs to keep idiocy clean, close to kenoticism—the humiliation and emptying out of Christ.

Dostoevsky's figure for stupidity, from which he tries continually to distance the sacred idiot, is Gogol's character, who is last seen scarfing a pie. In a gesture of extreme ambivalence, Dostoevsky escorts the reader to his literary father, the "great writer" Gogol, should the reader be invested in reading a brilliant exposition on stupidity. Making straight Gogol's territory, he clears the runway for essential idiocy. The image (fixed by Dostoevsky citing Gogol) of gorging on a pie offers a considerable contrast to the emptying out of self for which the Idiot stands.[4] The stupid subject, the Gogolian, is generally fortified, defended, living within a calculated economy of compensation and disavowal, holding it in and keeping it up. He subsists on a system of denial that does not deny itself a thing.

The Idiot?—Well, the Idiot can't hold anything down or be sure of very much. In any event, there is little material consolation here, and the confidence for which his simplicity allows falls on empty spaces. He lives on the edges of nihilist temptation, a permanent evacuee who cannot be said to appropriate much of a thought—nor do we witness him eating, that is, assimilating, digesting, ruminating. Judging from his elaborate condemnation of capital punishment, he remains a passionate advocate for social justice. Closed in on himself, unavailable to the registers of social anxiety, the subject of stupidity, here as in the novel's other examples, is nowhere in question, but protected, satiated, full . . . of himself. It—stupidity—is the closest we mortals come to an experience of plenitude. Myshkin, running on empty, keeps tripping over a body that will not hold still, much less hold him together; he is a traveling mark of insufficiency, open and exposed, politically anxious and socially improbable.

In a sense the sudden inclusion, the determined intrusion of Gogol in the novel seems to be saying, kettle-logic style (I've had to sacrifice a close reading of this passage here): I, Fyodor Mikhailovich, am not writing on stupidity, which has been beautifully addressed by my mentor, to whom I owe so much; frankly, it would be too tedious for me to be writing on stupidity, which is so ordinary; in any case, even if I were writing on stupidity, that subject, as I underscore, has been covered by the great writer, Gogol, to whom I refer you, especially if you want to experience a literature that flatters the moral outrage of the reader (to the extent that Gogol punishes his stupid protagonists, whereas Dostoevsky sympathizes, as Freud would say, with the predicament of the idiot).

THE LIBRARY PASS

Now my reading of the insistence of Dostoevsky's elaborate inclusion of Gogol involves a suspicion of a cover-up. I am interested in the link Dostoevsky refuses to make as he shuts down the border between stupidity and idiocy, and of which we get a clue regarding the occluded corpus in the harassed ending of Myshkin's narrative. When everything is closing in on him, the Idiot is bound in a secret yet troubling way by another scene of writing. Moved through cityscapes by unconscious promptings, Myshkin goes to meet his destiny. Something impels him forward; his mind fades and punctually returns. "Strange to say, he was at one moment keenly observant, at the rest absent-minded to an incredible degree." Shunted through an atmosphere of anguish and "terrible dread," he experiences "unutterable dejection" (585). The Idiot sketches one clear gesture. It verges on being illicit; in any case, objections are raised:

> All the ladies described afterwards how Myshkin had scrutinised every object in the room, had seen on the table a French book from the library, "Madame Bovary," lying opened, turned down the corner of the page at which the book was open, asked permission to take it with him, and not heeding the objection that it was a library book, put it in his pocket. (584)

The next scene, which provides a body, is cued. At this point we dwell on the level of unconscious motivation, following a kind of frenetic drive impelling Myshkin to stash the illicit book despite a chorus of objections. Why this particular volume, though? Why does he take *it* to heart? Is there a way to understand why this object he puts in his pocket behaves as true coin? Any number of reasons appear to justify why *Madame Bovary* would name an irreversible destiny for the Idiot. Such features could be a matter of braiding thematic destinies; monitoring linguistic synchronicities; or pointing up ironic mirroring and its structural reversals. Unhampered linkages could be forged: Charles, the incompetent doctor, and Myshkin, the idiot healer; Emma and Nastasya on the same destructive path; flunking out of school; the shared status of the clinic; the petite-bourgeoise Madame Bovary, the aristocratic Idiot Prince; deflected histories of desire, public censure, we all fall down, and on and on. Yet in this case we would do well to micromanage the reading protocols and stay away from smooth thematic promises. For if Myshkin's unconscious meanderings have led him to an open book, binding it somehow to his heart's desire, the gesture of appropriating the book also involves closing and hiding it, slipping it into the invaginated folds of an internal pocket. In the moment of greatest trouble, he reaches for a book, for another book or the book of the other. This book itself appears to have awaited him.

In his last pages of sanity, Myshkin takes in and inseminates himself with the seminal work of Flaubert, in what can be seen as a counterphobic act. The necessity of this act is based on a number of considerations. In the first place it suggests that the Gogol inoculation has by now worn off. The sensitive area Gogol had protected in Dostoevsky is now exposed to possible incursion. Gogol had kept something in the work out of harm's way; he maintained certain inviolable boundaries. At least he permitted the fantasy of such boundaries to stay in place. For some reason Dostoevsky has needed to keep the Idiot safe from the encroachment of the very concerns that belonged to Gogol's work.

But when the chips are down, he has Myshkin reaching for it. Now, what does this shift in loyalties tell us? (Or maybe we are confronted with another level of consciousness, and Flaubert arrives on the scene to collect an unconscious debt, or to gamble on another level of textual transaction?) Flaubert, in any case, would not have allowed for the clean distinctions the name of Gogol has arranged in the text of Dostoevsky. He could not be an accomplice to a transcendentalizing strategy separating off stupidity in order to guarantee the sanctity of idiocy. Admittedly, Emma and Charles sometimes read like the ancestral echo of dumb and dumber, and there is dumber still. But stupidity takes everywhere: it fans out, contaminates like an invisible toxin, without allowing for much of a free zone in the merciless economy of Flaubertian irony. In fact Flaubert is the unsurpassed thinker of stupidity, which is one reason why Myshkin must first clear him out, close and shut him up, in order to terminate.

Gogol, in other words, functioned as something of a decoy for Flaubert, where the ordinary meets its match in extraordinary inmixation. Stupid can be extraordinary, too, even transcendental: flailed by stupid expectations, Emma also has her transports. Charles Bovary occupies an undecidable limit between idiocy and stupidity (which covers the clinical and the functional, the touching and the mundane), as does the immortally simple Félicité of "Un Coeur Simple." But when he pockets Flaubert, taking him in or closing him off—taking him out of library circulation, interrupting the reading of someone else: "turned down the corner of the page at which the book was open"—the Idiot also stages an act of incorporation. Why would *The Idiot* enact the incorporation of Gustave Flaubert?[5] To what extent does the textual body get organized around the unassimilable fact of this foreign body, which lodges itself at its heart's center?

Beyond the critical reprimand Flaubert might represent in terms of the false containment of *bêtise* that Dostoevsky attempts (and the attendant disruption of the sacred, which poses Flaubert as a destabilizer of the project at hand) there is something else as well. Something that exceeds the strictures posed by anxiety of influence (another name for the interference Flaubert runs), which overwhelms the literary channels of transmission, and reverts to the elusive body of work both men share. Why does *The Idiot* pocket Flaubert, thereby protecting or exposing him, making him the chosen one, at once harassed and idolized?

Flaubert, namely, *is* the Idiot. That is, he fills the whole space of the concept, draws it around himself with sober dignity. Generously inhabiting idiocy, the author of *Madame Bovary* goes further. He not only thought the thought of *bêtise*, and assumed it in his greatest maturity; but early on he himself hadn't been able to read for an awfully long time—"Gustave *est bête*"[6]—and he was famously considered by his parents to be an idiot:

> [L]'idiotie d'abord, l'alarme du père . . . les années stériles de Paris et, pour finir, la crise de Pont-l'Evêque, le haut mal.

> First the idiocy, the father's alarm . . . the sterile years in Paris, and, to end it, the crisis of Pont-l'Éveque, the great illness.[7]

Finally he had himself committed to the maternal clinic to complete a life sentence (we know how greatly Flaubert struggled to complete the sentence).

There remains the other detail, a hidden name. Broadcasting from inside the head of little Gustave, Sartre claims that this dimension gathers the secret strand that ties all the syndromic aspects together, making sense of them:

> [D]ans le cerveau du petit, quelque chose c'était détraqué, peut-être dès la naissance: l'épilepsie—c'était le nom qu'on donnait à la "maladie" de Flaubert—c'était, en somme, l'idiotie continuée.

> (S)omething was malfunctioning in the child's brain, perhaps since birth: epilepsy— that was the name given to Flaubert's "illness"—that was, all in all, idiocy continued.[8]

These (over)determinations begin to offer a perfect if uncanny fit: they designate the epileptic fit that held both Flaubert and Dostoevsky in abusive custody. For Flaubert, any disclosure of his condition was taboo. This in part explains why Dostoevsky appropriates Flaubert to his work as an explicitly illicit act. Dostoevsky also has to defend himself against his formidable counterpart. It is not only that they share and inscribe the same body, or that Flaubert might rise up, in *The Idiot*, to demand retribution (or, more likely and equally scary, to point out a misplaced comma). Flaubert would not stand for the transcendence Dostoevsky hypes, or toward which he prompts the epileptic body. On the side of will and repression, Flaubert has refused to take the sort of metaphysical medication to which Myshkin resorts—a fact that, in itself, should not perturb the unfolding of Dostoevsky's incomparable insight. Nonetheless, the bad conscience named Flaubert appears to creep up on him in moments of serious doubt.

ON THE RELATEDNESS OF ETHICS TO MASOCHISM

What does Dostoevsky have on Flaubert? Or is it rather Flaubert who intrusively punctures a system of protection that his Russian counterpart has attempted to secure? In ways that are not yet comprehensible, the two are often at each other's throats. Both authors have something to say about the pathologized body. They understood the laws of submission to which the afflicted body points. Flaubert invented the addicted body; while Dostoevsky, himself an addict, stuck with idiocy and its cognates. Elsewhere, Dostoevsky would venture into the domain of addictive and criminal psychologies. In terms of their material-historical bodies, they shared the same disease. Though it seems unorthodox to look at their medical records, we need to remind ourselves that the history of certain pathologies belongs to literature and continues to occupy the space of the imaginary, eliciting a reading and calling for a sense of the world that opens up parergonal abysses. In Dostoevsky's case, Freud notoriously destabilized the status of the writer's accepted diagnosis, calling it, in part, a fiction.

The difference—or, let us say, one difference—between Flaubert and Dostoevsky can be seen in the persistence with which the Russian author imbricated the fact of epilepsy in his novels. Visible and acknowledged, if not thematically flaunted, the condition became an object of literary endeavor. On the other side of the line, the œuvre, like the family of Flaubert, remained silent about epilepsy. The name of the illness was never pronounced *en famille.* Instead, a masochistic process of disavowal was launched. The family maintained strict secrecy around Gustave's epilepsy, even though both father and brother were leading physicians who were attending him by using conventional methods for treating the condition. The payback for receiving house calls consisted of joining the familial repression of the disease.

Dostoevsky's gesture of uncommented appropriation in *The Idiot* indicates a double relation to Flaubert's phantom. He knew Flaubert's secret and was, in a sense, bound to out him. Myshkin was on his last lap when something propelled him toward *Madame Bovary.* At the same time, he is stopped short of exposing Flaubert's secret. When Myshkin spies the open book, he offers a seal of protection, closing rather than disclosing, in the end safeguarding and concealing its meaning in a hidden pocket. It could be said that Dostoevsky takes the secret upon himself in the way Myshkin assumes custody of Rogozhin's pain, namely by becoming the receptacle of a disavowed history. Custodian and keeper of Flaubert's secret, Dostoevsky inscribes

Flaubert as his double, as the living intimation of an unrepresentable experience of epilepsy. It is as if Flaubert held the key to the unavowable community of pain. A master at doubling the stakes, when the chips are down Dostoevsky zeroes in on his French other. In the end Madame Bovary and Prince Myshkin become a couple, hers being the only book to which he will hold on as he enters the irreversible closedown.

As medical observation or ontological index, as literary and historical figure, epilepsy remains elusive. And it is still not understood how this highly complicated condition commands textuality. Figuration begins with Greek mythology. Hercules, the herald of epilepsy, has mutated, as his illness has manifested itself historically, into Buddha, Alexander the Great, Julius Caesar, Napoléon, Lord Byron, Pascal, and Van Gogh, among others.[9]

FREUD

Perhaps the most significant knock that the literary elaboration of epilepsy received was introduced by Freud's work on the subject. Something happened to the ancient scene of epilepsy precisely when Freud intervened to consider the case of Dostoevsky. Occupying a special place in the unfolding of Freud's own œuvre, epilepsy was the only somatic illness about which Freud wrote after psychoanalysis was established. Where key researchers took pains to distinguish hysteria from epilepsy, Freud treated Dostoevsky as a hystero-epileptic—essentially, that is, as a severe hysteric. It could be that this heuristic decision gave Freud some leverage, given that epilepsy as such—a postulate Freud denies—rebuffs attempts at decipherment. As the contemporary psychoanalyst M.-H. Sutterman argues, it could also be the case that on still another level Freud was motivated by a parricidal impulse and wanted to overthrow the theories of his teacher and master, Charcot, the father of the hystero-epileptic division.[10] Indeed, the couple of hysteria and epilepsy was severed according to effects of sexual difference, with women acquiring hysteria and men epilepsy. The article treating Dostoevsky constitutes Freud's first discussion of hysterical attacks since his earlier paper on the subject written twenty years before (in 1909). Here Freud sheds light on the enigma of Myshkin's exaggerated kindness and trusting nature, qualities that acquire definition in an essential elaboration of social masochism.

The condition of epilepsy, when prompted out of its periods of latency, sends the subject out of consciousness, as it were; it mechanizes the body by means of the robotic lurches it encourages, thus configuring the automaton. In a sense it mineralizes a self that, according to the findings of a number of clinical studies, is sexuated indifferently—that is to say is asexual, seraphic, or often bisexual or androgynous. Wrung out by the punctual yet unpredictable manifestation of symptoms, the subject succumbs to the greatest extremes of passivity. The afflicted are plainly jerked around by a force exceeding their control.

As Freud and others claim, epileptics tend to be drawn into sadistic scenes dominated, as it were, by a masochistic attachment. Their sadism gets expressed outwardly in small doses, but more consistently when turned against themselves. Hence the many greatly humiliated and offended subjects of Dostoevsky's œuvre who repeatedly contend with infantile omnipotence. It is thus that the sadomasochistic engagements to which Dostoevsky held are of consequence for Freud.

At one point some light is shed on Dostoevsky's addictions, the most prominent of which were evinced, of course, in his gambling binges. Freud interprets these compulsive and hysterical qualities in terms of Dostoevsky's need for great punishment, the requirement he exacted of the world so as to provide him with humiliation and tangible debt—needs that gambling satisfied. Not surprisingly, perhaps, the development becomes classically Freudian, linking the depleting addiction to the truth of castration. Like all addictions, deriving from the "primal addiction" of masturbation, gambling pitches the subject toward the threat of castration while raising the stakes of terrific guilt.[11] Both the addiction and the epileptic attack are said to grow out of ambivalence toward a severe and sadistic father ("the boy wants to be in his father's place because he admires him and wants to be like him, and also because he wants to put him out of the way" [SE XXI, 183]). Ambivalence puts the death drive in gear.

Priming and miming the sexual act, the attacks also move beyond the pleasure principle to double for death. The lethargic, somnolent states Dostoevsky documented "had the significance of death: they were heralded by a fear of death" (SE XXI, 182) and produced what Freud subsequently calls "deathlike attacks." Several other sources have underscored the extent to which Dostoevsky anxiously awaited death with an almost daily regimen of rituals and preparations. Among other stunts, he left nightly notes on his pillow to those who might find him dead the next morning. And he ran over regularly to the house of his doctor, with whom he enjoyed nearly telepathic relations, and would spend the night there as his guest, in his care. The sleepovers staved off some fear, but could not arrest the symptom in the long run.

Back to Freud's couch. The attacks, in sum, indicate an identification with a dead person, "either with someone who is really dead or with someone who is still alive and whom the subject wishes dead" (SE XXI, 183). While identifying the subject with the dead center of the death-wish, this is how the attack in fact carries the "value of a punishment." One has wished another person dead, "and now one *is* this other person and is dead oneself." Hysterical epilepsy means that you have not gotten away with murder: you are the way. You have thrown your body in the way of the targeted object of a murderous impulse and will continue to trade positions with the intended other, dancing for the death commissioned by you.

Freud makes the macabre dance contingent on a death wish, but not on the death wish of the other (as Sutterman subsequently contends)—that is, on the likelihood, within the transmitted intimations of fantasy, that the infant has gotten the message of the near extinction wished upon her by the attending parent. Both views agree on the fantasy of an early murder scene, which the child, at once victim and perp, continues to perform into adulthood. Where Sutterman argues that the attack originates in the fantasy and dread of infanticide, Freud would age the infant and make this a secondary effect of a projected death wish. Psychoanalytic theory asserts that the target for a boy is usually his father and that "the attack (which is termed hysterical) is thus a self-punishment for a death-wish against a hated father." The punishing attack is the way of putting a restraining order on that part of oneself struggling to get the offending father and already locked in identification with his demise.

Thus Freud pins the violent attacks on the father complex. Aggravated or confirmed by Dostoevsky's latent homosexuality, the father complex is largely responsible for the passive positions occupied by Fyodor Mikhailovich when faced with the massive existential insults leveled at him, and, furthermore, informs his inordinate submissiveness to the Tzar and God—to "little father" and big daddy. Dostoevsky's attacks are in imitation of the dead, of that which he wished dead and which now wishes *him* dead, in a deadly karmic cycle according to which what goes around comes around to get you, especially because it stems from your unconscious. As we know from other texts, father is more alive when (wished) dead than he is while living.

Here the perished father stamps the coming to term of futurity, filling the meaning of a destiny. In a notable aside, Freud offers that destiny itself reverts, in the end, to paternal projection; the very concept of fate itself is fatherly: "Even fate is, in the last resort, only a later projection of the father." The unavoidable resonances of fate and FATHEr are fairly well set in place, at least since the Nietzschean hints of a homonymic cooperation between *amor fati* and *amor vati.* All kidding aside, the kid's symptoms of death-like attacks can thus be understood "as a father-identification on the part of his ego, which is permitted by his super-ego as a punishment" (SE XXI, 185). The internalized desire of the father gets the upper hand over the ego-identified father, in a rumble that has the subject falling to his death. The repetitive punishment, a punctual ritual, is the price exacted by superego's fury.

But how can two fathers rule and rumble? Freud narrates the split-off of the father function. The so-called epilepsy of our author has arisen as a consequence of the repression of the hatred of the father in the Oedipus complex. The repression gets supplemented. "There is something fresh to be added: namely that in spite of everything the identification with the father finally makes a permanent place for itself in the ego" (SE XXI, 184). Received into the ego, the identification establishes itself there as a separate agency, in contrast to the rest of the ego's contents: "We then give it the name of super-ego and ascribe to it, the inheritor of the parental influence, the most important functions" (SE XXI, 185). If the father was hard, violent, and cruel, those attributes are taken over by the super-ego and thus, in the relations it holds with the ego, the passivity that was supposed to have been repressed is reestablished. The super-ego has become sadistic; and the ego becomes masochistic, passive, even "feminized," by super-ego's control systems. "A great need for punishment develops in the ego, which in part offers itself as a victim to fate, and in part finds satisfaction in ill-treatment by the super-ego—that is, in the sense of guilt. For every punishment is ultimately castration and, as such, a fulfillment of the old passive attitude towards the father." To top it off, Freud writes:

> "You wanted to kill your father in order to be your father yourself. Now you *are* your father, but a dead father"—the regular mechanism of hysterical symptoms. And further: "Now your father is killing *you.*" For the ego the death symptom is a satisfaction in phantasy of the masculine wish and at the same time a masochistic satisfaction; for the super-ego it is a punitive satisfaction—that is, a sadistic satisfaction. Both of them, the ego and the super-ego, carry on the role of father. (SE XXI, 185)

When Dostoevsky was put under arrest by the Tsar's police, his symptoms were also arrested. The astonishing fact, reported by Dostoevsky himself, that in Siberia he was free from his attacks merely substantiates Freud's supposition that these attacks served as his punishment. When humbled by fate in this extreme way—serving time, serving father—he had no further need of the punishing attacks. All that can be made out is that Dostoevsky was released from having to punish himself when he "got himself punished by his father's deputy. Here we have a glimpse of the psychological justification of the punishments inflicted by society. Large groups of criminals want to be punished. The super-ego demands it and so saves itself the necessity for inflicting the punishment itself" (SE XXI, 186–87).[12] A rigorous psychology of the institution of penal systems would have to contend with this point raised by Freud, namely that super-ego casts about for strict external forms of punishment, the only condition under which ego can be relieved of unsparing symptoms. Lest one rush to authoritarian conclusions about the helpfulness of instituting systems of incarceration and the like, remember that Freud does not encourage the state to double for the punitive function or to satisfy its demands. Moreover it is no doubt important to observe that Dostoevsky was innocent, even though super-ego and the police had collaborated on the necessity of deporting him.

Freud's contemplation of this case advances an explanation for the fact that Dostoevsky passed unbroken through the Siberian years of misery and humiliation:

> Dostoevsky's condemnation as a political prisoner was unjust and he must have known it, but he accepted the undeserved punishment at the hands of the Little Father, the Tsar, as a substitute for the punishment he deserved for his sin against his real father. Instead of punishing himself, he got himself punished by his father's deputy. (SE XXI, 186)

The greater part of Freud's commentary refers to the epileptic criminal depicted in *The Brothers Karamazov* and the parricidal pact sealed by the dominant fraternity, both of which illustrate his theories. Both *The Brothers* and *The Idiot* lead to ethical hesitations, which urge, in turn, a critical review of what we think we know about ethics—or of what we have traditionally allowed ethics to exclude, discard.

On a number of occasions Freud appears to invite a comparison of the criminal with the epileptic. He observes that Dostoevsky has shown boundless sympathy when it comes to criminals. A recurrent symptom in his works involves an immoderate display of sympathy for the evildoer, a tendency itself at the same time associated with that of forgiving all. Allowing parenthetically that he has little interest in undermining an ethics of sympathy—"In saying this, we are not disputing the ethical value of this kindliness"—Freud goes on to say that his inquiry concerns a general quality that, to the degree that it underlies the mechanism of kindly sympathy toward other people, can be most readily gleaned from "this extreme case of a guilt-ridden novelist. There is no doubt that this sympathy by identification was a decisive factor in determining Dostoevsky's choice of material." Symptoms of excessive sympathy and extreme kindliness pervade his work, where a steady decriminalization of the protagonist takes place.

A complicated dossier has been opened. Freud takes some care to avoid destabilizing a possible ethics. Even so, his article takes on the presumed virtue of kindliness. Under scrutiny, the qualities of overlarge kindliness, including courteousness and politeness, point to an improbable source in perversity. The reportedly Christian values of love and sympathy, viewed in terms of Dostoevsky's masochistic rap sheet, are connected to a very strong destructive instinct. Dostoevsky could easily have been a criminal, as Freud says a number of times in a number of ways.

Literary critics have often been dissatisfied with Freud's uncompromising review of the symptom Dostoevsky. When reckoning the debt we have incurred to the great writer, Freud was unwilling to pass over Dostoevsky's retrograde submission to nation or religion: " . . . a position which lesser minds have reached with smaller effort. This is the weak point in that great personality. Dostoevsky threw away the chance of becoming a teacher and liberator of humanity and made himself one with their gaolers. The future of human civilization will have little to thank him for" (SE XXI, 177). Nor does he suppress mention of Dostoevsky's apparent confession to a sexual assault upon a young girl. The Freud that calls Dostoevsky to account knows the difference between rape and fantasy.

Yet Dostoevsky turned the criminal instinct against himself, in the form of a destructive pathos fueled by masochism. His personality retained sadistic traits "in plenty," traits that have shown themselves in his

> irritability, his love of tormenting and his intolerance even towards people he loved, and which appear also in the way in which, as an author, he treats his readers. Thus in little things he was a sadist towards others, and in bigger things a sadist towards himself, in fact a masochist—that is to say, the mildest, kindliest, most helpful person possible. (SE XXI, 178–79)

It is no doubt of some importance that even the reader gets pulled into the dragnet of sadistic intention, becoming inscribed in the small print of a published contract and positioned as victim to the abuses of Dostoevsky's sadomasochistic indulgences. In what way does the writer violate the implicit contract with the reader, submitting the reader to the manuscript and not the other way around? Freud does not motivate this inclusion, but, elsewhere, in *M & Mono*, he briefly explains how he is violently moved by textual controls. With Dostoevsky something like a masochistic alert goes off, or at least a feeling of disappointment. But for the moment let us steer clear of disappointed reading relations, at least until I clear out of here.

Reaching beyond the particular instance provided by the self-tormentor, Freud keys into a quality that affects the underpinnings of sociality and binds community with the glue of perversion. As it turns out, courteousness and helpfulness—what together resemble an outstanding ethical stance—involve a key feature of sadism turned inward. This apparent contradiction has not escaped current popular forms of expression, according to which notorious sadists, historical and fictional—such as Hannibal Lector, for instance—supplement their anal-sadistic sieges with princely postures of politesse. Consistent yet extreme forms of kindliness are traced back by Freud to the ironies of the sadomasochistic contract, possibly the most social of contracts.

P.S.

Now that we have entered the realm of lectors and readers, we can ask once again what it might have meant for Prince Myshkin to select *Madame Bovary* as the one indisputable item on his reading list. It is not as though he clutches Madame Bovary to his breast because she is the dominatrix of choice, though a case could be made for such an arrangement (her masochistic world appears to bear down on his, which it reflects, even duplicates at times). Sealing and concealing the book, Myshkin signs in, and, under the name of the other, binds himself irrevocably to this power that comes from elsewhere. He lends a countersignatory force to *Madame Bovary* by means of which he engages a reciprocal movement of countersigning, forming one body with the language of Flaubert. Henceforth Dostoevsky is bound up in Flaubert, who signs in turn and seals his fate. When Krafft-Ebing gave Leopold von Sacher-Masoch the credit for having refined a clinical entity "not merely in terms of the link between pain and sexual pleasure, but in terms of something more fundamental connected with bondage and humiliation," he was also pointing to cases of masochism without algolagnia.[13] The mobility of masochism on the grand chart of humiliation was established. The discovery, shared with regional differences by Dostoevsky and Sacher-Masoch, offers a *motive for opening onto other courses and objects, onto different figures or experiences of subjection*. The novel braces itself against the inevitability of such displacements, which it, in turn, also instigates. It is necessary to note, at the end of the novel, that the murder weapon will be taken from the pages of a book: a knife whose source and sorcery are located in the folds of a text. Dostoevsky's allowance for the book as a place of wounding, as the precise domain from which a knife can be drawn and thus a fatal blow incurred, reinforces the lacerating potential of the other book, whose retrieval is cleanly marked, even if the knife it wields remains as mysterious as it is untouchable. Feminized, even phallicized (no contradiction here), the book beckons and destroys, covers up and punishes.

The vow and disavowal are closely linked in the masochistic process. Deleuze reveals how the rhetoric of masochism consists in persuasion and education, guided by an effort to get the other to "sign," that is, to cosign a contract, to honor a reciprocal vow: "The masochist draws up contracts while the sadist abominates and destroys them."[14] In every respect, the masochistic "educator" stands in contrast to the sadistic "instructor," the one who knows it all already and has only scorn for the rhetoric of persuasion, the method of wimps and dummies. The masochist, trying to enroll the other in a course of surrendered complicity, gets his clause on a contract, and is ever on the lookout for the compliant signature. For whom is the other signing?

What the masochist carries in his heart, Deleuze argues, is the miniaturized image of the humiliated father: s/he has made contact with the secret of that humiliation. According to both Freud and Deleuze (though they are miles apart on key aspects of this analysis) the masochist remains prey to the paternal secret and is enlisted as a loyalist of the father's symptom. In the case of Dostoevsky, one could propose now that he has affected the corporeal absorption of the letter: "symptom," we recall, comes from *syn,* together, and *piptein,* to fall. Succumbing to the symptom, the "falling sickness," he produces an act of commemoration, or punctual reiteration, of the father's humiliation. Yet, too real, frozen out by trauma, the father's secret had to travel, to become symbolized, and even, in order to survive, to be redirected and fraternalized. To reclaim the safer bounds of the novel, the name or cryptaphor of Flaubert miniaturizes, folds; his fall is timed to occur together with the imminent collapse of Myshkin— or, more likely, he catches the fall.

Dostoevsky, out and open, needs the guarded and humiliated Flaubert to cosign. Needing to secure for himself a partnership with the humiliated other, the masochist works from a place of harried destitution. This is why I argued that the rapport with or relation to Flaubert was double (at least double) according to sadomasochistic protocols, involving the need to protect and the urge to expose. Tracked down for his signature at this crucial juncture, Flaubert is at once reassuring and disenfranchising, the accomplice and persecutor. Yet his status in the novel is left rigorously suspended— and remains part, henceforth, of the suspense, even suspended on the body, which carries the other writing to term. Suspense is not a stray shot, aleatory or random, but a strategic factor in the masochistic process. Masochism makes use of suspense. Deleuze points up the masochistic rites of torture and suffering, which imply actual physical suspension (the hero is hung up, crucified or suspended).

Let us now suspend this session.

NOTES

1. See Jacques Derrida, *États d'âme de la psychanalyse* (Paris: Galilée, 2000).

2. See Jean-Luc Nancy, "La douleur existe, elle est injustifiable," in *Revue d'éthique et de théologie morale* 95 (December 1995): 91–96.

3. See Emmanuel Levinas, "Responsibility for the Other," in his *Ethics and Infinity*, trans. Richard A. Cohen (Pittsburgh: Duquesne University Press, 1985), 93–101.

4. Fyodor Dostoevsky, *The Idiot*, trans. David Magarshack (New York: Bantam, 1955), 449.

5. In the interest of containment, we leave aside the issues of sexual difference marking these passages. Madame Bovary is spread open; Myshkin takes (her), but then he in turn is inseminated, and so forth.

6. Jean-Paul Sartre, *L'idiot de la famille: Gustave Flaubert de 1821 à 1857* (Paris: Gallimard, 1971), 612.

7. Unless otherwise noted, all translations are my own.

8. Sartre, *L'idiot*, 17–18.

9. For an outstanding analysis of epilepsy and temporality see Kimura Bin, *Écrits de psychopathologie phénoménologique* (Paris: Presses Universitaires de France, 1992), on a phenomenological psychopathology based on the existential analysis [*Daseinsanalyse*] of Ludwig Binswanger. Bin focuses on the ethical constitution of the epileptic, with observations on the heightened sense of duty and the exasperated sense of obligation on the part of the epileptic in relation to others.

10. See Jean-Martin Charcot, *Dostoïevski et Flaubert: Écritures de l'épilepsie* (Paris: Presses Universitaires de France, 1993).

11. Strachey notes that Freud's letter to Fliess of December 22, 1897, suggests that masturbation is the "primal addiction," for which all later addictions are substitutes. See Sigmund Freud, *The Origins of Psychoanalysis: Letters to Wilhelm Fliess*, trans. Eric Mosbacher and James Strachey (New York: Basic Books, 1954), 238–40.

12. Gilles Deleuze discusses the aggressive and hallucinatory return of the father in a world that has symbolically abolished him. The aggressive return of the father disrupts the masochistic situation. See Gilles Deleuze, *Coldness and Cruelty: Masochism* (New York: Zone Books, 1989), 40.

13. Ibid., 16.

14. Ibid., 20–21.

Family, Friends,
and
Other Relations

6. Sounds of Satan

Laurence A. Rickels

What a young fool he had been! Yet he was not sure that he regretted his action: had he stayed on Earth, he would have witnessed those closing years over which time had now drawn a veil. Instead, he had leapfrogged past them into the future, and had learned the answers to questions that no other man would ever know. . . .

But most of the time, with a contented resignation that comes normally to a man only at the end of a long and busy life, he sat before the keyboard and filled the air with his beloved Bach. Perhaps he was deceiving himself, perhaps this was some merciful trick of the mind, but now it seemed to Jan that this was what he had always wished to do.

—Arthur C. Clarke, *Childhood's End*

The Devil has two points of entry in Freud's science. He is along for the aside in which Freud, in your dreams, addresses philosophy and music. But then he also takes center stage when Freud analyzes cases of possession, in delusions and in dreams. The Devil of possession belongs to the rehearsal stage of Oedipal plot developments when father is your bosom body. In addition to the pre-Oedipal or phallic mother and the Oedipal father or parent, there is a pre-Oedipal father, the primal father in everyone's development, the one who, through monopolization of sexual difference or sexuality, gives rise to early theories of anal birth.

Both frames of Devil reference already appear in *The Interpretation of Dreams*. In the chapter 7 stretch of philosophical interrogation of reality, Freud makes reference to the Devil in Tartini's dream. The composer Tartini dreamt up the sale of his soul to the Devil, who, in this dream, then seized a violin and played the sonata the composer took back with him into the waking state. The Devil dream is an ornamental and parenthetical illustration dangling from the preceding paragraph in which precisely nothing was concluded about true reality: "The unconscious is the true psychical reality;

in its innermost nature it is as much unknown to us as the reality of the external world, and it is as incompletely presented by the data of consciousness as is the external world by the communications of our sense organs" (SE V, 613; emphasis added).

Freud's example of Devil dream possession in *The Interpretation of Dreams* is cited from the record of a nineteenth-century French pediatrician: the record shows a thirteen-year-old boy whose "sleep became disturbed and was interrupted almost once a week by severe attacks of anxiety accompanied by hallucinations. He always retained a very clear recollection of these dreams. He said that the Devil had shouted at him: 'Now we've got you, now we've got you!' . . . He woke up from the dream in terror, and at first could not cry out. When he had found his voice he was clearly heard to say: "No, no, not me; I've not done anything!" or "Please not! I won't do it again!" or sometimes: "Albert never did that!" (SE V, 585–86). Freud interprets the dream delusion as, one, referring to masturbation in the past, interrupted by denial and threatened punishment; two, as responding in the present to increased temptation arising, arousing with the onset of adolescence; and, three, as reflecting the present tension, what Freud terms the "struggle for repression," which transforms the suppressed libido into anxiety, and thus presses it into the service of punishment. There is an audio portion on the record that emerges with the loss of the boy's voice, which, once regained, belongs, at least in one instance, to a third-person party. While he is afflicted by the Devil of a nightmare, the possession seems to intervene after the dream crisis, which is first alleviated by the takeover of the boy's voice by an other's voice. Exorcism has often been analogized with therapeutic breakthrough. Possession, however, already nine-tenths of this law, takes steps toward recovery, which alternate with the interventions of exorcism. The person possessed has passed through a crisis and is now grounded in a delusion or a reality that allows this crisis to settle down for a demonic spell and thus become legible, audible, or, if you prefer, treatable. Two items in the original record that Freud leaves out of his sexological interpretation help fill in the blanks drawn between one voice and the other's. The boy's father makes an appearance in the hypothesis that "a past syphilitic infection in his father" (SE V, 587) may have deposited in the boy's brain a predisposition to mental illness. But the boy also describes how his nerves were overexcited to the point that he even contemplated the release of "'jumping out of the dormitory window'" (SE V, 586). The suicidal flight from or to the Devil is framed by an institutional inference that at age thirteen the boy was, in some sense, separated from his parents, including the father with the evil legacy to bear in his son's mind. The boy, who given time in the country was completely cured, went with the Devil down the fast lane of self-recovery associated with a healthy father function.

Serial dreaming stuck in the groove of traumatic impact, evidence presented by accident and war neurotics, first guided Freud beyond the bottom line of wish fulfillment in his interpretation of dreams. These dreams introduce repetition as that which lies beyond or before the pleasure principle and represents the first and last, but not least, entrenched attempt to build up a protective layer against mega-traumatizing stimuli. The compulsion to repeat opens up a new habitat for Devil reference in *Beyond the Pleasure Principle.* When manifestations of the compulsion to repeat act in strict opposition to the pleasure principle, they assume the aspect of a demonic force. In other words, whenever the compulsion to repeat comes into focus, is registered and is recognized as fitting a transitive sentence, it goes to the Devil. This new focus can be fixed on and in the analytic session: "It may be presumed, too, that when people unfamiliar with analysis feel an obscure fear—a dread of rousing something that, so they feel, is better left sleeping—what they are afraid of at bottom is the emergence of this compulsion with its hint of possession by some 'demonic' power." Once in analysis, this demonic force pops up within the transference. "In the case of a person in analysis . . . the compulsion to repeat the events of his childhood in the transference evidently disregards the pleasure principle in every way" (SE XVIII, 36). Repetition compulsion or the demonic appears as a decontextualized and sealed-off momentum in the transference, in the in-session doubling of the duo dynamic that Freud found, at least at first contact, haunting. Transference raises ghosts between the two of you; repetition compulsion in the transference raises hell in the third person.

The publication date of Freud's "A Seventeenth-Century Demonological Neurosis" sets this case study deep inside the second system that opened up around *Beyond the Pleasure Principle.* We're thus given ears to hear what's in the name of the monastery where exorcism was performed not once, but twice. In its name, Mariazell places Mary, ambiguous figure of immaculate reproduction, alongside the single cell or *Zelle.* The subsidized mode of existence the painter finds in the end as alternative to the Devil pact with the blood-related father still splits its share with the leader of the pact in relation to the *Zelle,* the monastery's social unit, but also in name the unicellular organism of replication that transmits the fantasy of body-based relations with father. To sign oneself over to your partner in pact, *sich verschreiben,* also means, same words, to make a mistake in writing, to commit a lapsus. It is in the phrasing of their contract that Freud discerns the fine print of their exchange: the painter vows to be the Devil's *leibeigener Sohn.* This can or should be translated as "bound son," as in duty-bound, beholden, or owned, serf-style. Literally the modifier means "of one's own body."

In person the Devil gives us a certain father, a blood-bonded father. In Freud's "A Seventeenth-Century Demonological Neurosis," the painter receives no sensational benefits in exchange for his immortal soul, but instead gets from the Devil a paternal replacement for the parents he had lost: a bodily father, yes, a father with maternal attributes, but not subsumable by the mother, not this time, nor by her missing place. Even when pumped up with breasts, the Devil is still the father who alone can cancel the painter's adoption of the deferred obedience plan. The painter's difficulty in earning a livelihood following the death of his parents belatedly obeys the father's veto of the son's wish to be an artist or—and it's never too late—administers punishment for the son's transgression. Exorcism of the Devil's hold over him, of a holding pattern that for a time served to stabilize the painter, leads, the second time around and by doubling as the painter's initiation into a fraternal church order, to an artist's life in a culture of subvention, the maternal care given by the church fathers at the monastery named Mariazell.

Christianity and the Devil, in it together, also help Wolf Man overcome his desire to surrender to his big bad but beloved father, the potent corporeal figure and pathogenic force of sexuality in his immediate family. Little Wolf Man's seduction by his sister carries out at one remove the paternal p-unitive trauma, love it or live it. He took care to breathe in the Holy Spirit, but always to breathe out evil spirits. The breathing-out exercise was also required whenever he saw any figures he would not like to be like. These "beggars, or cripples, or ugly, old, or wretched-looking people" (SE XVII, 67) followed the downbeat of how he saw his father. But heavy breathing, hot off the audio track of the primal scene, was also a resource for positive identification of or with the father.

But then one day a German tutor changed the frame of the teen's demonizations and idealizations when he introduced his charge to the free-thinking stance at attention. The military thus came to uniform Wolf Man's teen spirit. But the breathing rituals weren't stopped in these marching steps. And whenever Wolf Man saw three heaps of dung he still had to think of the Holy Trinity. A caterpillar dream Freud interprets recalls the tutor's influence: he had helped Wolf Man overcome his sadism toward small animals. But this brings back, at least in Freud's narrative, recollection of one Devil of a dream. Even while this dream is assigned to the period before the tutor's influence, it is nevertheless brought back in association with the tutor. And it is brought back to be exorcised within the analysis, and within the analytic and transferential relationship to Freud. The German tutor's influence is responsible for Wolf Man's fond rapport with all things German and that's a fact, Freud adds, "which was incidentally of great advantage to the transference during the treatment" (SE XVII, 69). In the earlier dream, the Devil was pointing to a gigantic snail, an image of childhood sexual research. Based on popularized high-cultural reference to the Devil, Wolf Man's dream representation includes the father's (and his own) idealization of the daughter-sister, whose accomplishments were read off the legend of the middlebrow map of high culture. This Devil father furthermore promises the complete answer withheld from the little boy when he was witness to the primal scene. The sister in the Devil father is on her role as transmitter of the father's influence or seduction and as intercessor between father and son, whereby she took the brunt of the grunting father. "When he heard that Christ had once cast out some evil spirits into a herd of swine which then rushed down a precipice, he thought of how his sister in the earliest years of her childhood, before he could remember, had rolled down on to the beach from the cliff-path above the harbor" (SE XVII, 67). The later caterpillar dream, the one that brought back, by contrast and association, the Devil and the snail dream, benefits from the switch from passivity to activity (in a military setting). But then Wolf Man remembers the waking experience of riding by a father asleep with his son in the fields. The son wakes his father, who shouts at Wolf Man as though his look at them was illicit, improper. The passive, feminine, or homosexual submission to the father had, then, really been only repressed. His psychoanalysis gave Wolf Man access to this repressed portion of his libido, each piece of which, upon being set free, sought out some sublimated goal or concern. But the tutorial in father-and-sonhood taken with Freud is the cover for his continued service to, for, as his undead sister. The Devil represented the father as blocked for Wolf Man by his sister. He was the contained, certain father. But the complications in the Wolf Man case, which lie in his relations with his sister, cannot contain themselves in the father. Daniel Paul Schreber occupies—through his older brother, who like Wolf Man's older sister committed suicide—the same uncontained projection booth of idealization and demonization with regard to his own father, the mad scientist who experimented on his sons. Just the same, the Wolf Man case shows how the fantasy of the certain father refers to a pre-Oedipal father, the father who holds the primally abusive monopoly of sexual difference (or, simply, of sex). At the time of the third person's first interruption of the dyad, there is only one "difference," and it belongs to the father. Little boy, little girl, and mother can only offer a back-end deal to obtain, sure thing, the father's penetrating certitude. The Devil father rules every military and paramilitary outfit in which sexual difference is similarly fantastically contained.

FIRST CIRCLE

In *Beyond the Pleasure Principle,* Freud admits a unicellular immortality that guarantees that we do not die naturally and, equally, that the death and reproduction plan propels our evolutionary development as a species. Then Freud jumps the gun, death-drive style, and formulates a tentative conclusion: the goal of life is death. How then do the self-preservative instincts fit in? They can now be seen as insurance that the organism will follow its own path to its proper death. The organism wishes to die only in its own fashion. But then Freud drops his role as devil's advocate, as he puts it, and, picking up the ambivalent track of the other, begins again: "But let us pause for a moment and reflect. It cannot be so. The sexual instincts . . . appear under a very different aspect" (SE XVIII, 39). Don't basic cells "work against the death of the living substance and succeed in winning for it what we can only regard as potential immortality?" In this way, however, we are only keeping up "the appearance of immortality." Even the so-called necessity of death only pays us the price of submission in place of the unbearable prospect of random chance, which always also represents the outside chance that the life lost could have been immortal (SE XVIII, 45).

As the realm of unlimited possibilities, biology draws Freud's speculations onward. Certain and conclusive scenarios are stated and then abandoned. The purposive statement about life and death, for example, is preceded by Freud's expression of his *wish:* "We seek only for the sober results of research or reflection based on it; and we have no wish to find in those results any quality other than certainty" (SE XVIII, 37). Before he unfulfills the wish in the main text, the footnote underworld sends up a warning shout; before 1925 the shout drops right before Freud pushes the "let us pause" button; after 1925 Freud sounds the alert even earlier and more expansively, right beneath the "certainty": "The reader should not overlook the fact that what follows is the development of an extreme line of thought. Later on, when account is taken of the sexual instincts, it will be found that the necessary limitations and corrections are applied to it" (SE XVIII, 37n2). In the wake of these stops and starts, and this movement extends well beyond the rebellion with a "pause," the disposable scenarios are, on their own, model Devil fictions. "It is surely possible to throw oneself into a line of thought and to follow it wherever it leads out of simple scientific curiosity, or, if the reader prefers, as an *advocatus diaboli,* who is not on that account himself sold to the devil" (SE XVIII, 59).

The death drive or the demonic is hard for Freud to follow. For all concerned, it's certainly hard to perceive in all its purity. It's like, says Freud, the silence in the background of the melody of the drives (SE XXI, 119, and SE XIV, 62). A demonic aspect in music was familiar to Freud early on at that influential remove of a follower's research. Max Graf, a music journalist and an academic historian of music, was one of two nonpractitioner members of the original Wednesday meeting group. Around the turn of the century Graf had already been publishing on music subjects—on Wagner in particular. The demonic force that was with Wagner, indeed a "Devilish curse" and the "curse of Satan," drove the composer to represent excessive passion and then to find release, if only by proxy, through renunciation.[1] With the exception perhaps of Graf's insistence that all this commotion fit the metabolization of one wound, in Wagner as in his protagonists, this biographical, intellectual-historical interpretation of Wagner is hardly psychoanalytic. In these early studies, the focus on the demonic inside Wagner is shared with the external Devil, the journalist friend of Brahms, Eduard Hanslick, who used Brahms "with Satanic cleverness" to fight the journalist's battles against Wagner, whom Hanslick despised. According to Graf, journalism is its own "mode of living," one that lacks religious or metaphysical sensibility, even connection with personal experience, and is thus anti-art, and part or projectile of Graf's fundamentally split position between art or art appreciation and analysis.[2]

In *Composer and Critic,* Graf cites the split between Hanslick and Wagner as the onset of "modern musical criticism in Europe," which is split-level: at first music critics targeted Wagner because they "sided with the readers of the papers—who looked for entertainment in theaters and concert halls of an evening—and in general opposed the independent artists and fought with all their intelligence and all their wit—and often with all their narrowness—against the great composers of the time."[3] But Wagner invented the generation gap: he made his cause that of the Teen Age.

Once all those Siegfrieds in the audience had replaced "the elder generation of the new industrial epoch," "the whole world turned Wagnerian" (243).

This modern splitting origin of criticism fighting music, and then under this cover together introducing middlebrow culture, repeats the original origin of music criticism, according to Graf: "It is a strange fact in the history of musical criticism that, at the moment it first entered the world, the first clash between this new force and creative power occurred. Similar conflicts have accompanied the whole development of music, from Bach to Stravinsky and Schoenberg. . . . Perhaps this is an inevitable and essential part of progress; perhaps it must accompany all great composers, just as military bands accompany an army into battle." Graf then performs the double inheritance of modern music criticism or modern music culture when he issues his policy statement for the history of music criticism: "Conflicts between critics and artists can be profitably analyzed only when they are the necessary result of different outlooks on the world: conflicts, for example, between generations or periods. These are not personal matters, but matters of logic; one might say that they are conflicts produced by the development of historical trends, by God himself, it may be, as He struggles with his own critic, the devil" (69).

Graf leaves himself the devil of a chance that he is neither God, nor the berated musical genius, but is caught up, just the same, within an inevitable context in which, in real time, one can't take sides. This context or contest—which even as it cites the Old Testament understanding of Satan, commences as social or group-psychological phenomenon only with the beginning of modern mass-media-music culture in the Teen Age—is one of testing. The relationship between Graf and Hanslick, which in Graf's historical perspective is the split-off side effect of the generational contest between critics and composers, was in fact just a reality test that both men were destined to pass, moving right along, transference-style, with the father-son identification. Indeed, Hanslick, who died in 1904, was one of Graf's mentors at the University of Vienna. The books Graf published while in the United States, for example, all open with the author's listing of his credentials as a music critic and historian, always including at the top of the list Hanslick's mentorship. When Freud gave his case study of the phobic five-year-old boy, who happened to be Max Graf's son, a nickname, he chose, perhaps in earshot of this father, Little Hans.

Freud's "Analysis of a Phobia in a Five-Year-Old Boy" is remarkable in his oeuvre for being, escapably, not his own. And yet many if not all the coordinates of the open-and-shut cases that cut to the crypt are pressing here, too. But this time it's not always also one big diversion. Little Hans's first contacts with technologization, for example, don't bear undead cargo. He suffers from phobias of transportation or *Verkehr*, which, from railway to the street, cover access to the mother's womb, which the dead father alone can gain for, while gaining on, the son. For little Hans, this speed race appears sexologically contained: his saving fantasy of marrying his mother and sending his father off to marry his own mother relieves the tension building the phobic symptoms

(SE X, 97). Displacement goes around and comes around as a happy ending because the father's father (the trans-parent figure) is both missing and at the remote controls: his more-than-absence guarantees that this farce—in which, while he's away, all the sons can play—will call curtains on the incestuous retention of the off-limits body. His place is represented by "the Professor," for whom little Hans and his father dictate and write down the case material. The course of the analysis does not rewind the course of the neurosis's development (SE X, 83), but constructs out of the material heading little Hans off at the impasse a transference neurosis and cure along a three-way free-way. Little Hans pounds this busy street or intersection where his life as a neurotic, the father's recording and programming of his associations, and the Professor's super-vision are traffic jamming.

> [FATHER:] "Once he knocked on the pavement with his stick and said: [LITTLE HANS:] 'I say, is there a man underneath?—someone buried?—or is that only in the cemetery?' [FOR FREUD:] So he is occupied not only with the riddle of life but with the riddle of death." (SE X, 69)

Although he knocks at portals of the anal and footnote underworld, where dead sausage children are internal and eternal occasions for grieving (SE X, 131n1), each return of the repressed the five-year-old rides out remains always only metaphorically "like an unlaid ghost" (SE X, 122). The three-way association passes from the almost improperly buried corpse (it can still be readily restored to the cemetery, which is just a question-to-the-father away) to the box-and-cart theories of birth that little Hans must apply to the riddle of his sister Hanna's arrival, the birth or death that he must metabolize: before Hanna traveled with them in the railway carriage, she was already with them in the box (SE X, 67ff). The conditions for haunting, which were there for Hans as they are in every development and transference, were nevertheless contained inside the transference neurosis and cure that the little patient could remember to forget. This forgetting, which is not repression but analysis, is the vanishing point of Freud's 1922 postscript: during his one-time-only follow-up visit, which is on the record, big Hans assures Freud that he did not recall his life as a neurotic, nor recog-nize himself in the study, but only began to feel the pull with the references to the fam-ily outing to Gmunden. This summer resort's place name is a last resort on the sliding scale of recall, one that regressively stammers *Munden* (to taste) and *Mund* (mouth), and at the same time thus touches on the retained wound of Freud's own dismembered name: *-mund*. In other words, the boxes and carts that stay, in Hans's case, on the one-way assembly line of interpersonal, couplified rapport with mourning through substitution and reproduction were (inside Freud and his haunted cases) the crypts crowding out and shutting down easy disposal of the separation or loss.

Graf's "Reminiscences" of Freud first appeared in English alongside Freud's "Psy-chopathic Characters on the Stage," the brief essay Freud presented to Graf, presum-ably in 1906, and which Graf gave to *The Psychoanalytic Quarterly* for publication (in translation) in 1942. The editorial note strongly suggests that the inclusion of his reminiscences was the deal Graf sealed with the offer that couldn't be refused of a brand-new Freud text. That the German version of Graf's "Reminiscences" insists on the openness of the invitation to publish gives us some cause to note the split and conflict running Graf's "I was there" histories of original conception. Still in 1946 Graf was fighting rounds in the Faustian pairing announced in the title of his American book, *Composer and Critic:*

> Only history could answer the question: Are the mistakes of musical criticism inherent in the system itself, or are they mere accidents, clinging to it like mud to the wheel of a moving car? Only history could teach me clearly to see the position of criticism in the musical life of our time, and its proper function within musical society. Musical criticism is the child of history, and only history, the greatest critic of human accomplishments could tell whether it is a legitimate child or a changeling. (29)

One day in the early days of psychoanalysis, Graf presented a paper to the Wednesday group on Wagner's *The Flying Dutchman.* Freud's blessing wasn't in disguise: he asked for Graf's leave to publish it in his series. The resulting 1911 monograph, Graf's best piece of writing and the only piece he made with Freud completely behind or in front of him, explored, once again, the "demonic" in Wagner's operas. But this time, this one time, Graf tracked back the force that was with Wagner to Wagner's relationship to his fathers. There was the bookkeeper, Wagner by name, who died when the composer was six months old. But his mother remarried and for the rest of his life and work Wagner played with, fantasized about the possibility that this man—Geyer was his name, which in a word, in German, means vulture—could have sired him before advancing to the official head of the family. Geyer was the only father Wagner ever knew and then he died, too, when the boy was seven years old. When forging a family crest for himself, the composer mixed and matched literalized, visualized references to the vulture and to the wagon or *Wagen* that the name Wagner mumbles. The wagon is given as many spokes as there were Wagner children. Thus the composer shared his special case of being son of Geyer, the family spokesperson, with his older siblings, too. Graf argues that Wagner had to play with this possibility for keeps on account of the implicated adulterous act of his mother that opened her up wide to the composer's unconscious visitations. "On the very day that Richard Wagner completed 'The Flying Dutchman,' he picked up the pen again to write his mother a letter. For years their correspondence had been interrupted. Now however the pressure of unconscious thoughts motivated him, for with 'The Flying Dutchman' the composer had returned to his home where he had once played as a boy and once again he had seen the large bright eyes of his mother resting upon him. . . ."[4] But as is suggested by the treatment of the names in rendering the fantasy family sign, Wagner also sought his physical connection with father, a connection that took the form of the demonic. The uncanny heroes of Wagner's operas are portraits of Geyer, but also of Wagner in Geyer's place.

The Wagner hero is born shortly after the death of the father, whom he therefore never really knows. But the son's arrival is associated with the lowering of the doom. If we include Wagner's fantasy calculation that Geyer was already siring him before the first father died, we recognize the two-timing of Wagner's identification:

> Doesn't the whole situation approximate the central plot of Wagner's operas and the topic of our analysis? Geyer would have arrived then as the Dutchman, like Siegmund, like Tristan. It is as if, while hiking up a mountain, the view suddenly opens wide onto a deep valley, which we would like to reach, but then with the next step the view disappears and we must again seek our way among cliffs. The Dutchman, Siegmund, and Tristan are not portraits of Geyer but rather of Wagner; they share his traits and his sensibility, there can be no mistake: Wagner speaks in these works of himself, not of Geyer—or, more precisely, he puts himself in the latter's place. By taking on the roles of the Dutchman and other figures, he puts himself into the same situation that he had conjured up in his fantasies for Geyer. He is now the man who approaches a union or marriage which his arrival destroys. (31)

In his parallel studies, for example *Wagner Problems*, Graf distinguished Wagner's rise to the heights of German culture as the victorious "slave rebellion of all dilettantish and literary natures, of the shady side of the musical world" (17; my translation). Wagner is thus under consideration as the unstoppable advent of the mass media Sensurround, which comes complete, split-level style, with the journalistic mediations and standards of middlebrow culture. In *The Case of Wagner*, Nietzsche finds the name to call the composer of the improv nightmare from which he has awakened: Wagner is an actor.[5] Nietzsche calls father Geyer an actor, too; but even if Geyer was a painter, as Graf tells the story, Wagner's dressing up in painter's drag was an acting identification. As a recovering Wagnerian, Nietzsche would nevertheless avow that to write and think in his day it was just as necessary to have fallen for this new middlebrow mascot culture and its pact psychology, its proxy relationship to so-called mass culture. Only in this way could Nietzsche conceive writing that risked being misunderstood, thus raising the stakes of reading and misreading to life or death within middlebrow culture.

If Graf is right about the exchange value of the essay he restored to the archive in 1942, Freud responded in "Psychopathic Characters on the Stage" to Graf's reading of the dramatic neurosis in Wagner's musical work with a diagnosis of another drama trauma, but without all the music. Freud adds to his double reading of Oedipus and Hamlet, which was rehearsed in the correspondence with Fliess and then repeated in *The Interpretation of Dreams*, the corollary notion that *Hamlet* is not psychological drama, but rather psychopathological drama and therefore requires a personalized audience: "Here the precondition of enjoyment is that the spectator should himself be a neurotic" (SE VII, 308-9). But, if we accept that Freud's sense of *Hamlet*'s audience is party to an exchange with Graf's Wagner investigations, then what Freud misses by not facing the music is the point of contrast. The culture that crawled out from under Wagner's "demonic" middlebrow is not the haunt of Hamlet neurotics. In *Hamlet* the father is a ghost and not the father; he's certainly not the father from hell, the unambiguous father. The neurotic component is stuck on the evidence of the mother's desire in the rush to replace the dead father and circumvent or repress proper mourning. Then there's a double background check that can't be covered: Shakespeare's unmournable child Hamlet can be conjured because, in some other secret place, Freud carried his mother's undead baby Julius, who made his fraternal orders and ghost appearances in earshot of Shakespeare's *Julius Caesar.* Like the unstoppable assumption among philosophical and intellectual-historical types that ghost status must be assigned to father as his exclusive right of passage, the Wagner split between passion and quiescence, life and death, is the commonplace of an uncomplicated or healthy mind. Neurotics don't go to the Devil. You have to be healthy, less inhibited, with an uncomplicated loss that only needs replacing, to deal with the Devil.

Like Nietzsche, Freud was not psychically constituted for association with the Devil. But he, too, took up the challenge of lifting the stakes and standards of interpretation within the unstoppable hell-raising of middlebrow culture. The Devil was the password that allowed Freud to join the big boys, the philosophers and journalists, and address Death, even one's own death (or is it father's?). With Dad certainty Freud could pass as philosopher. Devil reference is a passing mention in Freud because the death of the other or the dead other is in the psychoanalytic view, just like primal repression, one of the nonnegotiable facts of psychic life, based on the inconceivability of one's own death and, hence, of Death. It is this inside view that throws self for a loop through other and keeps us in the vicinity of mourning and unmourning, while also giving us the techno high of egoic immortality or, in the felt absence of replication, mass suicide. We saw the future of mass readership, or on a more staggered installment plan, the future leadership of the masses by the raising of the middlebrow, when what was legible began appearing as Devil doubles.

The Devil in Ernest Jones's study *On the Nightmare* is, by folk etymology or free association, always also a double, the demonization that fits the all-bad father in contrast to the all-good father.[6] In the precursor studies Jones dutifully tours, a certain A. Graf is cited for identifying the Devil's origin as lying in "the depths of the human soul" (154). Pfister and Silberer join the lineup for interpreting the Devil as, respectively, a throwback to "'infantile experiences of fear'" and the personification "'of the suppressed and unsublimated elements of the instinctual life'" (155). Freud can be found in the midst of this research review via his conjecture in "Character and Anal Erotism" that "'the Devil is certainly nothing else than the personification of the repressed, unconscious instinctual life'" (154). But Freud figures more directly outside this chorus line extolling the Devil's unconscious depths via another study that inspires or models Jones's new working hypothesis: "The belief in the Devil represents in the main an exteriorization of two sets of repressed wishes, both of which are ultimately derived from the infantile Oedipus situation: (a) The wish to imitate certain attributes of the father, and (b) the wish to defy the father; in other words, an alternating emulation of an hostility against the father" (155). The working part of the hypothesis is owed to Freud: "Since the origin of infantile terror is now known, it naturally suggests itself to one to investigate the descriptions of the belief in the Devil in the light of this new knowledge" (155). The footnote falls open to Freud's case study of little Hans (155n3).

Second Circle

With the onset of the second system, Freud cycles between ultimately demonic repetition as expression of the inertia in organic life and the combo energies of libido. But then repetition reemerges as the egoic and unicellular prospect of replication: immortality on the spot we're in with reproduction or death. The cycle of Freud's speculations in *Beyond the Pleasure Principle* passes through the metabolism of our worldly relations with or in the Devil as set out in 1965 by Vilém Flusser, mortal sin by mortal sin, within a lexicon adapted, for the duration of his *Die Geschichte des Teufels* (History of the Devil), to and from psychoanalysis.[7]

Flusser was born in Prague in 1920. He published what I've translated as "History of the Devil" in Brazil in Portuguese translation. The German original did not appear until 1993. By the late 1980s, Flusser had more or less established himself in the makeshift world of art magazine writing—all about the future now of media influences in theory, on art. But even though the leading international art magazines supported him, he remained a figure on the margin who was codependent on the notion of making it big. Published, as usual, by European Photography, a small press that seemed to exist only to have Flusser's books on list, his 1991 *Ein Gespräch* (A Conversation) was based on an interview Klaus Nüchtern conducted with Flusser the year before at the arts festival in Graz, Austria.[8] The subject is Flusser's account of the nomadic impulse, as presented in his plenary lecture the night before, and which is situated in the course of the interview as rivaling many well-known philosophical investigations in the receiving area of techno media. His collected works address photography, vampirism, the future of writing in an age of techno visualization, and a couple of plays.[9] His first book, completely out of context with his condensed all-out effort to be recognized many years later, is his best by far. It is the only work by Flusser that seeks a fit with Freud, though from a distance of the rationalization that the deadly sins required consultation with a sex theorist. But to his credit, it is the fit with Jung that would be noted by most scholars likely to proceed from an inquiry into the Devil.

The Devil is one immortal figure who also has a history, however. Human history, as progress, as evolution, is the history of the Devil. The Devil's job or purpose is to keep the world in this time, in time we keep with history's progress. The complete defeat of the Devil means the world would cease to exist. We would be one with God and nothing would be left of human existence. We are therefore more closely related to the Devil than to God. From the witch's flying broomstick to magic elixirs, the Devil's way has been one of technological enhancement or extension of our bodily existence.

Relations with the Devil begin or begin again in Lust, already inside the protoplasm from which life first evolved. The cell is immortal: it takes in life, moves in time and then divides or doubles itself, replicates itself. The multicellular organism, by contrast, is mortal, not by accident, which is the relationship of protozoa to death, but by plan, by law. Soul or psyche arises out of inhibitions, limitations, frustrations of our lustful striving to develop, to evolve, to rise to every occasion. To be more or less free of inhibition, either in the mode of great health or in the conscience-free condition of sociopathy, is to be in a position to part with soul or psyche and stand closer to the Devil than to God and His soul strain of inhibited, neurotic followers. Humans are, after all, essentially erotically uninhibited since human sexuality is not limited to the purpose of reproduction. This is the bottom line of human sinfulness. Our desires— self-sex, same-sex, unisex, fetish sex, self play, and foreplay—are perverse, not a reproductive part of society. However, if free love could be realized on this polymorphous basis it would be the end of human being. But when it's time for an example, Flusser points to the unlimited passion of nationalism, particularly in Europe, where each brand comes with its own underlying love of the mother tongue.

The second deadly sin, Anger, breaks limits and inhibitions and thus frees up passion. Laws, rules, and regulations breed Anger. In other words, the law transforms the world of the senses into the world or word of Anger, of power. In Lust and Anger we desire reality, we want our desires realized. But we end up—for example in the development of science out of lustful curiosity and angry transgression—in danger of losing our sense of reality.

As essential as lustful propagation, for example, is number three, the sin of Gluttony, of identificatory ingestion and digestion. We live in the excrement of human spirit. Shit rather than earth or clay is the Devil's creative medium. By passing through creature and creation first, shit is in a sense artificial, a repetition and a production, and as product it is moreover a blended mass of sameness. Shit stands for the equality of mothers and children of both sexes before the one and only difference, the one and only sexual difference, embodied by the Devil father. It is this world, at one irreversible remove from nature, that protects us against the natural world of accident and against God. The digested and excreted world has a purpose, that of serving mankind. The world thus becomes real again, believable. But what then finally is the difference between the undigested world of nature and the digested world of technology? We know as little about the future evolution of our machines as we know about the future development of any animal. What we do know is that machines develop or evolve more quickly than animals or plants. That's what makes our world so horrific. We eat the world to excrete the machines that devour us. We will die out and be replaced by technology just as we replaced our missing-link connection with the primates.

Envy and Greed are two deadly sins that are in it together, as the Devil's backup plan. In place of a phenomenal world that we see as unreal, we fall for the reality of the socius—and the power of language. Greed conserves the progressive work of Envy and thus fortifies the social hierarchies in the wake-up call of social upheaval. What's real, where the Devil grabs us, is what we thus take so interpersonally, namely the social relation. The bottom line is assigned to the world power of words, words as historic inheritance of generations, syntax as the tall glass from which we drink the wisdom of sentences. It is only within this perspective, which thus pulled up way short of the grammar or logic of relations and symbols (of symbols), that we can love language and yearn to preserve, greedily, language's purity, and look with envy at other speakers who would engage or enrich language. Language is a treasure haunt.

At bottom we find words, the doubly opened gateway, through which society penetrates us and we in turn enter society. Society is the gridlock of avenues composed of victory arches made up of words through which words move onward. That mankind is endowed with fundamental social being means that human life is nothing but an inner buzzing of words.

Language stands apart from all other aspects of the sensual world by all accounts of its hierarchical organization. Words have assigned places in the sentences in which they march. Whatever changes are introduced word by word, the principle of hierarchy is preserved. When Anger and Gluttony in seeking incorporation of the world in the word fail to convince us of this reality, in a word, of the phenomenal world, then it's up to Envy and Greed to affirm instead the reality of language and its manifestations, with society at the front of the line.

Language, as the only means of spiritualization that does not first subscribe to belief in God, is the crusade of the living and the dead against the Divinity. In this formation every word is a flaming sword in the Devil's service, and language as a whole is one big protest against the corporeality of humankind, an articulated cry of Envy against God. Creation thus becomes the gigantic attempt by the Devil to articulate himself—and to this end human society serves the Devil as mouthpiece and tongue.

Envy and Greed together generate society, its organizing principle as hierarchy, vengeance, and, with the same organizer, history. Vengeance is not beyond good and evil: it is good and evil at once. That's why, relatively speaking, vengeance requires no judge, and, therefore, the socio-historico-linguistic order (that vengeance fills out) no God. Envy is avenged by Greed, while Envy gets even with Greed. For each historical epoch, you can substitute for Envy and Greed one of the two defining antipodes or, anytime at all, you can fill them in, respectively, as son and father. Greed is the momentary success of Envy; Envy is Greed that has not yet realized itself. The Devil catches us in the choice to be made between hypocritical standards of self-betrayal (Envy and Greed idealized) and the enlightened opportunism that looks through the social and historical principle of vengeance onto a chessboard of manipulations.

With Pride we see through all of it, the whole world together with the Devil and God, all of the above, as our own egoic creation. This is the triumph of the will, the ego's motility. It is the ego's nature to go out of itself, to cast itself out and about, to realize itself, to make itself material, to project itself on the outside. The pressure is on, in the ego, to express oneself. Language is the net, the web, through which the ego exceeds its boundaries. The ego is like a spider: it collects its secretions, its thoughts, and keeps them crossing, back and forth, affixing them to the branches of trees, to our senses, and thus it weaves its web out of words and sentences. You can stretch language until it encompasses the infinitude of what's out there. Even the ego weaving it can be subsumed in language. But when it's too much of a stretch—as in the networking of logic and mathematics—then nothing can in fact be caught up in it, only covered like a shroud. This stretch belongs to the sorrow of the heart, apathy, depression, the deadly sin otherwise named *acedia*, popularly known as Sloth. But there are also moments of condensation or density—literally, of poetry or *Dichtung*—that capture what they encompass by holding the ego, reality, prisoner in this condensed form. Will can remove from this linguistic density all knots, connections, concepts. Then without any meaning we would still have a language, but one of relations only, one that no longer speaks but instead buzzes, hums. It's the sounds of music. Music can thus be seen as the highest and densest of art forms, of poetry or *Dichtung*. Music realizes the ego in a pure form: a meaningless song in praise of the will by the will.

It is a defect in the ego that in its role as creator it gives forth illusion, the illusions of good and evil, of wrong and right, and produces logic and ethics. Music grabs us because it is the final argument, the last stand or understanding—after music there's nothing left to say. God and the Devil are annihilated, dissolved in music. When the music plays we want only to submit to the glorious humming of language. The meaningless language of relations is reality, because it is ego. Music is the goal of human will. It is the ego's goal to transform all its works into music.

Music and mathematics could also be seen as two sides of language. On one side, one can award density to music and, in contrast, view mathematics as the stretch of language that covers everything but captures or holds not one thing. If math helps man control the world, this is only a by-product, a side effect. Indeed math has for its own sake the purpose of reducing all sentences to zero. The goal of human thought and speech is to be translated into math. Math realizes the complete silence that music realized in the ego's great pride of will. Music does not redeem us, deliver us from our sins, but only from ourselves. Music is thus a demon, a means of possession. Ego, if you must know, is a dissonance, a grammatical error that arises when math, the highest knowledge, and music, the most creative inspiration, connect, intersect, rather than merge with one another. With the music math loses the character of being for its own sake and becomes a means of delivering the ego, becomes an instrument of dissolution.

But mournfulness, apathy, laziness must renounce reality, because it is nothing. We have, in facing the music, delivered ourselves from God and the Devil—but also from every piece of the ego, from every shred of self-consciousness.

Between Freud's *Beyond the Pleasure Principle* and Flusser's *History of the Devil* there's Arthur Clarke's *Childhood's End*, another station in the crossing over or out that gives Death and the Devil direct address, whether by exception or as the rule. In *Childhood's End*, aliens, who are Devil lookalikes or were once upon a time taken by us for Devils, represent the highest development of consciousness, ego, reason. The future that comes toward the human species is an evolutionary version of reunion with God. It is a future that the alien Devil egos will never encounter. The Devils are ordered by the God-like Overmind to protect the human species from its innate mass suicide drive. The alien Devils come to earth as a way more advanced techno culture that can dictate its terms of peace on earth. But it turns out that all this protection was paid to maintain the conditions for the mutation that will end the human species, but send its dematerialized sequel into the Overmind.

Even though humankind appears, on the scale of its self-entitlement to intellectual and scientific penetration, evolutionarily inferior to the Devil aliens, there is something else in the human makeup that exceeds the understanding that came from outer space. This excess can be found on the margins of our own rational culture in the form of occult inquiry, in particular as evident in the study of telepathy. Alan Turing, one of the World War Two fathers of modern computing, advanced the thesis that it was possible to conceive of a form of artificial intelligence that would be indistinguishable from human intelligence.[10] The one exception to this equation of machine and man, Turing conceded, was the phenomenon of telepathy. Freud, too, after carefully including the role of the unconscious and wish fulfillment in his understanding of cases of alleged telepathy, concluded that telepathy did transmit, and that we could receive its frequency at the intersection between technology and the unconscious. Turing made explicit that if one accepted telepathy, the possibility of communication with the departed could no longer be pushed back as mere belief in ghosts. But this excess or access was the threat the Devil aliens were ultimately sent by the Overmind to contain. The lasting or last legacy of humankind is the relationship to our dead, the relationship of unmourning. It accompanies and exceeds the mass suicide along for the nuclear drive, the Oedipally complex realization of the primal scene between earth and sun. It is, in time, without God and the Devil, without the renewal through lazy thinking, without evolutionary jumping to conclusions, precisely un-containable.

Clarke resettled the Devil in 1953 within a science fiction about the proper timing of evolution beyond all links with the missing. In so many Faustian fictions and science fictions we see the Devil give time, in exchange for soul, specifically more time, more-of-the-same time, but at the same time more focused time, quality time. But the Devil cannot reverse time. The paraphysics of relative time—like the fantasy combinatorics of family identifications—remain accessible only to the human psyche or soul.

Owing perhaps to the novel's Jungian background and the opening shutting of its recent past, all that is relative or relational is annihilated or reborn as evolutionary progress marching as to God. One flashback comes up only to be dismissed as false analogy: "Somewhere long ago, he had seen a century-old newsreel of such an exodus. It must have been at the beginning of the First World War—or the Second. There had been long lines of trains, crowded with children, pulling slowly out of the threatened cities." But: "these who were leaving now were no longer children, whatever they might be. And this time, there would be no reunion."[11] The striving for union with God or Overmind, which leaves life as we know it behind, no longer misses the link that makes evolutionary change, a change that comes across like a break or a leap because the continuity shot with the stage of development that came right before is a lost loss in generation. But at the same time, what survives this break on the upbeat is lazy thinking that can't make out the big difference between Overmind Nirvana and the mass suicidal embrace of nothingness on death drive. And so an annihilating equation is the something for nothing that starts it all up again.

When you're not involved in the creative dynamic of excrement, when you swing low and lazy, you're frozen. But even the deep freeze reverses itself, doubles as turning point, as re-starter. Before (or after) you hit the icy bottom of your bottom's-up relationship to the world, to creation, to the Devil, you're in the start-up position (once again) of Lust and Anger, the two passions of self-sacrifice or soul sacrifice that are therefore tragic in dimension. Don Juan is driven by Lust to deal with the Devil, while Faust is inspired by Anger—at himself, his father, at his own limitations, at the limiting role of the mere word, his father's legacy. Anger (which can flip through internalized anger to deep depression) is our lasting relationship to the law. Transgressing against the law gets us off. We welcome the law's transformation of our world into the world of Anger because this new world order is also that of power. Then you pass on through ingestion and digestion of the world of our techno mediation. Greed and envy transmute this media metabolization into power-hungry, possessive, mixed-metaphorical relations of controlling the world through others. But then there's always our Pride, which drops us to the final position of sorrow and Sloth of the heart.

And, says Flusser, there is no way out of lazy thinking, out of the sadness of resignation, of being resigned to unreality. We're at the end and back at the beginning. The world is the Devil's instrument for dominating the world. Nothingness came from nothing and was annihilated by nothingness.

Flusser informs us at the end of his history, which is now our history, that all along the Devil has been only amusing himself, playing with himself. Whatever we do, say, write it's all about the Devil. And what we try to say about the Devil concerns the mirror image or doubling of the Devil. But we are neither satisfied, nor silenced by this realization. We are driven to transform into grammar and articulate word for word that which is hard to conceive, namely the lassitude and sorrow of the heart.

God created the Devil as his adversary and ally: the Devil was to create a world that could be redeemed for the timeless reality that would join God. But the Devil's world dissolved not into this reality, but rather into nothingness, death, which only the philosophical calm of lazy thinking and sorrow of the heart can contemplate. God and the Devil are there so the death we get—it is its only redemption value—is our own. One more last time: repetition or the Devil is all it can be within and with the exception of the pause we are given for lazy thought.

Third Circle

In his "Reminiscences," Graf turns to religion to characterize the ups and downs of the early years inside Freud's inner circle of application and submissions:

> I have compared the gatherings in Freud's home with the founding of a religion. How-ever, after the first dreamy period and the unquestioning faith of the first group of apostles, the time came when the church was founded. Freud began to organize his church with great energy. He was serious and strict in the demands he made of his pupils; he permitted no deviations from his orthodox teaching.[12]

The distance of Graf's withdrawal from the Freud group after Adler was excom-municated nevertheless remained compatible for the father of little Hans with unin-terrupted respect, perhaps even idealization, the right conditions, in any event, for his preservation of Freud's text and of his own "Reminiscences" of its author. That the pro-jection onto Freud of an unidentified influence upon coming events slips in between the lines of his reminiscences remains within the boundaries of the healthy. While Graf does not make the little Hans connection public, still for those of us by now in the know, the anecdote that most rocks the note to their historical collaboration concerns a gift Freud made to Graf's son, two years to countdown of the phobia: "On the occa-sion of my son's third birthday, Freud brought him a rocking horse which he himself carried up the four flights of steps leading to my house" (474).

The other side of the same distance dynamic, demonization, attended last and lasting words of resistance. In his Freud obituary, Jung, for example, wrote that he had been "permitted a deep glimpse into the mind of this remarkable man . . . possessed by a demon—a man who had been vouchsafed an overwhelming revelation that took possession of his soul and never let him go." When Freud died, Jung was the interna-tional leader of the German association of psychotherapy, which was being retrofitted to many of the specifics of National Socialism. However, given his negative transfer-ence, Jung could nevertheless count his willingness to serve as a concession and trib-ute to Freud since Freudians shared equally with Adlerians and Jungians in the new order's central institute in Berlin.

The demon that Jung refers to here can be good or evil, depending, for example, in what archetype the real father is set. Jung's 1948 updating revisions of his 1909 essay, "The Significance of the Father in the Destiny of the Individual," show the tension between this more neutral or historical notion of demon or genius and the earlier setting of God and the Devil. In 1909 Jung extends the findings drawn from the cases he presents—and the case of the bed-wetting boy Jung expressly offers as complement to Freud's study of Little Hans—to address his more-or-less normal public. The saga of demonic possession by the father is not restricted to the neurotic zone: "If we normal people examine our lives from the psychoanalytic perspective, we too perceive how a mighty hand guides us without fail to our destiny, and not always is this hand a kindly one. Often we call it the hand of God or of the Devil."[13] In 1948 Jung dropped "from the psychoanalytic perspective," thus, unwittingly perhaps, underscoring the consent of middlebrow normalcy to his destinal claims while at the same time marking the spot of overlap between Freud's alleged demon and Jung's certain Devil father, the one that gave a kind of order to Jung's life and corpus following the nervous breakup of idealizing relations with Freud, the good or God father. A second reference to the God or the Devil frame, which Jung deleted from his 1948 updating revisionism, reinforces the more-or-less healthy (or psychopathic) stereotype in which the Devil is set. We need only subtract the outer-limits stretch marks from the neurosis diagnosis to find our medium setting on the psychopathology continuum: "As soon as we enter the field of neurosis, this antithesis is stretched to the limit. God becomes the symbol of the most complete sexual repression, the Devil the symbol of sexual lust."[14]

Based on the many ready-made examples of Devil reference and fiction that have accrued to and within psychoanalysis, it is possible, in closing, to list a couple of conditions and distinctions. You need a neurotic-to-psychotic psyche, one that's inhibited, as in stuck on missing objects, to take the leap of faith called God or to cultivate more personalized occult relations with undeath. The psyche that signs up with the Devil is uninhibited and nonneurotic (or psychopathic passing as nonneurotic). For once and future reference: the psy-fi gadget lover or fetishist occupies yet another place of exception, one displaced with regard to the question of mourning or not mourning, which is not covered by this specific divide between faith and certainty. The Devil, remember, never grants immortality. Instead he grants quality time, which is really more-of-the-same time, but with the big difference that the Devil adds a deadline, an on-schedule certain death date. In other words, the Devil's powers, in person or by proxy, are linked and limited to this world. (In *Civilization and Its Discontents* and *The Future of an Illusion,* Freud considers whole epochs of religious belief in other worlds as "neurotic" [SE XXI, 144 and 43].) Even when the Devil extends or defers limits for a certain amount of time, the time will come when the limit or limitation must be observed.

What operates inside psychoanalysis in the Devil's name is not your usual occult foreign body. The Devil or the demonic or the Death Drive (in *Archive Fever* Derrida also argues for their interchangeability[15]) responds for psychoanalysis in the diplomatic context or contest in which Freud's science can find itself with philosophy or journalism. What psychoanalysis needed was a way to address what's strictly inconceivable according to psychoanalytic theory, but which remains the leading password across these disciplines, namely Death. At the same time, Freud was able to attend to the specific conditions of Devil fantasy or delusion, and under the rule of the exception to the overriding melancholic significance of all other occult relations give us ears to hear a case like that which Aleister Crowley makes for himself.

As chronicled in his *Confessions*, Crowley made it to Dad certainty through the perfect fit he threw between his death wish and his father's death. At first writing down his early years in the third person, Crowley identifies himself as his father's son. "In the case of Alick, he was the only son of a father who was naturally a leader of men. In him, therefore, this spirit grew unchecked. He knew no superior but his father."[16] But this continuity shot could only come about after the fact of the father's death. "In looking back over his life up to May 1886, he can find little consecution and practically no coherence in his recollections. But from that month onwards there is a change. It is as if the event which occurred at that time created a new faculty in his mind. A new factor had arisen and its name was death." This death was doubled and contained in line with the son's wish. On the night of the father's death, he dreamed this same death. To fix the quality of this connection he turns up the contrast with his mother's death. He keeps on dreaming that she's dead but she's still there. Eventually a dream death coincides with her passing. It's one hell of a coincidence. And this time, Crowley recalls, the dream had that special quality control he had sensed the one and only time he dreamt up the dead father. The mother's life or death position is uncontainable within the dream series; until, that is, the father's death is finally built up out of the repetition and catches up with the traumatic uncontrollability of the maternal body's presence and absence. But this maternal, material resistance, described, spectacularly without any identification whatsoever on Crowley's part, as the bouncing, escaping fallout from his wishes, which he followed relentlessly until one day the mother, over and out, was liquidated with Dad certainty, is not subsumable, via repression, denial, or displacement, by the early duo dynamic superintended by Mother to which all the other occult figures (vampire, mummy, werewolf, ghost, you name it) can in fact be seen to return with a haunting vengeance. With Dad certainty Crowley entered up-close and first-personal relations with his own life, which would henceforward be deadicated and dadicated to worship of the Devil in the pantheon of paganism.

> From the moment of the funeral the boy's life entered on an entirely new phase. The change was radical. Within three weeks of his return to school he got into trouble for the first time. . . . Previous to the death of Edward Crowley, the recollections of his son . . . appear to him strangely impersonal. . . . It is only from this point that he begins to think of himself in the first person. From this point, however, he does so; and is able to continue this autohagiography in a more conventional style by speaking of himself as I.[17]

NOTES

1. Max Graf, *Wagner-Probleme und andere Studien* (Vienna: Wiener Verlag, 1900), 44–45.

2. Ibid., 103, 100.

3. Max Graf, *Composer and Critic. Two Hundred Years of Musical Criticism* (Port Washington, N.Y.: Kennikat Press, 1946), 242–43.

4. Max Graf, "Richard Wagner im 'Fliegenden Holländer.'" In *Ein Beitrag zur Psychologie künstlerischen Schaffens* (Leipzig and Vienna: Franz Deuticke, 1911), 46.

5. Friedrich Nietzsche, *The Case of Wagner: The Birth of Tragedy and the Case of Wagner* (1888; New York: Random House, 1967), 178–79.

6. Ernest Jones, *On the Nightmare* (1910–12; London: Liveright Paperbound Edition, 1971), 158.

7. Vilém Flusser, *Die Geschichte des Teufels* (1965; Göttingen: European Photography, 1993).

8. Vilém Flusser, with Klaus Nüchtern, *Ein Gespräch* (Göttingen: European Photography, 1991).

9. Vilém Flusser, *Die Schrift. Hat Schreiben Zukunft?* (1987; Göttingen: European Photography, 1992); *Vampyroteuthis infernalis. Eine Abhandlung samt Befund des Institut Scientifique de Recherche Paranaturaliste* (1987; Göttingen: European Photography, 1993); *Deutsche Musik im neunzehnten Jahrhundert* (Berlin: Verlag Siegfried Cronback, 1898); *From Beethoven to Shostakovich. The Psychology of the Composing Process* (New York: Philosophical Library, 1947); *Die innere Werkstatt des Musikers* (Stuttgart: Verlag von Ferdinand Enke, 1910).

10. A. M. Turing, "Computing Machinery and Intelligence," *Mind* 59, no. 236 (October 1950): 433–60. For the more extended treaments of Turing test, telepathy, haunting, sexual difference, and Clarke's *Childhood's End*, see Laurence A. Rickels, "Satan and Golem, Inc.," *parallax* 30 (2004): 49–57.

11. Arthur C. Clarke, *Childhood's End* (1953: New York: Ballantine Books, 1990) 186.

12. Max Graf, "Reminiscences of Professor Sigmund Freud," trans. Gregory Zilboorg, *Psychoanalytic Quarterly* 11, no. 4 (October 1942): 465–76.

13. C. G. Jung, "The Significance of the Father in the Destiny of the Individual," in *The Collected Works of C.G. Jung*, ed. William Mcguire, Herbert Read, Michael Fordham, and Gerhard Adler, trans. R. F. C. Hull. (Princeton: Princeton University Press, 1989), 4:301–23.

14. Ibid., 321n22.

15. Jacques Derrida, *Archive Fever: A Freudian Impression*, trans. Eric Prenowitz (Chicago and London: University of Chicago Press, 1996).

16. Aleister Crowley, *The Confessions of Aleister Crowley. An Autohagiography*, ed. John Symonds and Kenneth Grant (London: Arkana, 1989), 52.

17. Ibid., 52–53.

7. Heteros Autos

Freud's Fatherhood

Silke-Maria Weineck

Die Liebe zu den Kindern ist immer eine unglückliche.
[Love of children is always unhappy/unrequited.]

—Arthur Schnitzler

In the first sentence of what must be the most famous subchapter of *The Interpretation of Dreams*, Freud writes: "Another series of dreams that may be called typical are those with the content that a dear relative, parents or siblings, children etc. has died."[1] The odd grammatical structure of the sentence, with its singular verb following multiple subjects, announces that it is really only one dear relative whose dreamed death will matter to psychoanalysis: the father, whose death, according to Freud's widely accepted autobiographical narrative, gave rise to his self-analysis and hence to psychoanalysis as we know it. In his later writings Freud will repeatedly stress that psychoanalysis stands—and falls—with the Oedipus Complex, an assertion echoed in the literature over and over again. Very recently, Slavoj Žižek wrote, "Whenever we talk about myths in psychoanalysis, we really talk about *one* myth, the Oedipus myth—all other Freudian myths (the myth of the primal father, Freud's version of the Moses myth) are variations thereof, albeit *necessary* variations."[2] Shortly thereafter he claims that "the Oedipus 'myth,' and possibly mythical naivete itself, serves to veil a forbidden *knowledge,* namely the knowledge of the father's obscenity."[3]

In the wake of psychoanalysis, to say that masculinity (or even becoming-human itself) emerges as Oedipal implies that it becomes defined and marked by the name of the quintessential son, whose mask even the most patriarchal of twentieth-century grand theorists could don without raising too many questions. While Freud, father of six, presents himself, in *The Interpretation of Dreams,* as the son reflecting on his father's death, he will still have much to say about dreams concerning the death of siblings and of parents of both sexes. But there is one of those typical dreams he will never explore: the father's dream of his son's death, what we may call King Laius's dream.[4]

I will argue that *The Interpretation of Dreams*, and the discipline that grew out of it, are characterized by an elision of far-reaching ramifications: the elision of fatherhood. Seeing the prominence of the very word "father" in psychoanalysis, this claim may sound counterintuitive, even absurd. Of course, I am suggesting neither that psychoanalysis does not reflect on fatherhood as an institution, nor that it does not reflect on fathers; it obviously has done both, to a great extent and to tremendous effect. At the same time, however, it fails to theorize the position of the father from within; we see him through the son's eyes only, as if fatherhood were a symbolic and phantasmatic extension of filiality, but not a distinct realm of masculine experience producing a subject position of its own.

In this light, the intense analytic preoccupation with the (name of the) father paradoxically blocks him from view. Like Laius, he is always already offstage, significant only after his death, to which he must consent in order to gain the power ascribed to the function he is called upon to embody.[5] If Freud's version of the Oedipus legend functions like a veil, what is veiled is indeed the father—perhaps in his obscenity, but, more important, in his impossibility. In 1902, Otto Weininger puts the matter in all bluntness: "[F]atherhood is a miserable delusion."[6] Miserable and necessary, of course, and everywhere at work, like God, that other grand and miserable delusion that does and does not come to an end at the same time, and for similar reasons.

THE NAME OF THE CHILD

Concerning his children, Freud writes in a well-known passage in chapter 6 of *The Interpretation of Dreams*:

> I held to it that their names ought not to be chosen according to the fashion of the day but be determined in memory of dear persons. Their names make the children into "revenants." And in the end, are children not for all of us the only access to *immortality?*[7]

If children are "'revenants'" (we will have to come back to this term later), who is returning in their name? The first sentence above suggests that it is "dear persons," *teure Personen;* the last suggests that it is the naming father. In isolation, neither claim— naming as commemoration of loved or admired others, children as a path to immortality—is especially striking or original, but the combination sets up a tension worth exploring. Freud names his oldest son Jean Martin, after Charcot; his second son, Oliver, after Cromwell; his third son, Ernst, after Ernst Wilhelm von Brücke. The encounter with Charcot and his work, needless to say, was a milestone in Freud's professional life, and in 1927, he writes of the physiologist von Brücke as "the greatest authority that ever has influenced me" (*der größten Autorität, die je auf mich gewirkt hat*).[8] Cromwell does not quite seem to fit in, but in the Dream Book itself, Freud notes that this "great historical personality . . . had attracted me mightily in my boyhood years, especially since my stay in England" (432), and he comments: "It is easily noted how the suppressed megalomania of the father is transferred to his children in his mind; yes, one will gladly believe that this is one of the ways in which the suppressions of the same, which has [sic] become necessary in life, takes place."[9]

To the extent that Charcot, Cromwell, and Brücke appear in this context as men with whom Freud identified to a greater or lesser degree (this is not all they are, of course), children provide access to immortality by returning as their father's ideal selves. Their names honor admired men and create a benign outlet for the megalomania that life has forced the father to suppress. Reading just a little more closely, however, it appears that the naming of the child is not only a mere consolation for an already suppressed megalomania, as might be expected, but constitutes one of the very avenues of such suppressions. Not unlike the fetish, the naming of the child thus marks an identification as well as its loss. When Oliver Cromwell returns as Oliver Freud, the effect is one of great satisfaction: "I had the resolve to use precisely this name if it were to be a son and, deeply satisfied, saluted with it the one just born."[10] But Freud's subsequent comment makes it clear that this satisfaction comes at a certain price: declaring the son to be Oliver is tantamount to the admission that his father is not.

At the same time, the loss of the fantasy of *being* Oliver (Jean-Martin, Ernst) may be compensated for or outweighed by the both symbolic and quite real power involved in making him return as one's child. Oliver Freud shows up with a curious delay; in the passage cited above, Freud returns to a dream he had already analyzed roughly twenty pages earlier, a dream concerning his father:

> After his death, the father played a political role with the Hungarians, he unified them politically, whereby I see a small, indistinct image: a crowd as in the Reichstag, a person standing on one or two chairs, others around him. I remember that on his deathbed he resembled Garibaldi so much, and I'm glad that this prophecy has come true after all.[11]

In analyzing this dream—and Oliver does not yet make an appearance in this section—Freud plays on the (etymologically metonymic) homonymy of the German words for chair and for excrement, *Stuhl*, analogous to English "stool," and interprets his father as "Stuhlrichter," judge of excrement. He remembers that "the most torturous of his sufferings was the total paralysis of his colon (*Obstruction*) over the last weeks" (415), an obstruction that, as we will learn only later, led to Jakob Freud defecating in his bed several times. Interestingly enough, Freud does not mention his father soiling his bed at this point, but makes the association to a fellow student:

> One of my contemporaries, who lost his father while he was still in high school, on which occasion I, deeply moved, offered him my friendship, once told me with derision of the pain of a relative whose father had died on the street and had been taken home, where it was found, while undressing the corpse, that during the moment of death or *post mortem* a *defecation* [*Stuhlentleerung*] had taken place.[12]

Through this double detour—the father of the friend's relative—Freud introduces the image of the defecating father, and the child's mortification at such a sight. One might expect Freud to read his own dream as fulfilling the wish to see his father's lost honor vindicated; but his final interpretation performs a curious displacement: "Now we have penetrated to the wish which embodies itself in this dream: *After one's death to stand before one's children pure* [also clean] *and great*, who would not wish for that?"[13] Who is dreaming this dream, Jakob or Sigmund Freud? Both? The one as the other's revenant?

It is only in the second telling of the dream that Freud explicitly acknowledges his own father's defecation. He repeats the last sentence of the first telling, and adds (some repetition is necessary here):

> (To this, a forgotten sequel.) From the analysis I can now insert what belongs in this dream-gap. It is the mention of my second boy, to whom I gave the first name of a great historical personality which mightily attracted me during my boyhood years, especially after my stay in England. I had the resolve to use precisely this name if it were to be a son and, deeply satisfied, saluted with it the one just born. It is easily noted how the suppressed megalomania of the father is transferred to his children in his mind; yes, one will gladly believe that this is one of the ways in which the suppressions of the same, which have become necessary in life, takes place. The little one gained his right to be included in the context of this dream through the fact that he had been subjected to the same—easily forgiveable in the child and the dying man—accident of soiling his linens. Compare here the allusion "*Stuhlrichter*" (judge of excrement) and the wish of the dream: To stand before one's children *great* and *pure*.

It is, of course, Freud himself who is the judge of excrement, standing on the chair, the stool, one or two of them. It is he who *forgives* both his father and his son for defecating, while dreaming himself first as son, second as father, but always in control of his own stool, clean-pure and great. While the dead Jakob Freud returns as the Garibaldi of the Hungarians, the new-born Oliver now appears as a revenant of Jakob in his excrement, in an association that places the child on the deathbed while he's still in his diapers. And while Cromwell may not qualify as a father figure, Charcot and Brücke surely do.

If Cromwell (Brücke, Charcot) returns as Freud's incontinent little infant, however, megalomania has hardly been suppressed; it has merely taken a little detour. The act of naming is, after all, an exercise of power. And so is the evocation of the dead that makes revenants of Freud's own children. The context of the passage is rather clear on this. The section that ends with the passage on the naming of his children follows his third reading of the famous self-dissection dream, in which Ernst von Brücke himself had told Freud to "prepare" anatomically his own lower body, an activity Freud understands to symbolize his self-analysis (438). The section itself presents his second reading of a double dream involving first the appearance of the dead Professor Ernst Fleischl in Ernst von Brücke's laboratory, and then his (dead) friend P., who joins Freud and Fliess for dinner. During the meal P. dissolves into nothing, after Freud, realizing that P. is already dead, pronounces, while penetrating him with his gaze, "non vixit," "he did not live," an error in tense that Freud realizes within the dream itself. The last affect Freud relates is again one of great satisfaction: "I am tremendously pleased about [P's disintegration], understand now that Ernst Fleischl as well was only an appearance, a revenant, and find it quite well possible that such a person exists only for as long as one wishes, and that it can be removed by the wish of the other."[14]

In the first telling, Freud had added a few mysterious sentences in which he notes that he would love to tell his audience the "full solution of these riddles," i.e., "the meaning of the dream which is well-known to me," but claims that he cannot "sacrifice consideration for such dear persons to my ambition, as I do in my dream" (409). "Dear persons" (teure Personen) reappear later as the namesakes of Freud's children. But even without this repetition, it is obvious that the dream concerns Ernst von Brücke rather than Ernst Fleischl, and that the dissolution of the "greatest authority" of his life is at stake. Freud himself feels reminded of his own disintegration at Brücke's gaze. His former teacher had once reprimanded him for coming late to the lab: "What he said was scant and firm; however, the words did not really matter. What overwhelmed me were the terrible blue eyes with which he gazed at me and before which I faded—like P. in the dream, who, to my relief, reversed the roles."[15] Revenants return as reversals, and, like dreams or the fairies of old, they appear to fulfill wishes, inverting the father's gaze, granting to the dreamer the imaginary power of the father he will never hold in his waking life—for the father's power is, and I will elaborate on this later, real only in its effects: it cannot be experienced.

When Freud returns to the dream later on, and once again mentions the satisfaction it gave him, he reflects on the "difficult self-overcoming involved in interpreting and communicating one's dreams. One has to uncover oneself as the only villain among all the noble ones with which one shares life." He continues, rather cryptically:

> Hence, I find it entirely understandable that the revenants exist only as long as one likes them, and that they can be removed by a wish. The revenants, however, are the successive incarnations of my childhood friend; hence I am also satisfied that I have replaced this person again and again, and a replacement for the one I am now in the process of losing [i.e., Fliess] will find itself. Nobody is irreplaceable.[16]

The passages cited thus far establish a number of equations concerning children. They are figures of return as well as replacement, repositories of selves that are and are not sacrificed to the demands of the reality principle, compensation for the death of beloved friends. Naming them is akin to an identity deposit. Similar to the logic by which the fetish allows the fetishist to both acknowledge and deny castration, the son allows his father to both acknowledge and deny death and replaceability: in other words, time. The son does not merely return as his father, but, perhaps as important, as his father's father, inverting a relationship of submission into one of power through the act of naming. The most troubling and perhaps the most extraordinary metonymical equation, however, is that of the child as revenant and the revenant as the figure who can be "removed by a wish." The passage that, in isolation, appeared as a benign and perhaps mildly self-ironical assessment of a father's ambition for his children, thus acquires a sinister filicidal undertone. To an extent, naming the son after another is always already a process of erasing the son's identity; of withholding him from his own time; of smothering his separateness in layers and layers of identities already established and meaningful; and, in its most benign intentions, a violent inscription on the softest of flesh. Questioning Levinas's conception of fatherhood, Luce Irigaray writes: "The child should be for himself, not for the parent. When one intends to create a child, giving the child to himself appears as an ethical necessity. The son should not be the place where the father confers being or existence on himself, the place where he finds the resources to return to himself in relation to this same as and other than himself constituted by the son."[17] Irigaray is right, but she perhaps underestimates the difficulty of "giving the child to himself" in a culture where father-son succession and substitution organize all foundational narratives.

NON VIXIT

There is nothing new, of course, in drawing attention to paternal violence in its many forms and guises. Especially in the wake of Freud, such violence has been taken for granted as fatherhood's defining feature, thus engendering and legitimizing patricidal fantasies and acts. The prohibitions against these fantasies and acts are, in fact, rather weak as soon as we enter metaphoric or symbolic realms. If anything, violent rebellion against all fathers has been the norm and, often enough, the ideal in cultural production (at least) since the Enlightenment, and it surely serves as a privileged (and not necessarily tragic) model of history. What remains underexplored in this familiar narrative is the position of the father himself, as well as the moment of transition, of becoming-father. Seen as the end of sonhood, patricide is the process by which the murderer usurps the place of the victim along with the seat of power. As Laius learns, gaining the woman means begetting the son, and begetting the son manifests more than potency and possession. The logic of fatherhood is bound to engender filicidal impulses in the father that are just as inevitable (and equally ambivalent) as the patricidal impulses of the prototypical son. This is not to deny that fatherhood is *also* marked by pride and by love, by the urge to protect and the (fantasmatic) pleasure at having extended the self into the future. The dilemma of fatherhood is precisely the simultaneity of encountering the rival one cannot destroy without destroying oneself. Fatherhood, in other words, is Laiusian, and the legend of Laius and Oedipus speaks as much to the sexuality of the adult male as to that of the child.

While Freud reads the Oedipal plot as a child's fantasy, we may want to read Freud's plot of the subordinate son, who displaces his desire in the interest of the patriarchal family, as the Laiusian fantasy par excellence, especially when it focuses on the six-year-old, the most reassuring rival a man could have. Except for the infant, the young child is no longer allied with the mother's body, whose womb and breasts he had usurped (providing her with a phallus that he in some regard has stolen from the father); and, unlike the young adult, he is socially dependent, physically weak, and sexually insignificant. By contrast, the Greek myth marks the two moments in which the promise of fatherhood is most critically threatened by the outbreak of filicidal violence: the birth of the son, which turns the man from lover into father (the moment in which Donald Hall addresses his newborn as "My Son, my Executioner"), and his transition to adulthood, in which he gains the very real power to challenge the father physically, sexually, and socially.

Two of Freud's own (filicidal) dreams mark these two moments very clearly:

> An elevation, on it something like an open-air privy [Abort], a very long bench, at its end a large privy hole. The edge at the very back densely occupied with little piles of excrement of all sizes and stages of freshness. Behind the bench, bushes [ein Gebüsch]. I urinate onto the bench; a long stream of urine rinses everything clean [rein], the pieces of excrement come loose easily and fall into the opening. As if something were left over at the end. . . .[18]

Freud happily receives his unconscious's assertion that he is "der Übermensch": Hercules, Gulliver, and Gargantua wrapped into one. And to the extent that he acknowledges the presence of his children in this dream, he comments: "I have discovered the childhood etiology of the neuroses and thus have saved my own children from falling ill."[19] It is difficult, however, not to at least speculate about a quite different reading. At the time of writing, Freud had six children, born in 1887, 1889, 1891, 1892, 1893, and 1895, "of all sizes and stages of freshness," so to speak. Even if the equation of defecation and birthing mostly belongs to a slightly later stage in Freud's work (he touches upon it in the section of birthing dreams, but in fact only develops the theme in the analysis of Little Hans), the equation of feces and gold and of children and wealth belongs to the *Interpretation of Dreams,* and so does the association of bushes and the female pubes.[20] The word Freud uses for "privy," *Abort,* is also the medical term for abortion, and finally, Freud himself characterizes the location of the dream as follows: "The elevation and the bushes belong to Aussee, where my children are staying at this point" (gehören nach Aussee, wo jetzt meine Kinder weilen) (452).

Freud, of course, does not interpret the little piles of feces as his children, whom or which he can rinse away with a powerful stream of urine—a penile act of abortion inverting the act of begetting—just as he does not draw a connection between the revenants he can dissolve with his gaze and the revenants he declares his children to be. In general, when Freud talks about himself as father in the Dream Book, he presents himself as especially benign rather than as the villain as whom he usually delights to pose. When he dreams of having "to flee my children," in a somewhat unusual transitive usage of the German verb *flüchten* (426), he finds in himself only sorrow at the prospect of separation and worry and care for their well-being (427). When, in the same dream, two of his sons appear with a father who is not Freud himself (426), he does not reflect on the appearance of another father as a possible inversion of the family romance, or as a variation on the ancient theme of paternal uncertainty;[21] rather, he realizes only that he, as a Jewish man, cannot provide them with a *Vaterland*, that he is barred from the metonymy of *pater* and *patria* that sustains fatherhood and the state alike.[22] When he dreams that his children's physician falls ill, he does not wonder whether he may be wishing for their illness as well. When he dreams of "my son the myop" (426), he does not ask what there may be to be gained in a son who does not see. The theme of filicide does surface in a passing joke—"A little bit later, a shingle hit my eye: Dr. *Herodes*, Practice Hours . . . I said, 'I hope the colleague isn't a pediatrician'"[23]—but the allusion is safely contained in the history of Jewish persecution; it is always the other father who kills. Only once in *The Interpretation of Dreams* does Freud come close to acknowledging in himself the Laiusian wish to destroy the child, and that is a passage added in 1919, concerning a son who has entered the privileged arena of masculine power, war:

> I tell my wife I have news for her, something very special. She is afraid and wants to hear nothing. I assure her that, on the contrary, it is something that will make her very happy, and begin to tell that our son's officer corps has sent a sum of money (5000 K?) . . . something about acknowledgment . . . distribution . . .

Freud enters a pantry, and suddenly

> I see my son appear. . . . He mounts a basket next to a cupboard as if to place something on top of this cupboard. I call to him; no response. It seems to me that he has his face or his forehead bandaged, he arranges something in his mouth, pushes something in. I think: Should he be so exhausted? And does he have false teeth?[24]

Freud, dreaming during World War I, realizes that this is a dream about his son's death: "It is easy to see that the conviction that he has been wounded or killed finds expression in the content of the dream," but when he begins to talk about the element of wish fulfillment which, by his own account, pervades all dreams, he takes a detour:

> the location of a pantry, the cupboard . . . these are unmistakable allusions to an accident of my own. . . . The deepening of the analysis then lets me find the hidden impulse that could find satisfaction in the feared accident of the son. It is the envy against youth,

which the older man believes to have stifled thoroughly in his life, and it is unmistakable that, should such a calamity actually occur, precisely the strength of the painful emotion discovers such a repressed wish fulfillment as its solace.[25]

To consider the dream as a wish fulfillment, Freud must soften death to accident, murderous fantasy to envy; and, in yet another double inversion of paternal and filial position, the accident repeats his own while his son appears as an old man with gray hair and false teeth.[26]

Such slides pervade Freud's writing on fatherhood, and it would be tempting to conclude that fatherhood and sonhood are so intimately bound up with each other that they cannot be kept apart. Under the influence of Lacan and others, it is certainly the case that Freud's concept of the Oedipal has become generalized to such a degree that the position of any *given* father (in contrast to "the" father, the symbolic one) appears to be subsumed under it. Claude LeGuen suggests as much when he writes: "I would say unequivocally that there is only an Oedipus Complex, the Laius complex being only an appendage. But what an appendage!"[27] To be sure, the citations from the Dream Book give strong evidence of the fact that father is always also son, and that he is more ready to present himself as son than as father. Moreover, it is difficult to decide whether sonhood precedes fatherhood or vice versa. Unlike fatherhood, sonhood is not optional, and thus (for all historical, cultural, individual differences) amounts to a universal situation. Every father has once been a son; for this reason alone his self-image will be contaminated by the remnants of his earlier, filial perspective. At the same time, in any given life, the father precedes the son, and the newborn, no matter how deeply embedded in the symbolic his life may already be, will have to come into awareness of his sonhood in encountering a father who is already there (or will be fantasized as always already having been there). Perhaps it is fair to say that to the son, the father *as father* comes first, and to the father, the son (both as a recuperation of his own sonhood and its phantasms and as the other, who, by his very appearance, moves him one generation closer to death and appeals to him to assent to this death).

Given these complications, as well as the mutual contamination or conceptual interdependence of terms, teasing out those elements of the father-son relation that belong to fatherhood alone is a challenge. As mentioned above, to us Laius is always already offstage; and his death is so constitutive of the myth as we read it that he is not merely dead, but appears as if he has never lived, that death is his existence: *non vixit.*[28] At the same time, the asymmetrical yet reciprocal entanglement of father and son does not imply that fatherhood and sonhood cannot be distinguished in important ways, just as the chicken-egg dilemma has never led anybody to claim that a chicken is the same as an egg. In a fascinating reading of the extant Greek sources, Marie Balmary has shown in great detail the extent to which Oedipus repeats his father Laius's transgressions, and she has suggested that Freud's disregard of Laius in his reading of the myth is a symptom of his failure to see "the fault of the father."[29] In a different revival of the figure of Laius, John Munder Ross has insisted that traditional psychoanalysis has overlooked or seriously downplayed the "pederastic and filicidal inclinations that I believe to be universal among fathers."[30] Both readings, while insightful and important, retain the original Freudian gesture of looking at the father through the son, reducing Laius to his transgressions (not just his attempted filicide, but also the rape of his adoptive father's favorite son, Chrysippus, a crime that according to at least some of the sources led to the curse that he would have to refrain from consummating his marriage or beget the son who would kill him). If, however, Oedipus is more than a patricidal motherfucker, Laius may well be more than a filicidal child rapist. And while Oedipus repeats, he also deviates in ways that shed light on precisely the specificity of the Laius position within the Oedipal dyad.

In a transgressive grab for immortality that is perhaps a more serious offense against the gods than patricide or incest, both Laius and Oedipus rebel against time. Laius, in attempting to bring about his son's death, refuses to accept his own substitutability. In fathering his siblings, Oedipus, within the generational structure that establishes kinship identity, aims to father himself and thus to take himself out of time in a different way.[31] Right before the anagnorisis of Sophocles' drama, Oedipus declares himself the son of mother fortune and the brother of the moons, with no father in sight. Right afterward, the chorus will tell him that he has been caught not by the law, not by the gods, not by truth, but by *time*, who sees all (*ho panth' horōn chronos*).[32] His downfall is intimately linked to his fatherhood. In the first line, he addresses his people in a markedly paternal gesture ("*ô tekna*," "oh children"); and the last scene shows Creon removing his children from him. His movement through the play is thus both one of ascending knowledge and one of diminishing fatherhood, of being forced to assume the filiality he had denied. It is fatherhood, then, that is linked with ignorance; and it suits this reading that, in his reascendancy, at Colonus, Oedipus is once again accompanied by his daugher, Antigone.

The task at which both Laius and Oedipus fail is a complex negotiation between simultaneity and succession: paternity is to incarnate—in one body and one identity—sonhood and fatherhood, but also to distinguish between them as relations to another, or rather to two others who, in turn, will fight for their individuation at the same time as they lay claim to their, our, and your identity. But while the father sees in his son both the enemy and an extension of his self, the son sees in his father the one who—benignly or maliciously—holds the place that is to be his. To repeat: this relationship is hardly symmetrical. While the child, as Aristotle argues in the *Nicomachean Ethics*, is *heteros autos* to the man (*ta gar ex autôn hoion heteroi autoi tôi kechôristhai*), both self and other, no son thinks of his father as another self in that way. Hence, fathers love their children more than children love their fathers (as Aristotle notes again with certainty, in the *Eudemian Ethics*).[33]

Freud's identification of children as multiple revenants adds one more complication: the child, as the self's extension into the future after death, is not merely other in his own right, but also incorporates a number of yet different others—the father's actual and symbolic fathers, as well as repressed phantasms of his own self. As if the ensuing multitude of simultaneous but irreconcilable relations were not enough, the most difficult tension fatherhood has to bear is the discrepancy between symbolic and actual that makes the experience of fatherhood one of incurable inadequacy. It is here that Freud's historical position as one who is thinking in the age of the death of god bears most decisively on his unwriting of fatherhood. In a footnote in *The Interpretation of Dreams,* he writes that "the father is the oldest, the first, and for the child the only authority out of whose omnipotence all other social authorities have developed over the course of human cultural history," but nonetheless it is also true that those "other authorities" have long served to produce the very paternal authority in which they purportedly ground themselves.[34] Fatherhood is the primal institution, but precisely as the first effect of pure signification, it is also inherently dependent on the feedback of power along the very metaphorical and metonymic chains it is said to anchor. More specifically, in monotheistic cultures, it is no longer the father who lends his authority to God, but God who lends his authority to the father, as the very principle of disembodied paternity. Precisely because paternity, Joyce's "legal fiction," is, in its distinction from material maternity, always disembodied in principle, incorporating it is thus a process of destabilization. The father may be the figure of omnipotence to his son, but never to himself, and least of all, perhaps, in gazing at his child.[35]

HETEROS AUTOS

The subjectivity of embodied fatherhood—as an experience of uncertainty, mortality, and, ultimately, castration—is in stark contrast to the concept of (symbolic) fatherhood in which psychoanalysis has so heavily invested itself.[36] If and when it surfaces, however, it comes with a strong flavor of lack and insufficiency. In the Rome Discourse, Lacan writes that "even when in fact represented by a single person, the paternal function concentrates in itself both imaginary and real relations, always more or less *inadequate* to the symbolic relation that essentially constitutes it."[37] And Jean-Michel Rabaté writes: "Who can be sure to be the father, who can be so self-confident as to utter without faltering, 'I am a fa . . .' and not crash down into the frozen lakes of doubt and incest that have nonetheless been safely crossed?"[38]

While the doubt is old, the faltering of the father's voice has a historical dimension as well. Around 1900, the stammering of the father is everywhere. We can hear it in a passage from Hofmannsthal's *Chandos Letter* (1902), a text that has been read as emblematic of the epoch at issue here:

> [T]he abstract words of which the tongue must by nature make use in order to bring any judgment to light fell apart in my mouth like mouldy mushrooms. It happened to me that I wanted to rebuke my four-year old daughter Catarina Pompilia for a childish lie of which she had become guilty and to lead her to the necessity to always

be true, and in this act the concepts that flowed to me in my mouth suddenly acquired such a glittering coloration and flowed into each other to such a degree that, stammeringly finishing the sentence as well as I could, as if I had become un-well, and indeed pale in the face and with a heavy pressure on my forehead, I left the child alone.[39]

Hofmannsthal acknowledges both the father's function to speak for the law—"to bring . . . judgment to light"—and the impossibility of embodying this function, pre-cisely at a time when fatherhood is no longer grounded by a monotheistic father-god who can serve as the ultimate moral instance guarding the distinction between truth and lie. Incapable of meeting the task of abstraction—i.e., the task of masculinity in the semiotic gender system that still organizes Hofmannsthal's writing—the father abdicates a discourse that has become purely external to him. The words "flow to him" as if of their own accord and disintegrate in his mouth, losing color, shape, and texture. Having to embody the function of the symbolic father, the real father's experience is one of an inadequacy that makes the voice falter in a mouth full of mush. True, this loss is recollected in some of the most exquisite German prose in existence, but the eloquence belongs to the gesture of abdication, and it cannot blind us to the fact that no voice can answer Kafka's *Letter to his Father,* a text that, like no other, demonstrates how the very gesture of acknowledging the father's superior power condemns him to silence.[40]

Kafka is simply the most audible and the most eloquent of sons. When Freud writes the *Traumdeutung,* the voice of the son has already begun to colonize literature, and the crisis of fatherhood manifests itself in a variety of (overdetermined) phenom-ena: the discovery of bachelorhood, to which Eve Kosofsky Sedgwick has drawn atten-tion; the cult of male youth; the late nineteenth-century horror of procreation that goes hand in hand and, to my mind, is an important constitutive element of the well-documented fear of the feminine marking the period;[41] the anti-organic themes of Huysmans's *À Rebours;* the fascination with dead children in the same author's *Là-Bas;* the pervasive anxiety concerning heredity (which always spells degeneration) in the wake of Darwin, to name just a few. Aesthetic innovation had been securely tied to patricide for quite a while, and the anxiety of influence may well be outweighed by the anxiety of *being* an influence. On the stylistic level, the most pertinent feature may be the famous catalogues of decadence, the endless enumerations and descrip-tions of the inanimate, that stall and undermine organic aesthetics, as well as narrative contracts built on the expectation of an integrating plot. These stalling narratives are indicative of the crisis of fathering, since father-son succession is the master plot of myth and every patriarchal culture's founding narrative, a succession that often enough is staged as the failure of filicide. (While their stories are very different, Zeus, Isaac, Oedipus, and Jesus are all sons who survive filicidal assaults.)

In centering his enterprise on the name of the son, Freud formalizes and final-izes a crisis and makes it productive. While the dilemma of fatherhood is both ancient and overdetermined, I think there is little doubt that Freud's voice—so paternal, so patriarchal, so Laiusian in his lifelong struggle with the psychoanalytic progeny—has, more than any other, generated the cultural space in which the sons will talk (and talk and talk and talk) about their fathers, in tones of derision and regret, fear and love—but hardly ever about their sons.[42] Since so many of these sons are fathers as well, both biologically and symbolically speaking, the son's son becomes the twentieth century's most repressed figure. Quite appropriately, he makes a barely veiled appearance in Freud's essay on "The Uncanny":

> The most prominent among the motifs that have an uncanny effect . . . [is] the *doppelgängerdom* in all its gradations and forms . . . [so] that one is led astray in contemplating one's I [*daß man an seinem Ich irre wird*] or puts [*versetzt*] the alien I in the place of the own, ergo I-doubling, I-splitting, I-substitution—and finally the eternal return of the same, the repetition of the same [*nämlichen*] facial features, characters, fates, criminal deeds, yes, of the same names through several successive generations.[43]

This *Doppelgänger* is the son. He is Oedipus as seen by Laius—familiar and alien, springing from the domestic uncanny of the lover's womb (*heimlich-unheimlich*), repressed but always returning, doubling the father, repeating his features, his crimes, his name, splitting his I, usurping his place, and at the same time, demanding to be loved without reserve.

Do fathers love their children? Of course they do. The love of the father, however, most prominently articulates itself upon the child's loss or death: Jacob mourns Joseph; David laments Absalom; Aegeus throws himself into the sea when Theseus's ship nears the harbor decked in black sails; Ben Jonson writes poems on his dead children; David paints Brutus watching the lictors bringing home the bodies of the sons executed at his command; Odoardo Galotti adores and stabs Emilia; Lessing writes the most moving letter after his son dies shortly after birth; Goethe's father rides on to the whispers of the Earlking while his son is dying in his arms—and there are Mallarmé's *Anatole*, Yeats's *On Baile's Strand*, and, more recently, Ian McEwan's *The Child in Time.*

Only the death of the child makes fatherhood speakable, because this death resolves fatherhood's profound ambivalence, or releases the tension, especially of fathering sons. Sons signify, simultaneously, a father's mortality and his immortality. Echoing the vicissitudes of biology, the father-son-relationship balances (or fails to balance) identity and difference. The logic between them is supplemental, echoing that of the *Doppelgänger,* and might in fact be the very model of the logic of the double itself.

The son is both promise and threat, beloved and feared, continuity and disruption, a gift and a monstrous imposition, another self and the worst possible rival, identity's futurity and its termination—and he is the one only *because* he is also the other. Precisely to the extent that paternity belongs to the public realm of order, law, and tradition, the son is *unheimlich,* the figure of the repressed other-self that comes from the home; and his death—real or fantasized—is the condition of love, or at least its articulation. Only the written child—written and hence both dead and alive—is the perfect child, or, as Ben Jonson has it, "his best piece of poetrie."

The son is intimately linked to writing itself. That writing erases the writer, that the author dies in every work he produces, are insights we owe to the late nineteenth and early twentieth centuries; we also owe them, I think, to the unacknowledged experience of fatherhood, which has so long functioned as creativity's ambivalent master metaphor.[44] Like writing, fatherhood is a form of suicide in the service of immortality, and every son is an executioner. Of course, this is never the whole story; but to begin telling that story, we have to begin to imagine Laius, and to finally imagine him from within, as a desiring subject, as the one who is called upon to say yes rather than no: yes to the child, and yes to his own death, thus releasing the son to the full potential of his otherness.

NOTES

1. "Eine andere Reihe von Träumen, die typisch genannt werden dürfen, sind die mit dem Inhalt, daß ein teurer Verwandter, Eltern oder Geschwister, Kinder usw. gestorben ist." Sigmund Freud, *Die Traumdeutung,* in *Studienausgabe Bd. II* (Frankfurt am Main: Fischer, 1972), 253. All quotations are from this edition; all translations are my own.

2. "Wenn wir über Mythen in der Psychoanalyse sprechen, dann sprechen wir in Wirklichkeit über *einen* Mythos, den Ödipusmythos—alle anderen Freudschen Mythen (der Mythos des Urvaters, Freuds Version des Mosesmythos) sind, wenn auch *notwendige,* Variationen davon." Slavoj Žižek, *Die gnadenlose Liebe* (Frankfurt am Main: Suhrkamp, 2001), 11.

3. "[D]er Ödipus-'Mythos', und möglicherweise die mythische 'Naivität' selbst, dient [dazu], ein verbotenes *Wissen* zu verschleiern, nämlich das Wissen um die Obszönität des Vaters." Ibid., 13.

4. It should be mentioned at the outset that the following remarks concern the father-son dyad almost exclusively. This is not because daughters or mothers do not matter, but because father-daughter relationships are a different story, and the elucidation of the role of the mother in the configurations sketched here would necessitate another article.

5. Discussing *Totem and Taboo,* Lacan writes, "[I]f this murder is the fruitful moment of debt through which the subject binds himself for life to the Law, the symbolic father is, in so far as he signifies this Law, the dead Father." Jacques Lacan, "On a Question Preliminary to Any Possible Treatment of Psychosis," in *Écrits: A Selection,* trans. Alan Sheridan (New York: Norton, 1977), 199.

6. Otto Weininger, "[D]ie Vaterschaft [ist] eine armselige Täuschung," in *Geschlecht und Charakter: Eine prinzipielle Untersuchung* (München: Matthes & Seitz, 1980), 307.

7. "Ich hielt darauf, daß ihre Namen nicht nach der Mode des Tages gewählt, sondern durch das Andenken an teure Personen bestimmt sein sollten. Ihre Namen machen die Kinder zu 'Revenants'. Und schließlich, ist Kinder haben nicht für uns alle der einzige Zugang zur *Unsterblichkeit?*" (Freud, *Die Traumdeutung,* 468–69).

8. Sigmund Freud, "Nachwort zur 'Frage der Laienanalyse,'" in *Studienausgabe Ergänzungsband,* 344.

9. "Es ist leicht zu merken, wie die unterdrückte Größensucht des Vaters sich in seinen Gedanken auf die Kinder überträgt; ja man wird gerne glauben, daß dies einer der Wege ist, auf denen die im Leben notwendig gewordenen Unterdrückungen derselben vor sich geht" (Freud, *Die Traumdeutung*, 432).

10. "Ich hatte das Jahr der Erwartung über den Vorsatz, gerade diesen Namen zu verwenden, wenn es ein Sohn würde, und begrüßte mit ihm hoch *befriedigt* den eben Geborenen" (ibid., 432).

11. "Der Vater hat nach seinem Tode eine politische Rolle bei den Magyaren gespielt, sie politisch geeinigt, wozu ich ein kleines undeutliches Bild sehe: eine Menschenmenge wie im Reichstag, eine Person, die auf einem oder zwei Stühlen steht, andere um ihn herum. Ich erinnere mich daran, daß er auf dem Totenbette Garibaldi so ähnlich gesehen hat, und freue mich, daß diese Verheißung doch wahr geworden ist" (ibid., 414).

12. "Einer meiner Altersgenossen, der seinen Vater noch als Gymnasiast verlor, bei welchem Anlaß ich ihm dann tief erschüttert meine Freundschaft antrug, erzählte mir einmal höhnend von dem Schmerz einer Verwandten, deren Vater auf der Straße gestorben und nach Hause gebracht worden war, wo sich dann bei der Entkleidung der Leiche fand, daß im Moment des Todes oder *postmortal* eine *Stuhlentleerung* stattgefunden hatte" (ibid., 415–16).

13. "Hier sind wir nun zu dem Wunsch vorgedrungen, der sich in diesem Traume verkörpert. *Nach seinem Tode rein und groß vor seinen Kindern dastehen*, wer möchte das nicht wünschen?" (ibid., 416).

14. "Ich bin ungemein erfreut darüber, verstehe jetzt, daß auch Ernst Fleischl nur eine Erscheinung, ein Revenant war, und finde es ganz wohl möglich, daß eine solche Person nur so lange besteht, als man es mag, und daß sie durch den Wunsch des anderen beseitigt werden kann" (ibid., 409).

15. "Was er mir sagte, war karg und bestimmt; es kam aber gar nicht auf die Worte an. Das Überwältigende waren die fürchterlichen blauen Augen, mit denen er mich ansah und vor denen ich verging—wie P. im Traum, der zu meiner Erleichterung die Rollen verwechselt hat" (ibid., 410).

16. "Man muß sich als den einzigen Bösewicht enthüllen unter all den Edlen, mit denen man das Leben teilt. Ich finde es also ganz begreiflich, daß die *Revenants* nur so lange bestehen, als man sie mag, und daß sie durch den Wunsch beseitigt werden können. . . . Die Revenants sind aber die aufeinanderfolgenden Inkarnationen meines Kindheitsfreundes; ich bin also auch befriedigt darüber, daß ich mir diese Person immer wieder ersetzt habe, und auch für den, den ich jetzt zu verlieren im Begriffe bin, wird sich der Ersatz schon finden. Es ist niemand unersetzlich" (ibid., 467).

17. Luce Irigaray, "Questions to Emmanuel Levinas," *The Irigaray Reader*, ed. Margaret Whitford (Cambridge: Basil Blackwell, 1991), 181.

18. "Eine Anhöhe, auf dieser etwas wie ein Abort im Freien, eine sehr lange Bank, an deren Ende ein großes Abortloch. Die ganz hintere Kante dicht besetzt mit Häufchen Kot von allen Größen und Stufen der Frische. Hinter der Bank ein Gebüsch. Ich uriniere auf die Bank; ein langer Harnstrahl spült alles rein, die Kotpatzen lösen sich leicht ab und fallen in die Öffnung. Als ob am Ende noch etwas übrigbliebe" (Freud, *Die Traumdeutung*, 452).

19. "Ich habe die Kindheitsaetiologie der Neurosen aufgedeckt und dadurch meine eigenen Kinder vor Erkrankung bewahrt" (ibid., 452).

20. "'How many children do you have now?'—'Six.'—A gesture of respect and precariousness.—'Girls, boys?'—'Three and three, that is my pride and my wealth.'" ("'Wieviele Kinder

haben Sie jetzt?'—'Sechs.'—Eine Gebärde von Respekt und Bedenklichkeit.—'Mädel, Buben?'—'Drei und drei, das ist mein Stolz und mein Reichtum'" [ibid., 302]). Also, see ibid., 360: "The male genitals symbolized by people, the female ones by a landscape."

21. On the theme of inverted family romance, see Marie MacLean, "The Heirs of Amphitryon: Social Fathers and Natural Fathers," *New Literary History* 26, no. 4 (1995): 787–807.

22. "The Jewish question, the worry about the future of the children to whom one cannot give a fatherland, the worry to bring them up in such a way that they can become free to move [*freizügig* also carries connotations of cosmopolitan, sexually liberated, loose], are easy to recognize in the relevant dream thoughts." (Die Judenfrage, die Sorge um die Zukunft der Kinder, denen man ein Vaterland nicht geben kann, die Sorge, sie so zu erziehen, daß sie freizügig werden können, sind in den zugehörigen Traumgedanken leicht zu erkennen" [Freud, *Die Traumdeutung,* 427]).

23. "Kurz darauf fiel mir ein Schild in die Augen: Dr. *Herodes,* Sprechstunde . . . . Ich meinte: 'Hoffentlich ist der Kollege nicht gerade Kinderarzt'" (ibid., 428).

24. "Ich sage meiner Frau, ich habe eine Nachricht für sie, etwas ganz Besonderes. Sie erschrickt und will nichts hören. Ich versichere ihr, im Gegenteil, etwas, was sie sehr freuen wird, und beginne zu erzählen, daß das Offizierskorps unseres Sohnes eine Summe Geldes geschickt hat (5000 K) . . . etwas von Anerkennung . . . Verteilung . . . Plötzlich sehe ich meinen Sohn erscheinen . . . Er steigt auf einen Korb, der sich seitlich neben einem Kasten befindet, wie um etwas auf diesen Kasten zu legen. Ich rufe ihn an: keine Antwort. Mir scheint, er hat das Gesicht oder die Stirn verbunden, er richtet sich etwas im Munde, schiebt sich etwas ein. Auch haben seine Haare einen grauen Schimmer. Ich denke: Sollte er so erschöpft sein? Und hat er falsche Zähne?" (ibid., 532–23).

25. "[D]ie Örtlichkeit, eine Speisekammer, der Kasten . . . das sind unverkennbare Anspielungen an einen eigenen Unfall . . . . Die Vertiefung der Analyse läßt mich dann die versteckte Regung finden, die sich an dem gefürchteten Unfall des Sohnes befriedigen könnte. Es ist der Neid gegen die Jugend, den der Gealterte im Leben gründlich erstickt zu haben glaubt, und es ist unverkennbar, daß gerade die Stärke der schmerzlichen Ergriffenheit, wenn ein solches Unglück sich wirklich ereignete, zu ihrer Linderung eine solche verdrängte Wunscherfüllung aufspürt" (ibid., 534).

26. When Freud finally does reflect on a father's dream at length, the son is already dead, and the only wishes Freud allows us to imagine are that he has come to life again, or that sleep goes on. It is striking that the dream of the burning child is explicitly framed as the one dream where the usual dream economy of fantasy, wish, and the outside does not apply. Cathy Caruth comments: "Unlike in other dreams, Freud remarks, what is striking in this dream is not its relation to inner wishes, but its direct relation to a catastrophic reality outside" (*Unclaimed Experience: Trauma, Narrative, and History* [Baltimore: The Johns Hopkins University Press, 1996], 94).

27. Claude Le Guen, "The Formation of the Transference: Or the Laius Complex in the Armchair," *International Journal of Psycho-Analysis* 55 (1974), 512.

28. See note 5, above.

29. Marie Balmary, *Psychoanalyzing Psychoanalysis: Freud and the Hidden Fault of the Father,* trans. Ned Lukacher (Baltimore: The Johns Hopkins University Press, 1982).

30. John Munder Ross, "The Darker Side of Fatherhood: Clinical and Developmental Ramifications of the 'Laius Motif,'" *International Journal of Psychoanalytic Psychotherapy* 11 (1985): 117.

31. In his brilliant annotations to his translation of *Antigone,* Hölderlin suggests that the conflict with "the spirit of time" is at the heart of tragedy: "The boldest moment in the course of a day or a work of art is the moment when the spirit of time and nature, the divine which seizes man, stands most wildly against the object he is interested in." (Der kühnste Moment eines Taglaufs oder Kunstwerks ist, wo der Geist der Zeit und Natur, das Himmlische, was den Menschen ergreift, und der Gegenstand, für welchen er sich interessiert, am wildesten gegeneinander stehen.) Friedrich Hölderlin, *Werke, Briefe, Dokumente,* Nach der Kleinen Stuttgarter Hölderlin-Ausgabe, hg. Friedrich Beißner, ausgewählt und mit Nachwort von Pierre Bertaux (München: Winkler, 1963), 671.

32. Sophocles, *Works,* ed. and trans. Hugh Lloyd-Jones, Loeb Classical Library (Cambridge: Harvard University Press, 1994), 2: 20–21, line 1214.

33. Aristotle, *Nicomachean Ethics,* ed., with an English translation, by Horace Rackham (Cambridge: Harvard University Press, 1934), 1161b; and Aristotle, *Eudemian Ethics,* ed. and trans. Horace Rackham (Cambridge: Harvard University Press, 1981), 1241b.

34. "[D]er Vater ist die älteste, erste, für das Kind einzige Autorität, aus deren Machtvollkomenheit im Laufe der meschlichen Kulturgeschichte die anderen sozialen Obrigkeiten hervorgegangen sind" (Freud, *Die Traumdeutung,* 226n).

35. The theme of paternal uncertainty (or its inversion in Oedipus's filial uncertainty) is the one red thread in the history of fatherhood: precisely because the bodily link between father and child is always dubious, paternity relies on and emerges as the archetype of signification.

36. Freud's blindness to the position of the father is, I think, intimately linked to his decade-long blindness to the phenomenon of countertransference. While he recognizes early on that the analyst's main task is to initiate, sustain, and bear the analysand's transference, within this transference he will always figure as the father, even though in a fatherhood he can construct as fantasized, displaced, not his own. In response, analysis develops the analyst as a counter-father, benevolent, nurturing, sexually abstinent, and—ideally, or in theory—silent, without features, present but invisible. Invisible to the analysand, but invisible also to himself, and that is, perhaps, the greater problem.

37. Emphasis added; see Jacques Lacan, "Function and Field of Speech and Language in Psychonalysis," in Lacan, *Écrits,* 67.

38. Jean-Michel Rabaté, "A Clown's Inquest into Paternity: Fathers, Dead or Alive, in *Ulysses* and *Finnegans Wake,*" in *The Fictional Father: Lacanian Readings of the Text,* ed. Robert Con Davis (Amherst: University of Massachusetts Press, 1981), 73.

39. "[D]ie abstrakten Worte, deren sich doch die Zunge naturgemäß bedienen muß, um irgendwelches Urtheil an den Tag zu geben, zerfielen mir im Munde wie modrige Pilze. Es begegnete mir, daß ich meiner vierjährigen Tochter Catarina Pompilia eine kindische Lüge, deren sie sich schuldig gemacht hatte, verweisen und sie auf die Notwendigkeit, immer wahr zu sein, hinführen wollte, und dabei die mir im Munde zuströmenden Begriffe plötzlich eine solche schillernde Färbung annahmen und so ineinander überflossen, daß ich, den Satz, so gut es ging, zu Ende haspelnd, so wie wenn mir unwohl geworden wäre und auch tatsächlich bleich im Gesicht und mit einem heftigen Druck auf der Stirn, das Kind allein ließ" (Hugo von Hofmannsthal, *Ein Brief,* in *Werke in zehn Bänden: Erfundene Gespräche und Briefe,* ed. Lorenz Jäger [Frankfurt am Main: Fischer, 1999], 25).

40. See Gilles Deleuze and Félix Guattari, "Exaggerated Oedipus," in *Kafka: Toward a Minor Literature* (Minneapolis: University of Minnesota Press, 1986).

41. Here is a (fairly representative) passage from Zola's *The Sin of Father Mouret:* "A

human smell rose from this heap of quivering houses. And the priest thought he was back in Desiree's barnyard, face to face with that endless swarm of multiplying animals. He felt the same heat of generation, the same continuous labor whose smell had made him sick. All day he had lived with this pregnancy of Rosalie's, and he finally thought of it as part of life's filth, of the flesh's drives, of the preordained reproduction of the species which sowed men like grains of wheat. The Artauds were a flock penned in by the four hills on the horizon, begetting, spreading out with each new litter from the females" (Emile Zola, *The Sin of Father Mouret*, trans. Sandy Petry [Lincoln and London: University of Nebraska Press, 1969], 57).

42. There are some notable exceptions here, of course: the most interesting one may be Yeats's work, especially his poems to his children and the Cuchulain plays culminating in filicide.

43. "[D]ie hervorstechendsten unter jenen unheimlich wirkenden Motiven . . . das Doppelgängertum in all seinen Abstufungen und Ausbildungen . . . so daß man an seinem Ich irre wird oder das fremde Ich an die Stelle des eigenen versetzt, also Ich-Verdoppplung, Ich-Teilung, Ich-Vertauschung—und endlich die beständige Wiederkehr des Gleichen, die Wiederholung der nämlichen Gesichtszüge, Charaktere, Schicksale, verbrecherischen Taten, ja der Namen durch mehrere aufeinanderfolgende Generationen," in Freud, "Das Unheimliche," *Studienausgabe* Bd. IV, 257.

44. Plato, "Symposium," trans. Michael Joyce, in *The Collected Dialogues of Plato*, ed. Edith Hamilton and Huntington Cairns (Princeton: Princeton University Press, 1961), 209a: "But those whose procreancy is of the spirit rather than of the flesh . . . conceive and bear the things of the spirit. And what are they? you ask. Wisdom and all her sister virtues; it is the office of every poet to beget them, and of every artist whom we may call creative." See also Aristotle, *Nicomachean Ethics*, trans. J. E. C. Welldon (New York: Prometheus Books, 1987), 1168a: "Every artisan feels greater affection for his own work, than the work, if it were endowed with life, would feel for him. But nowhere I think is it so true as in the case of poets; they have an extraordinary affection for their own poems, and are as fond of them as if they were their children." Freud, writing to Edoardo Weiss about his anonymous publication of *Moses and Monotheism*, says: "My relationship to this work resembles that to a love child . . . . Only much later did I make this non-analytic child legitimate" (*Briefe 1873–1939*, ed. Ernst and Lucie Freud [Frankfurt am Main: Fischer, 1968], 431).

8. "Non vixit"

FRIENDS SURVIVED

Elke Siegel

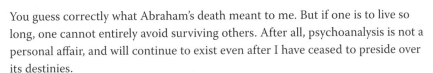

> You guess correctly what Abraham's death meant to me. But if one is to live so long, one cannot entirely avoid surviving others. After all, psychoanalysis is not a personal affair, and will continue to exist even after I have ceased to preside over its destinies.
>
> —Sigmund Freud, letter to Ludwig Binswanger, May 21, 1926

1900: YEAR OF "REVENANTS"

"This is the year of 'revenants,'" Sigmund Freud wrote to his friend Wilhelm Fliess on July 1, 1900, in and of the year that we have become accustomed to think of as the year of *The Interpretation of Dreams*.[1] Freud's statement refers to the guests he had been entertaining in Vienna: first, his half-brother Emmanuel from London, and then, unexpectedly, an old friend, the dermatologist Sigmund Lustgarten, who had emigrated to New York. Given that 1900 was overdetermined for Freud, his calling it "the year of 'revenants'" cannot be a mere coincidence.[2] It is not just a spontaneous eruption, joke, or slip—or better, it is all of these, and therefore carries precisely the weight that Freud himself attributed to such phenomena.

In the German sentence, the French word "revenant" comes close to being what it usually signifies: revenants are ghosts, uncanny apparitions, someone or something that comes back to you, for you. In the French word "revenant," Freud's time in Paris seems to be returning. On the one hand, "revenants" in this sentence merely means a literal return, a reappearance. But precisely because of Freud's time in Paris, he probably knew that the word "revenants" is usually reserved for those shadowy creatures haunting us from the grave. If Freud uses "revenant" for the living, for those who have left and return (maybe using the quotation marks to indicate that he was aware of the unusual use of the word), one still has to note the peculiarity that the living—the half-brother and the old friend—are designated by the (at the very least) ambivalent word "revenants." By the distancing marks of quotation, they are marked by a death that cannot be crossed out.[3]

This "year of 'revenants'" *and* of *The Interpretation of Dreams* also marks the further decline of the friendship without which the dreambook might never have been conceived.[4] Freud and Fliess met for the last time in August 1900. Much has been written about this relationship and about what psychoanalysis owes to it: in the first analysis—that is, in Freud's self-analysis—Fliess figured as proto/pseudoanalyst (without Fliess's knowing it).[5] As far as *The Interpretation of Dreams* is concerned, Freud called Fliess the godfather ("Gevatter") of this monumental book, the one who gave Freud "the gift of the Other, a critic and reader" and, substituting for Freud's lack of shame, stood in as the censor.[6] Freud had to write *to* somebody, and Fliess was his only audience, an audience of one.[7] He knew that not only self-analysis requires an Other, a stranger, but so does writing.[8]

Fliess is to Freud not merely the Other, but the "representative of the Other," a chameleon of a friend, the one friend who can stand in for all other people.[9] Fliess as friend is absolute changeability, absolute fluidity (the name "Fliess," of course, is related to the verb "fliessen," to flow). In *The Psychopathology of Everyday Life* (1901), dedicated to Fliess, Freud tells us about an incident in which he forgot to buy blotting paper—"Fliesspapier"—and goes on to show how the name of this particular kind of paper was connected with his friend.[10] Fliess becomes not only the one who blots out by being the censor of Freud's writing, but also the one who has to blot himself out, who has to be so much the constant friend (in and through his changeability) that, in the end, he will also be changed into an adversary, though maybe first of all into a revenant.

Friendships—the friendship with Fliess in particular—played an important role in Freud's life, yet he himself had surprisingly little to say about friendship, usually describing it only as a mode of sublimated sexuality, as in *Group Psychology and the Analysis of the Ego.* One should not forget, however, that Freud was acutely aware of the tension between publicizing the analyses of his own dreams and the responsibility to protect friends or particular friendships. He owed much to his friends, and he owed much to the friend, Fliess, regarding his work. And yet he had to pay back the debt with the risk of betrayal as the extreme limit of analysis and interpretation. It comes as no surprise that Freud—in a letter to Fliess from November 7, 1899, thus after the actual publication of *The Interpretation of Dreams*—should note: "The book has just been sent out. The first tangible reaction was the termination of the friendship of a dear friend, who felt hurt by the mention of her husband in the *Non vixit* Dream."[11] Freud was referring to Betty Paneth, the wife of his—dead—friend and colleague, Josef Paneth, who figured prominently and in an utterly unflattering way in the dream mentioned. It is in this dream that Freud makes the most explicit remarks about friendship found in his published works. And it is precisely the figure of the "revenant" that is closely connected to Freud's explications about friendship.

Klaus Theweleit, writing about Hilda Doolittle and elaborating on the figure of the female revenant, compares the revenant to a structural element in Freud's writing. This figure, says Theweleit, is

> a leading character in [Freud's] literary work since the *Interpretation of Dreams.* Freud learned from experience that not only did people from his childhood reappear (in dreams; then outside the dream), but also all the important people in his life had the inherent property of not disappearing from his life once they had entered it; the property of returning in other people, in another form, but clearly, all too clearly as the reappearance of past, abandoned, even forgotten or dead people; a figure whom he named the *revenant,* the one who returns, the never-ending doppelganger of all the important people who had entered his life.[12]

The figure of the "revenant" comes to stand in for the process of repetition, of return, for the importance of the past for the present. Before becoming a generalized name for this structure, however, the "revenant" is already intrinsically connected with friendship. In the course of the interpretation of the *Non vixit* Dream, Freud gives a summary of the history and meaning of friendship in his life, a remarkably explicit definition of what friends are and have been for him:

> I have already shown how my warm friendships as well as my enmities with contemporaries went back to my relations in childhood with a nephew who was a year my senior; how he was my superior, how I early learned to defend myself against him, how we were inseparable friends, and how, according to the testimony of our elders, we sometimes fought with each other—and made complaints to them about each other. All my friends have in a certain sense been re-incarnations of this first figure who "früh sich einst dem trüben Blick gezeigt": they have been *revenants.*[13]

Friends—no exception seems to be possible, unless there is a categorical difference between "all my friends" and *the* friend—have been "revenants."[14] In every friend, the first friend—the older nephew, John—returns. The year of *The Interpretation of Dreams* and of revenants is the year of friends: the book itself may be viewed as a book about revenants, friends, the friend, as a book about friendship as well as enmity.

BROTHER—COUSIN—FRIEND

On October 3, 1897, reporting to Fliess about the findings of his self-analysis, Freud writes about the important figures of his childhood. Concerning the latter he points out:

> I greeted my one-year-younger brother (who died after a few months) with adverse wishes and genuine childhood jealousy; his death left the germ of (self-)reproaches in me. I have also long known the companion of my misdeeds between the ages of one and two years; it is my nephew, a year older than myself, who is now living in Manchester and who visited us in Vienna when I was fourteen years old. The two of

us seem occasionally to have behaved cruelly to my niece, who was a year younger. This nephew and this younger brother have determined, then, what is neurotic, but also what is intense, in all my friendships. You yourself have seen my travel anxiety at its height.[15]

In this passage, friendship's origin is divided between the brother and the nephew John (whose real name was Johannes[16]), the son of Freud's half-brother, Emmanuel. Julius and John then merge to make up the "model" for friendship. Freud's relationship to his younger brother Julius, whose name Freud omits, is marked by the reproach "that regularly sets in among the survivors," as Freud put it after the death of his father.[17] The self-reproach he feels after the death of his brother might very well result from Freud's wish for the brother to disappear and even die—which he did, as if by the magic of the adverse wish.[18]

Julius, though constitutive, with John, in the determination of friendship, is never mentioned again. During the interpretation of the *Non vixit* Dream (which he dreamt in October 1898) Freud traces all his friendships back to the relationship with John. This relationship becomes the original model for all friendships, a model that has to omit Julius. But it might be exactly this death, and its omission in the further explication of friendship, that will turn out to haunt friendship. One might say: Freud reduces all of his friends to being the mortal remains in which John can reappear— or Julius, as the unnamed.

John now stands alone at the beginning of friendship, which for Freud is a relationship to somebody who is superior; against whom one has to defend himself; with whom one fights; about whom one complains. Nevertheless Freud and John were inseparable friends. This closeness seems to be the only friendly aspect of friendship. Keeping the letter to Fliess cited above in mind, these two were close as conspirators in crimes against others.[19]

THE *NON VIXIT* DREAM: MEMORIAL FOR A FRIEND

On September 21, 1899, Freud sends to Fliess what he called his "central accomplishment in interpretation"—the absurd dreams—and states: "It is astonishing how often you appear in them. In the *Non vixit* Dream I am delighted to have outlived you; isn't it terrible to suggest something like this—that is, to have to make it explicit to everyone who understands?"[20] Freud provides Fliess with an abbreviated interpretation of the dream, namely, that he (Freud) is delighted to have survived his friend in it. The statement is proleptic, a projection into a future after the death of the friend. The death of the Other determines friendship in this logic: even in the present, the Other is the one who will die first—that is the hope or wish. Since the death of the friend thus becomes decisive for friendship, even the friend who is still alive is seen from the perspective of death. Freud seems less apologetic about the dream-delight in surviving

Fliess than about the fact that, even if he does not explicate this interpretation, it is potentially clear to everyone. This conundrum haunts Freud's interpretation of the *Non vixit* Dream.

Freud gives this dream, which actually consists of a sequence of two dreams, considerable attention: almost eleven pages total in two rounds of interpretation. Two events or situations were on Freud's mind at the time: he had just attended the unveiling of a memorial in honor of Ernst Fleischl von Marxow, his by-then dead friend and former superior at the Physiological Institute of Ernst Brücke.[21] He was also worried about Fliess, whose relatives in Vienna had just informed Freud about a serious surgery his friend had undergone. The situation was even more troubling because Fliess had calculated that the age of forty—and he was forty at the time—would be critical for him. But there is no mention of Fliess until the second round of interpretation.

Freud's first interpretation takes place against the backdrop of Brücke's Institute. The personnel there consisted of four men in hierarchical positions: Brücke himself, the head of the institute and a veritable father figure, his two assistants, and, under their supervision, the demonstrator. "Wherever there is rank and promotion the way lies open for wishes that call for suppression," Freud writes during the interpretation of the *Non vixit* Dream, referring to himself and his friend Josef Paneth, who succeeded him as demonstrator.[22] Both Freud and Paneth shared the same ambition, but Paneth was more explicit about this than Freud. Fleischl, one of the assistants, inspired friendship and respect in Freud and Paneth, but also professional competition: the only hope for promotion inside the Institute was for one of the current assistants to make room, that is, to become the head of the Institute, to leave, or—to die.[23] In fact, Fleischl was seriously ill, which therefore opened the field for evil wishes in Paneth *and* Freud.

Freud introduces the dream as one that he dreamt very clearly. The motif of clarity will return in the dream itself:

> I had a very clear dream. I had gone to Brücke's laboratory at night, and, in response to a gentle knock on the door, I opened it to (the late) Professor Fleischl, who came in with a number of strangers and, after exchanging a few words, sat down at his table. This was followed by a second dream. My friend Fl. [Fliess] had come to Vienna unobtrusively in July. I met him in the street in conversation with my (deceased) friend P. [Paneth], and went with them to some place where they sat opposite each other as though they were at a small table. I sat in front at its narrow end. Fl. spoke about his sister and said that in three-quarters of an hour she was dead, and added some such words as "that was the threshold." As P. failed to understand him, Fl. turned to me and asked me how much I had told P. about his affairs. Whereupon, overcome by strange emotions, I tried to explain to Fl. that P. (could not understand anything at all, of course, because he) was not alive. But what I actually said—and I myself noticed the mistake—was, "NON VIXIT." I then gave P. a piercing look. Under my gaze he turned pale; his form grew indistinct and his eyes a sickly blue—and finally he melted away. I was highly delighted at this and I now realized that Ernst Fleischl, too, had been no

> more than an apparition, a "revenant" ["ghost": literally, "one who returns"]; and it
> seemed to me quite possible that people of that kind only existed as long as one liked
> and could be got rid of if someone else wished it.[24]

The first round of interpretation, which immediately follows Freud's narration of the dream, tries to explain the source of his gaze and of the phrase "non vixit," and is mainly concerned with the annihilation scene. Freud deduces his hostility toward Paneth first from the constellation Freud-Fleischl-Paneth and then from the childhood relationship with John.

It has already been mentioned that one of the reference points of the dream was the unveiling, which Freud had attended, of a memorial in honor of Fleischl. Fleischl received a memorial, Paneth did not. Rightfully so: that is one of the dream thoughts. Before his own premature death, Paneth was outspoken about his ambition to advance in the Institute, implying that he would welcome Fleischl's demise. Freud punishes Paneth in his dream, but later admits that he, too, had had such ambitious and perhaps fatal wishes. On the other hand, Freud claims that he built a memorial for Paneth with his dream. Thus the dream becomes a memorial for the loved and despised friend Paneth, whose death or disappearance Freud wished (with successful outcome in the dream), because Paneth himself had wished for the death or disappearance of a third friend, Fleischl. Maybe this memorial should bear the inscription "NON VIXIT," a fragmentary quote from a memorial for Emperor Josef,[25] which would fit the ambiguity of the memorial for Paneth, and maybe for all of Freud's friends: on the one hand honoring them, on the other hand not only pronouncing them dead (which would be "non vivit," "he is not alive," "he does not live") but as always having been dead, as never having lived: *non vixit*.

BRUTUS: THE PARATAXIS OF FRIENDSHIP AND ENMITY

Freud enters into a discussion of John through the antithetical, paratactic statement that encompasses his hostile and affectionate feelings towards Paneth: "Because he did a lot for science I build him a memorial; but because he was guilty of an evil wish (which was expressed at the end of the dream) I annihilate him" (423). This construction recalls for Freud the (according to him) only literary example containing a similar antithetical statement: Brutus's justification as to why he killed Caesar, whom he loved, in Shakespeare: "As Caesar loved me, I weep for him; as he was fortunate, I rejoice at it; as he was valiant, I honour him; but, as he was ambitious, I slew him" (424).[26] Here Freud assumes the role of Brutus, who kills Caesar for being ambitious.

After ten years of separation, John and Freud were reunited on stage (of all places):[27] John played Caesar and Freud played Brutus in front of an audience of children.[28] Thus John returns and is immediately killed. Freud does not explain the scene in this way, but instead defines the returning John as just another revenant: "He had come to us on a visit from England; and he, too, was a *revenant,* for it was the play-mate of my earliest years who had returned in him" (424). The origin of all revenants is himself a revenant. The dream, though, sets up the "revenant" as a ghost of the dead friend. If John also is a revenant, then he is an apparition of himself. "John" can signify a person on stage, a fifteen-year-old visiting Vienna, and a four-year-old playmate from ten years before with whom he seems not to be identical and who will have died. If "John" can in fact be all these personae, one has to ask the question: How is one to discern between a theatrical figure, a ghost, and a "real" person, between dead and alive? *Non vixit:* maybe he did not live, never lived.

Freud proceeds by stating again that the childhood relationship "had a deter-mining influence on all my subsequent relations with contemporaries. Since that time my nephew John has had many reincarnations"—including himself, we might add (424). But what, then, is the structure of this first friendship? If Freud puts all his friends into a series starting with John, we should recall that "John" is actually split into two moments: the child who disappeared or died (Julius/John) and the revenant. The reason for this absence/death is implicit in the temporality of the relationship itself, as well as in the intrinsic split within friendship into both friendship and enmity, or maybe we should call it: tyranny.[29]

Narrating a childhood scene that ends the first round of interpretation, Freud writes that John must have treated him badly and assumes that he, Freud, was coura-geous "in the face of my tyrant" (424). He concludes this from a little retort he had made and that was later reported to him. His father/John's grandfather asked: Why are you hitting John? Freud's reply: "I hit him cos he hit me" (425). John hits first, Freud hits back. An eye for an eye, a tooth for a tooth. His hostility toward Paneth, Freud concludes, must stem from his childhood hostility toward John: after all, Paneth, being Freud's superior, is just another version of the cousin.

It is important to note that this childhood recollection is formed from a sentence that was reported to Freud by his father. Freud can construct the childhood scene only because of the indiscretion of complaining to a third, who later will tell him what he said. Furthermore, the limit of the battle is no less than the removal, the death of the opponent. In the second round of interpretation, Freud narrates a fantasy or mem-ory (he does not specify) recalling the first fight scene with John, but with a twist: this time, the two of them fight over an object, about who came first, and Freud prevails. John has to make way, whereas Freud remains "in possession of the field" (483).[30] The themes of indiscretion and removal in order to possess the field alone are not only nodal themes of the *Non vixit* Dream: betrayal or treason and murderous feelings also constitute the extreme limit of friendship within friendship, since "John" is the origin of friendship and enmity:

> My emotional life has always insisted that I should have an intimate friend and a hated enemy. I have always been able to provide myself afresh with both, and it has not infrequently happened that the ideal situation of childhood has been so completely

> reproduced that friend and enemy have come together in a single individual—though
> not, of course, both at once or with constant oscillations, as may have been the case
> in my early childhood. (483)

In John, intimate friend and hated enmity coincide, and this is the "ideal" childhood situation. "John" stands for the matrix of ambivalence in friendship. One should not forget that "John" is not only the origin of two opposite feelings (both of which constitute friendship) and the original revenant at once dead and alive; but also that he bears the mark of the dead, unmentioned, unmentionable brother, Julius. "John" is friendship's origin in multiple folds, an unspeakable origin.

Maybe Freud wants to reassure himself and his friends that the reproduction of the ideal will never occur, that enmity and friendship no longer exist simultaneously, oscillating in one person, but occur in neatly separable periods or persons. In the dream Freud is satisfied that he can make the revenants disappear through his gaze and words. This is also the aim of analysis: to do away with repetition through remembering, to chase away ghosts with clarity.

THE INDISCRETION OF AMBITIOUS INTERPRETATION

> I can only express a hope that readers of this book will put themselves in my difficult
> situation and treat me with indulgence, and further, that anyone who finds any sort of
> reference to himself in my dreams may be willing to grant me the right of freedom of
> thought—in my dream-life, if nowhere else. (xxiv)[31]

The *Non vixit* Dream is a dream about the interpretation of dreams: about how to work through the haunting figures of the past. That the first dream is set in Brücke's laboratory points to this, as Freud himself explains. The element connecting his present work and that in Brücke's laboratory is "analysis." Both dreams contrast his present success in psychoanalysis with his past failure in physiological analysis, thereby humbling him.[32] According to Freud's explanation, dreams set in the laboratory are punishment dreams for his ambitions in analyses—at least until he later reintegrates these dreams into the wish-fulfillment theory (476).

As has been noted above, Freud counts the *Non vixit* Dream among those ambitious dreams that constitute his "central accomplishment in interpretation" (374). Although he praises this dream as a "fine specimen" (421) because it shows many characteristics typical for all dreams, nonetheless he is apparently forced to refrain from fully interpreting it. Freud writes that he "would give a great deal to be able to present the complete solution of its conundrums.[33] But in point of fact, I am incapable of doing so—of doing, that is to say, what I did in the dream, of sacrificing to my ambition people whom I greatly value" (422). The dream and its proper interpretation share the same problem: the sacrifice of "greatly valued people"—friends—to ambition, an act of supreme indiscretion and betrayal. To interpret the dream is to kill a friend. Friendship and interpretation thus seem to be mutually exclusive: to be discreet, to be a good friend, Freud has to be a bad interpreter, or a less ambitious one.

A full interpretation of the dream would repeat its sacrifice of the friend. On the other hand, any veiling would destroy "what I know very well to be the dream's meaning" (422). To unveil a memorial for Paneth or his friends, Freud would have to veil facts and findings of his interpretation. To do this, though, would mean to sacrifice his ambition. Freud's answer to this conundrum is to pick out only some elements of the dream for interpretation: "Any concealment, however, would destroy what I know very well to be the dream's meaning; and I shall therefore content myself, both here and in a later context, with selecting only a few of its elements for interpretation" (422). This solution does not really solve anything. There is no logical connection between the two parts: Any concealment would have destroyed the meaning—that's why I pick only a few elements. The betrayal interpretation always leaves the door open for revenants to return to their betrayer who, in turn, has to get rid of them again and again. Revenants haunt dreams as they haunt interpretation. The friend, the revenant, is therefore decisive for the problem of interpretation itself.[34] The *Non vixit* Dream is about the interpretation of dreams, which has to come to terms with the revenant, or with the revenant-like friend, in a way that would foreclose further repetitions and substitutions.

SUBSTITUTING FLIESS

In the *Non vixit* Dream, Fliess seems not to be a revenant like Fleischl and Paneth, both of whom Freud could make disappear. Instead, he is alive and apparently the recipient of the warm feelings of friendship, whereas Freud seems to save his enmity for Paneth, who in a way might be sacrificed for the good friend. But in the end, Fliess is not spared hostile thoughts, either.

Freud's ambivalence toward Fliess becomes apparent in the last section of the interpretation, which ends with the theme of survival and substitution: "No one is irreplaceable" (485). Since Paneth and Fleischl have turned out to be revenants, and since revenants are elements in a chain of substitution beginning with John substituting for himself and Julius, Freud can be satisfied that he has always "been able to find successive substitutes for that figure" (485). Regarding Fliess he now thinks: "I felt I should be able to find a substitute for the friend whom I was now on the point of losing" (485). This friend—Fliess—is presumed dead, thereby also becoming a revenant, since no friend can be spared becoming one. In the logic of the revenant, the loss of a friend never means simply a loss. Surviving the friend means to go on and substitute for the dead.

At the same time there is also a wish that Fliess be the one who ends the series of representations and revenants. Since censorship does not ban the thought of Fliess's substitutability, Freud deduces that the thought is not entirely objectionable. Now he tells the story of the substitutes differently, in a seemingly more humane way:

> What a number of valued friends I have lost, some through death, some through a breach of our friendship! How fortunate that I have found a substitute for them and that I have gained one who means more to me than ever the others could, and that, at a time of life when new friendships cannot easily be formed, I shall never lose his! (486)

Fliess would then be the substitute for all previous substitutes, the end of a series: to put it pointedly, the Messiah.[35] But even if Fliess-as-substitute will have been the last one, he is still a substitute: the logic of the substitute, the questions of life and death, of possession of the field, will still haunt this last relationship—and interpretation itself.

After having visited Fliess in April 1893, around Easter, Freud wrote about him in a letter to Minna Bernays:[36] "He is a most unusual person, good nature personified: and I believe, if it came to it, he would for all his genius, be goodness itself. Therefore his sunlike clarity, his pluck."[37] In the same letter Freud states that if his newborn child Sophie had been a boy, he would have named it Wilhelm after Fliess. This seems to allude to a desire to immortalize this particular being by circulating the name, by inserting the name of the friend into the generational chain.

It is certainly no coincidence that the second section dedicated to the interpretation of the *Non vixit* Dream should end, on a hopeful note, with the word "immortality," which is supposedly granted through children. This turn toward children in the interpretation is based on the fact that Fliess's daughter, Pauline (also the name of Freud's niece/John's sister), had just been born. In a letter to Fliess, Freud had already expressed the hope, or the certainty, that Fliess's daughter could replace, reincarnate Fliess's own dead sister, Clara. Freud states that children, by being given names in the memory of people one has been fond of, are made into revenants. They carry on the memory of loved ones and bear the reminder of us when we are dead: "And after all, I reflected, was not having children our only path to immortality?"

Of course, the hope for immortality projected onto the child is in itself highly unstable. Freud's daughter Sophie, whom, as I mentioned above, he would have named after Fliess had she been a boy, died in 1920. On April 12, 1929, the anniversary of Sophie's death, Freud writes to Ludwig Binswanger in reaction to the latter's loss of his oldest son, Robert:

> Although we know that after such a loss the acute state of mourning will subside, we also know we shall remain inconsolable and will never find a substitute. No matter what may fill the gap, even if it be filled completely, it nevertheless remains something else. And actually this is how it should be. It is the only way of perpetuating that love which we do not want to relinquish.[38]

Although this letter was written on the anniversary of Sophie's death, Freud is not actually referring to her loss. In a letter dated October 15, 1926, expressing condolences to

Binswanger (who at this time had already lost a first son), Freud notes that he and his wife had actually coped with Sophie's death remarkably well. More than Sophie, it is Sophie's son, Heinerle, who stands for an irreparable loss in Freud's life. Heinerle, who had died in June 1926, "had taken the place of all my children and other grandchildren, and since then, since Heinerle's death, I don't care for my grandchildren any more, but find no joy in life either" (78ff).

In Freud's interpretation of the *Non vixit* Dream, substitution was based on a notion of space allowing only for all or nothing, dead or alive, a substitution seemingly without memory. In the letter from 1929, there prevails a notion of irreplaceability, a space of loss that can simultaneously be filled and not filled, of a substitution that is not substituting for the dead one. The last quotation starts with a radical substitution, in which Heinerle comes to stand in for all others without himself being replaceable.[39] But with his death substitution ends, leaving Freud behind with the empty world of melancholia and the shattered dream of immortality, of surviving beyond death. The question will always be: is there a "representative of the Other" who is at once absolute changeability and yet completely singular?[40] And can there be friendship when only one survives?

Epitaph for an Epigraph: The Gift of Interpretation

We should be interested not only in Freud's use of the word "revenant" in the sentence: "All my friends have in a certain sense been re-incarnations of this first figure who 'früh sich einst dem trüben Blick gezeigt': they have been *revenants*" (SE V, 483), but also in the quote that qualifies the "first figure," i.e., John. It is taken from Goethe's "Dedication" (*Zueignung*), the poem placed at the beginning of *Faust.* This is neither the first nor the last time that Freud quotes from this "Dedication." Lines from this poem, which itself is marked by a return, keep returning.[41]

Freud did not always intend to use lines from Virgil's *Aeneid* as the epigraph for *The Interpretation of Dreams.*[42] These lines are in fact a substitute for a motto Freud apparently had preferred and had suggested to Fliess. His friend, though, left him at a loss for a motto when Fliess literally—in Freud's words of July 17, 1899—killed Freud's first choice: "A motto for the dream has not turned up since you killed [*umgebracht*] Goethe's sentimental one. A reference to repression is all that will remain."[43] The famous motto of *The Interpretation of Dreams* thus stands in, substitutes for the killed, "sentimental" Goethe motto. In this sense it is thus a remainder, a reminder of murder, of the friend's censorship. The quote referring to repression thus refers to a literal repression. The Virgil epigraph is an epitaph for the killed first one.

As Walter Schönau shows, the sentimental motto by Goethe probably would have consisted in a quote from the "Dedication."[44] Exactly which verses Freud would have chosen remains an open question; but Schönau narrows down the possibilities by looking into what Freud usually quotes from this text. He suggests that Freud refers either to lines one to three of the first stanza, or to lines three and four from the second: "Ihr naht euch wieder, schwankende Gestalten, / Die früh sich einst dem trüben Blick gezeigt. / Versuch' ich wohl, euch diesmal festzuhalten? / . . . Gleich einer alten, halbverklungnen Sage / Kommt erste Lieb' und Freundschaft mit herauf."[45] Because Freud used the adjective "sentimental" to qualify the murdered Goethe motto, Schönau proposes that Freud was probably referring to the latter lines.[46]

Goethe wrote the "Dedication" in 1797, more than twenty years after he had started working on *Faust*.[47] The poem addresses both the fictitious characters of *Faust* and the friends to whom Goethe read the text out loud before it was ever printed. In the "Dedication," these figures (the personae from *Faust* as well as the listeners, some of whom had since died) appear before the poet: they return as revenants. The Dedication *itself* thematizes revenants, addresses revenants, and, as a dedicatory poem, gives the work to these revenants, to old friends, dead friends, to friends survived. The "Dedication" makes *Faust* into a gift, into the property of another.

Quotes from the "Dedication" occur twice in Freud's letters to Fliess.[48] In a letter dated October 27, 1897, roughly a year after his father's death, Freud describes his state—tied to his self-analysis—as a quick variation of moods resembling a landscape one might see from a moving train. Given Freud's travel phobia, this is an image laden with fear. He then quotes lines two to four of the second stanza from Goethe's poem, which in a sublimated way express this state.[49] For Freud, Goethe's verses seem to signify the associative movement of remembering itself, of forgotten things resurfacing: shadowy creatures, which in turn bring along yet older figures—not only loved ones or friends, but in their wake, love and friendship, *first* love and friendship. But after citing these lines, Freud adds: "And also first fright and discord" (Auch erster Schreck und Hader). He does not abide by the tender words of the poet, which he chose precisely for their "sublimated" character: to love and friendship he adds fright and discord.

Two years later, in a letter of October 11, 1899, Freud again quotes from the "Dedication." Three months after Freud states that the "sentimental one by Goethe" has been killed, something returns that might very well bear the traces of this murder. During a phase of renewed ideas (*Einfälle*) yet unintelligible for him, Freud compares this flood of thoughts to the "first epoch of productivity."[50] We assume that he is indicating the year 1897. Again he uses Goethe's poem to describe the surfacing of the past—now including the immediate past of his discoveries and of the processes of analysis—in a wavering, indistinct form. This time he quotes the very first line of the "Dedication": "You come closer again, you hovering forms." Like the hovering forms themselves, Goethe's poem returns again and again in Freud's writing, describing the return of the past, the content of this return, as well as the history of psychoanalysis itself.

The intrinsic relationship that seems to tie Goethe's "Dedication" to psychoanalysis culminates in Freud's "Address at the Goethe-House," which Anna Freud delivered in her father's place when Freud was awarded the Goethe-Prize in 1930. In this speech Freud suggests that Goethe would have approved of psychoanalysis, and that it is no disgrace for Goethe if he or his texts become objects of it. Goethe's insights into psychic processes allow Freud to see in him a forefather and patron of psychoanalysis. Goethe, Freud says, already knew about the strength of the first affective ties of the child. It is exactly in the "Dedication," according to Freud, that Goethe celebrated these first ties. Freud thereby gives us his explicit reading of this poem as a beginning of psychoanalysis, insofar as what is acknowledged here is the meaning of the beginning of one's life—childhood. Resurrecting the dead Goethe motto, Freud cites lines one to three from the first stanza and lines three and four from the second. This quotation, says Freud, could be repeated with every psychoanalysis.[51] Goethe's "Dedication" thus has become an epigraph for psychoanalysis itself, for each psychoanalysis; a motto that is itself a revenant, since it had once been "killed."

The killed Goethe motto was thus not only about revenants; it was the quotation of a dedication to them. Had it been included, *The Interpretation of Dreams* would at least have borne the trace of being dedicated. It would have been a gift. The friend Fliess, to whom Freud wanted to give *The Interpretation of Dreams* as a birthday gift (which arrived too late), censored, cut this gesture, thereby, oddly enough, erasing the traces of the importance of friendship from *The Interpretation of Dreams*.[52]

Maybe then there is no such thing as a book about friendship, precisely because friendship is what cuts, what imposes limits—to representation and interpretation. All that survives of friendship's gift in *The Interpretation of Dreams* is the following inscription:

> All my friends have in a certain sense been re-incarnations of this first figure who "früh sich einst dem trüben Blick gezeigt": they have been *revenants*. (483)

Notes

The epigraph to this chapter is drawn from a letter from Freud to Ludwig Binswanger dated May 21, 1926; it is quoted in Ludwig Binswanger, *Sigmund Freud: Reminiscences of a Friendship*, trans. Norbert Guterman (New York: Grune and Stratton, 1957), 96.

1. In the German original this sentence reads: "Es ist das Jahr der 'Revenants.'" See Sigmund Freud, *Briefe an Wilhelm Fliess 1887–1904*, ed. Jeffrey Moussaieff Masson (Frankfurt am Main: Fischer, 1986), 462. The English edition of the Freud-Fliess correspondence renders this sentence as "This is the year of revenants!" See Sigmund Freud, *The Complete Letters of Sigmund Freud to Wilhelm Fliess 1887–1904*, ed. and trans. Jeffrey Moussaieff Masson (Cambridge, Mass., and London: Harvard University Press, 1985), 420.

2. As is well known, *The Interpretation of Dreams* actually appeared in 1899. Freud intentionally postdated its printed year of publication.

3. One is reminded of the other significance Freud gave to the new century: it announces the dates of his and Fliess's respective deaths: "The new century, the most interesting thing about which for us may be that it contains the dates of our deaths, has brought me nothing but

a stupid review in the *Zeit* by Burckhardt, the former director of the Burgtheater (not to be confused with our old Jacob)" (Freud, *Complete Letters*, 394).

4. For a discussion of the history and importance of the friendship between Freud and Fliess, see Ernest Jones, *Sigmund Freud: Life and Work*, 3 vols. (New York: Basic Books, 1953–1957); Didier Anzieu, *Freud's Self-Analysis*, trans. Peter Graham, preface by M. Masud R. Khan (London: The Hogarth Press and the Institute of Psycho-Analysis, 1986); Max Schur, *Freud: Living and Dying* (New York: International Universities Press, Inc., 1972); Patrick Mahoney, "Friendship and Its Discontents," in *Contemporary Psychoanalysis* 16 (1979): 55–109; M. Masud R. Khan, "The Catalytic Role of Friendship in the Epistemology of Self-Experience in Montaigne, Rousseau and Freud," in *Dynamische Psychiatrie* 3, no. 3 (1970): 168–78; Graham Little, "Freud, Friendship, and Politics," in *The Dialectics of Friendship*, ed. Ray Porter (London and New York: Routledge, 1989), 143–58; E. Buxbaum, "Freud's Dream Interpretation in the Light of his Letters to Fliess," in *Bulletin of the Menninger Clinic* 15, no. 6 (1951): 197–212; Th. Neyraut-Sutterman, "Le 'Portrait-De-L'Ami' de Freud," in *Revue française de psychanalyse* 36 (1972): 999–1019; and part 1 of Avital Ronell, *Dictations: On Haunted Writing* (Bloomington: Indiana University Press, 1986) on the constellation Freud-Goethe-Fliess and Freud's "haunted" writing.

5. For the problem of transference in the relationship between Freud and Fliess and the debate as to whether this transference ever ended, see Anzieu, *Freud's Self-Analysis*, 353, 385, 481, 524, and particularly 525ff., where Anzieu argues (against Buxbaum) that Freud tried to overcome transference toward the end of his friendship with Fliess. Mahoney modifies Erikson's statement that the friendship between Freud and Fliess was the first transference in history, which liquidated or liquified itself through its very discovery. For Mahoney, the transference was merely modified ("Friendship and Its Discontents," 71ff.). Little writes that Freud's friendships were marked by a "fundamental ambivalence in which a 'brother transference'—an equal partnership—was associated with a 'father transference' which would eventually take over, so that the friend/father had to be repudiated" ("Freud, Friendship, and Politics," 147). See William J. McGrath on the notion of a layering of father and brother transference in Freud's life in his *Freud's Discovery of Psychoanalysis. The Politics of Hysteria* (Ithaca and London: Cornell University Press, 1986).

6. Freud, *Collected Letters*, 376, 313, 369.

7. Ibid., 450.

8. "My self-analysis remains interrupted. I have realized why I can analyze myself only with the help of knowledge obtained objectively (like an outsider). True self-analysis is impossible; otherwise there would be no [neurotic] illness" (ibid., 281).

9. Ibid., 374.

10. SE VI, 159.

11. Freud, *Collected Letters*, 383.

12. Klaus Theweleit, *Object-Choice (All You Need Is Love . . .): On Mating Strategies and a Fragment of a Freud Biography*, trans. Malcolm Green (London and New York: Verso, 1994), 90ff.

13. SE V, 483. "[F]rüh sich einst dem trüben Blick gezeigt" translates as "Who long since showed themselves to my clouded gaze" (my translation).

14. On the critical question of the "number" of friends, see Jacques Derrida, *Politics of Friendship*, trans. George Collins (London and New York: Verso, 1997).

15. Freud, *Collected Letters*, 268.

16. Incidentally, the name "Johannes" comes up early on in *The Interpretation of Dreams*.

In chapter 1, Freud discusses the "Moral Sense in Dreams" as it has been seen by other authors. In this context there appears a quote referring to fratricide from 1 John [in German, Johannes] 3:15: "Whosoever hateth his brother is a murderer" (SE IV, 69).

17. Freud, *Collected Letters*, 202, November 2, 1896. For a discussion of the "guilt of the survivor," see Schur, *Freud: Living and Dying*; and Ronell, *Dictations*, 42ff.

18. In his essay on a childhood recollection from Goethe's *Dichtung und Wahrheit* [*Poetry and Truth*] (1917), Freud interprets a scene where Goethe throws dishes out the window as the staging of a magical act with which the writer tries to get rid of his newborn brother. Freud finds these adverse wishes in other patients, too.

19. The object of Freud's and his nephew's actions probably was Pauline, John's sister. For this constellation, see Freud's essay *Screen Memories* (1899) (SE III, 303–22).

20. Freud, *Collected Letters*, 374. The *Non vixit* Dream is actually not placed among the "Absurd Dreams," but in the subchapter "Calculations and Speeches in Dreams" in the chapter "The Dream-Work." The interpretation, which follows Freud's account of the dream itself, is interrupted by the subchapter on "Absurd Dreams" (which Freud begins with dreams about dead fathers) and is taken up again in "Affects in Dreams."

21. This ceremony had taken place on October 16, 1898, which thus allows for the approximate dating of this dream.

22. Freud, *Collected Letters*, 484.

23. In a letter to his fiancée, Martha Bernays, on June 27, 1882, Freud expresses his deep admiration for Fleischl and even plays with the thought that Martha actually would have deserved a man like him. Fleischl haunts many dreams in *The Interpretation of Dreams*, such as the Dream of Irma's Injection. It seems that Freud reproached himself for the fact that he gave Fleischl cocaine to alleviate his pain, not knowing that in the long run the use of cocaine would worsen his condition.

24. Due to limits of space I will not be able to discuss this dream comprehensively. Anzieu includes in his list of the dream's themes: lateness, indiscretion, immortality, and the rivalry with one's elders (*Freud's Self-Analysis*, 380ff.). For other interpretations of the dream and Freud's interpretation thereof, see Alexander Grinstein, *Sigmund Freud's Dreams* (New York: International Universities Press, 1980), 282–316; McGrath, *Freud's Discovery of Psychoanalysis*, 280–90; and Schur, *Freud: Living and Dying*, 153–70.

25. Freud, *Collected Letters*, 421. The Latin Freud provides as the source of "Non vixit" actually contains a mistake Freud only corrected in 1925: It is not "Saluti patriae vixit/ non diu sed totus" (For the well-being of his country he lived not long but wholly), but "Saluti publicae vixit/ non diu sed totus" (424).

26. Freud finds another proof for this association in the fact that in the dream Fliess came to Vienna in July, which was named after Julius Caesar. Freud never mentions Julius, the brother he survived.

27. It should be noted that *The Interpretation of Dreams* refers to the *Non vixit* Dream a third time, namely in the beginning of chapter 7. Freud here underscores the importance of an apparently trivial detail of the dream (the passage: "As P. failed to understand him . . . ," 421), which nonetheless eventually led him back to its underlying childhood memory: his affectionate yet stormy relationship with John. This association came about by way of a stanza from Heinrich Heine's poem "The Homecoming" from his *Book of Songs*, 77: "Rarely have you *understood* me, and rarely too have I understood you. Not until we both found ourselves in the mud ["Kot": excrement or dirt] did we promptly understand each other" (513).

28. Actually the scene acted out by Freud and his nephew was a song from Friedrich Schiller's drama *The Robbers*, a play about two rival brothers. For a short summary of this play as well as the implications of this text for the *Non vixit* Dream (namely, a text about brother-rivalry containing a song about the patricidal story of Brutus killing Caesar), see Grinstein, *Sigmund Freud's Dreams*, 293–305.

29. In his speech "On the Friend," Zarathustra asks: "Are you a slave? Then you cannot be a friend. Are you a tyrant? Then you cannot have friends." See Nietzsche, *The Portable Nietzsche*, ed. Walter Kaufmann (New York: Viking, 1954), 169. McGrath sees the political theme of (psychoanalytic) freedom/freedom of expression versus tyranny taken up in the *Non vixit* Dream: "[T]he dream suggested the possibility that psychoanalysis could open the way to freedom from the tyranny of the revenants" (290; see also 304 and 292 on the relationship between the issue of freedom versus tyranny in the Schiller play).

30. In a sense the fiasco in which the friendship between Freud and Fliess ended consisted in the dispute about who is in possession of the field, namely who can claim to have first discovered the importance of the notion of bisexuality.

31. Freud, *The Interpretation of Dreams*, "Preface to the First Edition" (SE IV). This sentence contains a hidden quotation of the famous imperative of the Marquis de Posa, expressed to the Spanish king in Schiller's *Don Carlos* (III, x): "Geben Sie Gedankenfreiheit" (Give freedom of thought).

32. The problem arising from these dream examples is, of course, how they align with Freud's thesis that all dreams represent a wish-fulfillment: these dreams do not express the pride or vanity of the "*parvenu*," but self-criticism. Freud concedes that he would have no objections to classifying these dreams as "punishment dreams," separate from wish-fulfillment dreams. The punishment is the consequence of the fact that (as Freud hypothesizes) "the foundation of the dream was formed in the first instance by an exaggeratedly ambitious phantasy" (Freud, *Complete Letters*, 475).

33. In the German original, Freud would not only "give a great deal," but rather uses the idiomatic expression "für mein Leben gern": read literally, this means he would give his life for being able to present a complete interpretation.

34. There is still another way in which friendship imposes a limit on Freud's interpretation: friends should not be interpreted. In the *Psychopathology of Everyday Life*, Freud tells us how he once saw fit "to reproach a loyal and deserving friend on no other grounds than the interpretation I placed on certain indications coming from his unconscious. He was offended and wrote me a letter asking me not to treat my friends psycho-analytically. I had to admit he was in the right, and wrote him a reply to pacify him" (SE VI, 169). While writing this letter, Freud broke a newly acquired Egyptian figure with his pen-holder. This, for him, is another instance of a "sacrifice" taking the form of breaking something, apparently by accident. This sacrifice, Freud goes on to write, was necessary to avert a greater evil that (we assume) would have been the loss of the friend. But: "Luckily it was possible to cement both of them together—the friendship as well as the figure—so that the break would not be noticed" (SE VI, 169ff.).

35. Freud called Fliess his "Messiah" in a letter of July 10, 1893, in regard to problems that Freud himself felt incapable of solving, but which he hoped Fliess would be able to solve.

36. Unpublished letter, quoted by Masson in the introduction to the Freud-Fliess correspondence (Freud, *Complete Letters*, 2). The date given for this letter is April 17, 1893, in the German edition, and April 7, 1893, in the English edition.

37. Freud, *Complete Letters*, 2.

38. Quoted in Binswanger, *Sigmund Freud: Reminiscences*, 84.

39. This structure reminds us of Freud's wish for Fliess to be the last in the series of substitutions.

40. The answer to this question might hinge on a different notion of space. In addition to using the French word "revenant," Freud also makes use of another French expression in the context of the *Non vixit* Dream: "Ôte-toi que je m'y mette!" (literally, "Get out of the way so I can get there") (484). In the second round of interpretation, Freud states that his attitude toward John and Paneth's attitude toward Fleischl are of the same reproachable kind and describes it by way of this French saying, alluding to the notion of space underlying the principle of substitution in Freud's interpretation. An extensive and critical discussion of precisely this "Ôte-toi que je m'y mette" can be found in a book by Freud's friend, the Swiss psychiatrist Ludwig Binswanger. His seminal work, *Grundformen und Erkenntnis menschlichen Daseins*, published in 1942, undertakes in its first part a phenomenological, ontological, and anthropological exploration of love. The book starts out with a section on *Die Räumlichkeit des liebenden Miteinanderseins* (The spatiality of loving-being-together). Binswanger reads "Ôte-toi que je m'y mette" as *the* imperative ruling everyday interaction (*Verkehr*). Ludwig Binswanger, *Ausgewählte Werke* 2, ed. Max Herzog (Heidelberg: Roland Asanger Verlag, 1993), 15. Tied to this imperative, the common notion of spatiality is that of "Körperdinge"—*res extensa*, things—being next to each other. According to this conception, "a thing cannot take the place of the other without the other changing its place" (Das räumliche Verhältnis zwischen den einzelnen Körperdingen ist das *Neben*einandervorhandensein, demzufolge nicht ein Ding den Platz des andern einnehmen kann, ohne daß das andere seinen Ort wechselt) (Binswanger, *Ausgewählte Werke* 2), 15. Binswanger contrasts this imperative with the absolutely different interaction found in loving-being-together. This loving-being-together is based on a spatiality that precisely does *not* involve having to make room or violently remove the other from his/her/its place. For Binswanger, love and friendship "show the same anthropological fundamental structure" (*Ausgewählte Werke* 2, 199).

41. For the significance of Goethe for Freud's writing, see Ronell, *Dictations*, part 1.

42. Mottoes mattered to Freud. Regarding a book he was working on at the time, he wrote to Fliess that he could only give him the mottoes that would precede the different chapters. (December 4, 1896, *Complete Letters*, 205). These mottoes seem to contain in a nutshell, so to speak, his not-yet-written work. Freud also treated mottoes as entities, as properties. The motto for the *Psychopathology* he humbly wanted to "borrow" from Fliess, who must have mentioned the particular Goethe poem once (October 14, 1900, *Complete Letters*, 427). He later writes that this motto was a gift from Fliess (August 7, 1901, *Complete Letters*, 447).

43. Freud, *Complete Letters*, 361.

44. Walter Schönau, *Sigmund Freuds Prosa. Literarische Elemente seines Stils* (Stuttgart: J. B. Metzlersche Verlagsbuchhandlung, 1968), 74ff.

45. "You come closer again, you hovering forms, / Who long since have showed themselves to my clouded gaze. / Shall I attempt to capture you this time? // And many beloved shades rise up / Like an old, half faded legend / First love and friendship rise up together with them" (my translation).

46. Schönau, *Sigmund Freuds Prosa*, 74.

47. It is not certain when exactly Goethe started working on *Faust*, but one assumes it was probably 1773–75.

48. One has to remember that Freud's father died in October 1896, and the month October might, even if Freud does not say so, be seen as the anniversary of this death.

49. "I am gripped and pulled through ancient times in quick association of thoughts; my moods change like the landscapes seen by a traveler from a train; and as the great poet, using his privilege to ennoble (sublimate), puts it: "Und manche liebe Schatten steigen auf; / Gleich einer alten, halbverklungnen Sage, / Kommt erste Lieb' und Freundschaft mit herauf" (Freud, *Complete Letters*, 274).

50. Ibid., 379.

51. SE XXI, 209.

52. See Freud's letter to Fliess of October 27, 1899, in Freud, *Complete Letters*, 380.

OTHER
DESIRES

9. The Dream between Drive and Desire

A QUESTION OF REPRESENTABILITY

Paul Verhaeghe

One of the major conclusions of Freud's *The Interpretation of Dreams* is, of course, that every dream comes down to the fulfillment of a secret wish. This is the main message of Freud's book, the one that has been kept intact for the last hundred years. The latent dream thoughts contain a forbidden unconscious desire, which finds its expression in the manifest dream content, albeit in a distorted way due to the dream-work. Every analysis has to follow the opposite road, meaning that the dream-work has to be countered by the analytic work. At the end of the analytic day, the patient will be consciously aware of his unconscious wishes; that is, he will be cured, because the dynamics of repression have been undone. This idea explains another well-known saying from Freud's Dream Book: that the dream provides us with the royal road to the unconscious, in this case the repressed desire and the latent dream thoughts.

I want to argue that such a reading of Freud is incomplete, to say the least. The way in which such a reading considers the dream, the unconscious, and the ends and goals of the analytic practice is rather naïve. First of all, I'd like to discuss this threefold naïvete.

Let us start with the central idea of wish fulfillment. Based on my clinical practice, I can say that this idea of a hidden wish in the dream is not all that clear. In a number of cases, it is rather difficult to find any wish whatsoever. In an even larger number of cases, there is a wish, but this wish is not hidden, or even, to the contrary, it appears as such in the manifest dream content, and the patient is fully aware of his desire during waking life. Freud mentioned this possibility when he discussed the dreams of small children, dreams in which the distortion owing to the repression has not taken place. Today, probably because of major changes in society, the process of repression seems to fail more and more, and our contemporary patients are confronted in their dreams with something beyond repression. This reminds me of a joke. A patient consults his analyst because of a recurrent dream: "Doctor, doctor, every night this last week I dreamt that I entered the bedroom of my new neighbor and that I fucked her like hell. I don't understand this, what does it mean?" Answers the analyst: "It means that you want to ride a white horse through your neighbor's front garden, armed with a long black spear."

So the idea of a hidden, repressed wish has to be abandoned in a large number of cases. Instead, I want to stress something else that is quite central in Freud's book: the main goal of every dream is to keep the dreamer asleep. And this wish to sleep is the central wish: dreams are the guardians of sleep (SE IV, 233–344; SE V, 678). This function is all the more interesting if we study the point where dreams fail to fulfill it—the nightmare. We'll come back to this.

My next point of discussion concerns the unconscious. The dream is the royal road to the unconscious, but the question is: to which unconscious? At the time of *The Interpretation of Dreams,* this unconscious came down to a number of repressed wishes, which are not too difficult to analyze. But when we study Freud's other works from the same period, things become a bit more complicated. Even in *The Interpretation of Dreams* itself, there is a remarkable idea that will persist through Freud's entire work. Every dream, says Freud, contains a nucleus that cannot be analyzed (SE IV, 111n1; SE V, 524–55), and this has to do with the kernel of our being (SE V, 603). This kernel or nucleus is the mycelium from which the dream wish springs, just like a mushroom (SE V, 525). So, this royal road to the unconscious is not that easy, and must necessarily lead to some kind of deadlock. As we will see, this deadlock has to be studied together with the failure of the dream's main function, that is, the wish to sleep.

My third point of discussion here is the most difficult one: it is the idea that the therapeutic goals of analysis can be restricted to the undoing of the process of repression. Even in Freud's time, the making conscious of the awareness of formerly repressed desires was something that did not work; hence his plea for the analysis of transference and for working through. Today, because of the lack of repression in our patients, we are obliged to redefine the goals of analysis in general and dream analysis in particular.

We have to leave this threefold naïveté behind us. Instead I wish to put forth three propositions. These propositions are based on my reading of Lacan, but as we will see, their core is already present in Freud: (1) Every dream contains a double level. On the one hand we have the level of desire, and on the other we have the level of *jouissance.* (2) These two levels correspond to two different layers in the unconscious, first those of the unconscious contents of repression, second the original or system *Ucs.* (3) This double level obliges us to reconsider the therapeutic goals of analysis.

Let us start with the first proposition, the one about desire and *jouissance*. To understand this we must study Freud's theory of the drive. The concept itself is coined after *The Interpretation of Dreams,* but the idea is very well present right from the start in his writings. I would go so far as to say it is one of Freud's main preoccupations. Every time he discusses the so-called Q-factor or quantitative energy, he is discussing the main character of the drive, that is, its very aspect of and as energetic.[1] And quite soon, he understands this Q-factor as something central, both in matters of sexuality and in matters of anxiety; hence his discussion about the transformation of sexual libido into anxiety. From his correspondence with Fliess, it is obvious that this Q-factor is something that needs representation, because without representation, the subject cannot cope with it in a normal psychological way. Once it has entered the realm of representation, all kinds of coping mechanisms can be applied to it, and these are summarized and gathered together by Freud in his idea of "defense." These mechanisms will find their first elaborate description in *The Interpretation of Dreams,* most particularly in the chapter on the dream-work, starting with the mechanisms of condensation and displacement. These mechanisms are fascinating. They are even so fascinating that we tend to forget the main thing: that they go back to an original infantile wish that needs to find a representation in one way or another, hence the first preoccupation of the dreamwork, the "considerations of representability."

From my point of view, this infantile wish is nothing but the original drive, although the concept is lacking in Freud's Dream Book. (I could argue this at length, but here, because of considerations of space, I cannot.) Thus considered, the dream is, first of all, a means of representing and expressing the drive in such a way that the dreamer can go on sleeping. Freud's further work on the drive will attest to the difficulty of this job. Indeed, being a concept on the border between the psyche and the soma, the drive is something that can never be fully represented. Hence that most beautiful Freudian definition: "[T]he drive is to be regarded as a measure of the demand made upon the mind for work" (SE VII, 168). Our dream life is one of the products of this demand.

Indeed, the dream-work starts from the drive, and proceeds in such a way that this drive becomes translated, that is, represented in a desire. Freud stressed the forbidden part of this desire, which was quite obvious in the Victorian era. Today, with Lacan, we can stress another clinical characteristic, also quite easy to recognize already in the Freudian examples. Every desire goes back to a desire of or for the Other, be it in the positive or the negative sense. In itself, this is already a very interesting thesis, because today it is more useful in clinical practice than the idea that every dream contains a hidden wish fulfillment. Moreover, it has the advantage of bringing dream interpretation right into the interpretation of transference, because sooner or later (usually sooner), the analyst is placed in the position of the Other. In itself, this last statement has some serious implications for interpretation, because it is not always clear who is interpreting whom.

Interesting as this might be, it nevertheless is not my main point here. What I want to stress is that desire and representability are to a certain extent synonymous. My desire is the desire of the Other, yes; but who or what is this Other? Following Lacan, the Other comes down to the representational unit from whom I draw all my identifications (remember that even for Freud, an identification is based on an object choice) or, to put it in Lacanian terms, all my alienations.[2] So, the upper level of the drive, in the dream, is the level of phallic desire, meaning the level of the Other, meaning the level of representability. These representational elements of the drive can be repressed, rejected, condensed, displaced—whatever. It is this phallic level that can be fully analyzed, because it is the very stuff upon which the model of free association is based. As I have already noted, such a full analysis implies the analysis of transference as well.

But what about the other level? As we have to deal with the drive, this other level concerns the unrepresented part of the drive, the Q-factor, the energy that has not entered the realm of the ever-phallic representation. I consider this to be Freud's kernel or nucleus, the mycelium that in itself is impossible to analyze. The reason for this impossibility is easy: as there is no representation available, this factor cannot enter into the associative material. It is this point Freud will encounter with traumatic neurosis, and he will baptize it as being "beyond the pleasure principle." It is this same point every one of us meets during a nightmare. Indeed, the nightmare is the most common example of traumatic neurosis: the dreamer meets with something he cannot put into words and which is impossible to represent, something from the Real. The dream fails in its attempt to represent this part of the Real; hence it fails in its function to keep us asleep, and we wake up in full anxiety. From a Lacanian point of view, this kernel or nucleus of the real is the object a or *jouissance,* that strange mixture of pleasure and anxiety beyond desire. In his later work, Lacan will call this *jouissance* the not-all—we shall return to this. To summarize: The dream is one way of coping with the drive by representing it through the desire of the Other. Where the mechanism of the phallic pleasure principle fails, we are confronted with the real of *jouissance.*

This brings us to my second statement: The dream is the royal road to the unconscious, but the question is, which unconscious? It is fairly well known that Freud distinguished three: (1) the unconscious in the descriptive meaning; (2) the unconscious in its dynamic meaning; (3) the unconscious as permanently unconscious system—the system *Ucs.*

The descriptive meaning is the least interesting, as it describes merely a state of mind. As such it has been assimilated by most contemporary psychological theories. The core problem resides in the dynamic unconscious and in the system *Ucs.* In his clinical work, Freud encountered the dynamic unconscious when he was faced with the split between energetic investment and representations. It appeared that the words, belonging to certain affects, disappeared from consciousness, and that the original cathexis became displaced onto other representations. The "forgotten"—

repressed—representations had been inscribed in another psychic system, from which they operated in a pathogenic way. This is the theory of repression, which explains the existence of *the dynamic unconscious.*

Based on this part of the theory, one might presume that the unconscious is the sole effect of such repression. This would imply that all the repressed contents can be made conscious again, as they first belonged to consciousness. This is not the case. In Freud's theory, repression proper is based on a primary form of defense, namely primal repression ("Psycho-Analytic Notes on an Autobiographical Account of a Case of Paranoia [Dementia Paranoides]," SE XII). For Freud, this primal repression concerns the somatic component of the drive, which is not so much repressed as left behind during psychological development. Primal repression must be considered as a primal fixation.[3] This process creates the kernel of the system *Ucs* by isolating it from any further development. This kernel will attract the material coming from repression proper, and thus it operates in a causal, albeit silent, way.[4]

Since Freud, all stress has been placed on the dynamic unconscious and on repressed thoughts. This is the core of most psychotherapies. The genuinely psychoanalytical question, the one concerning the nature of the "non-repressed unconscious" (*The Ego and the Id*, SE XIX; *New Introductory Lectures on Psychoanalysis*, SE XX), came to the fore with Lacan. In Lacan's first theorization, the repressed unconscious will be explicitly linked to language and to the speaking Other. Until 1964 he identifies this repressed unconscious with the unconscious as such, hence his saying: "The Unconscious is the discourse of the Other." The subject acquires its identity through the process of alienation, through the identification with the signifiers of the (m)other based on the desire of this Other. Repression proper operates on these signifiers, and is always related to the relationship with this Other. During the treatment, the repetition of this process in the transference implies both resistance and the possibility of the undoing of the repression, thus arriving at "full speech."[5] This expression of Lacan—"full speech"—indicates his conviction at that time that everything could be fully analyzed.

After 1964 Lacan will concentrate his theory on the system *Ucs.* His controversy with Ricoeur at the Bonneval Conference of 1964, and later the one with Laplanche and Leclaire, led him to a more distinct formulation of his theory in this respect. Ricoeur had defined primal repression as the process of translation, which turns the instinctual into the core of what could later become language.[6] In their joint paper presented at Bonneval, Laplanche and Leclaire voiced a different opinion. According to Leclaire, as a result of the analytic cure, the kernel of the system *Ucs* can be summarized in phonemes. According to Laplanche, this kernel consists of imagos, by which he means here sensory images without signifiers. With this idea, Laplanche reinterprets Freud's theory of thing-presentations and of the system *Ucs.*[7]

Such a reading is not without effect on the aim of the psychoanalytic cure. If, in one way or another, the kernel of the system *Ucs* is of a representational nature, then it can be verbalized and interpreted during the treatment. If not, then the final aim of the cure has to be redefined.

As long as Lacan stressed the linguistic aspect of the *Ucs*, the former position could be considered his. But from 1964 onward, his focus on the drive and the Real will oblige him to the latter position, and this will entail a new theory of them. In this respect, we have to acknowledge fully Lacan's ideas on determinism and causality.[8]

From a Lacanian point of view, the "Gothic" interpretation of the unconscious is totally wrong. In this romantic conception, the unconscious is viewed as the basement of the psyche, in which all ancient dreads and desires lay buried until the unavoidable day of their resuscitation. Freud's theory, which includes concepts such as "the return of the repressed," "repetition compulsion," and so on would be nothing more than the scientific elaboration of this inevitability. Obviously such a reading implies total determinism, inasmuch as a human being can only become what she or he already was. This tallies with the mechanistic-deterministic conviction of early twentieth-century science, but it does not leave much room for therapeutic hope.

Lacan not only distances himself from this substantialized interpretation of the unconscious, he even subverts it: the unconscious is of the order of the "not-realised," the "unborn."[9] As a process, it is always situated at the border; in itself, it is a void, an abyss: "For what the unconscious does is to show us the gap through which neurosis associates with a real—a real that may well not be determined."[10] And even when this unconscious becomes realized, this always happens in a bungled, failed way. The unconscious formations are "impediments" (*achoppements*), "failures" (*defaillances*), the most typical characteristic of which is their temporal scansion: the unconscious opens and at once closes.[11]

With this theory, Lacan rewords the Freudian opposition between the unconscious as dynamic and the unconscious as the system *Ucs*. On the one hand, we have the unconscious formations, including the dream; on the other hand, we are facing the drive nucleus, the object a. His reworking stresses the peculiar relationship between these two: the unconscious formations are failures because they fail to grasp, to cover the drive in a complete way. They manage to signify the phallic part of the drive, but they fail with the nonphallic other part. That is the point at which Lacan introduces his famous theory of the not-all, which must necessarily escape classical analysis. Indeed, only the repressed part of the unconscious is strictly determined and can be analyzed. Lacan explains this idea of determination in his theory on the so-called automaton. The drive kernel is not determined. On the contrary, even—it belongs to tuchè, to chance, and operates in a causal way. These two levels are in continuous interaction with each other.

The automaton is the level easiest to understand. It concerns the network or chain of signifiers, in which the "pulsational function of the unconscious" is at work. The barred subject pops up and disappears under these signifiers, hence "the signifier represents a subject for another signifier."[12] At this level the subject is indeed determined by the Other, as Lacan demonstrates time and again with his theory of the unconscious as being structured like a language.[13] The automatic character of this determinism was masterfully demonstrated in his seminar on "The Purloined Letter," where he shows how the chain of signifiers is just that, a chain.[14] This is the level of the lawful prediction at which mechanistic science aims, and here one may be convinced of the omnipresence of determinism.[15] This brings us to the second level. The unwinding of the associative chain succeeds only to a certain point, something that Freud experienced repeatedly in his therapeutic work, from the "Studies on Hysteria" onward. The process of remembering succeeds only to a certain limit, at which point the chain stalls and reveals an abyss, a gap (SE XII, 97–108, 145–46). This is what Freud termed the "primal repressed," and what he also called the navel of the dream and the core of our being (SE V, 603; SE XIV, 146–58). It is at this point that the real ex-sists outside the phallic order, the real in the sense of that part of the drive that cannot be assimilated by the phallic chain of signifiers. Hence the always-missed encounter, which is due to the lack of a signifier as meeting point. It is Lacan who conceptualizes this radical lack with his theory of the object a and the not-all. This is also the level of pure causality, where determinism and predictability fail.

Thus considered, it becomes clear that the unconscious operates on two levels. On the one hand, there is the chain of signifiers with the lack between them (in Freudian terms, the repressed or dynamic unconscious). This is the level of the automaton, and concerns the ever-predictable phallic desire. Underlying this chain, we find a more fundamental lack, which concerns the real, beyond any signifier (in Freudian terms, the primal repressed or system *Ucs*).[16] This is the level of the *tuchè*, of causality, where we are confronted with the other jouissance or the object a.

What is evident is that this opens up completely different perspectives on the subject of determinism. On the whole, Lacan is much more optimistic than Freud in this respect.[17] And this brings us to the last question: the aims and goals of the psychoanalytic treatment. My previous arguments have demonstrated that the core of the unconscious is itself not capable of being analyzed; it is only the repressed contents of the unconscious that lend themselves to the analytic process. The same reasoning can be applied on the level of the symptom. After Freud, symptoms were explained on the basis of defense, in which repression takes the prominent place. What is forgotten here is that repression in itself is already a secondary moment in the dynamics of pathogenesis. Indeed, repression is nothing but a coping mechanism that makes use of representational signifiers of the drive. Freud himself recognized a twofold structure within the symptom: on the one hand the drive, and on the other hand the symbolic.[18] The same reasoning goes for the dream as well—which is no surprise, since the dream itself is a symptom.

In the light of this twofold structure, every symptom has to be studied and treated in a double way. Following Lacan, dreams, phobic symptoms, even conversion symptoms come down to the formal envelope of the symptom; that is, they are the representational expressions of the real of the drive.[19] Thus considered, the symptom is a symbolic construction built around a real kernel of *jouissance*. The Real of *jouissance* is the ground or root of the symptom, while the symbolic concerns its phallic upper structure.

Both Freud and Lacan discovered that it is precisely this root of the symptom in the Real that obstructs therapeutic effectivity.[20] Analysis aims at the repressed part of the unconscious—the representational phallic system—and is powerless when confronted with the other *jouissance*. The very fact that today we are confronted with patients in whom repression is barely present implies a totally new challenge for psychoanalysis.

It is important to understand that these two levels are not separate in the manner of being opposed—in a binary opposition, for example. On the contrary: here we face a kind of fusion, with a situation that obliged Lacan to develop a whole new topology. This is expressed by his idea of the not-all, as elaborated in his *Seminar* XX. Freud expressed this beautifully in his metaphor concerning the impact of the somatic aspect: "[I]t is like the grain of sand around which an oyster forms its pearl" (SE VII, 83). Lacan speaks about the not-all and uses the metaphor of the jar, which illustrates the reasons why one can't spare oneself the trouble of an analysis. According to Lacan, the essence of making pottery does not reside in the raising of the sides of the jar, but in the hollow space that is created by these sides. The jar localizes the real within the symbolic. The resemblance to both the formation of a dream and the analysis of it resides in the fact that it is only through the elaboration and the analysis of the representational constellation that the Real of the drive appears. Or, to put it in Lacanian algebra, that the object a appears.

This object cannot be analyzed as such, nor can it be changed. Freud was rather pessimistic in this respect; he considered this level to be biological bedrock and spoke about interminable analysis. Lacan presents us with another solution. His theory on the object a acknowledges the impossibility of a final "full speech." The system *Ucs* remains unconscious and thus remains operative. Henceforth the aim of the treatment is not a final interpretation. The object a as such cannot be changed, but the position of the subject toward this object a can be revised.

In this way, Lacan presents us with the idea of a certain kind of identification, one based on a decision of the subject. Instead of the usual identification—the set of identifications with the Other—here the identification concerns the Real part of the drive, the part beyond phallic signification, and thus the identification here is identification with the symptom or the sinthome.[21]

Lacan describes this new subject, or this finally analyzed subject, as the subject that has made a choice for identification with the real kernel of its symptom or object a. To cite Lacan: "In what consists the sounding that is an analysis? Would it be— or not—to identify with one's symptom, albeit taking all the guarantees of a kind of distance?" "To know how to handle, to take care of, to manipulate . . . to know what to do with his symptom, that is the end of the analysis."[22]

NOTES

1. "The Neuro-Psychoses of Defence" (SE III, 60). It must be noted that Freud uses several denominations (energetic investment, instinctual power, pressure, quantitative factor, and, of course, libido). This impossibility of finding one denomination and one only testifies already to the fundamental difficulty of, to the impossible relation between, drive and representability.

2. For further discussion, see Paul Verhaeghe, "The Lacanian Subject: Causation and Destitution of a pre-Ontological non-Entity," in *Key Concepts of Lacanian Psychoanalysis*, ed. D. Nobus (London: Rebus Press), 164–89.

3. This idea of fixation does not solve the problem. On the contrary: closer study of the concept of "fixation" reveals that it contains both a somatic and a representational element, so the problem remains. Even in his most explicit discussion, Freud uses a strange word to denominate the psychological component of the drive: *Vorstellungsrepräsentanz*, "ideational representative" (SE XIV 14, 152–53). Lacan will meet the same difficulty. In the final part of his work he will develop a new theory on the "letter" as his way of understanding the primal fixation of the drive on the body.

4. I have discussed this evolution in Freud extensively in *"Does the Woman Exist?"* (New York: The Other Press, 1999), 123–48.

5. J. Lacan, "Fonction et champ de la parole et du langage en psychanalyse," in *Ecrits* (Paris: Seuil, 1966), translated by Alan Sheridan as "Function and Field of Speech and Language in Psychoanalysis," in *Ecrits: A Selection* (New York and London: Norton, 1977); *Le Séminaire, Livre XI, Les quatre concepts fondamentaux de la psychanalyse*, ed. J. A. Miller (Paris: Seuil, 1973 [Seminar of 1964]), translated by Alan Sheridan as *The Four Fundamental Concepts of Psychoanalysis* (Harmondsworth: Penguin, 1977); *Le Séminaire, Livre XXII: R.S.I.*, ed. J. A. Miller, in *Ornicar?* 3 (1975), 106–7 (see sessions of January 21 and February 18).

6. Paul Ricoeur, *De l'Interprétation* (Paris: Seuil, 1965), translated by Denis Savage as *Freud and Philosophy: An Essay on Interpretation* (New Haven: Yale University Press, 1975).

7. J. Laplanche and S. Leclaire, "L'Inconscient: une étude psychanalytique," in *L'inconscient*, ed. H. Ey (VIme Colloque de Bonneval) (Paris: Desclée de Brouwer, 1966), 95–130, translated by Patrick Coleman as "The Unconscious: A Psychoanalytic Study," *Yale French Studies* 48 (1977): 118–75 .

8. Lacan, *Four Fundamental Concepts*, 16–64.

9. Ibid., 22–23, 128.

10. Ibid., 22, my translation. In the published translation, the French "la béance par où la névrose se raccorde à un réel" is translated as "the gap through which neurosis recreates a harmony with the real." The whole point of Seminar XI comes down to the demonstration that any harmony with the real is lost forever, so the official translation is wrong. With this idea, Lacan associates himself with an almost forgotten part of Freudian theory, namely the fixation of the drive, which implies that the body is decision-making instance. See Paul Verhaeghe and Frédéric Declerck, "Lacan's Analytic Goal: Le Sinthome or the Feminine Way," in Luke Thurston, ed., *The Symptom* (London: Rebus Press, 1999).

11. Lacan, *Four Fundamental Concepts*, 25. It is important to understand that this always failing realization does not take place against a hidden (because unconscious) background of totality or unity. On the contrary, the background is never there. Lacan summarizes this subversion with a pun on the "un" of unconscious: "Let us say that the limit of the 'Unbewusste' is the 'Unbegriff'—not the non-concept, but the concept of lack" (26). I remember having read

somewhere in Freud the uttering of the question about whether the latent dream thoughts do really exist, or if we have to consider them as essentially absent, meaning that the dream analysis is an attempt to construct an originally failed process.

12. Ibid., 157.

13. See Lacan, *The Seminar, Book VII: The Ethics of Psychoanalysis* (Seminar of 1959-60), ed. J. A. Miller, trans. D. Porter (New York and London: Norton, 1992), 32, 44–45.

14. See Lacan's "Seminar on 'The Purloined Letter'" of 1956, trans. J. Mehlman, *Yale French Studies* 48 (1972): 39–72. This translation does not contain Lacan's three appendices to his original paper: "Presentation of the sequel," "Introduction," and "Parenthesis of parentheses." For these texts, see Lacan, "Le séminaire sur 'la lettre volée,'" in *Ecrits* (Paris: Seuil, 1966), 11–61.

15. For "efficient cause," see Aristotle, *Physics*, trans. W. Charlton (Oxford: Oxford University Press, 1970), 198a.

16. What is this real all about? Seminar XI is quite clear on this point. The real beyond the signifier, functioning as cause, is drive-ridden, and this is why Lacan took the drive as his starting point. With this aspect of the real any meeting is always a failed one, because there is no signifier. In the course of his teaching, Lacan enumerated the various imaginary elaborations of the real: The Other of the Other, the Sexual Relationship, The Woman, all of which are summarized in the notation of the barred Other. For "the Other of the Other ," see Lacan, "The Subversion of the Subject and the Dialectic of Desire in the Freudian Unconscious," *Ecrits: A Selection*, 311; for the "Sexual Relationship" and "The Woman," see Lacan, *Le Séminaire* livre XX: *Encore*, 35, 68.

17. "It is always a question of the subject *qua* indeterminate" (Lacan, *Four Fundamental Concepts*, 26).

18. This is clearly present in Freud's first case study, of "Dora." Here Freud does not add to his theory on defense, which had already been elaborated in his two papers on the psychoneuroses of defense (SE III). It can be said that the core of this case study is precisely a matter of this twofold structure, as Freud here focuses on the real, drive-related element, what he denominates as the "Somatisches Entgegenkommen." Later, in *Three Essays,* this will be called fixation of the drive. From this point of view, Dora's conversion symptoms can be studied from two sides: a symbolic one, which concerns the signifiers or psychical representations that are repressed; and a real one, related to the drive, here the oral drive.

19. Lacan, "De nos antécédents," *Ecrits*, 66.

20. Thus it is not a matter of surprise that Lacan considers the drive to be central in what he calls Freud's will. Indeed, after fifty years of clinical practice, Freud's conclusion can be summarized as follows: It is the drive that decides on the lasting success of the treatment, and this is precisely the reason for his pessimism. See "Analysis Terminable and Interminable," SE XXIII, 224ff. The same evolution can be discovered in Lacan's work. The early Lacan will focus on the Symbolic and the Imaginary, but from Seminar XI onward, the Real and the drive come to the fore of his attention. Nevertheless, Lacan will present us with another solution, beyond Freud's pessimism.

21. The fixations, considered by Freud as primary symptoms, are for Lacan of a general nature. It is the symptom that defines mankind, and, as symptom, this cannot be rectified or cured. That is Lacan's final conclusion: *there is no subject without a symptom.* In his last conceptualizations, the idea of the symptom receives a new meaning. What is at issue is a purified symptom, one stripped of its symbolic component parts. This is precisely the part of the symptom that ex-sists outside the unconscious considered as structured as a language. Here what is

at issue is the object a or the drive in its pure form. See Lacan, Seminar of 1974–75, "R.S.I.,"
Ornicar? 3 (1975), 106–107. The real of the symptom, or the object a, demonstrates the particular *jouissance* of the real body of this particular subject. Lacan prefers the idea of symptom
to that of the object a because of his thesis that there is no sexual relationship. If there is no normal sexual relationship as such, every relationship between sexual partners is a symptomatic
one. As a result, the analytic treatment, in its final phase, has to focus on this analyzed, denuded
version of the symptom. We must stress the fact that this identification with the symptom does
not come down to surrender. On the contrary, surrender is an expression of impotence, and
thus would qualify the attitude toward the symptom as one of belief. Thus the failure would be
considered as isolated and individual, and the conviction would persist that other people—that
the Other has succeeded in installing such a sexual relation. This is not the case for the subject
that has identified with its symptom and who has verified—during his analysis—that the failure
of the sexual relationship is not a matter of individual impotence, but of structural impossibility. The analysis has made clear that the essence of the subject—"son être de sujet"—is situated
at the place of the lack of the Other, at that place where the Other does not provide us with an
answer. The analysand has experienced the fact that the subject is "an answer of the Real," and
not "an answer of the Other." See Lacan, "L'étourdit," *Scilicet* 4 (1973), 15.

22. "En quoi consiste ce repérage qu'est l'analyse? Est-ce que ce serait, ou non, s'identifier,
tout en prenant ses garanties d'une espèce de distance, à son symptôme?" "Savoir faire avec, savoir
le débrouiller, le manipuler . . . savoir y faire avec son symptôme, c'est là la fin de l'analyse." Lacan,
Le Séminaire 24: "L'insu que sait de l'une bévue, s'aile a mourre," *Ornicar?* 12/13 (1977), 6–7.

10. Is Lacan Borderline?

Judith Feher-Gurewich

One hundred years after *The Interpretation of Dreams,* Freud's discovery of the unconscious continues to sap the comfort of our received notions on love, desire, reproduction, violence, and death. Freud's unconscious is a seductive delinquent, always on the go, tracking down desire and its infinite partial objects. Oblivious to debts, to logic and justice, it moves steadily toward death in search of the intervention of a father figure in front of whom it refuses to yield. No wonder that, among Freud's epigones, Lacan stands quasi-alone to plead for that which defies the proper functioning of the law of social and economic exchange. But if Lacan defends the motivations of the unconscious and has fought long and hard for the probation of the Oedipal fantasy and its representation in the dream-work, many of his fellow psychoanalysts, especially colleagues on the other side of the Atlantic, have declared the Oedipal complex a quasi-obsolete historical phenomenon. Consequently, they have reverted to a pre-Freudian vision of psychic functioning, according to which the dream-work must necessarily be reduced to mere affective states, referring more to anxiety and narcissistic wounds than to the complex relation between the incestuous wish and its prohibition. The effect of this shift brings to the fore either the real of neuro-psychiatry or the imaginary relation between analyst and analysand.

It is as if the unconscious would only speak of the vicissitudes of desire in French, while the pathologies of psychic life have found, in the official language of science or pseudo-science, the means to circumvent the return of the repressed. If I single out American psychoanalysis, it is mainly because it appears to have rejected Freud's discovery, while at the same time keeping the psychoanalytic institution alive. In this sense, Lacan and American psychoanalysis are at opposite extremes: on the one hand, the ethics of desire and an unshakable allegiance to the name of the father, and on the other hand a rejection of the Oedipal fantasy, but also a tolerance for social change matching American psychoanalysis's call for adaptation.

I would like to believe that attempting a rapprochement between these two extremes speaks directly to the question that occupies us today, namely the status of psychoanalysis a hundred years after Freud encountered the psychic reality of the Oedipal drama in his own dream. Psychoanalysis is not a school of thought—Freudian, Lacanian, Kleinian, Kohutian—but is rather a practice that permits us to detach the workings of the unconscious from the intentions and aspirations of the conscious ego. Since Freud, many psychoanalysts have had ideas about how to revise his original discovery. All of them have been sincere in their belief that their own approach would better serve the direction of the cure, and most of them indeed have had something useful to contribute. But breaking through theoretical divides, or even political and ideological differences, is rarely at the forefront of analysts' preoccupations. They are caught in the comfort zone of their theoretical and institutional framework, and therefore offer a deaf ear to any theoretical or clinical approach that contradicts their own.

There are, of course, many good reasons for the present "dialogue de sourds" that is pervasive in the psychoanalytic milieu. On the one hand, we have the Lacanians, who apparently refuse to think in terms of adaptation, of affects, of parental deficiencies, of good behavior, and therefore appear to themselves as having been saved from the traps of normativity and the orthopedics of good intentions. These are among the chosen people, who have successfully broken down the divide between good and evil. The unconscious speaks directly to them and it is in its name that they will condemn whatever social formations seem to contradict the good functioning of the Oedipus complex and the desire it produces. Because they have the inside story—and have gone through the Lacanian Seminary on top of that—they set themselves above their critics and are therefore extremely vexed when they are accused of preaching a return to what appears to be traditional family values. When they are pushed too far by radicals of all sorts, whether feminists, queers, or even American therapists, they pull out their secret weapon, the ultimate proof of their anti-conventionalism, of their profound allegiance to the truth of desire: the formula of sexuation, or the rather mysterious and unfathomable feminine *jouissance*, which only a few, a very happy few, have been invited to encounter. The conversation then stops, since Lacan's "not-all" is neither a proper diagnostic category, nor is it perceived as an effect of postmodernity on the vicissitudes of psychic life. On the other side of the Atlantic, psychoanalysis, which sits firmly on the side of a good fit between the individual and his social milieu, has long since given up on the Oedipus complex and its vicissitudes, and it is therefore free, to a certain extent, to observe the new psychic effects of postmodernity without being encumbered by the complexities of Freudian theory. Psychoanalysis in America started as a medical science and has never left the auspices of psychiatric nosography.

If social change has modified the classical definition of good behavior by including within it the various effects of the sexual revolution, it nonetheless remains to a certain extent wedded to the suture of science. In this sense, psychoanalysis only defends the course of human desire as long as it remains at the service of the social order. But since the social order has reworked the definition of good and evil, at the end of the day, American psychoanalysis appears paradoxically more liberal than its Lacanian counterpart, which deplores the effects of social change on the good life. This is not to say, however, that American psychoanalysis is better equipped to define the terrain of its transmission. Its contribution seems to consist in having understood that the psychiatric formulations that have informed its teachings are now obsolete. It has discovered, for better and for worse, that hysteria and perversion have given way to borderline and narcissistic disorders because, as Kohut points out, the effects of shame have replaced the neurotic effects of guilt. Social change has a direct impact on the formations of new pathologies, and therefore the Freudian model no longer holds. New therapeutic approaches need to be invented in order to face the new challenges of the actual.

So, for American psychoanalysis, there has been a shift both in theory and practice: new diagnoses have forced new therapeutic approaches. The borderline and narcissistic disorders reveal that something in the relation between the subject and its milieu has changed, and that this transformation affects psychoanalysis and its transmission. The problem with the American approach is that, by focusing on the maladies of the ego, which it considers to be central in the new pathologies, it leaves behind the relation of the unconscious to the *object a* or the Oedipal fantasy. On the other hand, the problem with the Lacanians is that they perceive social change as detrimental to the symbolic function, and in that sense they refuse to a certain extent to reevaluate the foundations and applications of their theory.

Yet to assure the transmission of psychoanalysis, it is paramount to define a terrain that would allow for a dialogue between different schools and different clinical approaches. Something of our analytic experience must be amenable to translation. All psychoanalysts will certainly agree that, through the transference, something of the unconscious is bound to appear so as to allow a psychic shift in the patient to occur. After all, it is through their own transferential experiences that people such as Kohut and Kernberg, both originally classical Freudian analysts, have come to decide that new pathologies are in the making. Yet their suggestions for the treatment of these patients remain deeply imbedded in a concept of transference that Lacanians would call imaginary. At the same time, their work is not unproductive and their clinical results cannot be simply attributed to a simple strengthening of narcissism; something of the unconscious must have been heard, otherwise they would not have convinced so many clinicians of the value of their contributions. But from the way Americans describe their cases, we get the distinct feeling that the Freudian unconscious cannot breathe under so many resistances, defenses, and aggressions; that the analytic space is filled by the ego and its deficiencies, placing the analyst either in the slot of the law (Kernberg) or in the slot of the positive self object (Kohut).

The cleft between American and Lacanian psychoanalysis does not only reveal a cultural divide between two radically different ideologies or visions of the world. The unconscious feeds on the super-ego, both maternal and paternal, which in turn both affirms and undermines the symbolic function, which finds its support in social ideals, whatever they may be. But to bridge the gap between Lacan's defense of the ethics of desire (which seems to exclude social change and its effects on narcissism) and the American condemnation of the Freudian unconscious (in the name of science and social adaptation), one must move beyond this theoretical and ideological divide and ask a straightforward clinical question: underneath the aggressive defense mechanisms of the borderline patient, do we not discover a classic structure of desire, whether hysterical, phobic, obsessional, or perverse? And further: can we acknowledge that social change has indeed affected our classical psychoanalytic models, and that therefore Lacan's contribution needs to be revised? Or that these new pathologies, namely the narcissistic and borderline disorders, which have helped cause the downfall of Freud in the United States (and which contradict the importance of the Oedipus complex) have shed, paradoxically, a different light on the clinical relevance of one of Lacan's most apparently abstract contributions to psychoanalysis, the formula of sexuation and his strange statement that woman is not-all, regarding her inscription in the symbolic order?

Such an unlikely rapprochement might, with hope, break down a false dichotomy within the psychoanalytic world and thus allow Freud's revolutionary discovery to return refreshed onto the psychoanalytic scene. As the talking cure has amply demonstrated, resistance and obedience are often the flip side of each other. To resist psychoanalysis may actually be more instructive than to surrender blindly to its teachings, as we see is done every day in our psychoanalytic circles. Wouldn't the value of Freud's ideas best be recognized if Lacan's insights could be discovered in the very folds of America's resistance to the power of the unconscious? What better way to assure the transmission of psychoanalysis than to let the borderline phenomenon push American psychoanalysis straight into Lacan's arms?

Therefore I would like to suggest that borderline and narcissistic disorders might lose their antisocial characterization so well described by Kernberg—in other words, their bad reputation—if their peculiar behavior could be understood within the Lacanian cartography, as a certain inability to rely fully on an unconscious fantasy thanks to which our neurotic construction of the world can be supported. Hence I would suggest that patients manifesting such phenomena are not-all inscribed in the world of phallic signification. In other words, the Oedipal fantasy does not cover over completely the lack in the symbolic order; and this in turn causes these patients to confront head-on the arbitrary and therefore nonsensical nature of the social order. So what appears in the psychiatric nosography as evil behavior is, in fact, an attempt to fence off the threat of the meaningless nature of social interaction. Such an approach might also offer us a better understanding of how the world appears when the *object-a*-cause-of-desire cannot support the necessary distortions that make life meaningful. Bringing Lacan's concept of the "not-all" together with those of borderline and narcissistic disorders not only offers new therapeutic strategies, but also brings Lacan's mysterious and quasi-mystical notion of feminine *jouissance* down to the painful reality of psychic suffering.

For those who are less familiar with Lacan, let me try to explain in a few words what I understand by his idea of feminine *jouissance* and his famous dictum that "the woman is not-all."[1] Basically, Lacan's crucial contribution to Freud's discovery lies in his attempt to break down the fundamental deadlock that led Freud to declare that, because he could not figure out what a woman wanted, he felt unable to move beyond the bedrock of castration and therefore could not find the secret formula to resolve the transference and bring analysis to a close. What Lacan explains is that to a certain extent Freud himself was trapped in the Oedipal fantasy because he believed an answer could be given to the enigma of femininity. Thus Freud himself could not see that what he had thus discovered was in fact the limit of psychoanalytic knowledge. There is no mystery beyond castration anxiety and penis envy. Instead there is a hole. The system of phallic signification of language, of science, of social interaction falls short in offering the ultimate answer to the enigma. The system in which we are inscribed as human beings does not include an explanation either of its origin or of its function. Beyond the fantasy we create as desiring subjects, there is no secret meaning to be revealed. But this fantasy, or *object a*, is the best we have to assure the good functioning of desire.

But Lacan also says (and I am simplifying to the extreme) that there are some people—more often women, but not necessarily—who are not-all protected or directed by this unconscious fantasy, which would plug the hole in the symbolic order. Something of their drive or their body is left, so to speak, open to receive a peculiar non-message from the place in the Other that is barred. The way I understand this is that the "not-all" neurotic self of such beings—because these patients are not psychotic, which of course is the most interesting characteristic of borderlines—has a way of being involved in the world that is peculiar: something of the realm of illusion has been punctured. These people see the world without the glasses of neurotic distortions. Yet this highly metaphysical approach to human existence is not experienced outside the narcissistic boundaries of the ego. It is the ego that bears the brunt of the relation of the body to the hole in the symbolic order. In this sense, feminine *jouissance* enters into the realm of diagnosis if we agree to say that in psychoanalysis the term *diagnosis* can only be read as a name for a certain psychic position appearing within the transferential relationship. Therefore we can expect (and here I think are the contributions of Kernberg and Kohut) that borderline patients are prone to experience the transference as particularly taxing on the boundaries of the ego, and therefore that they present a symptomatology that cannot be qualified as purely neurotic.

As Kernberg points out, these patients have enormous narcissistic issues, even though they appear on a purely social level to be particularly well adapted—on the surface—to the demands of their surroundings. This is what Kernberg says about borderline disorders:

> Direct exploitativeness, unreasonable demandingness, manipulation of others without consideration or tact are quite noticeable. These patients may feel superficially quite insecure, uncertain, and inferior in regard to their capacities or dealings with others. These feelings of insecurity and inferiority may be in part a reflection of the more realistic aspects of their evaluation of their relationships to significant others, work, and life in general, and often reflect a realistic awareness of some of their shortcomings and failures. Yet on a deeper level feelings of inferiority often reflect defensive structures. It is striking when one finds so often underneath that level of insecurity and uncertainties omnipotent fantasies and a kind of blind optimism, based on denial, which represent the patient's identification with primitive all good self and object images.[2]

The narcissistic disorders are not far from this either. Kernberg says, "It is as if they feel they have the right to control and possess others and to exploit them without guilt feelings—behind a surface which very often is charming and engaging one senses coldness and ruthlessness. Very often such patients are considered to be dependent because they need so much tribute and adoration from others; but on a deeper level they are completely unable actually to depend on anybody because of their deep distrust and depreciation of others."[3]

Let us not be too judgmental of Kernberg's own judgmental perspective. We are all susceptible to coming up with similar descriptions of our patients, especially when we have become the objects of their scorn. But we may also choose to think that, since Kernberg has not read Lacan, his ignorance of psychoanalysis proper has led him to confuse classic neurotic structures of desire with narcissistic and borderline disorders. This is precisely the kind of reaction I find counterproductive if the survival of psychoanalysis remains our principal focus and interest. It may be more productive to give Kernberg the benefit of the doubt (after all, he was trained in Argentina and Kohut was trained in Vienna!). It may be more productive to think that the effects of modernity on the psyche (in which I include the particular effects of American life, including the vicissitudes of emigration) need to be elaborated further.

Although it was not Lacan's intent to apply the concept of the "not-all" to a new psychic position that may be related to the effects of modernity (his own tendency was more to look on the side of perversion), this does not mean, a generation later and on a continent once removed, that such a connection cannot be made.

As always, it is my clinical practice that permits forays into theory. Probably due to the fit between the patient I shall describe and myself, certain circumstances in the following account do not quite resemble Kernberg's description. Thus, in my presentation of the following case material, I leave it to your imagination, and to the fact that this patient had abandoned several previous therapies, to make the connections between the profile of this patient and those of narcissistic or borderline disorders.

An intelligent and insightful young woman—herself clearly a femme fatale for men, extremely successful in her work, highly regarded by her male friends, adored by her husband—came to see me because she felt invisible to others and to herself. It is not that she was clueless, but that she experienced herself as only partly inscribed in a world where people appear to know what they want. While she is dimly aware of the fascination she exercises on men, in turn she is not quite sure whom she desires and why. While sex is for her a source of pleasure and curiosity, she is not particularly invested in uncovering the mysteries of erotic desire.

Her *jouissance* seems located elsewhere—but in an elsewhere that divests her of any possibility of giving an appropriate libidinal charge to the objects surrounding her. Everything is the same. Although she is a fairly good judge of character and situations, she can never tell if she likes one person more than another; if she should adopt a child or have her own; if she should live in one place or another. Despite her efforts, she cannot find, in the phallic order, the means to situate herself in relation to others.

By being in part excluded from the phallic order, my patient attempts to discover its meaning, yet fails to discover the order of things. More remains equal to less. Her father's small business, where she worked as a child, is for her of the same magnitude as the big corporation of which she is a director. In other words, she cannot appropriately translate one situation into another. If she is given a project, and her secretary forgets to photocopy a document, she does it herself, working late hours as if the question of hierarchy in her company had no impact on who does what. Unlike the hysteric, who would readily transgress the law, my patient focuses on the task at hand and does whatever needs to be done, assuming that if she is not heard it is because she is invisible and therefore there is nothing she can do about it. Because of her intelligence, efficacy, and charm, she is respected by her superiors, yet she never takes credit for work well done. Her job is her job: not to do it well is not an option. She can identify with her project, yet she cannot fully occupy the position of power the project grants her. Her metaphysical evaluation of the metaphors we live by puts a strange and interesting spin on our own system of values. But she cannot enjoy—in the phallic sense— the originality of her perspective. For her, society operates according to arbitrary laws, and the best she can do is to learn them "by heart." When she encounters a law she does not recognize, she fills in the gaps with the set of received notions she has at her disposal—spending hours photocopying papers, for example, since she cannot figure out why her secretary did not comply with her request. For her to ask the employee why is not an option.

As the analysis progresses, she discovers slowly that what fascinates her in our work is my deep interest in the ways her unconscious operates. She discovers that what she wants is the analytic process itself. The desire of the analyst becomes for her a space in which this other *jouissance*—the *jouissance* of the lack in the other—can be accepted. The analyst's desire becomes a support that allows her to discover, bit by bit, the links between signifiers and the strange beauty they radiate. It is crucial here to introduce the notion that Lacanian analysis is predicated not on the well-being of the patient per se, but on the analyst's desire for the emergence, in the transference, of the unconscious fantasy that causes the dialectic of desire. Yet because such fantasy provides the illusion that castration can be avoided, the neurotic classically resists the analytic process in the sense that he or she believes that the rule of free association is at the service of the realization of the fantasy, thus refusing to entertain the possibility that this fantasy is precisely what needs to be disposed of.

For my patient, however, transference is not structured according to the parameters of the neurotic. I do not possess the secret combination of her desire, because her unconscious fantasy is not the predominant cause of her psychic structure. As she discovers the chain of her unconscious signifiers through my desire for their appearance in the transference, she is given a status she did not experience before. For the first time she discovers who she is, not at the level of her fragile ego, but at the level of the signifiers that have constituted her as a subject of language.

Recently she told me that the stewardess on a flight she takes regularly for her job recognized her, and that when she got to Avis to rent her usual car, instead of getting it herself in the lot, the agent saw her and drove the car to her. She said to me, "I realize that I am no longer invisible." The more meaningful recognition she had gotten in her life, including a big promotion at work, could not match the beauty of being recognized by mere strangers. My patient as "not-all" found, through the desire of the analyst, the means to give a more bearable orientation to her other *jouissance*. She reached a psychic position that made more visible those aspects of her life that are usually indifferent to us common folk, who are trapped in the vicissitudes and rewards of phallic *jouissance*.

I was presenting this patient to an American colleague, whose clinical acumen I trust deeply, and who surprised me when she suggested that this patient was a classic borderline case. After being somewhat baffled by her reaction, I realized that the turn the transference had taken had protected me from being the target of her narcissistic fragility. It is interesting to note, by the way, that Kernberg specifically says that a good match between a borderline and his analyst is crucial for a positive outcome of the treatment.[4] After all, it would not have been difficult to fail the test, to have entered into an imaginary deadlock with her. I must have been so intrigued by the ways this woman described the minute details of the vicissitudes of everyday life that I was able to keep, without consciously knowing it, a strong symbolic position in the transference. I remember that once I made her wait for over ten minutes, and she left and came back twenty minutes later. She told me that if she was so unimportant to me, she was not going to stick around because if she was invisible to me, there would be no point to the analysis. I reacted quite spontaneously by saying that lately I had been late too often, that I was going to try to make an effort, and that she was right to be upset. But I also said that we should use my mistake to her advantage, so that she could come to understand how her perception of the circumstances led her to dismiss my lack of punctuality and only concentrate on her being unimportant. She was able then to retrace other circumstances of the same sort. By keeping my lateness as a fact against which she could test how she lacked the necessary symbolic space to be able to wait and be angry at the same time (she had actually left, gone for a walk, and come back) gave her the means to begin to read the world slightly differently. It was after this episode that she got a raise and a promotion at work. Recently she pushed the experiment further by quitting her job and trying to live for a while without the protective identity it had provided.

Another aspect of what I realized, after the fact, could be perceived as a borderline characteristic had to do with the importance of competition in her life. She was for a while very competitive with a woman friend, a repetition of her childhood experience when she was jealous of her younger sister's privileged relation with her mother. To see this competition as a signifier, rather than as an effect of the mirror stage, was also helpful because it shed some light on the paradoxical position of the father in the family. Feeling competitive operates as a border against feeling invisible, yet at the same time it leaves her confronted with a profound sense of disarray because she does not want to have or be what the other has or is. It confuses her totally. In fact, competition with another woman never has a man as an object, but rather the vision of a woman's envy. She envies the possibility of feminine envy. In this case, she envied her friend's envy of a necklace the friend could not afford. In other words, she envies hysterical desire, and in this way she is confronted with the fact that she lacks it. She suffers from lack in the strict sense of the word. The work we have been doing has been to capitalize on the signifiers that circle around the lack in the symbolic and to take advantage of the knowledge that her peculiar position provides her, instead of thinking that this "knowledge" is the proof of her inadequacy. In other words, every time the space she occupies begins to shrink, the focus of our discussion turns to the circumstances that lead her to feel that way. Invariably she discovers that a signifier has been missing in order to make sense of the world around her. In the process, something of her physical presence is called into question, and she feels she does not have permission to inquire either within or without so as to figure out what is happening. Instead she dies inside, feeling herself to be at the mercy of an unknown that is not the *jouissance* of the Other, but rather the lack of such a *jouissance*. There is nothing there.

A story she told me gave me a clue to the origin of this feminine *jouissance* that plagues her, and this in turn gave us a better sense of the paradoxical position of her father in relation to phallic power. When she was seven years old, she went with her family on a guided tour of an old American village, during which, in front of each house, she saw a boot scraper. Since she did not know what it was, she asked the male tour guide, who did not answer. She asked again and again, so eventually someone on the tour explained to her what a boot scraper was and she was very pleased. When she

came home her father screamed at her for having humiliated the tour guide and exposed his ignorance, which is something she should never do. She was very impressed
by her father's violent reaction and never forgot the lesson: what is incomprehensible
must remain so, otherwise the man collapses. She never ventured again onto the terrain where phallic knowledge could be questioned. While this experience certainly
helped her in her career, it also prevented her from wanting to plug the unknown with
a fantasy of how to get to that knowledge. For her, the desire to know can only reveal
the fragility of phallic signification. My patient understood too soon that, for her father,
castration was an irreparable wound, and that therefore she could not supplement it
as a classical hysteric would. If she could become the object of a man's sexual fantasy,
she never felt she could become an object of desire; it was as if she felt instinctively the
Real of the Other, but not the other's desire of the other. For her to relate to a man
meant to sleep with him and to act out his most secret sexual fantasy. Even if the man
felt in love with her, this never made any sense to her except on the level of sex.

Here we can see the thin line separating the not-all from the hysteric. The "not-
all" "knows," to a certain extent, that phallic signification is thwarted. Had her father
distinguished the tour guide from other men, no doubt she would have become a
hysteric, but he did not. Every situation that involved her desire brought back to her a
sense that something was impending; that the other is, by definition, always barred;
and that she needed to make do with her own resources, since the Other does not
have the answer. Thus her feeling of being invisible was the best defense against the
hole in the symbolic. Her analysis has brought her to the realization that she was right
all along to doubt the power of the other, and that she did not need to turn upon herself what she perceived as an outside truth. This gave her a sense of her own boundaries so that she no longer abandons herself to others by doing whatever they want
because she now knows that the narcissistic rewards she got (a short-lived sense of
power) failed to get her in touch with her desire. Yet each time she encounters it, her
desire appears to her almost by surprise: one by one, instance by instance, moment
by moment, and only partially predicated on the Oedipal fantasy or *object a*. In other
words, the objects of her desire are not obviously connected by a chain of signifiers.
Rather they seem to operate in discrete units, and when her punctual desire is satisfied, she does not experience, as we do, a sense of sadness or loss. Each experience
comes with a quota of gratification, but the next step is never readily available.

Of course I consider myself lucky to have found a patient who allowed me to
elaborate a potential link between borderline and "not-all." I shall never know whether
Kernberg would have perceived my patient as a typical borderline case. But my analyst-
friend's reaction had been enough to make me wonder if the hypothesis of the "not-
all" cannot help clinicians of all persuasions to think differently of their position in
the transference, given that what this entails is that it is not exclusively the place of
object a that they occupy. It seems to me, rather, that if analysts could understand that
the borderline symptomatology masks the nothing that interrupts the flow of phallic

signification, which in turn is sustained by the Oedipal fantasy, they would not be so tempted to push through the false self to the narcissistic defenses. Instead they would be able to explain these defenses not only by exposing the castration of the analyst, but also in reference to the metaphysical truth, which plagues the existence of the borderline. In a sense, such persons are right to doubt that the phallic order can provide all the answers, but they are wrong to believe that there is no knowledge on the side of castration. That knowledge is desire, yet desire is a dotted line—for them in particular. Their Oedipal fantasy cannot fully sustain the position they occupy in the world. Something of the real of their existence remains open, and this may cause a fundamental bewilderment at the place where the other is powerless to bring solace, since that other is, by definition, lacking.

While the history of the femme fatale though the ages has given us many examples of the fascination such borderline figures exercise on men, who find in these women the incarnation of mystery, the actual providers of such fascination can only derive limited pleasure from such a position of power. Their only resource is to discover, in the knowledge of their own castration, enough proofs that it is the Other, and not they themselves, who does not exist. In other words, the truth of psychoanalysis is in the symptom of the borderline.

Notes

1. Jacques Lacan, *Feminine Sexuality, Jacques Lacan, and the Ecole Freudienne*, ed. Jacqueline Rose and Juliet Mitchell, trans. Jacqueline Rose (New York: Norton, 1982), 151.

2. Otto Kernberg, *Borderline Conditions and Pathological Narcissism* (Northvale: Aronson, 1985), 5.

3. Ibid., 17.

4. Ibid., 150.

11. Dream Model and Mirroring Anxiety

SEXUALITY AND THEORY

Claire Nahon

Translated from the French with the help of
Alehé Mir-Djalali and Amanda Bay

Freud's *Interpretation of Dreams* is generally acknowledged to interrogate the very status of the sexual. Yet it is striking to observe that the psychoanalytic literature of the past fifty years virulently challenges the Freudian model—*Vorbild*—of the dream and the transference. We are actually witnessing a perplexing evolution characterized by the always more profound denial of the very essence of the Freudian discovery and its foundation—namely, the existence of the images created by autoerotic sexuality, i.e., the unconscious (infantile) images—*Bild[er]*—that shape the dream as well as the neurotic symptom, and even psychosis. Already in the preface to the first edition of *The Interpretation of Dreams*, Freud emphasizes the "theoretical value [of dreams] as a paradigm." Indeed, he writes, "Anyone who has failed to explain the origin of dream-images [*Traumbilder*] can scarcely hope to understand *phobias, obsessions or delusions* or to bring a therapeutic influence to bear on them" (SE IV, xxiii; my emphasis). Freud usually indicates the connection between dream images and all psychopathological formations—those "abnormal psychical phenomena" that interest him—and he clearly highlights their link to psychosis in the section of *The Interpretation of Dreams* dealing with "The Relations between Dreams and Mental Diseases":

> It is quite likely, on the contrary, that a modification of our attitude towards dreams will at the same time affect our views upon the internal mechanism of mental disorders and that we shall be working towards *an explanation of the psychoses while we are endeavouring to throw some light on the mystery of dreams.* (SE IV, 92; my emphasis)

This is what Freud actually writes, with all due deference to his detractors, who seem quick to challenge the Freudian heritage, to reduce it hastily to the neurosis model and to the vicissitudes of the Oedipus complex, and then to a sexuality that, no longer understood in its unconscious dimension, frequently becomes confused with genitality.

Yet such an evolution was predictable. Indeed, as far back as 1932, while preparing his "Revision of the Theory of Dreams," Freud is already compelled to deplore the striking decrease in references to the dream:

> Let us look through the volumes of the *Internationale Zeitschrift für (ärztliche) Psychoanalyse* [International Journal of (Medical) Psycho-Analysis], in which, since 1913, the authoritative writings in our field of work have been brought together. In the earlier volumes you will find a recurrent sectional heading "On Dream-Interpretation," containing numerous contributions on various points in the theory of dreams. But the further you go the rarer do these contributions become, and finally the sectional heading disappears completely. *The analysts behave as though they had no more to say about dreams, as though there was nothing more to be added to the theory of dreams* [*als wäre die Traumlehre abgeschlossen*]. (SE XXII, 7–8; GW XV, 7, my emphasis)

This statement is all the more noteworthy because, in this contribution, Freud precisely confers upon the theory of dreams an almost initiatory virtue, referring to it as a *"shibboleth,"* "the use of which decided who could become a follower of psychoanalysis and to whom it remained forever incomprehensible" (SE XXII, 7). Nevertheless, the very essence of the Freudian discovery has already begun to fade, whether due to a gradual dissolution, distancing, or misunderstanding. Thus the true foundation of psychoanalysis is overlooked, and what is preserved instead are its most superficial features, formulas that are, furthermore, truncated, misused, distorted. It is as if the advent of this inward gaze—so emblematic of the process at work in dreams and transference, as well as of all imaginative capability—could concern no more than a privileged few, the initiates of a "science" whose theory of dreams constitutes "what is most characteristic and peculiar" (SE XXII, 7), a true "turning-point," as Freud puts it, in the history of psychoanalysis. It is as if this inward gaze, no longer able to contemplate the eminently plastic images unfolding on the psychic stage,[1] had to drag down with itself, in its blindness, the sexual, unconscious truth that auto-erotism determines and which confers on the dream the paradigmatic value that Freud first glimpsed while watching the astonishing ballet of hysterical bodies.

During his stay in Paris as a fervent admirer and disciple of Charcot, Freud saw *Théodora* on stage (1885), and was, like his contemporaries, captivated by Sarah Bernhardt.[2] She performed with a wide variety of masks and embodied on stage, as in her own life, some of the most recurrent fantasies of her time: those dealing with the very essence of the difference between the sexes. Sarah Bernhardt was by turns the "golden voice" fascinating the crowd and the "great hysteric" exasperating her critics.

While performing both female and male parts, she highlighted the very uncertainty of the relations between sex and gender that Charcot underscored on his own stage at La Salpêtrière. This is the same uncertainty that the upcoming debate on bisexuality would attempt to resolve, and that Charcot tried to capture among other hysterical symptoms through highly visual, even photographic, procedures. Georges Didi-Huberman develops this idea at length in his *Invention de l'hystérie*, where he focuses on the inextricable link between hysteria and the gaze. He emphasizes the visual essence of the hysterical symptoms and the plasticity of bodies, which take on or lose shape at will, responding to an observing, suggestive, or demanding gaze. In Freud's words, Charcot "was, as he himself said, *a* 'visuel,' *a man who sees*. . . . He used *to look again and again* at the things he did not understand, *to deepen his impression of them* day by day, till suddenly an understanding of them dawned on him" ("Charcot," SE III, 12, my emphasis). As an heir to a medical tradition in which faith in observation is absolute, Charcot bears witness to this ever so exterior gaze, whose violence can appear extreme. He first pretends to let himself be overtaken by the disorderly and unworkable material, whereas in fact his gaze tolerates no secret, demanding full submission to its infinite power of organizing and classifying: "In his mind's eye the apparent chaos presented by the continual repetition of the same symptoms then gave way to order: the new nosological pictures emerged, characterized by the constant combination of certain groups of symptoms" (SE III, 12). This is what Freud writes, thus indicating that the alleged submissiveness to the phenomenon is pure artifice, that this eye that scrutinizes, hungry for understanding, is actually not willing to give up its power. Nevertheless Charcot's knowledge was rooted in seeing. And by means of photography he made the most out of "the figurative possibility to generalize the *case* into a *picture*," as Didi-Huberman puts it.[3] Indeed as an artist and a collector, Charcot called up the realistic virtues of photography and its absolute objectivity to capture the reality of nervous disorders. He could then refer to the "living pathological museum" he was creating.[4] In "directing" hysteria both theatrically and scientifically, Charcot was building an entity compelled to exist and move at will through a gaze: an entity that was to be exposed and exhibited on the stage of "this big optical machinery of La Salpêtrière," in Didi-Huberman's words, until the Master could theoretically and immutably frame its slightest (de)formations and *trans*formations.

The narrative of Emmy von N.'s treatment reveals that at the beginning of his practice, Freud remained attached to a similar perspective. During that time, he was convinced of the "external" etiology of hysteria, the trauma being considered as a foreign body—*Fremdkörper*—invading the internal space.[5] Nevertheless Freud unceasingly emphasizes the primacy of the visual sense, while insisting on the pathogenic character of the visions assailing his patient. Indeed, these images that haunt Emmy, far from being considered attributable to her own singular psyche—images emerging directly from her unconscious, "an autochthonous theory of oneself" (Pierre Fédida)— are, on the contrary, dedicated to destruction. For instance, Freud writes: "My therapy consists *in wiping away these pictures,* so that *she is no longer able to see them* before her"; "*I extinguished her plastic memory of these scenes*"; "I made it *impossible for her to see* any of these melancholy things again, not only by *wiping out her memories of them in their* plastic *form* but by *removing her whole recollection of them,* as though they had never been present in her mind."[6] Freud does not recognize yet, in Emmy's hallucinations, what he will conceive, in Elisabeth's cure, as a "secret": the return of the repressed.[7] Nonetheless, in its visual dimension the dream model is incipiently present. It will not fully appear until Freud takes into account the *sexual* etiology of hysteria, when he begins to cast an inward gaze on specific productions such as dreams and symptoms. Indeed, in *The Interpretation of Dreams,* when Freud emphasizes the regression at work in dreams, as is obviously the case in the inaugural Dream of Irma's Injection (and Lacan's commentary on this dream makes very explicit the paradigmatic vision of the "*informe*" [formless] as well as the *imaginary* "decomposition of the function of the ego," in the sense that the latter can no longer allow for the preeminence of consciousness or of the *person*[8]), when Freud discovers the eminently sexual nature of the therapeutic solution, through the trimethylamin formula, he continually insists on the plasticity of dream images. This plasticity is identical to that of hysterical symptoms, and transcends the anatomical difference between the sexes. It is the same plasticity that is ultimately rooted in the highly creative and transgressive nature of sexuality, a sexuality that is irreducible, in the unconscious, either to the concept of bisexuality—in the sense in which it is currently used—or to the opposition between masculinity and femininity. The "dream of dreams," which plays with unconscious vision in the extreme and which indeed is driven by it, diffracts viewpoints and subverts conscious optics ("We can see the series of egos appear," as Lacan declares[9]), revealing the unrepresentable itself, this mouth-throat-sex of Irma, terrifying in its state of decay, comparable to Medusa.[10] Thus the Dream of Irma's Injection not only represents this critical moment of the *mise en abyme* concerning the meaning of the dream on its own stage; it also represents the primacy of a gaze that no longer looks at an external object but is fundamentally concerned with the internal images it encounters. Here is Lacan's commentary: "Just when the hydra has lost its heads, a voice which is nothing more than *the voice of no one* causes the trimethylamine formula to emerge, as the last word on the matter, the word for everything. And this word means nothing except that it is a word."[11] This word is nevertheless inextricably connected to Fliess's hypotheses concerning human sexuality. Indeed, if the Dream of Irma's Injection appears foundational because it reveals the nature of the unconscious as well as the psychic ability to let mental images occur on the inner stage, the dream also illustrates the very nature of the transferential bond and the power of the word. As Lacan explains: "iS—imagining the symbol, putting the symbolic discourse into a figurative form, namely the dream. / sI—symbolising the image, making a dream-interpretation."[12] This word, which in itself means nothing, remains, however, what links Freud to Fliess and what establishes their relationship on the very basis of the sexual at the precise moment when the dream puts on stage the analyst's anxiety regarding the resistances of his patient, who is compelled to "open her mouth"!

Hence we realize that the Freudian *Vorbild* of the dream and of the transference is eminently sexual, and represents a model or prototype that allows an understanding of the mental images created by auto-erotism. Does not its signifying form—*Vorbild*—as well as its semantic content reveal the primacy of the image on the psychic stage, and, in this sense, the manifest interweaving of the sexual and the visual, the eminently visual nature of the sexual? In fact, we need to refer to the chapter of the *Three Essays on the Theory of Sexuality* dealing with "The Manifestations of Infantile Sexuality." Taking thumb sucking or sensual sucking—*Ludeln* or *Wonnesaugen*—as an example, Freud examines the nature of auto-erotism and shows to what extent the latter constitutes the fundamental moment of fantasy's emergence, the presence-absence of the nourishing object, the *hallucinatory* rhythm of the sexual object destined to disappear at the very moment it arises. What is emphasized here is not, as is often reductively assumed, that auto-erotism occupies the inaugural position upon which the first object relations are then grafted. Rather, Freud actually defines auto-erotism as an *après-coup* in which the sexual drive finds some appeasement through images: this is a hallucinatory moment *par excellence.* While attaching itself to the self-preservative drive, the sexual drive in fact occasions the moment where the nourishing object (milk) is at once lost in its reality and shifted onto, or subsumed by, the organ from which it comes. The breast, a part-object, thus becomes the sexual object, the object of an infinite tension—the object *a*, as Lacan calls it.[13] Sexuality appears this way, through a shift, in the inevitably hallucinatory quest for what is destined never to satisfy.[14] This is the destiny of sexuality that Freud recounts in the chapter of the last of the *Three Essays on the Theory of Sexuality,* which deals with "The Finding of An Object," in a passage that clearly reveals the Freudian meaning of *Vorbild,* because the image of the "child sucking at his mother's breast" is designated as prototypic—*vorbildlich*—of all love relations.[15] In this sense, Freud writes, "The finding of an object is in fact a refinding of it." Thus the *Vorbild* works as an idealized model, a preexisting image, which prefigures the destinies of sexuality: dream, being in love—*Verliebtheit*—transference. The verb form—*"(sich) vorbilden"*—stresses in one of its older senses the power of representation, of imagination; and it is not surprising that Freud refers to the *Vorbild* when he evokes the infantile in the dream or when he highlights the forthcoming effects of the first love object-choice. Unceasingly he underscores its visual characteristics, emphasizing the crucial fact that auto-erotism and the model it engenders—the model of the dream and of the transference—proceed from the necessary diverting of the organ. This is the way the self-preservative function is driven out by the sexual drive: lips kissing themselves, for instance, through the act of sucking, which "is determined by a search for some pleasure which has already been experienced *and is now remembered*" (SE VII, 181, my emphasis), or the eyes, which, when overexcited, are blinded to conscious images. That Freud, in a highly striking insight, qualifies as "*Vorbild*" the deformations of "the genital organ in its states of excitation" ("On Narcissism: An Introduction," SE XIV, 84) should not be surprising. Equivalent to the mouth-throat-sex of Irma, this organ, "that is in some way changed and that is yet not diseased in the ordinary sense," allows us to understand not only the libidinal cathexis at work in hypochondria, but more specifically the erotogenicity characteristic of every part of the body. And the dynamic, deformed image it offers—the image of a uniquely animated flesh—can be likened to the kaleidoscope that dream images make and unmake. Thus a veritable subversion is at work: It is the prerogative of a sexuality that only bothers with the organ the better to transgress it—flesh and psyche substituting for each other—and that thrives only by feeding itself the images it ceaselessly produces, unconscious formations located well beyond the anatomical difference between the sexes. The strategies of desire of Freud's "clever woman patient," the famous butcher's wife, are quite revealing. Freud remarks: "I saw that she was obliged to create an unfulfilled wish for herself in her actual life" (SE IV, 148). And the analysis of her dream clearly exposes the plasticity of the sexual identifications at work: "my patient put herself in her friend's place in the dream because her friend was taking my patient's place with her husband and because she (my patient) wanted to take her friend's place in her husband's high opinion" (SE IV, 150–51). Freud insists on the sexual community between these two women, while another identification appears— one that does not escape Lacan—namely the identification with the husband, who, although he usually "admires a plumper figure" (SE IV, 148), finds his wife's friend attractive in spite of her inability to satisfy him.[16] This "transgressiveness" of sexuality is pictured in the most explicit manner in the hysterical attack, which obeys the same rules of distortion and condensation as the dream (cf. "Some General Remarks on Hysterical Attacks," SE IX). Indeed it not only allows itself to be deciphered as does a dream, but it also exhibits the same plasticity that drives it, like the dream, to mock the anatomical yoke, while the body offers to the eye, without any mediation, the intimacy of fantasy. This is quite well illustrated by the hysterical woman mimicking desire and defense, in a scenography worthy of Charcot (cf. "Hysterical Phantasies and their Relation to Bisexuality," SE IX): she tears her dress away with one hand, while keeping her clothes against her body with the other one. A situation that Freud attributes to the bisexuality that was so extraordinarily subversive in his time, and could be qualified today as still too much attached to the representation of a normativity of sex and gender: "As the woman," "as the man"—this is the way Freud describes the hesitation of the patient. He thus remains in a fixed dichotomy probably still too far from the continuum that characterizes the unconscious: a passage, fluid and constant, from one sex, one gender, to another. This is the sexuality psychoanalysis is based on and deals with, a sexuality intrinsically linked to the visual. And it is precisely the *Bild* or the dream or the symptom that makes the psychic apparatus thinkable, by providing the *Vorbild* of its very functioning—this *Vorbild* being, as we know, paradigmatic not simply of neurosis, but rather of all psychopathological formations.[17] Its misrecognition leads straightaway to therapeutic deadlocks, as in the treatment of Dora and the young homosexual woman. If we fail to understand that the polymorphously perverse child of the *Three Essays on the Theory of Sexuality* and the hysteric are both emblematic of the fact that sexuality is not only irreducible to the genital sphere, but, on the contrary, is bound continually to transgress it, we might be heading for a blunder, which, if not dogmatic, at least ideological or normative, would lead us to think that Dora could not experience a homosexual love for Frau K., or that the homosexuality of the young woman was only due to a disappointment that turned her away from men. Hence any imagination of the sexual gets short-circuited.

The elimination of the sexual and its images in contemporary psychoanalytic thought seems to constitute a rejection of the visual dimension that characterizes the unconscious and gives access to its formations; that is a rejection of the singular dialect to which only regression gives access. In fact, an unfortunate confusion has spread for the last fifty years: it is as if the emphasis on the "new patients" had radicalized the opposition between the ego and the object to the point of making this opposition seem insurmountable, thus consecrating the idea that narcissism excludes otherness, whereas, as we know, even auto-erotism does not. Because the psychopathological descriptions of the patients presenting a borderline personality insist on the weakness of these patients' ego (with all that such a qualification implies with regard to manifestations of "lack of anxiety tolerance," "lack of impulse control," "lack of developed sublimatory channels," "primary-process thinking"), because these descriptions emphasize the poor quality, even the absence, of internalized object relationships, because they stress the diffusion of their identity and the pregenital level of their functioning,[18] these psychopathological descriptions may have contributed to splitting the field of identity even further from the field of sexuality, assimilating the latter to sexual behavior and inscribing it in a strictly developmental perspective. As a consequence of such a way of thinking, sexuality is deprived of the unconscious meaning that is its very essence and that prohibits confusing it with genitality,[19] unless the entire meaning of the Freudian discovery be misconstrued. How are we to understand that psychoanalysis has developed in such a manner that it virtually excludes from the cure the idea that the drive is at the very basis of psychic conflict and thus of the analytic process, that it clearly plays its role in the dynamics of desire? Should the acknowledgment that the "new pathologies" and especially the narcissistic personality disorders are based on more archaic mechanisms than those met in neurosis lead to the belief that there are nonconflictual zones in the psyche where no drive energy circulates?

Let us return to the source of these theoretical trends. In Hartmann's ego psychology, one discovers that the unconscious and its transgressive nature are hardly of interest. Rather, Freud's "biologizing" tendency here becomes radicalized, so that the scientific aspiration prevails over the "mytho-theoretical"—thus sexual—dimension that forms the essence of psychoanalysis. Here gender seems to proceed naturally from the anatomical difference between the sexes,[20] and the ego finally appears to be endowed with a *phallic* attractiveness. Many of the concepts developed by Hartmann appear to reject auto-erotic sexuality more and more blatantly, while the reference to reality is exalted. For Hartmann, indeed, psychoanalysis is expected "to become a general *developmental psychology*" and he holds it as "one of the basic sciences of sociology."[21] It is noteworthy that an allegiance to Freud is continually reaffirmed, and yet leads very subtly to the dismissal, to a kind of eradication of the sexual drives and their vicissitudes, by way of the magnified reference to the primacy of the ego and its functions. This almost orthopedic vision of psychoanalysis can then praise the "dominance of the ego," "ego strength," "ego control." In Hartmann's conceptualization, the prevailing role attributed to the ego is in fact ascribed to the very genesis of the ego, conceived of as an *autonomous* agency clearly separated from the id instead of being differentiated *out of* the id:

> I should rather say that both the ego and the id have developed, as products of differentiation, out of the matrix of animal instinct. From here, *by way of differentiation, not only man's special "organ" of adaptation, the ego, has developed, but also the id; and the estrangement with reality, so characteristic of the id of the human, is an outcome of this differentiation,* but by no means a direct continuation of what we know about the instincts of lower animals.[22]

Thus from Freud to Hartmann the emphasis has shifted: the human being, far from being considered as essentially dominated by the unconscious, the id, satisfying its requirements, as Freud puts it,[23] seems on the contrary ever more distant from the force of the drives, and constantly involved in an effort of mastery over them. And the exaltation of the ego, "a specific organ of learning and adaptation,"[24] goes with a will for desexualization, something Freud himself treats with more nuance. For Freud, as we know, "the character of the ego is a precipitate of abandoned object-cathexes and . . . it contains the history of those object-choices" ("The Ego and the Id," SE XIX, 29). And in Lacan's reading, as his thoughts on the mirror stage make clear, the ego results from the libidinal cathexis of the image, being thus the product of identifications. Furthermore, the sublimation to which Hartmann refers consists, in Freud's metapsychology, of the abandonment of the sexual aim, but not of the drive pressure, which remains the leading force of the process. Nevertheless, for ego psychology, sexualization—as well as aggressivization—seems basically conceived as a disturbing force that dooms neutralization to failure and threatens the autonomous factors of the ego. We thus understand that regression, far from being considered a privileged access to the unconscious with which the analyst works, represents, on the contrary, a remoteness from reality that implies the necessity of defensive recourse to secondary autonomy.[25] However, it is in a more subtle manner that ego psychology consecrates the evacuation of the drives from the psychoanalytic sphere, paving the way for the upcoming hegemony of narcissism understood as utterly opposed to the object and to otherness. And this is made possible by dividing the ego into the ego and the self, the self being the one of these entities to be invested with libido.[26] While stating that "the ego's capacity for neutralization is partly dependent on the degree of a more instinctual cathexis being vested in the self,"[27] Hartmann seems de facto to consecrate the truly narcissistic isolation of the ego—in the sense "narcissism" is currently used—which is then considered only from an intrasystemic point of view and is therefore stripped of all that connected it to the drives and to the unconscious.

In other words, we have a phallic narcissistic ego that ultimately corresponds to the ideal of scientificity so valued by ego psychology, which thus appears in search of a psychoanalytic technique diametrically opposed to the very meaning of *The Interpretation of Dreams*. Concern over this is developed by Pierre Fédida when, evoking "the difficulties inherent in the countertransference of the analyst" and the sense of the latter's identity, he wonders, on the basis of the Dream of Irma's Injection, "whether the theory of the 'borderline personality' grew in the favorable soil of ego psychology in order to constitute, simultaneously, its critical challenge and its doctrinal confirmation."[28] Borderline personalities would then be "fundamentally captives of the ideological crisis of analytic practice and the crisis affecting the theory of the regression of the ego."[29] Indeed the fragmentation of the ego in the dream reveals precisely what borderline patients let us see. We thus notice that the psychopathological descriptions of their being may actually refer to the idealized vision of a "normal" ego which would be stable and unitary. "We might even dare to conjecture that nothing is closer to the analyst's dream than the borderline personality!" as soon as the analyst ceases to believe in "the integrity of the therapeutic identity of [his] ego," as Fédida proposes.[30] The ego appears somehow *phallicized* by such a theorization, and this process gives rise, furthermore, to a "modernist clinical consciousness concerned with empathy" (Fédida), which refutes ego psychology's practical implications with a laudable therapeutic solicitude, but scorns the drives even more than ego psychology itself. It is as if this overvaluing of the ego made any imagination of the sexual impossible, while *unconsciously* keeping its most superficial feature: *the sexual polarity*. If Kohut's emphasis on the self indeed corresponds to a radicalization of the rejection of the drives and intrapsychic conflict;[31] if Oedipus is definitively opposed to Narcissus;[32] if the self consists of an asexual entity that emerges through empathic mirroring, in a symbiotic bond with an identical other, a self-object or idealized imago allowing for self-esteem to develop; and if the process of sexuation ultimately and magically occurs, shaped outside of conflict and through empathy;[33] then this rejection of unconscious sexuality has as its corollary the emphasis on the *maternal,* a clinical and *feminized* positioning that exalts the notions of holding and bearing, as well as the notion of receptivity to the other. Echoing the phallic attractiveness of the ego, this clinical practice highlights the maternal and feminine, namely self-psychology. In this way psychoanalysis meets a paradoxical fate: a theorization concerned with excluding the sexual unwittingly reintroduces it in a return of the repressed. Here it is as if the plasticity of infantile sexuality, irreverent as it is about sexual difference, had been deflected from its first

meaning and then given way to a true *sexuation* of the theory itself! And this is precisely the imagination of the sexual—the psychic (animistic) ability to create images—
as elaborated in *The Interpretation of Dreams,* namely the visual capacity to split ad
infinitum and to do so where least expected. In other words, even though the imagination of the sexual does not explicitly appear in the theorizations aiming to refute it,
it nevertheless emerges in the *hallucinatory* attempt to reflect on these theorizations,
namely in the "dream of interpretation" this chapter is dealing with.

The ability "to picture"—*das Zeichnen*—is dear to President Schreber: for him it
means the ability to have voluntary recourse to the soul's potentialities to imagine—
to shape images—so that they become visible to God's gaze. At the foundation of this
ability, Schreber refers to the "Ein*bild*ungskraft": The strength and power of creating
images,[34] among which is the "picturing" of female attributes on his body.[35] And
besides his own subjective sensations, we know that he expects irrefutable proof of his
metamorphosis into a woman through a mirroring reflection. According to Schreber,
his anatomical changes are such that everyone could henceforth confirm by looking
at him that he is indeed a woman, since his breasts have developed: "anybody who sees
me standing in front of a mirror with the upper part of my body naked would get the
undoubted *impression of a female trunk*—especially when the illusion is strengthened
by some feminine adornments."[36] Thus he appeals to an exterior gaze that would fit
the interiority of his own, like a shared hallucination or like an animistic temptation,
close to Nathaniel's imaginary capture induced by the doll Olympia in Hoffmann's
tale. This imaginary capture makes him go mad as soon as he confuses his inner world
and outer reality, as well as the woman in the flesh and the automaton with human
eyes: he is persecuted by an exacerbated visual sense, a vision that splits ad infinitum
(cf. "The Uncanny," SE XVII). In fact, this gaze upon Schreber's body, which plays on
the organ and subverts the real of sexual difference, also accounts for "the rapid
sequence of ideas in dreams" to which Freud refers, and which "is paralleled by the
flight of ideas in psychoses" (SE IV, 91). Here we approach the *mirroring anxiety—
Augenangst*—that characterizes the fleeting impression of *uncanniness* that often occurs
when encountering transsexual patients. There is an unavoidable visual disturbance
affecting anyone who emancipates himself from taxonomies and breaks with accepted
discourse—the sacrosanct splitting between sexuality and identity!—in order to listen
to these patients and be touched by their words. Who would deny that anxiety can
emerge from the inability to attach the words expressing the patient's pain to the body
that refutes them, from one's fascination with a suspended, always fleeting identity,
from the palpable sensation, as in a dream vision, of the flickering of the ego evoked
by Lacan in his reading of Freud's Dream of Irma's Injection? Schreber's body (an
object under God's gaze) and the transsexual's body (in the process of being transformed, hallucinated, imagined, or just watched) alike demonstrate the vanity of theories that ignore the extraordinary capacity of the psyche to continue producing unique
forms—unconscious forms subverting the male/female polarity. Such forms induce,

ultimately, a mirroring anxiety very similar to what one experiences in an anxiety dream and to the "*informe*" at work in dreams. "The possibility of creating composite structures stands foremost among the characteristics which so often lend dreams a fantastic appearance" (SE IV, 324), as Freud indicates. This is the very basis of psychoanalytic practice. It is utterly contradicted in those peremptory statements denying transsexuals any capacity for working through, since their wish for a sex-change opposes the traditional psychotherapeutic aim of curing the psychic by means of the psychic—as if such a fantasy were not typical of the human psyche! This is the model of the dream and the transference: the patient's speech touches us and, through regression, elicits unprecedented images in us. We are then compelled to imagine, for instance, that the transsexual patient illustrates—even more than Schreber does— the dream-work as soon as (s)he *literalizes* the dream image, casting the unconscious out of the enclosed space of the psyche and instead embodying it deeply in his/her flesh. Imagine, in a total subversion of conscious optics, that the flesh, in its animation, would substitute itself for the psyche: the better to restore the latter's plasticity. Such imagining is a way of not closing oneself to the transsexual's request, which, far from being only or merely a matter of identity, as it is so often read, expresses the vicissitudes of unconscious sexuality. Working with transsexual patients can inure one to their "uncanniness." Rather than suggesting that one has become more receptive to the other, more tolerant, this loss of the capacity to regress and imagine is perhaps a detrimental loss of the interlocutor's own *Einbildungskraft*. It may well signify the rejection of what fundamentally constitutes these patients and their extraordinary capacity to capture the gaze. In this sense this rejection could amount to the defensive preservation of the interlocutor's shaken sense of his/her own cohesion.

In short, gazing at Schreber's body, as well as at the transsexual's, would compel us to further examine the *emancipatory* and *transgressive* potentialities of unconscious sexuality—*trans-sexuality* as such—as well as to seriously consider the danger threatening psychoanalysis when it praises (masculine, feminine and even ego-based) imagos so as better to repress its very foundation, namely the dream.

NOTES

A first and shorter version of this chapter was presented in 2000 at "The Dreams of Interpretation/*The Interpretation of Dreams*" conference held in Minneapolis. The essay was revised and expanded in 2002 for the present volume. It is based on my prior experience as an in-hospital clinical psychologist working with transsexual patients who wished to have sex-reassignment surgery. For further and more recent developments on my understanding of trans-sexuality, see my article "La trans-sexualité ou l'en-dehors des formes (défiguration, déformation, déchirement)" in Claire Nahon, ed., *Cliniques méditerranéennes* n°74: "La trans-sexualité: défiguration, déformation, déchirement," *Érès*, Autumn 2006.

I also wish to thank John Brenkman for his help with the translation.

1. Freud clearly reproduces the plastic characteristics of the dream images in his presentation. Beginning with the "technique of dream-interpretation," he explains his choice as follows: "[I]t will present a more concrete appearance [*es wird plastischer ausfallen*] and make a more vivid impression on you." And his description of the characteristics of the manifest dream draws its very fluidity: "It may be coherent, smoothly constructed like a literary composition, or it may be confused to the point of unintelligibility, almost like a delirium; it may contain absurd elements or jokes and apparently witty conclusions; it may seem to the dreamer clear and sharp or obscure and hazy; its pictures may exhibit the complete sensory strength of perceptions or may be shadowy like an indistinct mist; the most diverse characteristics may be present in the same dream, distributed over various portions of it; the dream, finally, may show an indifferent emotional tone or be accompanied by feelings of the strongest joy or distress" (SE XXII, 10; GW XV, 9–10).

2. See Freud, *Correspondance 1873-1939* (letter to Martha Bernays, November 8, 1885), trans. A. Berman, J.-P. Grossein (Paris: Gallimard, 1979).

3. G. Didi-Huberman, *Invention de l'hystérie—Charcot et l'iconographie photographique de la Salpêtrière* (Paris: Macula, 1982), 33.

4. "Nous sommes, en d'autres termes, en possession d'une sorte de *musée pathologique vivant*, dont les ressources sont considérables." J.-M. Charcot, "Leçons sur les maladies du système nerveux," *Œuvres complètes* III, 3–4, quoted in "Appendice 1: Le 'musée pathologique vivant,'" in Didi-Huberman, *Invention de l'hystérie*, 275.

5. "But the causal relation between the determining psychical trauma and the hysterical phenomenon is not of a kind implying that the trauma merely acts like an *agent provocateur* in releasing the symptom, which thereafter leads an independent existence. We must presume rather that the psychical trauma – or more precisely the memory of the trauma—acts like a foreign body which long after its entry must continue to be regarded as an agent that is still at work" (*Studies on Hysteria*, SE II, 6). Also, see the analysis proposed by Monique Schneider in her "L'admission du 'corps étranger' dans l'espace interne," in *Monographies de psychopathologie*, "Les addictions" (Paris: Presses Universitaires de France, 2000), 133–46.

6. SE II 53, 58, and 61, my emphasis.

7. Here is what Freud writes about Elisabeth's "knowledge" of her suffering: "From the beginning it seemed to me probable that Fräulein Elisabeth was conscious of the basis of her illness, that *what she had in her consciousness was only a secret and not a foreign body*" (SE II, 138–39, my emphasis). Such a remark clearly indicates that "foreign body" is actually related to what does not belong as such to the field of consciousness, that it refers in fact to the source of psychic conflict.

8. See *The Seminar of Jacques Lacan II: The Ego in Freud's Theory and in the Technique of Psychoanalysis*, ed. J. A. Miller, trans. S. Tomaselli, with notes by J. Forrester (1954–55; Cambridge: Cambridge University Press, 1988).

9. Ibid., 165.

10. "The phenomenology of the dream of Irma's injection led us to distinguish two parts. The first leads to the apparition of the terrifying anxiety-provoking image, to this real Medusa's head, to the revelation of this something which properly speaking is unnameable, the back of this throat, the complex, unlocatable form, which also makes it into the primitive object *par excellence*, the abyss of the feminine organ from which all life emerges, this gulf of the mouth, in which everything is swallowed up, and no less the image of death in which everything comes to its end" (ibid., 163–64).

11. Ibid., 170.

12. Ibid., 152.

13. "You see, the object of desire is the cause of the desire, and this object that is the cause of desire is the object of the drive—that is to say, the object around which the drive turns." J. Lacan, *The Four Fundamental Concepts of Psychoanalysis*, ed. J. A. Miller, trans. A. Sheridan (New York: Norton, 1981), 243.

14. For this whole development, see J. Laplanche, *Vie et mort en psychanalyse* (1970; Paris: Flammarion, 1989).

15. Here is what Freud writes: "At a time at which the first beginnings of sexual satisfaction are still linked with the taking of nourishment, the sexual instinct has a sexual object outside the infant's own body in the shape of his mother's breast. It is only later that the instinct loses that object, just at the time, perhaps, when the child is able to form a total idea of the person to whom the organ that is giving him satisfaction belongs. As a rule the sexual instinct then becomes auto-erotic, and not until the period of latency has been passed through is the original relation restored" (SE VII, 222).

16. See J. Lacan, "The Direction of the Treatment and the Principles of Its Power," in *Ecrits: A Selection*, trans. A. Sheridan (London: Tavistock Publications, 1982).

17. "The model [*Vorbild*] of the formation of symptom [*Symptombildung*] remains, in a certain sense, the *dream image* [*Traumbild*] that at once designates images as the behavior of the *dream content*, the *image* as the hallucinatory formation, and also *the dream as theory of the image*," in Pierre Fédida, "The Movement of the Informe," trans. M. Stone-Richards and M. Tiampo, *Qui Parle* 10, no. 1 (1996): 53. See also P. Fédida and P. Lacoste, "Psychopathologie/métapsychologie: La fonction des points de vue," *Revue Internationale de Psychopathologie* 8 (1992): 589–627.

18. See, for instance, O. Kernberg, *Borderline Conditions and Pathological Narcissism* (1975; New York: Jason Aronson, 1981).

19. For example, Kernberg writes: "There was a time when a typical misunderstanding of the implications of psychoanalytic theory and practice was the assumption that sexual activity in itself was a therapeutic factor. We have advanced a long way from such misunderstandings, and have learned that often what appears on the surface to be genital activity is actually in the service of aggressive, pregenital aims. With patients presenting borderline personality organization the opposite danger of seeing only their pregenital, destructive aims, to the neglect of acknowledging their efforts to overcome their inhibited sexual orientation, appears to be a frequent clinical problem" (ibid., 103). We can notice here the alleged equivalence between sexuality and genitality.

20. About the relationship between the psychological and the biological, Hartmann writes: "In our opinion the psychological is not an 'antithesis' to the biological, but rather an essential part of it." In this sense, he further remarks: "Precisely because the psychological is a part of the biological, under certain conditions our method sheds light on physiological developments, particularly on those pertaining to instinctual drives. We can trace the course of these developments, using psychological phenomena as their indicator or symptom. *This relationship has still another aspect: for instance, though we can describe the differences between masculine and feminine to some extent psychologically, it does not follow that there must be fundamental psychological concepts which correspond to masculinity and femininity.*" In H. Hartmann, *Ego Psychology and the Problem of Adaptation* (1939), trans. D. Rapaport (1958; New York: International Universities Press, 1977), 34–35 (my emphasis).

21. Ibid., 8, 20.

22. H. Hartmann, "Comments on the Psychoanalytic Theory of the Ego," *The Psychoanalytic Study of the Child* V (1950): 79 (my emphasis). In a preceding passage, Hartmann writes: "Some aspects of early ego development appear in a different light if we familiarize ourselves with the thought that the ego may be more—and very likely is more—than a developmental by-product of the influence of reality on instinctual drives; that *it has a partly independent origin*— apart from these formative influences which, of course, no analyst would want to underestimate; and that we may speak of *an autonomous factor in ego development. . .* in the same way as we consider the instinctual drives autonomous agents of development. Of course, this is not to say that the ego as a definite psychic system is inborn. . . . This statement also implies that *not all the factors of mental development present at birth can be considered part of the id*—which is, by the way, included in what I have said elsewhere in introducing the concept of an undifferentiated phase" (ibid., 78–79, my emphasis).

23. Freud uses an evocative comparison to emphasize to what extent the control of the ego over motility and action and its submission toward reality may also appear as a compromise actually satisfying the requirements of the id: "Thus in its relation to the id it is like a man on horseback, who has to hold in check the superior strength of the horse; with this difference, that the rider tries to do so with his own strength while the ego uses borrowed forces. The analogy may be carried a little further. Often a rider, if he is not to be parted from his horse, is obliged to guide it where it wants to go; so in the same way the ego is in the habit of transforming the id's will into action as if it were its own" ("The Ego and the Id," SE XIX, 25).

24. H. Hartmann, "The Mutual Influences in the Development of Ego and Id," *The Psychoanalytic Study of the Child* VII (1952): 14.

25. Secondary autonomy is defined as "this resistivity of ego functions against regression" (ibid., 25).

26. "It therefore will be clarifying if we define narcissism as the libidinal cathexis not of the ego but of the self" (Hartmann, "Comments," 85).

27. Ibid., 86.

28. P. Fédida, "A Borderline State of Humanity and the Fragmented Ego of the Analyst," in *The Subject and the Self: Lacan and American Psychoanalysis*, ed. J. Feher-Gurewich and M. Tort, in collaboration with S. Fairfield (Northvale: Jason Aronson, 1996), 67.

29. Ibid., 68.

30. Ibid., 69, 67.

31. "For our present purposes I will concentrate on a single issue: the drive concept in psychoanalysis and its consequences. And I will immediately emphasize once again that it is not the presence of the drive concept *per se*, not *the isolated inconsistency of the intrusion of a vague and insipid biological concept into a marvelous system of psychology* that would have spurred me toward scientific action—and the same can be said with regard to my attitude *vis-à-vis* the concepts of 'dependence,' 'autonomy,' 'identity,' and 'adaptation' imported from social psychology. It was not theoretical inconsistency that prompted my reflections but only *my conviction that the drive concept* (as well as the aforementioned sociological intruders into depth psychology) *has had significant deleterious consequences for psychoanalysis*." In H. Kohut, "Introspection, Empathy, and the Semi-Circle of Mental Health," *The International Journal of Psycho-Analysis* 63 (1982): 401 (my emphasis). Beyond the clearly expressed rejection of the drive, we notice Kohut's scorn toward the aim for objectivity underlying ego psychology's concepts.

Also, *"Under normal circumstances we do not encounter drives via introspection and empathy. We always experience the not-further-reducible psychological unit of a loving self, a lusting self, an assertive self, a hostile-destructive self. When drives achieve experiential primacy, we are dealing with disintegration products:* in the realm of Eros, the fragmenting self watching helplessly as it is being replaced by a feverishly intensified pleasure experience, by the ascendancy of a pleasure–giving erotogenic zone, and thus of the drive over the self; or, in the realm of Thanatos, the fragmenting self watching helplessly as it is being replaced by a feverishly intensified rage experience, by the ascendancy of a detructive and/or self-destructive orgy, and thus, again, of the drive over the self" (Kohut, "Introspection," 401, my emphasis).

32. See the opposition Kohut makes between the "guilty man" of "traditional" psychoanalysis and the "tragic man" of self psychology. "[I]ntergenerational strife, mutual killing wishes, pathological 'Oedipus complex' (as distinguished from the normal 'Oedipal stage' of development) refers not to the essence of man but . . . they are deviations from the normal, however frequently they may occur" (ibid., 402).

33. Kohut writes, for example: "[I]f there is *empathic mirroring* acceptance of the little girl's self, *if she can merge with the idealized admired parental imago,* then the recognition of the sexual difference will cause no permanent harm, will not lead to a lasting disturbance of narcissistic equilibrium." In H. Kohut, "A Note on Female Sexuality" (1975), in *The Search for the Self: Selected Writings of Heinz Kohut* 2 New York: International Universities Press, 1980), 791.

34. See D. P. Schreber, *Memoirs of My Nervous Illness,* trans. and ed. by I. Macalpine and R. A. Hunter (London: Dawson, 1955), especially 136–37 and 180–81. Here we can notice the distinction Schreber makes between his "mind's eye" and his "bodily eye"; see for instance 137n73.

35. *"I can also 'picture' myself* in a different place, for instance while playing the piano I see myself at the same time standing *in front of a mirror* in the adjoining room *in female attire;* when I am lying in bed at night *I can give myself and the rays the impression that my body has female breasts and a female sexual organ. . . . The picturing of female buttocks on my body— honni soit qui mal y pense*—has become such a habit that I do it almost automatically whenever I bend down. 'Picturing' in this sense may therefore be called a reversed miracle. In the same way as *rays throw on to my nerves pictures they would like to see especially in dreams, I too can in turn produce pictures for the rays which I want them to see"* (ibid., 181, my emphasis).

36. Ibid., 207.

Focuses *on* *the* Apparatus

12. Closing and Opening of the Dream

MUST CHAPTER VII BE REWRITTEN?

Jean Laplanche

Translated by Mira Reinberg and Thomas Pepper

It is from the point of view of *communication* that we wish to reexamine the theory of the dream. But this word takes on two different meanings: *communication of the dream* (notably its account in treatment) and *communication in the dream,* whether or not there exists a communication in the dream itself. As to "communication of the dream," a purely idealist, intersubjective, linguistic conception of the cure would consider this problem outmoded. Such a view would consider it nonsense to wish to analyze the dream, since there is never anything but the account of the dream, which is merely an account like any other, situated solely in the transference and the *hic et nunc* of the cure.

All Freud's thought and technique comes to oppose such a theory. For him the dream is a formation of the unconscious to be analyzed as such, independent of its own interference with its enunciation in treatment. The dreamed dream is a reality, and the account we give of it is but the façade (*Fassade*). Surely we side with this Freudian realism. But Freud pushes his "objectivism" much further, whence our second question arises: "Is there communication in the dreamed dream?" Certain formulations are radical: no communication as such would be at the origin of the dream. And the dream itself would not bear any communicative intention: "The dream doesn't mean anything to anyone; it is not a vehicle of communication."

These two assertions are hard to accept. To discuss them, it is advisable to enter into the Freudian theory of the dream with its three aspects: wish fulfillment, hallucination, and function of the dream. It is this critique we shall try to sketch. We shall ask if a conception of the *unconscious*—one that places at its origin the communication of enigmatic messages of the other and their partial repression by the subject—

would allow us to pose the dilemma in a new way, as that between a narcissistic closing of the dream on the one side versus a potential opening of the dream to communication on the other.

For this Freud himself gives us a path in suggesting the rolling (back) up of the diagram of the psychic apparatus. It is in following this indication that we might arrive at a new chapter VII, not symmetrical to the first version, but nonetheless opening it up to the discussion of the primacy of the other.

Thus the theme with which I would like to begin is that of the relation between the dream and communication. This problem is broader than that of the relation of the dream and language (*langage*), a relation to which, notably after Lacan, it would tend to be reduced. There are communications without language (in the verbal sense of the word); and, inversely, there are elements of language that have lost all relation with a communication.

But the question—renewed as it is by the discovery of psychoanalysis and by the role the dream plays in our practice—is, in fact, much older than Freud. One can even say that in the case of the human being, interrogation concerning this matter is coextensive with the enigma posed to such a being by the dream, this fragment of our life that is so astonishing: something that always has appeared as speaking (*parlant*), and, at the same time, as radically eluding our will to communicate—even our will, period.

For more clarity, I would like to divide the question in two. On the one hand there is the communication *of* (*du*) the dream, notably in treatment; on the other hand there is the dream *as* communication. Or, put more generally and concerning the latter, there is the question of the relation of the phenomenon of the dream to interhuman communication in general. These two problems are intertwined, but distinct.

THE PROBLEM OF THE COMMUNICATION OF THE DREAM

Obviously this problem is to be discussed in relation to the communication *analysis* itself *is*. In effect, our practice has widened what one might call the quantum of verbalization of the dreamed dream; and, above all, it has radically widened the manner of "handling" (*traiter*) this material.

Today, one hundred years after the *Traumdeutung*, numerous evolutions have taken place—voluntary changes, ones justifiable in theory, but also surreptitious changes in our practice—and we may distinguish two main attitudes among analysts that we might oppose in a somewhat caricatural manner: the purely subjectivist or intersubjective attitude, and the objectivist attitude. I say "caricatural," since in fact we encounter many more nuanced positions.

The Intersubjective Attitude

Here everything is taken as what happens in the analytic dialogue itself, in its *hic et nunc.* To introduce this attitude, I would like to relate a memory of my own that is, in fact, rather banal. I had been invited to a certain colloquium or conference as a respondent to the presentation of an analyst in training. In his well-prepared presentation, he asked the question, precisely, of how to interpret the dream today. Unfortunately, the answer had come before the question. Scarcely had the young analyst begun the account of his patient's dream when my fellow discussants, his elders, began to interrupt him to teach him a thing or two. The young analyst had not understood what the patient had said *in telling him* this dream. Transference—indeed countertransference—was evident. In short, the problem of the interpretation of the dream had vanished at the expense of what is pompously called the intersubjective dynamic.

This is a common attitude: we stick to the manifest content. More precisely: the manifest content is taken up exclusively in terms of its enunciative value (*valeur d'énonciation*), and not in terms of the question: What does the dream mean? And not even: Why has this analysand dreamed this at this moment of the analysis? But rather: What is he telling me *in recounting* this dream?

These on-the-spot interpretations—we all know them in the analytic session. Most often, they rely on symbolism of a very general nature. The manifest content is not considered to be dissimulating something fundamentally heterogeneous to it. It is taken as a whole other discourse, even if it does mean applying certain simple modifications: transformation of an element into its opposite, denegation, wordplay, puns.

One cannot exaggerate the extent to which the Lacanian path of listening to signifiers, when followed in an exclusive fashion, has been detrimental. Because here—and this is to push things to the limit for the sake of clarity—the listening is never "authorized," save by the listener himself. It is the listener, and he alone, who decides that the expression "take it upon oneself" entails an allusion to a sexual relation. It is the listener, and he alone, who chooses to hear "oh it's so (*que c'est*) difficult to say" as "oh a dick is so difficult to say" (*ah queue c'est difficile à dire*).[1] We cannot endlessly invoke Freud's example without precautions, nor his frequent recourse to more or less "good" jokes in order to support his interpretations. For Freud's interpretations—and we shall return to them—are far from claiming the sovereignty so often declared by our master interpreters. According to this mode of thinking, if we push this so-called sovereignty to its foundations, the only recourse left is to maintain that it is solely the unconscious that is hidden within common language, independent of the way in which the individual believes himself to make use of it, while—as it would be maintained from this position—in fact he does nothing but serve it. Hence, a collective unconscious.[2]

Let us sum up: Within a certain conception of the analytic dialogue, dream analysis appears to have been definitively superseded. According to this conception,

Freud believed—wrongly—that he was speaking of the dream, while in fact he was only speaking "of the verbal fashion by which the dreamer renders his dream."³ The analysis of the dream would allow the bringing to the fore of certain mechanisms, which would in turn make us aware of their being universal or proper to language: "Listening to the dream as a discourse has enabled analysts to listen to discourse as dream, that is to say as obeying the same grammar as that of unconscious discourse."⁴

I just mentioned Lacan. But this deserves some nuancing: nowhere, it seems to me, did Lacan advocate either this sort of reintegration of the dream into discourse in general, or the neglect of the rules proper to dream interpretation. And furthermore, this scorn for the famous "royal road" is a phenomenon that, in the analytic world, is in no way restricted to the Lacanian sphere. It seems to me to go hand in hand with the decline of the reference to the individual unconscious in the practice and theory of the cure.

This is not to say that Lacan is a stranger to this drift, particularly by virtue of his pure and simple assimilation of the mechanisms of the dream-work—displacement and condensation—to universal modes of functioning of language, that is, metonymy and metaphor. Although a thousand times criticized, arguments at the ready, this assimilation has nevertheless reinforced the rumor according to which the dream is a discourse like any other.⁵

To this factor is added yet another: the assimilation of the analytic rule—free association on the part of the analysand, and equally hovering attention on the part of the analyst—to a sort of bracketing of reality in the sense of a "phenomenological reduction," to a suspension of all referential dimensions of discourse, with which one should henceforth no longer be concerned. Henceforth it would be completely immaterial to know whether the discourse of the analysand refers to a dream, to a fancy (*fantaisie*), to an everyday event, to the words of a third person, and so forth.

Winnicott says somewhere that in the presence of the patient, the analyst must reasonably not pretend not to know that King George did die on that day. Now, precisely for those whom Winnicott implicitly criticizes here, the statement (*énoncé*) "King George is dead" would only be part of the enunciation of the analysand, and for the analyst, this psychic asceticism would be such that this enunciation alone should occupy his own psychic field.

If analysis is suspension of reality, it is certain that the "dream-referent" loses all privilege. We should, however, think of this little experience, which is not rare, and which I will call the distraction of the first minute: during the first seconds of a session, the analyst's thought process, having been distracted by some external or internal circumstance, is sometimes belated in its relation to the patient's discourse. Here then is the analyst who emerges into attention, and hears these words: " . . . so the car lightly struck the cyclist," etc. I challenge any of our colleagues to claim not at least to have asked himself: Is this a dream he is telling me, or is it an incident that actually occurred? And I challenge him to admit to not having attempted, within himself, to pick up on the clues that would allow him to catch up with the moving train, so to speak, of the discourse.

Let us tighten things up. With the subjectivist point of view, which suspends all reference to anything exterior to the discourse within the session—even reference to the unconscious and to this privileged phenomenon that is the dream—close to three quarters of Freud's work becomes void: not only the interpretation of the dream, but the works on the psychopathology of everyday life, jokes, humor, and so forth. And his works on so-called applied psychoanalysis as well, if it is true, as Viderman sometimes states, that the suspension of reference must, here once again, be the rule: "[L]ittle does it matter what Leonardo saw . . . little does it matter what Leonardo said . . . what matters is that the analyst . . . makes it exist in saying it."[6]

The Objectivist Attitude

Freud's point of view concerning the dream will remain objectivist throughout his lifetime. It is "objectivist" in that it supposes that the "dreamed dream" exists; that the memory of it is something else; and the account (*récit*) of it is something else yet again. It is not without interest that we read a passage such as the one from chapter VII about the forgetting of the dream, and of the further acts of censorship (*censures*) the account itself may introduce. To demonstrate this, Freud does not hesitate to make the dreamer repeat the dream a second time, in order to note the differences between the two accounts:

> But the parts of the dream which he describes in different terms are by that fact revealed to me as the weak spot in the dream's disguise. . . . That is the point at which the interpretation of the dream can be started. My request to the dreamer to repeat his account of the dream has warned him that I was proposing to take special pains in solving it; under pressure of the resistance, therefore, he hastily covers the weak spots in the dream's disguise by replacing any expressions that threaten to betray its meaning by other less revealing ones. In this way he draws my attention to the expression which he has dropped out. (GW II–III, 519–20; SE V, 515)

Here we see Freud's realist attitude. The dream exists outside its account (*récit*), outside of what analysis will make of it. And for him, the best proof is that the psychic phenomenon of the dream globally goes beyond the mere use the analysis has made of it as "the royal road toward the unconscious." As late as 1923 Freud is still steadfastly disputing the objection according to which the analysand's dreams might be entirely shaped by the analytic situation and by the suggestion of the analyst. His conclusion merits citation:

> [The patient] recollected some dreams which he had had before starting analysis and indeed before he had known anything about it; and the analysis of these dreams, which were free from all suspicion of suggestion, led to the same interpretations as the later ones. (SE XIX, 118)

And Freud concludes:

> I think that in general it is a good plan occasionally to bear in mind the fact that peo-
> ple were in the habit of dreaming before there was such a thing as psycho-analysis.
> (GW XIII, 309; SE XIX, 117)

To admit that there exists a dream-object, revelatory independent of its inclusion in
the transference, is to admit the possibility of a different attitude regarding it—as there
is regarding any discourse in the cure—an attitude that could be called, following Guy
Rosolato, "technological," with the following caveat: the term "technique" is not pejo-
rative, it should be associated with that of suppleness, and it implies only that the
activity of listening (*écoute*) and the intervention are adapted to their particular object.
Despite its prosaic sense, the word "technique" refers to the major discovery of Freud,
namely when he defined analysis foremost as a procedure that allows knowledge of
processes that would otherwise remain pretty much inaccessible.

I shall refer here, very quickly, not only to Freud's time, but to a contemporary
psychoanalyst, Danielle Margueritat, whose approach seems to me to be marked here
by a genuine fidelity to the Freudian line.[7] But first let us cite Ferenczi, who, concerning the activity of listening to dreams, advocates an entirely different kind of listening from that of "hovering attention." In listening to dreams, he says, "we must strive
to note the text of dreams in the smallest detail. I often make the analysand repeat
complicated dreams a second time, even a third if necessary."[8]

Let us now cite Danielle Margueritat: "What happens to me when someone
tells *me* a dream? First something happens to me, since I tend to isolate dreams, not
from the context of the analysis, but from the whole of the discourse of the session."
And the same theme returns as a leitmotiv, that of the dream-event, that is to say what
in the end Freud calls "the other scene": "Then, when I am told a dream, the alarm
goes off, my attention is mobilized" (attention and vigilance, not at all a pure and simple letting it flow [*abandon*]). "Thus a dream happens, and I am prey to a troubling
of the rhythm of time. . . ."

"Then a dream comes forth, with its associations. . . ." "*With* its associations":
I insist on this and it is a second essential aspect. The dream is not assimilable to
its associations. And this to the point that Freud (still in 1923) enumerates different possible rules, different ways (*ordres*) of approaching and obtaining associations.
And once again, we have this astonishing sequence in Danielle Margueritat, concerning a dream where it is a matter of contact lenses (*lentilles de contact*):

> I no longer knew if we were in the account of the dream or in the associations, and
> when I asked her the question, she answered: "it was in the dream, but in the dream
> it was contact lenses [*lentilles*, literally lenses or lentils], and I didn't feel like saying
> that word."[9]

Here yet again is a strictly Freudian approach, one that considers the difference in formulation between the dreamed dream (lenses, lentils) and its account (contact glasses)—itself already more censored than the dream—as revelatory. Let me be clear: analysis since Freud, and even more so after him, cannot do without the dimension of enunciation, or, to use other terms, address or transference. But inversely it cannot use this pretext in order to completely dissolve the dream into its "address," into its account (*récit*), that is precisely into what Freud considers as even more misleading or more disguised than the dream "*itself.*"

I'm afraid we cannot go much further concerning this matter of the "communication of the dream" than to stick with the dilemma that exists between Freudian realism, on the one hand, which admits the existence of material or psychic realities to which all discourse *refers*—including in analysis—and on the other hand a kind of idealism of discourse, first of discourse in analysis, and then of all discourse in general. This last is an attitude that renews a sophistical position while radicalizing it. According to this tendency, the dream is only the discourse on the dream, in the same way that love, or paternity, etc., are only the words "love," "paternity."

COMMUNICATION AND THE DREAMED DREAM

Having rallied myself unambiguously to the Freudian position on this point, I feel even more at ease to freely take on the question of "communication *in* the dream," which I formulate thus: The dream itself, the dreamed dream, does it have something to do with interhuman communication?

Here we bump up against two unambiguous propositions of Freud, both of which are shocking and revelatory in their abrupt formulation. From the "efferent" side, that is, at the exit of the process: "A dream does not want to say anything to anyone. It is not a vehicle for communication; on the contrary, it is meant to remain ununderstood" (GW XI, 238; SE XV, 231). And, from the "afferent" side: "The words of the analyst . . . act in a way analogous to that of somatic stimuli that exert their action on the dreamer while sleeping" (GW XI, 238; SE XV, 231). Taken absolutely, this last statement signifies that the dream does not take any message into account—or, which amounts to the same—that it treats all message as purely material stimulus.

The term message, *Botschaft* (embassy, embassage), is relatively rare in Freud, and it is all the more instructive to note the passages where it occurs, which are mainly about telepathy. Let me briefly summarize what this is about. During the 1920s, Freud, influenced particularly by Ferenczi, was interested in so-called "occult" phenomena, and these in two forms: prediction of the future and transmission of thought. These are two phenomena that could be translated notably and eminently into *premonitory* dreams on the one hand and *telepathic* dreams on the other. Freud's position on this subject will hardly change.[10] Theoretically speaking, premonition is inadmissible simply because it would invert the arrow of time, and has never been demonstrated by experiment (*expérience*). On the other hand, mostly based on personal experience (*expériences*), Freud formally admits the possibility of transmission, or "transference," of thoughts, or of memories of strongly affective tonality.

But what interests us here is not to take a stand concerning telepathy itself. It is rather the relation between this telepathic message and the dream in which we eventually pick it up again. Would this not be a case where the dream would be the receiver of a certain speech, and this in whatever manner it might reach us? Freud is going to be radical here. The theory of the dream need not change one iota to take account of this possibility. In fact, in the same way as any other message, the telepathic message does not reach the dream as speech; rather it is treated just like any other material stimulus:

> A telepathic message will be treated as a portion of the material that goes to the formation of the dream, like any other external or internal stimulus, like a disturbing noise in the street, or an insistent organic sensation in the sleeper's own body. (GW XIII, 176; SE XVIII, 207)

This assimilation of the message to a *noise* is evidently what we shall have to contest. And to do so, it is indispensable to enter to some extent into the psychic machinery, "the apparatus of the soul," as Freud calls it, as it is described in chapter VII of the *Traumdeutung*.

Here, then, is the apparatus Freud describes and makes evolve under our eyes:

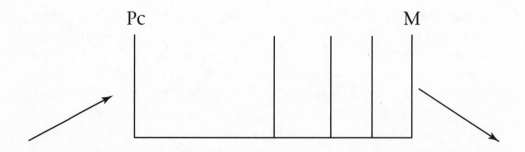

First point: This is not a somatic apparatus. The body, one could say, is represented by or consists of the two arrows, the afferent and the efferent. Second point: Neither is it a neurological apparatus. The systems are virtual, psychic. They are perhaps produced by (the material treated by) neurology, but without any direct correspondence with it.

Let us then grant that this is the "psychic apparatus." And yet another nuance: This is a one-dimensional section (*coupe*) of a three-dimensional apparatus, which is a kind of a parallelepiped bucket containing photographic plates, the memory systems.

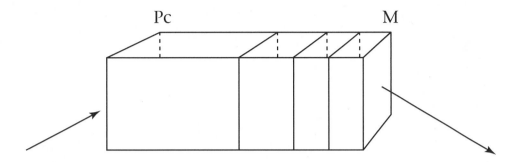

For our purposes, let us stop at the two ends: perception (the afferent arrow), and motility (the efferent arrow). There is no communication or message either at the entry or at the exit. At the entry and at the exit, there are nothing but material actions. Thus this is a purely behaviorist apparatus, the model for which, says Freud, is the reflex (arc): "Reflex processes remain the model of every psychical function" (GW II–III, 543; SE V, 538).

Now I shall proceed immediately to the state of sleep, in which afferent forces and efferent forces are—*almost*—completely cut out.

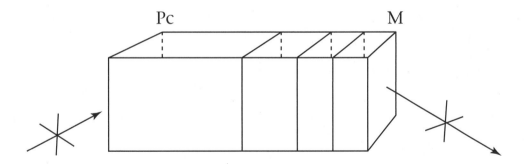

But it is precisely here that a differentiation would be instructive: one that should be made between, on the one hand, that which is of the order of perception without signification, and, on the other hand, that which is of the order of the message. It is thus that Bourguignon gives instances of numerous experiments that show that stimuli that have meaning (*significatifs*)—words, for example—are much better perceived by the sleeper than material stimuli, regardless of whether they awaken him, or whether they are eventually integrated into the dream thoughts.[11]

These remarks leave us in perplexity as to the Freudian diagram. If the human psychic apparatus cannot be lodged between two poles, that of stimulus and that of reaction, as Freud would wish, but rather between a pole of received messages and a pole of emitted messages, then it would perhaps be wisest to leave the diagram on hold, even if only to take it up again on the basis of other data.

The *Traumdeutung* is an immense work. Most of chapters II through VI are consecrated to two trajectories, which are considered as reciprocal, even if they are not identical. On the one hand there is the interpretative trajectory, which goes back from the account of the dream to its original elements; and, inversely, there is the trajectory of the dream-work, which is presumed accurately (*réellement*) to account for the genesis of the dreamed dream and the told dream. As for chapter VII, it develops two or even three major theses, which are, moreover, bound together: (1) that the dream is the fulfillment of the wish; (2) that the dream is hallucinatory (which remains to be explained); and (3) that the dream is the guardian of sleep.

Concerning the second thesis—hallucination—Freud will remain dissatisfied up until the end, proposing varying explanations for this recrudescence of dissatisfaction. In contrast, the thesis of "wish-fulfillment" (*accomplissement de souhait*) is fundamental. *In its very statement* (*énoncé*) it gives food for thought: not that the dream expresses a wish, nor even that it presents a wish as fulfilled, but that the dream *is* the fulfillment of wishing, and this with no distance whatsoever between the wish and its fulfillment. Moreover, Freud says that the dream is expressed in the present, and not in the optative. (We shall pass over the apparent inexactitude in opposing a tense—the present—and a mood—the optative. In fact, the dream is expressed in the present indicative.)

In the last instance, Freud always refers this wish to an archaic one; and, despite certain denegations, to a sexual one, which is always, according to the well-known metaphor, the "capitalist" of the dream. Now the basis of this whole demonstration refers to a theory, to a model of the origin of infantile wish—or desire—namely, "the experience of satisfaction." This "Befriedigungserlebnis" (experience of satisfaction) here is itself taken up from the *Project for a Scientific Psychology*, and we must linger upon it for a moment.

The infant is subjected to an internal tension, that of need. Here the need in question is explicitly that of hunger, which evidently goes back to the experience of nursing. The alimentary need for food is conceived, very plausibly, as a continuous increase of tension from which the organism cannot escape. Despite the triviality of the example, let us imagine a kettle on the stove. The water boils, the lid rattles. There are two possible scenarios here: if no one intervenes, and the caloric energy continues to be discharged in a disorderly way, then "the starving infant will cry or squirm." But this series of actions is not capable of stopping the stimulus. Otherwise what can happen is what Freud calls specific action: *"fremde Hilfeleistung,"* "outside help"—a curious word to designate the mother,[12] who, alerted by the crying, will bring food, thus stopping the excitation for an extended moment (GW II–III, 571; SE V, 565–66).

This is how Freud explains the birth of the *wish:* A psychic connection gets created, henceforth associating the memory of hunger's excitation with that of food.

At the moment of the reappearance of the state of tension, hunger will cause the image of food to be reborn; and, if real food does not arrive, its image will be invested with such force that it will acquire a hallucinatory intensity.

> An impulse of this kind is what we call a wish; the reappearance of the perception is the fulfillment of the wish; and the shortest path to the fulfillment of the wish is a path leading direct from the excitation produced by the need to a complete cathexis of the perception. . . . [T]hus the wishing ended in hallucinating. (GW II–III, 571; SE V, 566, translation modified)

This is a well-known model, even a hackneyed one. In it we might even try to see the very birth of infantile sexuality. But to do so we should have to go beyond two major insufficiencies. On the one hand, communication is hardly mentioned here; nor, *a fortiori*, is dialogue between mother and child. The child's message is reduced to purely mechanical movements. As for the mother's message, we read in Freud only *a purely material supply of food.* What is most important here is that the action unfolds on the level of a single need, namely the alimentary. The supplied object is food, milk. And we don't see how the mnemic trace of the perception could be anything other than an *alimentary* image.

This experience of so-called satisfaction is surely a very fecund model, one that might be developed in the direction of the emergence of the sexual on the basis of a self-preserving relation. Even then we must *give up believing in the illusion Freud proposes to us.* From the hat of hunger, from an instinct for self-preservation, Freud the illusionist pretends to pull out, magically, the rabbit of sexuality: an impossible thing, unless sexuality had already been hidden there somewhere beforehand. From the image of milk, by association, that of the breast can be derived. But this is only then a breast-object, the symbol of alimentary satisfaction, and nothing more. The experience of satisfaction could only be doubled, or open onto the sexual, if something of the sexual had been lodged there from the start; thus if the object had already been at once double, ambiguous, and, in sum, enigmatic.

From then on, to introduce this duality of the sexual and of self-preservation, there are only two solutions. Either we can suppose from the start that two needs of internal origin operate in the infant, one alimentary, the other sexual. In its most simplified version, this is the so-called theory of an object choice leaning up (*étayé*) against another one.[13] Infantile sexuality is thus claimed to be present from the beginning, endogenous; but, in order for it to be asserted, it needs to lean upon the alimentary function. I have said more than once how unsatisfying such a theory is, in its going back to the positing of an innate oral sexual drive, which nothing in the psychology of the infant allows us to presuppose.

The second interpretation appears to me much more plausible, and allows us to preserve the experience of satisfaction as a ground. Yes, this experience is first of all of the order of self-preservation. It is, moreover, a much more complex experience, more charged with significations and affects than the simplistic model of the boiling kettle: It is the beginning of a reciprocal communication, one that is instituted from the first moments of life, probably on the basis of certain innate setups (*montages*), which themselves will develop rapidly ("Attachment," "Bindung").

But for the psychoanalyst the main thing is not here. Rather it is in the introduction of the sexual element, and this not from the side of the physiology of the child, but from that of the messages coming from the adult. Very concretely, these messages are situated on the side of the breast, the *sexual breast*, the inseparable companion of the milk of self-preservation.

Thus I have attempted to give a model for what is here a true genesis of the unconscious and of the drive, of which the unconscious thing-representations are henceforth the source. I shall not linger on this model, called the translational model of repression, and which, on the one hand, implies an attempt by the child to translate the enigmatic double messages of the mother, and on the other hand the partial failure of this translation, of which the nontranslated remains constitute precisely the elements of the unconscious. I shall only add, without being able to insist on it, that we may no longer keep to a conception of the birth of the sexual drive that would be limited to a single time (such as is precisely the case for the experience of satisfaction). For it is Freud himself who teaches us that indeed any unconscious inscription at all necessitates at least *two times:*[14] there is both the experience itself as well as its signifying retake (*reprise*), which I, for my part, call translation (necessarily an imperfect one).

Thus in order to complete the model of the experience of satisfaction, we must modify it profoundly. We must substitute the notion of message for that of perception; we must introduce the duality—that is, the compromise—between the sexual and the self-conservative on the side of the adult message; and finally, we must set the notion of afterwardsness fully into play.[15]

But what I would like to call attention to now is that introducing the notions of message and signifier does not leave unchanged the problem referred to as that of "the identity of perception," and that of hallucination. In the Freudian perspective, it is the perceptual remains, those of the satisfying object, which are reproduced, and with such force that they are even hallucinated—indeed to the degree that it may well be asked how the child might be able to get out of a hallucination that fully satisfies its need, and why it would seek more food when it possesses it completely in a hallucinatory manner. *But if* the notion of message is introduced—explicitly that of the messages of the adult—what will be found rejected in the unconscious are not inert perceptions, which are fortuitous and without intersubjective signification, but rather pieces of message, signifiers that, extracted from their context, take on the consistency of quasi-things. These signifiers divested of meaning (*désignifiés*) are certainly something other than memories; having lost their meaning-relations (*liaisons de sens*), their contextual relations in time and in space, they impose themselves entirely naturally as though they have the strength (*valeur*) of psychic reality. Henceforth it is not a question of figuring out how an intensity supplement can be added to a perception so as to transform it into a hallucination—a problem that will not cease to haunt Freud, and to which he gives the most diverse and most contradictory solutions, from the *Project for a Scientific Psychology* up to the "Metapsychological Supplement to the Theory of Dreams." In this latter text, it seems indeed that Freud finally runs aground over the major difficulty he himself has brought forth: namely that an extreme regression toward "very clear visual mnemic images" may be produced "though we do not on that account for a single moment take them for real perceptions" (GW X, 421–22, SE XIV, 231).

Without so much as presuming to resolve the question, I would like to suggest a path that appears to me to be fertile, namely that the *question of the hallucination* of the dream cannot be detached from that of clinical hallucination. Now, here Freud will stick to a so-called clinical model, that of Meynert's Amentia, an entity that disappeared almost as soon as it was described.[16] In contrast, all psychiatrists are in agreement in considering hallucination as primarily of the order of speech, whether heard or spoken again. In clinical experience, visual hallucinations are relatively rare and, most important, very localized.

In addition, to go further, the question under discussion is not exactly that of the "sensorium" (vision or hearing), but whether a message is present. The visual, as well as the auditory, can be the bearer of a message. Since Clérambault, since Freud with the Schreber Case, since Lacan and his Seminar on *The Psychoses,* the old notion of "perception without object" fades before the much more fertile one of a *message without a sender,* or *with an indeterminate sender.*

With this key in hand, research concerning dream hallucination should be oriented toward a more elaborated or even phenomenological description. For example, we must delimit what pertains truly to the visual, to the auditory (spoken words), and particularly to conviction and to internal discourse, to what are called, in clinical experience, verbal psychic hallucinations, as, for example: "*I was saying to myself* that my friend Pierre was in the room."

On the other hand, it would be necessary to rethink the articulation between two factors mentioned by Freud, and which are far from equivalent: hallucination proper on the one hand, and on the other the fact that the dream only possesses the "present" of the indicative, to the point of leaving no distance between the expression of the wish and its fulfillment. Moreover the analogy Freud establishes with the grammatical tense of the present ("my father dies") might be the very analogy in need of reexamination in relation to the infinitive ("my father [to] die") and the subjunctive ("that [or lest] my father die").[17]

Let us simply note this: If we accept the idea that the unconscious is characterized by the disappearance of discursive links, then the diverse modalities of enunciation (grammatical moods) should therefore be absent. In this way the unconscious would always be in the "present," that is, always presenting its contents as "perfected" (*accompli:* in general usage finished, fulfilled). It would hardly be forcing things to say that the unconscious, by virtue of its consistency as thing, is *in and of itself* "hallucinatory"—except for the fact that it remain(s)—unconscious.

All of this is to make palpable the very idea that the hallucinatory fulfillment of an unconscious wish bears within it something of the tautological. As actuation, this fulfillment—that is, the abolition of the distance between signifier and signified—is *in and of itself* a hallucinatory presentation, and this precisely when what is at issue is the unconscious wish.

It is in this sense that I have always considered it superfluous to attribute a psychic, clinical reality to the so-called hallucination of the nursling. This was only a metaphor that would allow us to sense the constitution of an atemporal unconscious, one thus always present and contemporaneous (*actuel*)—actuated (*actué*), one might say.

I want to return to my primary question: Is the *dream* itself a *communication?* Yes or no? But before that I will try, briefly, to take up a major problem, which is linked to the Freudian model referred to in chapter VII as that of the psychic apparatus.[18]

In the different versions he gives of the model, Freud slightly varies the position of the letters on the extreme right-hand side. Thus I give the following two-dimensional diagram:

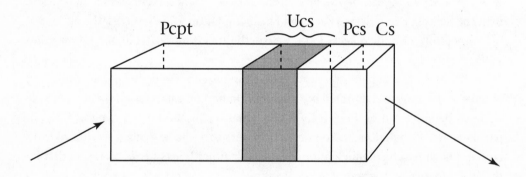

This diagram has the advantage of posing a problem. Consciousness is to be found at both ends of the apparatus: to the left, as perceiving consciousness of the external world, and to the right, immediately after the censorship agency of the preconscious, as consciousness of internal processes. Now for Freud these two types of consciousness are but one, and are both linked to a perception.

It is here that a note is introduced in 1919. I cite:

> The further completion of this diagram, which has been unrolled in a linear way, should have to reckon with the fact that the system next beyond the *Pcs.* is the one to which consciousness must be ascribed—in other words, that *Pcpt.= Cs.* (GW II–III, 546; SE V, 541, translation modified)

Despite appearances, this note is clear. It tells us that the diagram of the bucket is only linear because it has been *unrolled.* And that therefore it must be rolled back up so as to make the two extremities—that is the two modalities of consciousness—coincide.

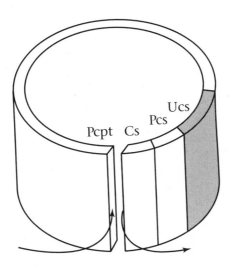

This is such a model. Despite what he promises in this note, Freud never explicated it afterward. Almost no one has noticed this rolling-[back]-up. Already since January 1972 (in *Problématiques* I), and then again in 1980, I have kept referring to it.

It is a *model,* and as such, we must not hasten to apply it to a single reality. It is more rich, more multivalent. It is neither (1) the model of a body, nor (2) of a neuronal system, nor even (3) that of a psychic apparatus, for it lacks everything necessary to provide for a psychology: emotions, affects, reasoning, and so forth. Nor is it a model of the unconscious, which constitutes only one part of it. This diagram can be drawn from above, which has the advantage of bringing out the aspect of the tangency of two circuits, and about which we cannot help but think that they are language circuits (*circuits langagiers*):

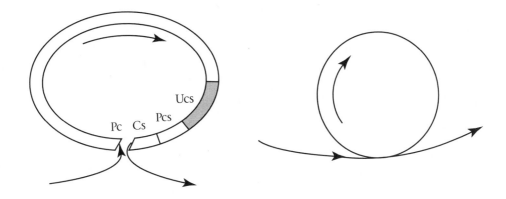

We must note that this idea of tangency corresponds very closely to that of marginality (such as is the case with the prefix *neben*), which Freud ceaselessly uses to designate the surging up of the sexual and/or of the unconscious as byproduct (*produit marginal, Nebenprodukt*). This is a multivalent model, but one that works primarily to explain the surging up of what one might call, after Lacan, the "formations of the unconscious"—and thus, among other things, as a model of the dream. But we must also admit that the arrows of the external circuit can be discharged in a more subtle fashion than the simple "all or nothing" of deep sleep. In all these formations, the external circuit should be conceived of as the totality of everyday, self-preservative messages. At the point of tangency, the two circuits touch each other for an instant; but there and then, the internal circuit, the sexual one, begins to function by itself, and in the opposite direction from that of the other. These formations of the unconscious—dream, bungled action, etc., and *doubtless the analytic session as well*—do not constitute an "other thing," which would exclude everyday discourse pure and simple; but rather here something happens, is thus launched, as it were, at the point of tangency, at which it separates off (*se marginalise*) so as to become autonomous.

Furthermore, with this rolling back up of what had been unfolded in a linear fashion, something paradoxical has happened. The preceding model, "linearly unrolled," was a model of closing; it was a black box functioning according to the behaviorist principle of stimulus-response. With the rolling back up suggested by Freud, paradoxically enough the model becomes a *model of opening* by means of (*par le bias de*) the tangency between the two circuits.

To recall once more the experience referred to as that of satisfaction and the criticisms we have made of it, we might show that our model would be adequate enough to give figure to what I would call, henceforth, *the experience of seduction.* At the point of contact, the external circuit—itself the enigmatic message of the adult, self-preservative but contaminated by the sexual—comes to be inscribed and then to be submitted to repression. What we are witnessing here is the real neogenesis of the sexual in the infant, and not at all an endogenous hatching. In this version of the model, nothing should stop us from figuring the body precisely at this point of tangency.

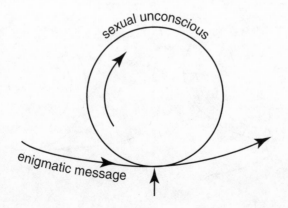

I return to my question of the dream as communication or as embryo, as seed of communication. It is here that the locution, "royal road toward the unconscious" need not lead us to confuse the two, that is, the unconscious and the dream. That the dream has no communicative intention, as Freud sometimes says, is perhaps an excessive formulation, one that, strictly speaking, is valid only for the unconscious, the it (*le ça*) itself. When he reexamines the question in 1923, in his "Comments on the Theory and Practice of the Interpretation of the Dream," Freud is much less categorical. Doubtless "the employment of dreams in analysis is something very remote from their original purpose" (GW XIII, 310; SE XIX, 117). But Freud concedes very willingly that in analysis dreams are the site of a "superior yield," a "motor," an "unconscious potential" (*puissance*). That he attributes this potential to suggestion is not satisfactory to us, but with the term *transference* we are more at ease. Nonetheless it still remains for us to agree about the word!

Do dreams follow the dictates of a communicative aim during analysis? Certainly. But no matter how unprecedented (*inouïe*, unheard of), or even inaugural the analytic situation is, we cannot be unaware that it is somehow prefigured in other interhuman situations. Thus it cannot be denied that *at all times and all places* dreams have borne within them a certain perlocutionary opening. Most certainly the dream does not speak to anyone directly. It functions fully even if it is forgotten. Thus a multitude of dreams fall into oblivion. But it cannot be denied that there has always existed a certain compulsion to tell the dream to others, to open it onto the other.

Once again, it is Ferenczi who writes this short fragment, which is worthy of being cited in its entirety: "To whom does one tell one's dreams? Psychoanalysts know that unconsciously one feels compelled to tell one's dreams to the very person his latent dreams concern. Lessing, it seems, already had this premonition when he wrote this distich: 'Somnum/Alba mihi semper narrat sua somnia mane/Alba sibi dormit: somniat Alba mihi' (Dream/Alba always tells me her dreams in the morning/Alba is asleep to herself: may she dream for me)."[19]

We must go further; that is we must surpass the notion of an addressee, a simple receiver marveling at a story in the mode of the fantastic. The poetic reception of the dream, whether by the German Romantics or the Surrealists, far from satisfying us, risks leading us astray. Divinatory art has always *asked for* dreams *for interpretation,* and it is difficult not to think that it is the soothsayer, and the *enigma* he incarnates, that is the element provoking certain dreams.[20]

"Provocation by the analyst": this is the phrase I have employed concerning transference. So if transference in the cure is rather provoked by the enigma embodied by the analyst, how would it not be the same for dreams during the cure, or at its margins, such as at the moment of resuming sessions? The diagram of tangency applies well in both cases, both for transference in the dream and transference in the cure. In both cases it is the discourse, the address of the analyst—real or supposed, but always enigmatic—that elicits this transference, and provokes the sort of libidinal neo-genesis linked to it.

To give homage to the primacy of the other as originary in the constitution of our unconscious, I have wanted to favor—counter to the mechanisms at whose origin is the subject—the verbs and the actions where *the subject is the other.* Thus, beside the central term of seduction, there are those of provocation, even of inspiration. Today it comes to mind to add to these the one of looking for something, of asking for it (*chercher*), in its popular sense, in which one says, "you are looking to provoke me," or "you are asking for it" (*tu me cherches*).

He is "looking for" it from me and I find him. This is a formula in which come together Picasso, with his "I don't seek, I find," Freud, with his "finding" of the object (*Objektfindung*), and even Pascal, with the words he hears from the mouth of Christ: "You wouldn't seek me if you hadn't already found me." In this way it can be said that the dream, in certain circumstances, is sought after (*cherché*), provoked by a potential addressee (*allocutaire*). And, in its turn, so to speak, the dream will "look for"—or seek out—unconscious desire.

All by itself, chapter VII is a monumental work within this monument that is the *Traumdeutung.* In translating it step by step, and with such difficulty, I have learned yet again that Freud is not always, as is claimed, a great writer, nor, a fortiori, is he an author to be read on the train; rather, he is an immense thinker. One more time I wish to put him to work. But what a joy to discover, as if in a nook, the main instrument for this work. With this three-line note on the unrolling of the diagram, what we are given is something like a door, a corridor opening onto another chapter VII: virtual, but no less effective. This "other" chapter VII is not the mirror image of the first. Rich with a thousand developments, it takes into account, if its consequences are developed, Freud's main and initial discovery, even if this discovery is always buried anew: the primacy of the message of the other in the constitution of the sexual unconscious.

NOTES

This essay is published here for the first time in English. It has appeared in German under the title "Sollen wir das siebte Kapitel neu schreiben?" in *Der Traum in der Psychoanalyse,* ed. Jürgen Körner und Sebastian Krutzenbichler (Göttingen: Vandenhoek und Ruprecht, 2000), and in the original in the proceedings of the Association pour la recherché sur la psychiatrie et la psychanalyse de l'enfant (ARPPE) (Paris: Dunod, 2002). The editors wish to thank Dr. Laplanche most kindly for his offering us this article for publication in lieu of being able to deliver it in person in Minneapolis in October 2000. The translators also wish to thank the author, as well as M. Christian Fournier, for their energy and time, as well as their generous and meticulous care in answering queries, solving problems, and going over the translation. All remaining errors are the translators'. At the time of querying Professor Laplanche concerning the translation, he supplied us with another, almost identical typescript of this essay bearing the title "Rêve et communication" (Dream and Communication), and bearing the same subtitle. Comparing this second typescript with the one from which we had made the draft of our translation, we found there a few additions to the first. We have interpolated these here. The Fischer edition of the *Gesammelte Werke* also contains the "Entwurf einer Psychologie" in its unnumbered *Nachtragsband. Texte aus den Jahren 1885–1938.* All notes and references henceforth are those of the author, except for material in square brackets, which, unless otherwise stated, is that of the translators and editors.

1. Examples are borrowed from J. C. Lavie, "Parler à l'analyste," *Nouvelle Revue de la Psychanalyse* 5 (1972).

2. Collective and specific to each language: "que (queue) de que (queues) dans la langue française!" (that there is only dick, how many dicks and tails there are in the French language!)

3. Lavie, "Parler," 294.

4. Ibid.

5. Among many other critiques, see J.-F. Lyotard, *Discours, figure* (Paris: Klincksieck, 1971), 250–60.

6. Serge Viderman, *La Construction de l'espace anaytique* (Paris: Denoël, 1970), 164.

7. Danielle Margueritat, "L'analyste et le rêveur," in *Le fait de l'analyse* 4 (March 1998): 172–73.

8. Sandor Ferenczi, *Oeuvres complètes* (Paris: Payot, 1974), 3:198.

9. Margueritat, "L'analyste," 186.

10. This position is already the object of the last paragraph of *The Interpretation of Dreams.* For a short summary, see Freud, "Die Okkulte Bedeutung des Traumes" (GW I, 569-73; SE XIX, 135–38).

11. See André Bourguignon, "Neurophysiologie du rêve et théorie psychanalytique," in *La Psychiatrie de l'enfant* XI, 1 (1968): 1–67, 6.

12. Freud writes *fremde Hilfe* and "experienced individual," *erfahrenes Individuum,* in the *Project* (*Nachtragsband,* 410).

13. Laplanche uses the word *étayage* as the translation of the German *Anlehnung,* which Strachey and others have unfortunately rendered as "anaclisis," or "anaclitic object choice," a translation Laplanche and Pontalis thus are themselves compelled to list in their *Vocabulaire de la psychanalyse.* While Jeffrey Mehlman, in his translation of Laplanche's *Life and Death in Psychoanalysis,* uses the phrase "propping up," Laplanche has told the translators that his dissatisfaction with this expression has to do with its implying the idea of *holding something up,* as opposed to that of *leaning upon* or *up against,* which is Freud's obvious meaning.

14. "As soon as this need [of food] occurs once again, a psychic motion is produced by virtue of the established connection; this motion will want to invest the mnemic image of this perception anew, and to provoke the perception itself once again, thus, properly speaking, to reestablish the situation of the first satisfaction. Such a motion is what we call a wish; the reappearance of the perception is the fulfillment of the wish" (GW II–III, 571; SE V, 565–66). The words I have added here—"of food"—come directly out of the text two lines above. But in this text the second time is not a reelaboration of the first, but only the hallucinatory repetition of perception. Square brackets here are those of the author.

15. Laplanche himself has introduced this word as a translation for the German *Nachträglichkeit,* which in French is well served by the expression *après coup,* but which the translators of the *Standard Edition* render rather prosaically—and not at all consistently—as "deferred action."

16. See Christine Lévy-Friesacher, *Meynert-Freud, "L'amentia"* (Paris: Presses Universitaires de France, 1983).

17. See a discussion of this point regarding the "Rat Man" in J. Laplanche, *Problématiques* I (Paris: Presses Universitaires de France, 1980), 273–80.

18. For a more detailed development, see J. Laplanche, *Problématiques* V (Paris: Presses Universitaires de France, 1987), 34–83.

19. Ferenczi, *Oeuvres complètes* 2:32.

20. See the dream "Tyre is thine" and my commentary on it in *Problématiques* V, 217–18.

13. Dreaming and Cinematographic Consciousness

Laura Marcus

The year 1895 is key in the history of psychoanalysis and cinema. On July 24, 1895, Freud dreamed the Dream of Irma's Injection, the Specimen Dream of *The Interpretation of Dreams.* "Do you suppose," Freud wrote to Wilhelm Fliess in a letter describing a later visit to Bellevue, the house where he had had the dream, "that someday one will read on a marble tablet on this house" that

> Here, on July 24th, 1895
> the secret of dreams
> revealed itself to Dr. Sigm Freud.[1]

During September and October 1895, Freud wrote the uncompleted *Project for a Scientific Psychology*, which, as James Strachey notes in his editorial introduction to *The Interpretation of Dreams*, contains sections constituting a first approach to a coherent theory of dreams. (SE IV, xv). *The Interpretation of Dreams* was, Freud himself claimed, "finished in all essentials at the beginning of 1896" (SE XIV, 22).

The Lumière brothers' Cinématographe gave its first public presentation (to the Société d'Encouragement de l'Industrie Nationale in Paris) on March 22, 1895, exhibiting their film "Workers Leaving the Lumière Factory" as an example of the progress being made in photography. Its immediate success was unexpected. The film is both the most unmediated of early *actualité* films and a complex act of historical reflexivity: the workers at Lumière *père*'s photographic plate factory look into the camera, which would transform the very act of looking and turn still images into moving ones. George Meliès's trick films, which directly exploited the relationship between dream and film, followed soon after.

Psychoanalysis and cinema thus emerged in tandem at the close of the nine-teenth century: twin sciences or technologies of fantasy, dream, virtual reality, and "screen memory." In the following century, a vast body of literature explored the complex historical and conceptual relationship between the two fields. Psychoanalytic film theory has turned to a wide range of Freud's writings—on fetishism, on femininity, on fantasy, on "scopophilia"—as part of this exploration, and with a focus on cinematic spectatorship. Dreams and dream theory have nonetheless retained a privileged role in the "parallel histories" of psychoanalysis and cinema, just as dreams have a privileged role in psychoanalysis itself.

Practioners and theorists of psychoanalysis have found the film–dream relationship compelling for their understanding of unconscious processes; while philosophers have turned to this relationship in their explorations of the workings of consciousness, and of the relations of space and time, in particular, to dreams and to cinema. From the first decades of the twentieth century on, cultural commentators have explored the primacy of "wish-fulfillment" in the narrative structures of films, and as equivalent to its function in dreams and daydreams. The cinema as a "dream factory" is an early designation. For filmmakers themselves, dreams and dream states seemed from the outset to be an essential part of film's ontology: while "dream sequences" within films may seem to be bounded, they are never fully sealed off from the film-space containing them. It has been said, moreover, that we can watch films precisely because we are dreamers: for Hugo von Hofmannsthal, "a secret instinct is appeased" in film spectatorship, "an instinct familiar to the dreamers of dreams."[2] Elsewhere we find the implication that the film has in some sense replaced the dream in and for the twenti-eth century: the argument might thus run that we know how to watch films because we have in the past been dreamers.

Such ideas suggest a "total world" equivalence in their accounts of filmic and oneiric universes. Yet the fascination with film and dream seems as often to situate their interrelationship on borderlines and thresholds: between sleeping and waking, inner and outer, visual and verbal, stasis and motion, reality and simulacra. It is such borderlines and thresholds that this article in part explores.

"Cinema" (Kino) and "film" are absent from Freud's theoretical work, appearing neither as topics, nor as analogies in the *Standard Edition*, though we can find references to photography and other optical technologies and instruments of vision, including the microscope and the telescope, deployed as analogues for the workings of consciousness and the unconscious. By contrast, Freud's contemporary Henri Bergson made the "cinematograph" and the "cinematographical" central to his theorizations of mind and reality, even as he expressed doubts about film (the "movement," which is in one way illusory, and which mechanistically segments and spatializes time into discrete and identical units, rather than producing it as continuous flow) as an appropriate analogue for time and motion: "[R]ests placed beside rests will never be equivalent to a movement."[3] A number of film theorists—in both the early and late twentieth century—have wanted to argue that Bergson's understandings of time and consciousness are ultimately cinematic, despite his expressions of ambivalence and even hostility toward film, and that his writings—whether overtly debating the question of the cinematographic or not—are the founding texts of philosophy and film.[4] It is also worth noting that Bergson's models of the cinematographic would have been drawn largely from late nineteenth- and early twentieth-century (pre)cinematic experiments (beginning with Etienne-Jules Marey's "chronophotography," which experimented with the representation and analysis of movement) rather than with the later narrative cinema.[5]

Underlying Freud's silence on the question of cinema may well be a resistance to the "modernization" or mechanization of thought and consciousness. As I discuss below, Freud, in the essay on "The Uncanny" (SE XVII) in particular, is resistant to the connection of "the uncanny" and its manifestations with the "novel and unfamiliar" (SE XVII, 221) (which could include the new technologies of vision and animation), firmly linking it instead with the archaic and the always known. For Freud to embrace photography as an analogue for unconscious life, as in his use of Francis Galton's "composite photography" to analogize "condensation" in the dream-work, but to remain silent on the question of cinema, may suggest a habit of nineteenth-century thought resistant to some of the innovations of the twentieth century. There may also have been an ambivalence toward the primacy of the visual, which, in *The Interpretation of Dreams*, is represented as a regression, redeemed for meaning and for culture by the highly verbal and textual work of secondary revision, narration, and interpretation. We could usefully compare Freud's approach with that of Bergson in his essay on dreams (published in France in 1901 and in an English version in 1913). There are similarities, including foci on inscriptions and on the unfathomable mysteries of dream-life—the latter taking both thinkers into the realms of psychical research and telepathy. Bergson's account, however, is more overtly concerned than Freud's with the hallucinatory and visual aspects of dreams, including the phenomena of hypnagogia and the phantasmagoric, a concern linked to Bergson's understanding of human subjectivity as both mingled with and emerging out of a universe of images.[6]

The approach of Havelock Ellis's *The World of Dreams* to the visual arena also provides a significant contrast with Freud's. Ellis writes that "[t]he commonest kind of dream is mainly a picture, but it is always a living and moving picture, however inanimate the objects which appear in vision before us would be in real life." Fascinated by the hypnagogic state—"the porch to sleep and dreams"[7]—he discusses the ways in which hypnagogic imagery crosses the threshold from waking to sleeping. Imagery in motion is at times analogized through the kaleidoscope, as a way of representing the renewal of the stream of sleeping consciousness. Echoing Baudelaire's image of the flâneur as "a kaleidoscope gifted with consciousness," Ellis writes: "[I]f the kaleidoscope were conscious we should say that each picture had been suggested by the preceding pattern—but yet definitely novel." Elsewhere Ellis makes the magic lantern the more appropriate analogue: "The movement of the cinematograph, indeed, scarcely corresponds to that fusion of heterogeneous images which marks dream visions. Our dreams are like dissolving views in which the dissolving process is carried on swiftly or slowly, but always uninterruptedly" (36). This is the only reference in *The World of Dreams* to the cinematograph, and it is striking that Ellis includes it as one among a number of optical instruments or shows, not only undifferentiated from its precursors, but less absorbing in its assumed inability to fuse and dissolve images. Freud may not, or not only, have neglected the cinema on the grounds of its modernity, its seeming lack of attachment to the already known, but because of its association with toys such as the kaleidoscope, which, for so many of the nineteenth-century commentators he critiques in the first chapter of *The Interpretation of Dreams*, implied not a pattern of difference (as it does for Ellis) but a disordered and chaotic visual regime—precisely the charge from which Freud wishes to redeem dreams and dreaming.

The absence of "film" in Freud's work does not, however, diminish the perception that there is a profound relationship between psychoanalysis and cinema, and the few "glancing" references to film in Freud's writings and in the biographical literature on Freud become highly charged. In the second volume of *Sigmund Freud: Life and Works*, Ernest Jones writes of a visit to the cinema in New York in 1909: "We all dined together in Hammerstein's roof garden, afterwards going on to a cinema to see one of the primitive films of those days with plenty of wild chasing. Ferenczi in his boyish way was very excited at it, but Freud was only quietly amused; it was the first film they had seen."[8] Stephen Heath argues that if Jones is right in claiming that this was Freud's first encounter with cinema, his disinterest becomes even more marked: there were some eighty cinemas in Vienna at this time.[9] In fact, a letter written by Freud to his family from Rome in September 1907 (published in Ernst Freud's edition of Freud's letters and in a different English translation in Jones's biography of Freud,[10] though Jones himself notes no contradiction) provides an earlier, and much fuller and more appreciative, account of cinematic viewing, as Freud describes watching open-air projections of lantern slides on the Piazza Colonna:

> They are actually advertisements, but to beguile the public these are interspersed with pictures of landscapes, Negroes of the Congo, glacier ascents and so on. But since these wouldn't be enough, the boredom is interrupted by short cinematographic performances for the sake of which the old children (your father included) suffer quietly the advertisements and monotonous photographs. They are stingy with these tidbits, however, so I have had to look at the same thing over and over again. When I turn to go I detect a certain tension in the attentive crowd which makes me look again, and sure enough a new performance has begun, and so I stay on. Until 9 p.m. I usually remain spellbound; then I begin to feel too lonely in the crowd, so I return to my room to write to you all.[11]

As Jonathan Crary notes at the close of his recent study, *Suspensions of Perception: Attention, Spectacle, and Modern Culture*, Freud says nothing of the content of the cinematographic performances.[12] The spellbinding nature of the spectacle is precisely the display of its own visibility, and this is to be situated as a historical moment in the early history of cinematic reception. I would add that Freud's account is interestingly structured around the phrase and the concept of "look[ing] again," which itself is multiplied as repetition (seeing the same thing over and over again), return (being called back to look again), and renewal (looking again as seeing anew). For Crary, Freud's account offers a specifically modernized, urban vision, as the advertisements and the images of foreign lands as touristic spectacle play over the surfaces of the ancient city and its buildings.

Freud's vivid description provides a counter to the view that he was hostile to cinema where he was not indifferent to it. There is no overt suggestion, however, that he saw in the cinematic spectacle an analogue for psychic life, or that he wished to transmute the Roman holiday experience into the work of theoretical reflection. By contrast, Lou Andreas-Salomé's journal entry of February 15, 1913, recounts both her pleasure in the movies and her thoughts on film and psychic life:

> A few purely psychological considerations deserve to be added to the many things that might be said in vindication of this Cinderella of aesthetic criticism. One has to do with the fact that only the technique of the film permits the rapid sequence which approximates our own imaginative faculty; it might even be said to imitate its erratic ways. . . . The second consideration has to do with the fact that even though the most superficial pleasure is involved, we are presented with an extraordinarily abundant variety of forms, pictures, and impressions. . . . Here in Vienna it was Tausk who took me to the movies despite work, weariness, and lack of time.[13]

Andreas-Salomé makes the crucial link between cinema and consciousness. This connection was explored at length by the psychologist Hugo Munsterberg, author of one of the earliest works on film aesthetics, *The Film: A Psychological Study* (1916), for whom film "unfold[s] our inner life, our mental play [in] tones which are fluttering and fleeting like our own mental states"[14]: "The massive outer world has lost its weight, it has been freed from space, time, and causality, and it has been clothed in the forms of our own consciousness" (95). His post-Kantian aesthetic not only connects cinema and consciousness, but makes cinema (as does Andreas-Salomé) the reflector of a particularly modernized consciousness, imaged in the terms of a Baudelairean metropolitan modernity, in which "the fleeting, passing surface suggestion" is imbued with depth and fullness only through "our mental mechanism," as the gift of consciousness to the phenomenal world. Linking "cut-back" or flash-back to "the mental act of remembering" and close-up to "the mental act of attending," he says, "It is as if the outer world itself became molded in accordance with our fleeting turns of attention or with our passing memory ideas" (41).

Freud was silent on the topic of film's capacity to "unfold our inner life." He did speak out, however, on the issue of using film as a way of representing psychoanalytic theory. The most charged moment came in 1925, when Karl Abraham wrote to Freud, telling him that he had been approached by a director (Eric Neumann) of UFA (*Universum Film Aktiengesellschaft*) about the possibility of a film exploring psychoanalytic concepts. Letters between Abraham and Freud chart Abraham's growing enthusiasm for the project and Freud's continuing resistance:

> My chief objection is still that I do not believe that satisfactory plastic representation of our abstractions is at all possible. We do not want to give our consent to anything insipid. Mr. Goldwyn was at any rate clever enough to stick to the aspect of our subject that can be plastically represented very well, that is to say, love. The small example that you mentioned, the representation of repression by means of my Worcester simile [a reference to the analogy of the invader to illustrate repression and resistance], would make an absurd rather than instructive impact.[15]

Freud may well have felt that his *Introductory Lectures* had already analogized and dramatized psychoanalytic abstractions to a sufficient degree. To represent analogies in cinematic form would thus be to further substantiate the dramatized example, rather than the concept of which it was an illustration. The film was made, however, as *Secrets of a Soul*, directed by G. W. Pabst. Abraham and Hanns Sachs acted as advisors, and Sachs wrote the pamphlet that accompanied the film and explained some of the psychoanalytic concepts it explored.

Sachs's own introduction to psychoanalysis had come with his reading of *The Interpretation of Dreams* in 1904. He abandoned his law career in its early stages and followed Freud into psychoanalytic work, initially through writing and editing, and, in 1920, through the training of analysts. Freud's Dream Book remained a key text for him, as did Freud's 1908 essay, "The Creative Writer and Day-dreaming." Fascinated by the application of psychoanalysis to the creative process and to the reception of works of art, as well as by the concept of the work of art as a "collective day-dream," Sachs explored the idea of "day-dreams in common," a concept that became central to the articles he wrote on film in the late 1920s and early 1930s for the film journal *Close Up*.[16] In an article on "Film Psychology," Sachs also opened up the relationship between conscious and unconscious knowledges in relation to dream and film, suggesting that the film-work functions not only by analogy, but by contrast with the dream-work.[17] While the dream disguises unconscious wishes and desires as a way of eluding the censor, the film reveals them. In this sense, the film could be said to be closer to dream interpretation, with its emancipatory potential, than to the dream itself.

The *Secrets of a Soul* pamphlet describes at length and in detail the action of the film as an illustration of central Freudian concepts: repression, sublimation, displacement, condensation.[18] There is, however, virtually no analysis of the ways in which the filmic medium might itself be operating in ways that are analogous to the psychic apparatus; the film seems to function at this stage for Sachs as pure illustration, though the dream sequences in the film use devices, such as superimpositions and fade-outs, which others among his contemporaries were readily mapping onto the processes of the dream-work. In some senses, then, the pamphlet serves to neutralize or, at least, to instrumentalize the cinema.

Sachs's partial occlusion of the cinematographic in the *Secrets of a Soul* pamphlet is found in a different guise and in a far more extreme form a few years earlier, in Freud's comments on Otto Rank's study, *The Double*, in the essay on "The Uncanny" (SE XVII). Freud discusses Rank's exploration of the connections "which the 'double' has with reflections in mirrors, with shadows, with guardian spirits, with the belief in the soul and with the fear of death," as well as his theories of the evolution of the idea of the double as a preservation against extinction. In a footnote he adds: "In Ewer's *Der Student von Prag*, which serves as the starting point of Rank's study on the 'double,' the hero has promised his beloved not to kill his antagonist in a duel. But on his way to the duelling-ground he meets his 'double,' who has already killed his rival" (SE XVII, 236). Ewers indeed wrote the script for *The Student of Prague* (1913), but it is striking that Freud makes no reference to the film itself, referring to the narrative in entirely literary terms.

If we turn to Rank's *The Double* (1914), however, we find in his first paragraph the following lines: "Psychoanalysis need not shy away even from some random and banal subject, if the matter at hand exhibits psychological problems whose sources and implications are not obvious. There should be no objection, then, if we take as a point of departure a 'romantic drama,' which not long ago made the rounds of our cinemas."[19] While Rank does add that "[t]hose whose concern is with literature may be reassured by the fact that the scenarist of this film, *The Student of Prague*, is an author currently in vogue and that he has adhered to prominent patterns, the effectiveness of which has been tested by time" (3–4), he goes on to make a direct connection between cinematic and psychic processes. As he writes:

> Any apprehension about the real value of a photoplay which aims so largely at achieving external effects may be postponed until we have seen in what sense a subject based upon an ancient folk-tradition, and the content of which is so eminently psychological, is altered by the demands of modern techniques of expression. It may perhaps turn out that cinematography, which in numerous ways reminds us of the dream-work, can also express certain psychological facts and relationships—which the writer often is unable to describe with verbal clarity—in such clear and conspicuous imagery that it facilitates our understanding of them. The film attracts our attention all the more readily since we have learned from similar studies that a modern treatment is often successful in reapproaching, intuitively, the real meaning of an ancient theme which has become either unintelligible or misunderstood in its course through tradition. (4)

The broader context for Rank's discussion is the uncanniness of cinema itself, described so often by early commentators as a world of shadows. "This is not life but the shadow of life and this is not movement but the soundless shadow of movement," Maxim Gorki wrote in July 1896, describing a showing of the Lumière brothers's first films: "It is terrifying to watch but it is the movement of shadows, mere shadows. Curses and ghosts, evil spirits that have cast whole spirits into eternal sleep come to mind and you feel as though Merlin's vicious trick is being played out before you."[20] For cinema's first spectators, the realism of early films, combined with their unlifelike absence of sound and color, seems to have provoked, in Yuri Tsivian's words, "the uncanny feeling that films somehow belong the world of the dead" and that "cinema is a convenient metaphor for death."[21]

There is a phenomenological fear embodied in the early reception of cinema that is strikingly reinvoked in German expressionist cinema of the 1910s and 1920s: films such as *The Student of Prague*, *The Cabinet of Dr. Caligari*, and *Nosferatu* do not merely constitute an episode in the history of cinema, but act as figurations of the materiality and the phenomenology of film *and* of fear. Such films, with their shadows, their mirrors, and their doubles, inform—in however oblique and occluded a way— many of the terms and the images of Freud's writings of the period, in particular the essay on "The Uncanny." This, like Rank's *The Double*, attempts to negotiate the rela- tionship between the archaic and the modern: the animations and automations— anthropologically conceived—of primitive mentation and belief, and of the new tech- nologies, with their power to bring still things to life and to represent (though Freud does not of course make the connection to filmic representations) "dismembered limbs, a severed head, a hand cut off at the wrist . . . feet which dance by themselves" (SE XVII, 244). Moreover, and as Friedrich Kittler suggests, psychoanalysis and film— science and technology—together extend *and* implode the life of the Romantic dou- ble.[22] The fundamental link between the two fields overrides Freud's silence on the question of the cinematic in his thoughts on "the double" and "the uncanny."

In the quotation from Rank cited above, a specific equation is made between cin- ematography and the dream-work. The plethora of psychoanalytic and psychological studies of dream-life in the 1920s and 1930s was, I would argue, linked to the devel- opment of film aesthetics, while writings on dreams and dream-life in the early twen- tieth century found new forms of association and analogy in film. The intense debates over visual-verbal representations in the transition from silent to sound film in the 1920s had highly significant counterparts in the discussions over the visual or verbal dimensions, and the alphabetical or pictorial scripts, of dream-language. Time and again in early film theory we find the paradox that this art or science or modernity is being framed in the terms of a primitive or archaic consciousness, mapping onto Freud's exploration of the "regressive" transmutation of ideas into visual pictures in his dream, and his account of visual thinking as "primitive" mentation.

Freud's account of the "apparatus" of the mind had a crucial influence on later filmic "apparatus theories," most notably the work of film theorists such as Jean- Louis Baudry and Christian Metz, who, in the 1970s, made a theoretical return to the machinery and apparatus of the cinema, constructing, as Stephen Heath notes, a conceptual synthesis of the technological and the metapsychological.[23] Film theory's fascination with psychoanalysis also has its counterpart in psychoanalytic literature's deployment of film. Analysts and theorists have taken up the cinematic dimensions of such concepts as "projection," "scene," and "screening." I have discussed elsewhere the centrality of such terms for Ella Freeman Sharpe, in her book *Dream Analysis,* for Bertram Lewin, in his work on the "dream screen," and, most recently, for Didier Anzieu, in his formulations of "the skin ego."[24] For these psychoanalytic theorists, projections, such as we have in dream images, require a screen. As Ella Freeman Sharpe stated in her account of the dream mechanisms of "dramatization" and "secondary elaboration": "A film of moving pictures is projected on the screen of our private inner cinema." One of the dreams Sharpe analyzes is an anxiety dream in which

> [a] man is acting for the screen. He is to recite certain lines of the play. The photographers and voice recorders are there. At the critical moment the actor forgets his lines. Time and again he makes the attempt with no result. Rolls of film must have been spoilt.[25]

In Sharpe's analysis of the dream the associations reveal an infantile situation in which "the dreamer was once the onlooker when his parents were 'operating' together. The baby was the original photographer and recorder and he stopped the parents in the 'act' by noise. The baby did not forget his lines!"

> The "return of the repressed" is given in the dream by the element "rolls of film must have been wasted" telling us by the device of metonymy, of a huge amount of faecal matter the baby was able to pass at that moment.
>
> Illustrated in this dream are some of the profoundest activities of the psyche. We have the recording of sight and sound by the infant and the incorporation by the senses of sight and hearing of the primal scene. We have evidence of this incorporated scene by its projection into the dream dramatization. The modern invention of the screen of the cinema is pressed into service as the appropriate symbol, the screen being the modern external device corresponding to the internal dream picture mechanism. (76–77)

Sharpe's analysis echoes (while also making explicit the film-dream analogy) Freud's account of one of the most famous dreams of psychoanalysis, his patient "the Wolf-Man," whose childhood dream was of observing, through a window, a number of white wolves sitting on a tree and looking at him. "He had woken up and seen something," Freud comments. "The attentive looking, which in the dream was ascribed to the wolves, should rather be shifted on to him. At a decisive point, therefore, a transposition has taken place" (SE XVII, 34–35). Behind the content of the dream, Freud suggests, lies the "primal scene," the "Urszene," in which the very young child observed the parents' sexual intercourse.

In Sharpe's analysis, the transposition from observer to observed noted by Freud revolves around the image of the "screen" as both interior (the "inner private cinema") and "exterior" ("the modern external device"). The perception both extends and renders cinematographic Freud's claim in "A Metapsychological Supplement to the Theory of Dreams" that "[a] dream is . . . among other things, a *projection:* an externalization of an internal process" (SE XIV, 223), and, in "The Ego and the Id," that "The ego is first and foremost a bodily ego: it is not merely a surface entity, but is itself the projection of a surface" (SE XIX, 26). Freud's emphases in this essay on the ego as a bodily "projection," and on the body and its surface as a "place from which both external and internal perceptions may spring" (SE XIX, 25), allow us to bring together the concepts of "projection" as "prosthesis" (the body extended or projected into the world) and as a "screening," whereby not only the subject's body but his or her relationship to the "skin," the screen-surface of the other (the mother) is projected or imaged.

In Bertram Lewin's important work of the 1940s, the "dream screen" becomes the hallucinatory representation of the mother's breast, which once acted as a prelude to sleep, while the forgetting of dreams is often imaged as a rolling up or away of the dream screen, repeating the experience of the withdrawal of the breast.[26] In a more recent study, and returning to the Wolf-Man, Lewin explores the ways in which events in motion (paradigmatically the parents "operating" together in the "primal scene") are remembered as "stills": "They are as if immobilized for better viewing."[27] "Screen memories," it could be said, "freeze-frame" the moving picture. By extension, Freud's photographic analogies could be taken not merely as pre-cinematic concepts, but as ways of understanding the stillness of which the moving (cinematic) image is truly composed.

In making a distinction between the screen and the dream-images projected onto it, Lewin allows for a distinction to be drawn between sleep (the blank screen) and dream (the play and projection of visual images). The distinction between sleep and dream is relatively untheorized in *The Interpretation of Dreams*, as are threshold states between sleeping and waking. It is to such states that I now turn, in relation to cinema and film spectatorship, in part as a way of pursuing the question of the archaic, the modern, and their interrelationship.

My starting point comes in the opening section of chapter 2 of *The Interpretation of Dreams*, the preamble to the analysis of the specimen dream, the Dream of Irma's Injection. Freud is describing his development of the techniques of free association and their relationship to dream interpretation. This method of interpretation, he writes, "involves some psychological preparation of the patient. We must aim at bringing about two changes in him: an increase in the attention he pays to his own psychical perceptions and the elimination of the criticism by which he normally sifts the thoughts that occur to him" (SE IV, 101). The distinction Freud draws—as Strachey translates it—is between the "frame of mind of a man who is reflecting" and "that of a man who is observing his own psychical processes." While attention is concentrated in both cases, the man who is reflecting is exercising his *critical* faculty, and censoring his thoughts. The self-observer, by contrast, need only suppress his critical faculty to enable "innumerable ideas [to] come into his consciousness of which he could otherwise never have got hold." Freud continues:

What is in question, evidently, is the establishment of a psychical state which, in its distribution of psychical energy (that is, of mobile attention), bears some analogy to the state before falling asleep—and no doubt also to hypnosis. As we fall asleep, "involuntary ideas" emerge. . . . [and] change into visual and acoustic images. (SE IV, 102)

The abandonment of the critical function is also to be found, Freud argues, in poetic creation.

The significant phrase in this section of *The Interpretation of Dreams* is "mobile attention," and I want now to link the concept to those modes of (in)attention and reduced wakefulness that so preoccupied critical theorists such as Siegfried Kracauer and Walter Benjamin, and which the film threorist Christian Metz explored in a different conceptual and historical context, one more directly in relation to film and dream, in *The Imaginary Signifier*.[28] The film-dream analogy functions not only as a correlation between dream-work and film-work, but through the concept of states— film states and dream states—which converge in the transitional space between sleeping and waking. As Kracauer stated in his *Theory of Film:* "Lowered consciousness invites dreaming."[29]

The work of Benjamin is of significant interest here. Axel Honneth has argued that Benjamin took from American pragmatism and French versions of *Lebensphilosophie* (especially the work of Bergson) a fascination with religious and aesthetic experiences as "borderline experiences in which reality as a whole is experienced as a field of subjective forces."[30] Hence Benjamin's preoccupation with situations of reduced attention or half-wakefulness—flâneurie, reading, listening to music, intoxication, artistic creation—and above all, moments of awakening, "when the environment's perceptual stimuli cannot yet be instrumentally classified in accordance with everyday routine."[31] In ways that are at least analogous to Freud's distinction between reflection and self-observation—the latter allied to free association—Benjamin suggests, in Honneth's words, that "when our purposively directed concentration is low, we tend to experience reality as a field of surprising correspondences and analogies."[32] For Benjamin, modernity, with its demands for instrumental, purposive, rational attention, threatens the "anthropologically based potential for intensifying experience by reducing attention."[33]

Film plays a most complex and ambiguous role in this model. The loss of aura, which the cinema—among other modern technologies—embodies, could be seen (as Honneth sees it) as a deprivation of those experiences of the shattering of the self and of reduced attention. Yet Benjamin's film viewer is also a centerless subject, responding to the "shock" of cinematic experience—its radical disruptions and "changes of place and focus which periodically assail the spectator"[34]—"in a state of distraction." The cinema trains the spectator, Benjamin seems to suggest, in the transformed mode of perception demanded by modern life. For Siegfried Kracauer, writing a decade earlier, "distraction"—originally a negative attribute, as opposed to contemplative concentration—takes on a positive aspect as it becomes anchored in a nonbourgeois mode of visual and sensorial experience, a form of attention or inattention appropriate to the fragmentary, discontinuous nature of the modern visual media.

Kracauer's *Theory of Film* (published in 1960, but including earlier material) explores the relationship between dreaming and cinema through "the two directions of dreaming": toward and into the object and "away from the given image into subjective reveries." These apparently opposed movements of dreaming are in fact intertwined:

> Trance-like immersion in a shot or a succession of shots may at any moment yield to daydreaming which increasingly disengages itself from the imagery occasioning it. . . . Together the two intertwined dream processes constitute a veritable stream of consciousness whose contents—cataracts of indistinct fantasies and inchoate thoughts—still bear the imprint of the bodily sensations from which they issue. (166)

The relations of "inside" and "outside" here strongly recall Freud's emphases, noted above, on the ego as a bodily "projection," and remind us of the extent to which mind-body and inner perception-outer world dichotomies are dissolved in Freudian dream theories.

The work of Christian Metz leads us back to the question of cinema spectatorship as a mode of reduced attention on the borderlines of sleep and wakefulness:

> [T]he filmic flux resembles the dream flux more than other products of the waking state do. It is received, as we have said, in a state of lessened wakefulness. Its signifier (images accompanied by sound and movement) inherently confers on it a certain affinity with the dream, for it coincides directly with one of the major features of the dream signifier, "imaged" expression, the considerations of representability, to use Freud's term.[35]

Throughout part three of *The Imaginary Signifier*—"The Fiction Film and its Spectator"—Metz sets dream, daydream, and film alongside and against each other through the question of degrees of sleep and wakefulness. Film and dream "are interwoven . . . by differences." The filmic state "is marked by a general tendency to lower wakefulness"; "[t]he filmic and dream states tend to converge when the spectator begins to doze off [*s'endormir*] . . . or when the dreamer begins to wake up. But the dominant situation is that in which film and dream are not confounded: this is because the film spectator is a man awake, whereas the dreamer is a man asleep" (198). Nonetheless, "the filmic situation brings with it certain elements of motor inhibition, and it is in this respect a kind of sleep in miniature, a kind of waking sleep. . . . To leave the cinema is a little like getting up: not always easy (except if the film was really indifferent)" (117). "The spectator puts himself into a state of lessened alertness. . . . Among the different regime of waking, the filmic state is one of those least unlike sleep and dreaming, dreamful sleep" (128). Metz's procedure, however, is not to rest with such formulations, but to introduce new terms for comparison; in this case, it is the daydream, so he concludes with the image of the film as a force field, in which distinct regimes of consciousness—reality, dream, and daydream—are momentarily, but only momentarily, reconciled.

I want to draw my discussion to a close by pointing to the significance of the borderline for film, dream, and modernism. The transitional states between sleeping and waking, and the experiences of going to sleep and of waking up, are central to modernist literature. Proust is the crucial example here. The most intensely cinematic or cinematographic works of modern literature are also those that are most preoccupied with the representation of states of going to sleep, sleeping, and awakening: for example, Virginia Woolf's *To the Lighthouse*, which is so bound up with the representation of reduced attentiveness and lowered wakefulness, as in Mrs Ramsay's evening reverie: "All the being and the doing, expansive, glittering, vocal, evaporated; and one shrunk, with a sense of solemnity, to being oneself, a wedge-shaped core of darkness, something invisible to others."[36] The central section of the novel, "Time Passes," is highly cinematic in its representations of sound "folded into silence" and of the animation of the object world. It begins and ends with the processes of going to sleep and awakening—the last word of the section is indeed "Awake"—while its center is a correlation between dream and the play of projected images on surface, which implies a cinematographic realm or consciousness. The last part of the novel, "The Lighthouse," returns to the realms of daydream, reverie, memory, and hauntings.

The importance of "the borderline" and of transitional states emerges, in a rather different way, in the film writings of the poet H.D., a central figure for the interrelations of psychoanalysis and cinema, historically and conceptually. In her articles for the film journal *Close Up* in the late 1920s (also the forum for Hanns Sachs's writings on cinema), H.D. describes the processes of an initial resistance to film, which we could link to the resistance to sleep, understood as a fear of the loss of identity and even of death. As Freud writes in "A Metapsychological Supplement to the Theory of Dreams," the ego, in extreme cases, "renounces sleep because of its fear of its dreams" (SE XIV, 225).

In her article on the Russian film *Expiation*, H.D. writes of the ways in which, about to enter the cinema to watch the film, she finds herself impelled to create a form of prefilmic experience from the vision of the street: "I so poignantly wanted to re-visualize those squares of doors and shutters and another and another bit of detail that of necessity was lost at first that I did illogically (I was already late) climb back."[37] She enters the cinema when the film is a third over: "Rain poured over a slab of earth and I felt all my preparation of the extravagantly contrasting out of doors gay little street, was almost an ironical intention, someone, something 'intended' that I should grasp this, that some mind should receive this series of uncanny and almost psychic sensations in order to transmute them elsewhere; in order to translate them" (39–40). Film and prefilm (the "dimensional dream-tunnel" of the street) are brought into an "uncanny" relationship, allowing H.D. as spectator, to "translate" the "remote and symbolical" dimensions of the film. *Expiation*'s destructive beauty is perceived by H.D. as an "excess" having echoes of the Romantic sublime: it is something beyond the limit, "the word after the last word is spoken," "taking the human mind and *spirit* further than it can go." Her film aesthetics and her model of vision are predicated on symbol, gesture, "hieroglyph," and her film writing tends to provide not retrospective judgment on a film, but a performative running commentary on the processes of spectating, which becomes a form of "inner speech," acting as a screen onto which the film images can be projected.

H.D.'s article on *The Student of Prague* describes or enacts a spectatorial procedure similar to that in *Expiation*, an initial resistance to film, an irritated awareness of her surroundings, a disorder: "Something has been touched before I realise it, some hidden spring; there is something wrong with this film, with me, with the weather, with something," and then a moment of understanding and an increasing absorption in the film, until its close, when she "awakens" to the discordant voices of her fellow spectators: "A small voice . . . will whisper there within me, 'You see I was right, you see it will come. In spite of "Gee" and "Doug Fairbanks" and "we must have something cheerful," it must come soon: a universal language, a universal art open alike to the pleb and the inititate.'"[38] The promise of the film as "universal language"—which did not survive the transition to film sound for H.D.—becomes increasingly inseparable from a model of the "universal language" of the dream.

For H.D. the intertwining of (silent) cinema and psychoanalysis was cemented by the cinema of Pabst, whose *Secrets of a Soul* was, as I have noted, supervised by Hanns Sachs, H.D.'s analyst for a brief period. H.D. not only wrote for *Close Up*; she also acted in the films directed by one of the journal's editors, Kenneth Macpherson.[39] The most ambitious film, *Borderline*, in which H.D. acted alongside Paul Robeson, took *Secrets of the Soul* as a central model, including the publication of a pamplet, written by H.D., to explain the film.

In the spring of 1933, as *Close Up* entered its final year, H.D. traveled to Vienna for psychoanalysis with Freud, bearing Sachs's recommendation. She did not refer to her work in and on film in her accounts of the analysis—"Writing on the Wall" (1945–46) and "Advent" (1933–48), published together as *Tribute to Freud* in 1985—but it seems likely that she saw her sessions with Freud as a way of continuing, or perhaps replacing, the work of film, finding in dream and symbolic interpretation an equivalent to, and extension of, the "language" of the silent cinema, which she invested with both individual and "universal" meaning.

The "shapes, lines, graphs" of dreams are, H.D. writes, "the *hieroglyph of the unconscious*."[40] In an echo of Freud's repeated references in *The Interpretation of Dreams* to the popular newspaper *Fliegende Blatter*—in one of which he compares the work of "secondary revision" with "the enigmatic inscriptions with which *Fliegende Blatter* has for so long entertained its readers" (SE V, 500)—H.D. discusses "the newspaper class" of dreams, implicitly suggesting the ways in which the diurnal newspaper itself provides the materials for the "day's residues":

> The printed page varies, cheap-news-print, good print, bad print, smudged and uneven print—there are the great letter words of an advertisement or the almost invisible pin-print; there are the huge capitals of a child's alphabet chart or building blocks; letters or ideas may run askew on the page, as it were; they may be purposeless; they may be stereotyped and not meant for "reading" but as a test.[41]

The passage strongly recalls the debates about film captions and intertitles in the 1920s, and their indeterminate nature as speech or writing, as in the Hungarian film theorist Béla Balázs's account of the ways in which emotions in the silent film were "made visible in the form of lettering. . . . It was an accepted convention, for instance, that alerting alarm-signals rushed at us from the screen with tousled letters rapidly increasing in space. . . . At other times a slowly darkening title signified a pause full of meaning or a melancholy musing."[42] The "enigmatic inscriptions" to which Freud refers are also the alphabets or hieroglyphs of film and dream.

In *Tribute to Freud*, as in others of her autobiographical writings, H.D. represents her childhood memories and dreams as moments of vision, which are also moments in a history of pre-cinema and cinema, and autobiography becomes intertwined with a history of optics (lenses, daguerrotypes, transparencies). Most strikingly, there is the "writing on the wall," her "visionary" experience in Corfu in the early 1920s, which Freud saw as "the most dangerous symptom" and H.D. herself viewed as her most significant life experience. She recounts, frame by frame, the inscription of hieroglyphs, images projected on a wall in light, not shadow. The first are like magic lantern slides, the later images resemble the earliest films. "For myself," she writes, differentiating her position from that of Freud, "I consider this sort of dream or projected picture of vision as a sort of halfway state between ordinary dream and the vision of those who, for lack of a more definite term, we must call psychics or clairvoyants" (41). Later in the text, she recalls an earlier dream or "flash of vision" of a carved block of stone, a solid shape that appeared before her eyes "before sleeping or just on wakening" (64). "Crossing the line," "crossing the threshold," are H.D.'s signature phrases. They refer both to the blurred borderline between ordinary experience and "psychic" life, and to the threshold between the states of sleeping and waking. In this indeterminate zone, films and dreams share a reality.

For H.D., remembered scenes, recalled in the analytic session, "are like transparencies, set before candles in a dark room," and the network of memories builds up to become a surface, onto which "there fell inevitably a shadow, a writing-on-the-wall, a curve like a reversed, unfinished S and a dot beneath it, a question mark, the shadow of a question—*is this it?*" (30). Throughout *Tribute to Freud* (and its companion text, *Advent*) we are led around (as in a cinematic panning-shot) the space of Freud's consulting room in Vienna, following the line of its walls, the fourth of which is a wall that is not a wall, its folding doors opening onto a connecting room, the "room beyond," which "may appear very dark or there may be broken light and shadow" (23). She links this "fourth wall" and the room beyond, which contains Freud's books and antiquities, to the "fourth dimension," the dimension that, for Sergei Eisenstein, writing in *Close Up*, was the dimension of the Kino. It is the "fourth wall" and the "room beyond" that both H.D. and Freud face or look toward, as she lies on the couch with Freud seated in the corner behind her, his cigar smoke rising in the air.

In *Advent*, the account of her analysis with Freud based most closely on the notes she made at the time, H.D. represents Freud as absorbed by particular aspects of her Corfu experience, the Writing on the Wall of her hotel room, including

> the lighting of the room, or possible reflections or shadows. I described the room again, the communicating door, the door out to the hall and the one window. He asked if it was a French window. I said, "No—one like that," indicating the one window in his room. (170)

In *Advent*, the space of the hotel room, the scene of the Writing on the Wall, becomes increasingly identified with the space of Freud's consulting room, an identity to which his own insistent questioning would seem to point. If both spaces are the sites of projection, of picture-writing, of a Writing on the Wall, then psychoanalysis, too, becomes a cinematographic arena, with both analyst and analyand facing toward a surface—wall or screen—onto which memories and imaginings are projected.

As H.D.'s *Tribute to Freud* helps us to understand, Freud's silence on the question of cinema (a silence with which H.D., despite all her then recent and intense engagement with film, appears to have colluded) conceals the profundity of the relationship between psychoanalysis and film. Psychoanalysis is itself cinema, the projection and play of sign, image, and scene upon a screen that, like H.D.'s representations of Freud's "fourth wall," is at once past, present, and future and is simultaneously absent and present, wall and not-wall. In this reading, the absence of filmic analogies in Freud's writings does not signal an indifference toward cinema. In the absence of analogy, a more fundamental relationship—the identity between psychoanalysis and film—begins to emerge.

NOTES

1. Jeffrey Moussaieff Masson, *The Assault on Truth: Freud's Suppression of the Seduction Theory* (New York: Penguin, 1985), 417.

2. Hugo von Hoffmannsthal, "A Substitute for Dreams," *The London Mercury*, November 1923 to April 1924, 177–79, translated from "Der Ersatz für die Träume" (1921).

3. Henri Bergson, *Creative Evolution* (London: Macmillan, 1911), 329, trans. Arthur Mitchell, from *L'Evolution creatrice* (1907).

4. See in particular the work of Gilles Deleuze, especially *Cinéma 1: L'image-mouvement* (Paris: Minuit, 1983), trans. Hugh Tomlinson and Barbara Habberjam as *Cinema 1: The Movement Image* (Minneapolis: University of Minnesota Press, 1986); and *Cinéma 2: L'image-temps*

(Paris: Minuit, 1985), trans. Hugh Tomlinson and Robert Galeta as *Cinema 2: The Time-Image* (Minneapolis: University of Minnesota Press, 1989).

5. Mary Ann Doane has argued for a conceptual and historical link between Freud and Marey, in that both psychoanalysis and chronophotography were attempts to correlate storage and time. See Doane, "Freud, Marey, and the Cinema," in *Endless Night: Cinema and Psychoanalysis, Parallel Histories*, ed. Janet Bergstrom (Berkeley and Los Angeles: University of California Press, 1999), 57–87.

6. Henri Bergson, *Dreams* (1914), trans. Edwin E. Slosson (London: Unwin).

7. Havelock Ellis, *The World of Dreams* (London: Constable, 1911), 32.

8. Ernest Jones, *Sigmund Freud: Life and Work* (London: Hogarth, 1955), 2:62.

9. Stephen Heath, "Cinema and Psychoanalysis: Parallel Histories," in *Endless Night: Cinema and Psychoanalysis, Parallel Histories*, ed. J. Bergstrom (Berkeley and Los Angeles: University of California Press, 1999), 25.

10. Jones, *Sigmund Freud*, 40–41.

11. Sigmund Freud, *The Letters of Sigmund Freud*, ed. Ernst L. Freud, trans. Tania and James Stern (New York: Basic Books, 1975), 261.

12. Jonathan Crary, *Suspensions of Perception: Attention, Spectacle, and Modern Culture* (Cambridge, Mass: MIT Press, 1999).

13. Lou Andreas-Salomé, *The Freud Journal*, trans. S. A. Leavy (London: Quartet, 1987), 101.

14. Hugo Munsterberg, *The Film: A Psychological Study* (New York: Dover, 1970), 72.

15. "A Psycho-Analytic Dialogue: The Letters of Sigmund Freud and Karl Abraham, 1907–1926," ed. Ernst L. Freud and Hilda C. Abraham, trans. Bernard Marsh and Hilda C. Abraham (New York: Basic Books, 1965), 80.

16. The *Close Up* essays discussed in this chapter have been anthologized in *Close Up 1927–1933: Cinema and Modernism*, ed. James Donald, Anne Friedberg, and Laura Marcus (London: Cassell, 1998).

17. Hanns Sachs, "Film Psychology" (1928), in ibid., 3, 5.

18. Hanns Sachs, *Psycho-Analyse: Rätsel des Unbewussten* (Berlin: Lichtbild-Buhner, 1926).

19. Otto Rank, *The Double: A Psychoanalytical Study*, trans. Harry Tucker (London: Maresfield, 1989). 3.

20. Richard Taylor and Ian Christie, eds., *The Film Factory: Russian and Soviet Cinema in Documents 1896–1939* (London: Routledge, 1988), 25.

21. Yuri Tsivian, *Early Cinema in Russia and Its Cultural Reception*, trans. Alan Bodger (Chicago: University of Chicago Press, 1994), 6.

22. Friedrich Kittler, *Literature, Media, Information Systems* (Amsterdam: Overseas Publishers Association, 1997).

23. Stephen Heath, *Questions of Cinema* (Bloomington: Indiana University Press, 1981), 223.

24. Laura Marcus, *Sigmund Freud's The Interpretation of Dreams: New Interdisciplinary Essays* (Manchester: Manchester University Press, 1999).

25. Ella Freeman Sharpe, *Dream Analysis* (London: Hogarth, 1937), 76–77.

26. Bertram Lewin, "Sleep, the Mouth, and the Dream Screen," *Psychoanalytic Quarterly* 15 (1946): 419–34.

27. Bertram Lewin, *The Image and the Past* (New York: International Universities Press, 1968), 16–17.

28. Christian Metz, *The Imaginary Signifier: Psychoanalysis and the Cinema*, trans. C. Britton, A. Williams, B. Brewster, and A. Guzzetti (Bloomington: Indiana University Press, 1982).

29. Siegfried Kracauer, *Theory of Film: The Redemption of Physical Reality* (New York: Oxford University Press, 1965), 163.

30. Axel Honneth, "A Communicative Disclosure of the Past: on the Relation between Anthropology and Philosophy of History in Walter Benjamin," in *The Actuality of Walter Benjamin*, ed. L. Marcus and L. Nead (London: Lawrence and Wishart, 1998).

31. Ibid., 122.

32. Ibid.

33. Ibid., 123.

34. Walter Benjamin, "The Work of Art in the Age of Mechanical Reproduction," trans. Harry Zohn, in *Illuminations* (New York: Schocken, 1968), 238.

35. Metz, *Imaginary Signifier*, 124.

36. Virginia Woolf, *To the Lighthouse* (Harmondsworth: Penguin, 1992), 69.

37. H.D., "Expiation," *Close Up* 2, no. 5 (1928): 5-49.

38. H.D., "Conrad Veidt: The Student of Prague," *Close Up* 1, no. 3 (1927), 34–44.

39. *Close Up* was edited by Kenneth Macpherson and by Bryher (Winifred Ellerman). Bryher was also analyzed by Hanns Sachs, and writes about him in her memoir, *The Heart to Artemis: A Writer's Memoirs* (London: Collins, 1963).

40. H.D., *Tribute to Freud* (Manchester: Carcanet, 1985).

41. Ibid., 92.

42. Béla Balázs, *Theory of Film*, trans. Edith Bone (London: Dobson, 1952), 183.

14. A Knock Made for the Eye

IMAGE AND AWAKENING IN DELEUZE AND FREUD

Yün Peng

THOUGHT AS THEATER

This essay is part of a larger project in which I try to trace certain links in twentieth-century thought among thinkers such as Freud, Deleuze, Benjamin, Heidegger, and Blanchot. I introduce my theme by referring to Foucault's 1970 essay on Deleuze, "Theatrum Philosophicum." Here Foucault writes that the most important question for philosophy now, as Deleuze shows us, is the relation between thought and non-thought, or stupidity. Thinking is therefore an *act* in the double sense of the word. It is first of all an act of giving birth to itself, from *and* in relation to stupidity. The act of birth—and here comes the second sense of the word—is enacted in what Foucault calls "a theater of mime," in which thought "approaches" and "mimes" stupidity by remaining "motionless to the point of stupefaction," and lets stupidity "slowly grow" within itself, all the while awaiting "the shock of difference."[1] Deleuze's "philosophy as theater" is the *scene* of thought: "multiple, fugitive, and instantaneous *scenes* in which blind gestures signal to each other" (190, 196).

I wish to call attention to the word *scene* here. In *What Is Philosophy?* Deleuze and Guattari speak of philosophy as being dependent on a prephilosophical act, namely, the laying out of a plane of immanence. The plane of immanence "*is not a concept that is or can be thought* but rather the *image* of thought" (my emphasis).[2] The question I ask here is, why image, or scene? Why does the scene or the image crop up precisely at the critical moment when it is the relation between thought and its outside that is at stake?

In "Theatrum Philosophicum," the most important gesture Foucault sees in Deleuze's philosophy of immanence is an affirmation of both the event and the phantasm:

> Thinking . . . requires the release of a phantasm in the mime that produces it as a single stroke; it makes the event indefinite so that it repeats itself as a singular universal. It is this construction of the event *and* the phantasm that leads to thought in an absolute sense. A further clarification: if the role of thought is to produce the phantasm theatrically and repeat the universal event in its extreme point of singularity, then what is thought itself if not the event that befalls the phantasm and the phantasmatic repetition of the absent event? (178)

I propose that Deleuze's concept of the "crystal image" is precisely the image of thought with which I am concerned. In the crystal image Deleuze has found a different place for phantasm other than the one defined by the dichotomy of "essence" versus "appearance." A crystal image is a redoubling, a "small circuit" in which the real and the imaginary, the actual and the virtual "chase after each other, exchange roles and become indiscernible." It is the "coalescence of an actual image and *its* virtual image, the indiscernibility of two distinct images."[3] In the crystal image, the two sides—the real and the imaginary, the virtual and the actual—are linked only by the heterogeneity between them, and this in the same way that, for Foucault, the theater of thought affirms both the event and phantasm, but affirms only in *disjunction*. The crystal image is thus a *scene* in which event and phantasm are constantly in exchange with each other.[4]

A fuller understanding of the crystal image takes us to Freud, a thinker who, as we shall see, tackled a very similar problem.

FREUD'S DREAM: A CRYSTAL IMAGE

The Dream of the Burning Child is introduced by Freud in chapter 7 of *The Interpretation of Dreams*, where Freud is about to embark on his general psychology. The dream, which Lacan considers to be "in a category of its own," goes as follows:

> A father had been watching beside his child's sick-bed for days and nights on end. After the child had died, he went into the next room to lie down, but left the door open so that he could see from his bedroom into the room in which his child's body was laid out, with tall candles standing around it. An old man had been engaged to keep watch over it, and sat beside the body murmuring prayers. After a few hour's sleep, the father had a dream that *his child was standing beside his bed, caught him by the arm and whispered to him reproachfully: "Father, don't you see I'm burning?"* He woke up, noticed a bright glare from the next room, hurried into it and found that the old watchman had dropped off to sleep and that the wrappings and one of the arms of his beloved child's dead body had been burned by a lighted candle that had fallen on them.[5]

With a gesture uncharacteristic of him, Freud quickly sets aside the question of meaning: the dream, he says, "raises no problem of interpretation" (SE V, 510). The peculiarity of the dream is rather the structural symmetry, the "quasi-identity," as Lacan puts it, between the burning in the dream and the burning in reality.[6] But precisely because the distance between dreaming and waking is here at its smallest limit, the difference between them is all the more irreducible. The first question that arises is thus: what is the relation between the dream scene and the reality?

In analyzing Freud's dream, Lacan offers an example. Suppose someone knocks at the door when he, Lacan, is asleep. Because of the knock, he begins to have a dream, though in the dream the knock is disguised, as it often happens in so-called "awakening dreams" (i.e., dreams in which the instigating disturbance is masked so as to prolong the sleep). He then wakes up and is aware of the knocking. But how—since the knocking is thus absent from perception? Here is Lacan's main point: the knock that finds its place in consciousness is a re-presentation. In other words, the knock is *re-presented* in the subject's consciousness insofar as it becomes caught up in a web of coordinates reestablished upon awakening ("I'm here," "I am waking up," etc.). There is a split between perception (as reception) and consciousness. When the knocking occurs in the subject's sleep, its impression is received, but not registered in consciousness. It only enters the subject's consciousness in the form of representation, thus at the very moment when it has already and definitively been left out of perception. The knock *itself*, as an event, therefore, eludes the subject through the irreducible gap between perception (which comes too early) and consciousness (which comes too late). The event of the knock is encountered neither in dream, nor in waking.[7] Meanwhile, the dream, though it does not reproduce the knock, nevertheless transmits its effect; the subject is "knocked up."

The Dream of the Burning Child has a similar structure. The reality (noise, glare, etc.) recognized by the waking consciousness is—as in the case of the knocking—a representation, or, in Lacan's words, a representation "*by means of* reality." The dream scene, on the other hand, is the counterpart of the conscious representation. It is that which takes the place of the representation. In other words, the dream is not a representation; it is rather a placeholder for something that is not present. This something is the real.[8]

Precisely because the dream is not a representation (but is rather, like Freud's soldiers' dreams, already a repetition, an afterimage, as it were, of the missed encounter with the real) it is, for Lacan, more "real" than the noise, glare, and so on by which the father also recognizes the reality of the fire in the next room. It is "only in the dream" that the father's encounter with another reality, in the form of the child's voice, can occur. But that is not all. Lacan is rather more interested in the "forking" that has taken place between reality and dream, a forking in which lies the "ambiguity of awakening." It is "between dream and awakening" that the encounter is missed.[9] The real is therefore located precisely in the gap, in the parting of the two corresponding lines: the real is what binds them by dispersing them. Though absent, the "knock" of the real impregnates the dream, which rises up as the effect of the missed encounter and also forms the empty core around which consciousness weaves together its representations. A bullet of void, the "knock" shoots through, and binds together, the two walls of the symmetrical structure of awakening: "I am *knocked up.*"[10]

As described in Lacan's reading of Freud, this structure is precisely that of a crystal image. The crystal image is pivotal to Deleuze's attempt at extracting such notions as the "cause" and the "social whole" from their Hegelian dialectical entanglement. Following Spinoza, he argues that the real cause, which is "coextensive with the whole social field" can only be an immanent, "absent cause." The immanent cause is a cause that manifests itself only in the effects it produces; it is "'not above' but within the very tissue" of its own effects. The immanent cause realizes itself "only by taking diverging paths, splitting into dualisms, and following lines of differentiation." [11] In other words, the virtual actualizes itself by dispersing into two forms: between these two is an irreducible "non-place." In Lacan's version, this gap forced open by the virtual is the place—or non-place—of the unconscious, or the real. The unconscious is a limbo: it is "neither being, nor non-being, but the unrealized"—in other words, the real is the virtual.[12] It is a gap in causality: "[T]he Freudian unconscious is situated at that point, where, between cause and that which it affects, there is always something wrong."[13] But the gap is precisely the cause, because the encounter with the real is always missed and an entire series of repetitions is generated. Thus, in the Dream of the Burning Child, the real is neither the dream, nor the reality: it is rather the power that has connected the two by setting them apart, the absent "knock" that has produced the crystalline structure.

In the Dream of the Burning Child, as with a crystal image, the imaginary (the dream scene) comes into relation with the real, and "there is no longer any linkage of the real with the imaginary, but [rather an] *indiscernibility of the two,* a perpetual exchange."[14] First, there is the indiscernibility between the dream scene and the traumatic void behind: the awakening takes place precisely *in* the dream. Then there is an exchange between the actual and virtual at another level: for what is the accident? As Freud shows in the Wolf-Man Case, an accident, such as the witnessing of the "primal scene," is a contingent event in an individual's life; but it "becomes necessary" as soon as it marks the point of contact between the individual and phylogenetic development (SE XVII). If we think of the latter as a circuit of repetition that exists independently outside the individual, we begin to understand that the unconscious is at once "the inside that lies deeper than any internal world," and the outside that is "farther away than any external world."[15]

CINEMA AND THE PRIMAL SCENE

The resemblance between dream and crystal image is not a coincidental one. According to Deleuze, the crystal image emerges out of a crisis that marks the "break" between modern (postwar) cinema and classical (prewar) cinema: the crisis of the sensory-motor link. For him, the breakdown of the sensory-motor link—or, in other words, the link between perception and action—is what characterizes the postwar period as a new phase of modernity. In cinema, the rupture changes the nature of image. Classical cinema makes an attempt to contain the crisis by reestablishing the link between images and extending it into action. In modern cinema, this is no longer possible. Action, as well as narrative, becomes fragmented. Thus being cut off from motor development, an image comes into relation only with *its* virtual image. For the modern subject, the breakdown of the sensory-motor link means that s/he no longer has the ability to act; s/he is lost in a purely optical and acoustic situation that no longer extends into action. The character becomes a *seer* rather than an *agent*.[16]

The breakdown of the sensory-motor link has left us profoundly in the condition of dreaming. Like images in cinema, dream unfolds in a suspended world in which no action is possible. Indeed, it is the paralysis of the subject in dream that puzzles Freud in his interpretation of the Dream of the Burning Child: at a moment when immediate action seems most necessary, why dream at all?

For Deleuze, the loss of one's ability to act is the consequence of the condition of modernity. It is part and parcel of the shock experience characteristic of this era of the subject. The subject's perception no longer extends into action because s/he is confronted with something "too powerful, too beautiful, too painful" for him/her to act.[17] The modern experience is too overwhelmingly shocking to be absorbed by consciousness. Likewise, modern cinema becomes a scene that unfolds by itself in front of one's eyes, one both too overwhelming and too fascinating—this is the *primal scene.*

To compare cinema to the primal scene is not invariably to reduce cinematic images to castration. The fundamental resemblance between the two lies rather in the peculiar temporal structure these share, namely, the structure of deferral Freud discovers in the Wolf-Man Case. In cinema as in dream, time is "out of joint." There is an essential passivity on the part of the subject. The position of the *seer*—the subject in dream and the character involved in optical and acoustic situations—is "profoundly that of someone who does not see. The subject does not see where he is leading, he follows."[18] If the subject is paralyzed in its action, it is because there is an essential piece, something fundamentally missing. Vis-à-vis the scene, the subject is always either too early or too late. This also amounts to saying that the scene is never entirely a presence, never fully present.

The temporality of deferral brings the question of visibility to the fore, inasmuch as perceptual images are associated with consciousness and therefore with representation. In every perceptual image, a traumatic "knock" is always missed. It is in this sense that Lacan maintains that the gaze is what is always elided in vision.[19] However, the "knock," which bypasses the shield of consciousness to leave a trace in the unconscious, comes back in dream and is what motivates dream images. Images in dream therefore unfold in the gap between perception and consciousness. Likewise, consciousness is always belated in the "purely optical and sound situation" of the postwar cinema. Thus in dream as well as in cinema, one sees precisely what is invisible, what is eluded in the "normal" perception. In other words, what distinguishes the image of Irma's throat in Freud's dream, or the butterfly in the Wolf-Man's dream, from "normal" perceptual images is that they are stripped of the "wandering shadow" of the ego and are rather haunted by the encounter with the Real.

For Deleuze, image is distinguished from perception because it is neither hidden, nor visible. The visible in modern cinema is haunted by the invisible, and what one sees in cinema is precisely the invisible. How can something be "neither hidden nor visible"? We have first to realize that here we are not dealing with the opposition between the surface and what is hidden beneath it. In other words, this is not a question of depth. The invisible is not hidden. We are rather dealing with something like a film strip—to use Jean-Clet Martin's metaphor—on which images are superimposed.[20] Everything is on one single surface; one only needs the right running speed for what is on this surface to become legible. This is precisely the problem Freud faces in the Wolf-Man Case. The importance of the "primal scene" as an analytic—and, shall we say philosophical—construct, lies in that it enables Freud to make a temporal cut into the entangled and superimposed threads of the case. The primal scene holds together two irreconcilable things, namely, the unconscious, which is timeless, and the analytic process, which is necessarily temporal. To extend the metaphor a little bit, shall we say that with the primal scene Freud has discovered the cinematic apparatus necessary to run the film strip?

Understood in this way, image becomes a matter not so much of visibility as of "legibility" or "readability."[21] Here Deleuze's concern converges with that of Freud when the latter compares dream images to hieroglyphic signs, and also with the concerns of Walter Benjamin when he likens modern photographic images to "scenes of crime" and maintains that captions are obligatory for such images to be readable.[22] For all three thinkers, image (the visible) has to be understood in conjunction with speech (the articulable). Thus, for Deleuze, what modern cinema does for philosophy is to bring to the fore this relation—or rather "non-relation"—between image and speech. By raising the two to a common limit, which separates them but connects them precisely in separating them, both image and speech are opened up to the outside.[23] An aberrant event, indeed: a crime scene.

THE IRRATIONAL CUT OF AWAKENING

The dream "raises no problem of interpretation": what remains enigmatic is rather the very nature of dream. This is how Freud ends his discussion of the Dream of the Burning Child. But here the writing suddenly turns dark. From now on, "every path will end in darkness" (SE VII, 549). What is the anxiety behind this moment of darkness, if not the question that has also haunted Descartes, namely, the question of distinguishing "toilsome wakefulness" from the "bedeviling hoaxes" of dreams?[24] In other words, how does one know that one's interpretation is "awake," that it has reached the moment of "awakening"? Now, near the end of the dream book, this question is at once more acute and more difficult: awakening in relation to what? Awakening to what? Awakening as what? (Where is the subject *at?*) Awakening forces Freud to confront the limit of interpretation, not as an infinite plenitude of meaning, but as the *beyond* of meaning. When it comes to the Dream of the Burning Child, it is no longer a question of inquiring about the "hidden meaning." For here the dream is all about the scene of a wake as well as about awakening—at an hour when all are asleep. Lacan's question is therefore: *awakened by what? Or, what is a knock?*

Perhaps Deleuze also precisely has awakening in mind when he suggests, quoting Antonin Artaud, that image in cinema should be a "knock made for the eye."[25] The essence of the image, Deleuze says, is only realized when it produces "*a shock to thought.*"[26] This is because, like "a matron who has not always existed" (Artaud), thought "has no other reason to *function than its own birth, always the repetition of its own birth,* secret and profound."[27] Thought, which "has not always existed," needs to be *provoked.* Here we encounter Heidegger: "*Most thought-provoking in our thought-provoking time is that we are still not thinking.*"[28] What provokes thought is stupidity, i.e., what withdraws from thought, yet must be thought. The withdrawal, like a maelstrom, exerts an attraction in the place of the void. Thus Deleuze says that what forces us to think is the "impower" (*impouvoir*) or powerlessness of thought.[29] The question is: how does thought "introject" stupidity, which long ago "has turned away" from thought?[30]

Thought's relation—or nonrelation—to its outside is the structure of awakening; thought as an act must be understood as the repetition of the moment of awakening. Awakening is no longer a matter of certainty, as it is with Descartes. As we have seen from the Dream of the Burning Child, the "knock" is encountered neither in dream, nor in waking, but is rather missed in the gap between the two. Between dream and reality (considered as representation), awakening is a void, an interval that binds the two by setting them apart. It is precisely what Deleuze calls an irrational cut.

Cinema's potential for thought therefore has to be sought in its ability to set the power of the interval into relief: "[T]he interval is set free, the interstice becomes irreducible and stands on its own."[31] The interval is "power" because it is not a secondary term added to two existing primary terms; the interval *is primary* to that which it separates, but connects in separating. In Deleuze's words:

> [T]he whole undergoes a mutation, because it has ceased to be the One-Being, in order to become the constitutive "and" of things, the constitutive between-two of images. The whole thus merges with [what] Blanchot calls the force of "dispersal of the Outside," or "the vertigo of spacing."[32]

In other words, the force of the Outside is the "constitutive 'and'" that creates through bifurcating and evacuating itself.

The primary spacing demands a different understanding of both space and time. Spacing is no ordinary space. Once again we think of Freud's assertion that dream is a *different locality.* Lacan also elaborates on this in his discussion of the Dream of the Burning Child. The dream is "another locality, another space, another scene, the *between perception and consciousness,*" because it unfolds in the causal gap, in the liminal space breached by the "knock."[33] Dream is precisely a matter of "spacing," and its secret is not to be sought in fantasy and wish fulfillment, but rather in its nature as an *envelope* of the real. This space, where the "knock" is repeated but not represented, is a feminine sort of space. It is a space that is "knocked up," impregnated. As Shoshana Felman argues, the space of dream, like the navel, does not simply lead to the unknown, but is rather the "pregnancy" of the unknown and the "fecundity" of feminine resistance.[34]

In cinema, one finds the same enveloping structure in what Deleuze calls framing. For him, framing in modern cinema is not to be understood in the classical out-of-field sense; rather, sound image and visual image become frames themselves and are, in turn, framed by the common limit, the interstitial space, between them. In this way, speech is made to confront the visual image as its irreducible internal spacing, while the visual image is raised to the level of legibility by moving toward the limit set by speech. Image as frame draws what essentially cannot be thought into the heart of thought; it "colors" stupidity, as it were.

Benjamin once wrote that "the past can be seized *only as an image* which flashes up at the instant when it can be recognized and is never seen again."[35] The reason that the past "can be seized only as an image" is because the past is an absolute past; it is time itself. When Foucault says that thinking produces the phantasm and "repeat[s] the universal event in its extreme point of singularity," what is at stake is the same problem Freud was also facing in the Wolf-Man Case, namely, how does something timeless, such as the unconscious or the event, cut into something temporal? Image should be considered as situated precisely in this radical heterogeneity. Impregnated with the seed of time, image's delicate, enveloping structure is opened up by the power that is time and that continuously bifurcates.

It is because void haunts image that image, like Eurydice's face in the night, fascinates thought. Thought, fascinated by image, is the thought of becoming, or the becoming things of thought.

> To experience an event as image is not to free oneself of that event, to dissociate oneself from it, as is asserted by the esthetic version of the image and the serene ideal of classical art, but neither is it to engage oneself with it through a free decision: it is to let oneself be taken by it, to go from the region of the real, where we hold ourselves at a distance from things the better to use them, to that other region where distance holds us, this distance which is now unliving, unavailable depth, an inappreciable remoteness become in some sense the sovereign and last power of things.[36]

NOTES

1. Michel Foucault, "Theatrum Philosophicum," in *Language, Counter-Memory, Practice* (Ithaca, New York: Cornell University Press, 1977), 190.

2. Gilles Deleuze and Félix Guattari, *What Is Philosophy?* trans. Hugh Tomlinson and Graham Burchell (Chicago: University of Chicago Press, 1994), 37.

3. Gilles Deleuze, *Cinema 2*, trans. Hugh Tomlinson and Robert Galeta (Minneapolis: University of Minnesota Press, 1989), 127.

4. Ibid., 83–84.

5. Sigmund Freud, *The Standard Edition of the Complete Psychological Works*, trans. James Strachey (London: The Hogarth Press, 1953), 509.

6. Jacques Lacan, *The Four Fundamental Concepts of Psycho-Analysis*, trans. Alan Sheridan (New York, London: Norton, 1977), 57.

7. Ibid., 56.

8. Ibid., 58–60.

9. Ibid., 59–60.

10. Ibid., 56.

11. Gilles Deleuze, *Foucault*, trans. Seán Hand (Minneapolis: University of Minnesota Press, 1986), 37.

12. Ibid., 30.

13. Ibid., 22.

14. Deleuze, *Cinema 2*, 273.

15. Deleuze, *Foucault*, 96.

16. Deleuze, *Cinema 2*, 272.

17. Gilles Deleuze, *Negotiations*, trans. Martin Joughin (New York: Columbia University Press, 1994), 51.

18. Lacan, *Four Fundamental Concepts*, 75.

19. Ibid., 73.

20. Jean-Clet Martin, "Eyes of the Outside," in *Deleuze: A Critical Reader*, ed. Paul Patton (Oxford, England, and Cambridge, Mass.: Blackwell, 1996).

21. Deleuze, *Negotiations*, 52; *Cinema 2*, 22.

22. Walter Benjamin, *Illuminations* (New York: Schocken Books, 1968), 226.

23. Deleuze, *Cinema 2*, 260.

24. René Descartes, *Meditations* (Indianapolis, Ind., and Cambridge, Mass.: Hackett Publishing Company, 1993), 17, 16.

25. Deleuze, *Cinema 2*, 169.

26. Ibid., 156.

27. Ibid., 165.

28. Martin Heidegger, *What Is Called Thinking?* trans. J. Glenn Gray (New York: Harper and Row, 1968), 6.

29. Deleuze, *Cinema 2*, 168.

30. Heidegger, *What Is Called Thinking?* 7.

31. Deleuze, *Cinema 2*, 277.

32. Ibid., 180.

33. Lacan, *Four Fundamental Concepts*, 59.

34. Shoshana Felman, "Postal Survival, or The Question of the Navel," in *Yale French Studies* 69 (1985): 49–72. In this light the "narrative envelope" of the Dream of the Burning

Child is worth noting. According to Freud, the dream was told to him by a woman patient, who herself had heard it in a lecture on dreams. The woman then repeated it in her own dream (SE V, 509). Who else, at the time, was giving lectures on dreams other than Freud himself? (I owe this point to Thomas Pepper and his two seminars on Freud.) But when Freud says that the actual source of the dream was unknown, he is not simply lying. For what does it mean to ask who dreams the dream, anyway? One finds here a relay between the virtual and the actual, between the analyst and the patient. This is the becoming hysteric of Freud.

35. Benjamin, *Illuminations*, 255.

36. Maurice Blanchot, "Two Versions of the Imaginary," in *The Station Hill Blanchot Reader* (Barrytown, N.Y.: Station Hill, 1999), 424–25.

MATTERS *of*
INTENSITY

15. Insomnia

Pablo Kovalovsky

Translated by Cecily Marcus

Through insomnia
the rain slips its painful phrasing. . . .
—Pedro Arturo Estrada

THE ISAKOWER PHENOMENON

The withdrawal of stimuli coming from the external world, and which Freud deemed necessary to the onset of sleep, entails, according to Otto Isakower, a phenomenon that occurs in some people at the moment just prior to falling asleep.[1] In his descriptions Isakower notes how this "falling" reveals a subjective destitution, and how the subject later reencounters itself as an object in the dream scene. This phenomenon consists of sensations that imply the dissolution of the corporeal limits between the inside and the outside, a loss of corporeal integrity, and a predominance of the oral zone. In his text Isakower also compares this to other phenomena, such as déjà vu and the epileptic aura. The visions and sensations described in his work of 1938 have the virtue of linking the fall into sleep with the undoing of personhood and with estrangement—crepuscular states linking the dispersion of the phantasm into its components, the subject and the object. Isakower argues that this withdrawal is gradual and that it presupposes an irregular distribution of cathexes, which, once withdrawn from external world, flow back into the I. As a consequence of this irregular distribution, the body is confused with the external world. On the other hand, in casting the oral zone—not the return to the maternal breast, as Freud had done—as the paradigm of the fall into sleep, something between the child and the mother is left unresolved, remaining open to the elaborations of another author, Bertram Lewin.

Lewin affirms Isakower's theory, especially since the incorporation of oral stimuli, Lewin tell us, dissolves the limits between subject and object; and it is this that

227

grants the reversibility characteristic of dream images.[2] Moreover, Lewin adds that the squashing of the breast by the nursling literally flattens the breast, so that it serves as the projection screen for the dream dreamed by the sated child.

This screen *is*—it doesn't *represent*—the wish to sleep. It doesn't enter the representational field of the dream. This is to say: the dream screen is the border of the dream, it is the real of sleep. Invoking Freud again, Lewin later adds that the transcription of the dream renders it useless for the purposes of analysis because the transcription emphasizes the screen rather than the dream itself. As an example, he describes how a supposedly transcribed dream is found, upon awakening, to be a blank page. That empty page, Lewin says, was the screen for the dream that wasn't.

IN FREUD'S WORK

The two functions of dreams—wish fulfillment and guarding sleep—underwent divergent fates in Freud's work. It is only from 1914 on, with "An Introduction of Narcissism," in which Freud develops the imaginary structure of the ego, that certain clinical consequences of these differences appear. One year later, in the "Metapsychological Supplement to the Theory of Dreams," Freud will announce that he is addressing such affective states as grief and falling in love (significantly, he does not say "melancholia"), as well as sleep and the phenomenon of dreaming. Freud writes:

> We are not in the habit of devoting much thought to the fact that every night human beings lay aside [*ablegen*] the wrappings in which they have enveloped their skin, as well as anything which they may use as a supplement to their bodily organs (so far as they have succeeded in making good those organs' deficiencies by substitutes), for instance, their spectacles, their false hair and teeth, and so on. We may add that when they go to sleep they carry out an entirely analogous undressing of their minds and lay aside most of their psychical acquisitions. Thus on both counts they approach remarkably close to the situation in which they began life. (SE XIV, 222)

The nakedness of the state of sleep and the peaceful isolation from the external world's stimuli that Freud calls "primitive narcissism" concur with the tendency to go from the lowest possible level of excitation to nirvana. On the horizon of an imaginary formation, Freud places the impossible absolute *jouissance* in the confines of horror.

The so-called wish to sleep is now defined as a passion: "not wanting to know anything about the external world" *(will nichts von der Aussenwelt wissen).*

Here affirmed as disturbers of sleep, dreams—and the wishes fulfilled in them—become knowledge. The strangeness[3] the dream bears[4] is produced by the collapse of the scenic perspective,[5] which supposes the vacillation of the structure of phantasm. In the dream the gaze "shows itself" and disturbs us, while the I seems to have multiplied, at once to have been disseminated everywhere and nowhere.

At the border of the dream—neither external nor internal to it, neither separate from nor part of it—the function of secondary revision is to keep watch so the dream may continue, and thus to prolong the state of sleep. If the dream is an "awakening that begins," the secondary revision is what makes it intelligible, setting it on a stage and supplying it with a façade that integrates phrases and locutions, material from waking life ready and available for use—"prêt à porter," as Lacan calls it.[6] The dreamer's I makes itself present in the form of a negation: "It is only a dream" provides the strangeness of the dream image with a stage upon which perspective is restored and the undetermined parts of the dream dissolve. On the edge of the dream, negation serves as the "shifter" linking the event with its legibility. This negation not only makes the dream legible, but it provides the frame that allows sleep to continue. By putting a veil over the dream's strangeness it shows up as writing. The double nature implicit in the renunciation "it is only a dream" is clear: at once it shows and hides the letter of the dream itself.

Heine's humor served well for Freud's attempts to describe this negation (or secondary revision) and its function, which Freud compares to Heine's "sleepless philosopher": "With his nightcaps and the tatters of his dressing gown he patches up the structure of the universe." Of secondary revision itself Freud writes: "It fills up the gaps in the dream structure with shreds and patches."[7]

If the imminence of anxiety brought on by the possibility of wish fulfillment interrupts both dreaming and sleeping, then secondary revision separates these, provoking a first awakening even while one still sleeps.

The Treatment of Insomnia

The temporal gap introduced between dream and sleep is an index of the suspended *jouissance* sustaining the dream scene. This economy of *jouissance*, which is linked to the introduction of the imaginary of narcissism, leads Freud to ponder the treatment of insomnia. Until this point, insomnia had merely been considered an annex to actual neuroses as a toxic excess of excitations.[8]

What can be taken from the above is that neither the absence of the ego, which localizes the dream through negation ("it is only a dream"), nor the case in which the ego doesn't emit the signal of anxiety to the subject (because for Freud, the signal of anxiety comes from the ego toward the subject, and for this reason is distinct from other states described here) will cause the subject to awaken, on account of a deficit of the imaginary function of the ego. Indetermination and strangeness persist because of the lack of delimitation of the dream scene, which has its correlate in the body. In this way, the dream is narrowly tied to the imaginary function. We find ourselves in the nightmare from which there is no waking up and sleep is never interrupted. Marked by the *jouissance* of the Other, and beyond the subjectivation of anxiety (inasmuch as here the ego does not emit any signal to the subject), the function of the Other's desire reveals the effect of madness characteristic of many clinical pictures that coexist with insomnia, that is to say where the imaginary function is also deficient.[9]

Further on Freud outlines the relationship between melancholia and insomnia. He will explain the exacerbation of narcissism or its deficit. The point from which one cannot remove the object to which the I is tied—a piece of clothing or something that supplements a part of the body—corresponds, in insomnia, to an equivalent retention where the superego is the sleepless guardian. A supplemental body part, though, is not just a prosthesis. It is the real of an apparatus that refers to everything mediating the body, expanding toward anything that is "incorporated" into the body but that still subsists at the limit of the corporeal: the objects "a" for Lacan, for example, are "incorporated" as extensions of the body—the pain of a mutilated limb as much as the pain of a phantom one both demonstrate the phantasmatic character of the image of one's own body. In 1915 Freud also speaks about hypochondria. It is known that the passion to "want to know nothing about the external world," as in the passion for ignorance Freud ascribes to the sleeper, is authenticated in hypochondria as the passion for "wanting only to know." This "wanting only to know," the incessant and undetermined exteriorization by which the body makes itself aware, is the insomniac's greatest warning. The insomniac evokes for us the pathetic figure of the mythological guardian, Argos. With one hundred eyes surrounding his head, fifty of which are always open even as he sleeps, Argos is nonetheless hypnotized by Hermes' flute and beheaded.

The relationship between hypnotized and hypnotist, which Freud compares to the sleeping mother's attentiveness to her baby's cry, represents this part of the subject that is always irremediably awake, even while in the depths of sleep. The absolute of sleep is disturbed by something exceptional, and in this case it is a unique object.

The melancholic's self-reproach is consistent with his imaginary deficit of self-recognition, the only trait Freud situates as a specific difference contrasting melancholia to mourning. The critical sleepless instance persecutes the I in a savage and incessant way. The hypnotist takes on this vigilant function of the super-ego. He acquires the power of the object that supports the tyranny of the pulsation to make this object coincide with the ego-ideal.

In *Group Psychology and the Analysis of the Ego*, Freud is aware that at the root of the passionate phenomenon of falling in love (which, significantly, he already placed in this context along with mourning and melancholia in 1915) is a homologous conjunction in which hypnosis can be used for enchantment or for terror.

In sleep the part of the subject that is still awake will be inhabited either by the wish fulfilled of the dream or by the phantasm of the hypnotist. The hypnotist occupies the place corresponding to the subject who sleeps, annulling the dream. The hypnotic sleep keeps a part awake, which corresponds to the dream inasmuch as the dream is the awakeness of sleep: if there is no sleeping subject, the hypnotist is a recourse, a parapet that doesn't keep the reward of the *jouissance* of the Other from the sleeper, sending him to nirvana. This part that stays awake puts a limit on the *jouissance* of the Other and can be used for the worst things—as is seen in *Group Psychology*. This is the price paid by the subject for erecting a barrier against the *jouissance* that ravages him.

From the beginning Freud was aware that the hypnotist localizes and gives a fixed border to this part of awakeness existing within sleep in a way that prevents the sleeper from being at the mercy of the absolute *jouissance* of primary narcissism. Maximum *jouissance* is conjoined with the imaginary and incestuous horror, the return to the mother's womb. One could well interrogate the analyst's own position in examining determinate structures or in moments of the cure where, by a lack of outlining the oneiric scene, the nightmare of insomnia reappears.

THE ANALYST'S POSITION

The phrase "It is only a dream" opens the dream space and allows the dream scene to advance beyond its own negation. The enunciation of the negation makes possible both the dream and play.

In this sense, the place that Freud provides for humor is significant.[10] In humor, the super-ego is kind, caring for the I of the subject like a child and creating the effect of illusion (*Illusion*) in the place of a painful reality (*Realität*). These are Freud's terms, and it is important to point out that one might confuse them with *Wirklichkeit*, a reality represented as both framed and less painful. Humor, though, sets a stage, turning the real of the dream into fiction while caricaturing the imaginary side of power by increasing it out of all realistic proportions. By stressing these traits, solemnity fades. The ideal detaches itself from the object, underlining the hypnotic power of their union. Access to the comic comes not via the joke—which is the way of the unconscious—but via disavowal, just as the disavowing "it is only a dream" hides the dream's strangeness at the same time that it shows the letter of the dream. It is a way of turning the unreal event of the dream into a text, like a transcription of another reality— an Other scene that prolongs the negated event and allows it to coexist in the manner of one dream inside another.

On the other hand, hypnosis prevents the passage of the dream scene to the waking scene, as the phenomenon of passionate infatuation shows. The person is awake, but the subject is asleep, a situation that evokes somnambulism.

DORA 1923

In 1923 Dora visits a clinic because of the hearing difficulties accompanying the migraines she has suffered since childhood. She is interviewed by Felix Deutsch[11] and complains of insomnia. She relates that her son, whom she suspects has started to date women, comes home in the night's wee hours. She lies awake listening for his footsteps.

Deutsch interprets that Dora cannot sleep because she is unable to keep from hearing her son's footsteps. Suffice it to say that she is stunned. The problems that brought her to consult a doctor improve immediately. We should differentiate, however, between the character of footsteps that are surprising and continuous on the one hand, and those that make sleep possible on the other. The state of being stunned blocks the localization of the lost object; and when there is no respite, the object retains its voraciousness because of the indeterminate source of the noise. Dora is stunned precisely by the footsteps she did not hear. On the contrary: the footsteps she actually hears localize a time and delimit a field of an absence.

BY WAY OF CONCLUDING

The passage from the phantasm's screen to the dream screen implies an imaginary buoying up of an object or of a place as a support for the I, which has cut itself off. The same I will later say: "It is only a dream." This development coincides with Winnicott's mention of a zone in his dreams he called "My Club," a place that established itself in his dreams after he stopped being a member of the Athenaeum. The equivalence between insomnia, nightmare, melancholia, and hypochondria supposes for the analyst a position in the cure that opens the scene to free association, while hypnosis, inasmuch as it blocks the possibility of both dreaming and play, brings together the suggestion of prescribed knowledge and the addictive fixation on an object—a magical, chemical object that will never be incorporated.

NOTES

1. O. Isakower, "A Contribution to the Psychopathology of Phenomena Associated with Falling Asleep," *Journal of Psychoanalysis* 19: 331–34.

2. B. Lewin, "Sleep, the Mouth, and the Dream Screen" *Psychoanalytic Quarterly* (1946), and "Reconsideration of the Dream Screen," *Psychoanalytic Quarterly* 15 (1946): 419–34.

3. See Freud, "Metapsychological Supplement to the Theory of Dreams," GW X, 412–26; SE XIV, 219–20.

4. J. Lacan, *Crucial Problems for Psychoanalysis,* unpublished seminar, session of December 16, 1964 (Library of the "Escuela Freudiana de Buenos Aires"). In the course of this, Lacan articulates the strangeness of dreams with the Other scene, in particular with the topology of the surface of the Klein Bottle.

5. Freud, *The Interpretation of Dreams,* SE IV–V, 31, 54, 595–96.

6. J. Lacan, "The Logic of Fantasy," unpublished seminar (Library of the "Escuela Freudiana de Buenos Aires").

7. Freud, *The Interpretation of Dreams*, SE V, 490. Referred to "Die Heim Kerh of Heime" (LVIII).

8. See Freud, *Three Essays on the Theory of Sexuality*, n. 52, and his letter to Fliess of October 6, 1893, as well as "Neurasthenia and Anxiety Neurosis," SE I, 185.

9. J. Lacan, *The Seminar II: The Ego in Freud's Theory and in the Technique of Psycho-analysis* (1954–55) (Paris: Edition du Seuil, 1978). Here Lacan defines madness as distinct from psychosis: the former is a disruption on the imaginary plane, while in psychosis there is a deficit in the symbolic order: "A madman is he who adheres to the imaginary purely and simply" (Lecture of May 25, 1955).

10. S. Freud, *Jokes and their Relation to the Unconscious* (SE VIII, 1). The function of self-observation linked to the super-ego had also been ascribed to secondary revision in relation to the "dream within a dream" structure such as it figures in an appendix to *The Interpretation of Dreams* in 1911. This explains the "dreamt" character of dreams. Freud says the intention is to rob the dream of its reality. (See chapter VI, section C, "Conditions of Representability," SE IV, 338.) The function of the scene within the scene allows the dream the possibility of passing through censorship by fooling it, as may be observed in Hamlet's play scene, which is a sort of whimsy.

11. F. Deutsch, "A Footnote to Freud's *Fragment of an Analysis of a Case of Hysteria*." This contribution was first published in *The Psychoanalytic Quarterly* (XXVI, 159–67) in 1957.

16. Strange Intelligibility

CLARITY AND VIVACITY IN DREAM LANGUAGE

Rei Terada

Where the sheets are not rumpled, poetry has not spent the night.

—Osip Mandelstam

"Most prominent among [the] formal characteristics, which cannot fail to impress us in dreams," Freud asserts, are the "differences in intensity" within them (SE IV, 329). Freud notes that "differences in intensity between particular dream-images cover the whole range extending between a sharpness of definition which we feel inclined, no doubt unjustifiably, to regard as greater than that of reality and an irritating vagueness which we declare characteristic of dreams because it is not completely comparable to any degree of indistinctness which we ever perceive in real objects" (SE IV, 329). In Freud's experience—and in our own, we would probably agree—dreams are both sharp and dim, vivid and pallid, in whole or in part. The logic by which we account for these varying intensities matters because it promises to explain how some ideas appear more significant than others. In the sensorium, intensity signals emphasis, prioritizing impressions to create sense; it seems reasonable to ask whether in a dream, intensity is the perceptual correlative of affect.

Freud's account of dreams' variable intensities is complicated from the outset by the co-presence of different kinds of intensity. He associates "intensity" (*Intensität*) with "sharpness of definition." But as he points out, there is also a second kind of intensity, vivacity, and it's easy to confuse clarity and vivacity. This confusion appears in chapter VI of *The Interpretation of Dreams* when Freud proposes to examine, separately but in the same breath, the "distinctness [*Deutlichkeit*] of particular parts of dreams or of whole dreams as compared with one another" and the "sensory intensity" or "vividness" (*Lebhaftigkeit*) of "particular dream-images" (SE IV, 329):

> In the former case clarity [*Deutlichkeit*] is contrasted with vagueness, but in the latter case it is contrasted with confusion [*Verworrenheit*]. Nevertheless it cannot be doubted that the increase and decrease of the qualities in the two scales run parallel. A section of a dream which strikes us as perspicuous [*klar*] usually contains intense elements; a dream which is unclear [*unklarer*], on the other hand, is composed of elements of small intensity. Yet the problem presented by the scale which runs from what is apparently clear [*Klaren*] to what is obscure and confused [*Undeutlich-Verworrenen*] is far more complicated than that of the varying degrees of vividness [*Lebhaftigkeit*] of dream-elements. (SE IV, 331, translation modified)

Got it straight? Probably not. Not the same, yet intimate, these qualities scintillate in dizzying trompe-l'oeil effects. To make matters worse, clarity also *metaphorically* denominates the *intelligibility* with which we associate *properties* of clarity and vivacity. Clarity and vivacity contribute to impressions of intelligibility, sometimes deceptively; they belong to the *rhetoric* of intelligibility. Hence we arrive at the category of the "apparently clear."

Freud's discussions of all of these features bear particularly on language. His extended reflections on dreams' deployment of words as objects point back to the central fact that the ability to associate invisible ideas and feelings with perceptible words creates excitement. His privileged illustration of dream intensity is the formula for trimethylamin in his Dream of Irma's Injection; appropriately enough, this paradigm of oneiric intensity operates both as an idea and as a word. In chapter IV Freud remarks that in his dream he saw the *formula* for trimethylamin "printed in heavy type, as though there had been a desire to lay emphasis" on something (SE IV, 116). He does not reproduce the formula, however, but uses the word to exemplify the modulation of intensity:

> The case is the same as when, in preparing a book for the press, I have some word which is of special importance for understanding the text printed in spaced or heavy type; or in speech I should pronounce the same word loudly and slowly and with special emphasis. The first of these two analogies reminds us at once of an example provided by the dream-work itself: "*trimethylamin*" in the Dream of Irma's Injection. (SE V, 595, translation modified)

Strachey translates this phrase, "the word '*trimethylamin*'" (SE V, 595). But the *word* "trimethylamin" does not appear in the dream. What does appear is hard to say: something unrepeatable that holds the place of the formula—unrepeatable language, paraphrasable but not phrasable, translatable but not readable. Comparing dream intensity to emphatic language, Freud embodies the comparison in his own emphasized type. Typographical alteration, of course, represents special stress. I would suggest that Freud's analogy to heavy type also compares intensity to language as such.[1] Language *is* stress for us; it marks what is important and likely to recur. We routinize its intensity, and so apply boldface and volume as supplements. In the murky environments of dreams, however, language recovers the power to electrify by sheer articulation.

How might Freud understand this electrification, and what impact might it have on interpretation? In the first section of this chapter, I'll trace Freud's attempts to discern repression and condensation through the clarity and vivacity of dream language. Intelligible language, as Lyotard has pointed out, is a serious problem for Freud's hypothesis that "the dream-work does not think." Dream language shows that thoughtfulness and thoughtlessness are logical distinctions, which cannot be formally distinguished. Thus, it turns out that specific instances of intensity cannot be interpreted as such. Rather, as I suggest in the second section, we are left to speculate about the dynamics of the feelings of clarity and vivacity in general. Freud's examples of dream language reveal that we strategically forget the thoughtlessness within language so as to create feelings of clarity and vivacity that support our sense of our own intellectual intensity.

THE CHALLENGE OF VIVACITY

"Trimethylamin" supplies the starting point for Freud's treatment of vivacity in his *Project for a Scientific Psychology*. More concerned in the *Project* with waking than dreaming states, Freud uncontroversially argues that vivacity signals importance in normal sensory life—a function that becomes problematic when censorship must conceal import. His vision of the chemical formula for trimethylamin in the Irma Dream was "immensely vivid" (*sehr lebhaft*), he recalls (SE I, 342). Before recounting part of the dream, Freud opines that "in dreams the vividness of the hallucination is directly proportionate to the importance—that is, to the quantitative cathexis—of the idea concerned. This indicates that it is Q [quantity] which determines the hallucination" (SE I, 339). As Strachey points out, the mysterious concept of "quantity" is defined in the *Project* only as "what distinguishes activity from rest . . . subject to the general laws of motion" (SE I, 295).[2] Freud states that both vivacity and quantitative cathexis are "proportionate to . . . importance," hence aligning the two. Further, we learn that vivacity indicates greater significance than "interest"; Freud connects interest, in contrast, to clarity. A perception of the external world "in waking life . . . is no doubt made clearer" by a "cathexis (interest)" from within, "but not more vivid; it does not alter its quantitative characteristic" (SE I, 340). In other words, I'm not going to see you more vividly—or as more important—just because I'm focusing my attention on you. I can, however, work backward from vivacity to significance. If I see you more vividly than other entities in my perceptual field, that does mean you must be important to me—so important that my cathexis to you has overcome the natural dominance of perception over ideas and forced its way upstream from the mind to the perceptual system. *The Interpretation of Dreams* reiterates the potential signal function of vivacity. "If we are considering a psychical process in normal life and find out that one out of its several component ideas has been picked out and has acquired a special degree of vividness [*Lebhaftigkeit*] in consciousness," Freud writes, we can regard this as "evidence that a specially high amount of psychical value [*Wertigkeit*] . . . attaches to this pre-dominant idea" (SE IV, 306).

The natural connection of sensory vivacity to value obligates the censorship to dispel its telltale stress. Freud goes so far as to assert that it is in response to the threat of vivacity that the dream-work invents its tactics. In the struggle of the dream-work the dreamer's values are "stripped" from objects:

> [A] psychical force is operating which on the one hand strips the elements which have a high psychical value of their intensity, and, on the other hand, *by means of overdetermination,* creates from elements of low psychical value new values, which afterwards find their way into the dream-content. If that is so, *a transference and displacement of psychical intensities* occurs in the process of dream-formation, and it is as a result of these that the difference between the text of the dream-content and that of the dream-thoughts comes about. The process which we are here presuming is nothing less than the essential portion of the dream-work; and it deserves to be described as "dream-displacement." (SE IV, 307–8)

The old, direct relation between psychical intensity and sensory vivacity survives in only one respect: "In most dreams it is possible to detect a central point which is marked by peculiar sensory intensity . . . . this central point is as a rule the direct rep-resentation of the wish-fulfillment" (SE V, 561). Aside from this instance, the ratio between subjective import and vivacity is utterly destroyed. Not only is there a trans-valuation of all "psychical intensities" in dreams: that process "is nothing less than the essential portion of the dream-work," and it is "as a result of" the necessity of displac-ing intensities that dreams are as they are (SE IV, 308).

What does this transvaluation consist of? According to the *Project,* in waking life powerful psychic intensity simply *yields* sensory vivacity. Yet in chapter VII Freud notes that in the dream "the *psychical* intensity of the elements in the dream-thoughts has been replaced by the *sensory* intensity of the elements in the content of the actual dream" (SE V, 561–62). Value-stripped dream elements and elements of low value exchange qualities to create misleading impressions, exploiting the fact that "*psychical* intensity or value or the degree of interest of an idea is of course to be distinguished from *sensory* intensity or the intensity of the image presented" (SE IV, 306n). The dream-work trades endlessly on the ambiguity of the conjunction of these two things that must be distinguished. It is not simply that when psychical intensity is "replaced by" sensory vivacity in dreams, psychical intensity drops from consciousness, leaving a seemingly inexplicable sensory vivacity. If that were all that happened, we would always know how to interpret vivid elements, by connecting them to their missing associations. Freud insists more radically that the dream-work pulverizes any connec-tion between psychical and sensory intensities:

> [I]t might be expected that the *sensory* intensity (that is, the vividness) of particular dream-images would be related to the *psychical* intensity of the elements in the dream-thoughts corresponding to them. In the latter, psychical intensity coincides

with psychical *value:* the most intense elements are also the most important ones—those which form the centre-point of the dream-thoughts. We know, it is true, that these are precisely elements which, on account of the censorship, cannot as a rule make their way into the content of the dream; nevertheless, it might well be that their immediate derivatives which represent them in the dream might bear a higher degree of intensity, without necessarily on that account forming the centre of the dream. But this expectation too is disappointed by a comparative study of dreams and the material from which they are derived. The intensity of the elements in the one has no relation to the intensity of the elements in the other: the fact is that a complete "transvaluation of all psychical values" [in Nietzsche's phrase] takes place between the material of the dream-thoughts and the dream. (SE IV, 330)

Similarly, displacing vivacity from one element onto another nearby would not be enough to obscure what is going on; something more serious occurs:

[A]nalysis shows that the most vivid elements of a dream are the starting-point of the most numerous trains of thought—that the most vivid elements are also those with the most numerous determinants. We shall not be altering the sense of this empirically based assertion if we put it in these terms: the greatest intensity is shown by those elements of a dream on whose formation the greatest amount of condensation has been expended [*für deren Bildung die ausgiebigste Verdichtungsarbeit in Anspruch genommen wurde*]. (SE IV, 330)

Not only are features of strong psychic value prohibited from appearing in the dream in the first place; the vivacity that once was theirs is scattered, kept away even from "their derivatives," so that "no relation" remains between vivacity and psychical value. Vivacity is dispersed, not annihilated; scattered vivacity is pressed together again wherever condensation is strongest. It accumulates in condensed dream elements that register the tectonic energy that has pushed them together. Vivacity is reconstituted, but is now more substance than signal.

Freud thus arrives at a new, quantitative standard of significance in which numbers of determinants still warn of import, but without any relationship—direct or indirect, positive or negative—between the warning and any specific meaning. Vivacity reflects density as though measuring particles in air. The standard of this intensity is still subjective: we expend energy on dispersing and condensing things only when they have mattered to us. But from vivacity, we cannot know more than *that* this happened: we cannot know what is important.

Clarity and Intelligibility

If vivacity is defeated by censorship, what of clarity, dream language that is sensorily (literally) and conceptually (metaphorically) clear? Presumably, if vivacity can be melted down and redistributed, then so can clarity or any feature. For Freud's theoretical purposes, it is actually preferable that this be the case with the intelligibility of dream language: the unintelligibility of dreams is crucial evidence for the very existence of unconscious processes.

Freud maintains the uniqueness of unconscious processes by dividing dream-thoughts from dream-work (a maneuver that has been investigated with great profit by J.-F. Lyotard).[3] Dream-thoughts are ideas compiled before dreaming and consciously organized; in the course of the dream-work, repression deforms the dream-thoughts, generating the compromise of the dream and obscuring its sense. Compartmental-izing dream-thoughts and dream-work allows Freud to assert that the dream-work mentions language without using it: the dream-work cannot do "intellectual work" (SE IV, 313) or craft new sentences. It cannot perform mathematical calculations, but "merely throws into the *form* of a calculation numbers which are present in the dream-thoughts and can serve as allusions to matter that cannot be represented in any other way" (SE V, 418). It follows, however, that Freud's prohibition on dream thought is imperiled whenever intelligible phrases or accurate-looking mathematical operations do appear in dreams. Proposing that dream words specially illuminate the pressures of dream-work through their very resistance to those pressures, Freud also admits their potential exceptional thoughtfulness:

> The work of condensation in dreams is seen at its clearest [*am greifbarsten*] when it handles words and names. It is true in general that words are frequently treated in dreams as though they were things, and for that reason they are apt to be combined in just the same way as are presentations of things. Dreams of this sort offer the most amusing and curious neologisms. (SE IV, 295–96)

Freud tries to turn the hardest case to greatest advantage: *even* words are diced and recombined by the dream-work, which does not recognize their integrity. Thus we learn how vigorous the condensation is. His examples are convenient: neologisms bear scars of manipulation that can be interpreted as traces of censorship; portmanteau words show the seams of condensation. When words are at *their* clearest, however, the presence of condensation is not clear.

Sensory and cognitive clarity are inextricable because there are minimal distinct-ness conditions for intelligibility. If we cannot read, hear, or remember the content of some instance of dream language, it serves only as an allusion to language in general. Cy Twombly's writing-like paintings operate in this generically suggestive way, as do stylized depictions of letter-writing in films, in which the actors don't really write, but make gestures that mean "here imagine a letter being written." These instances raise no obstacle to Freud's hypothesis that the dream-work does not produce language. His concern must be for words with both sensory clarity and intelligibility intact.

Freud offers two explanations for the strange presence of such language: down-loading and secondary revision. First, since the dream-work relies exclusively on form for expression (SE V, 506–7n), words may get through the censorship when they are processed as objects. An analogue for this process might be PDF file format, which treats a text *en bloc* as an image, rather than recognizing characters as units. This language is intelligible, but doesn't belong to the dream:

> [A]ll spoken sentences which occur in dreams and are specifically described as such are unmodified or slightly modified reproductions of speeches which are also to be found among the recollections in the material of the dream-thoughts. A speech of this kind is often no more than an allusion to some event included among the dream-thoughts, and the meaning of the dream may be a totally different one. (SE IV, 313)

Freud thus calls words in dreams "reproductions" of words. An emblem of this conception of dream language appears in his dream of a bookstore window.[4] Freud spots "a new volume in one of the series of monographs for connoisseurs which I am in the habit of buying . . . . *The new series was called 'Famous speakers' or 'Speeches' and its first volume bore the name of Dr. Lecher*" (SE IV, 268). Here we see Freud's description of dream language—"reproductions of speeches"—literalized. The reproducibility of language is underlined by the volume's being part of a series and by Freud's "habit" of buying other volumes in similar series. The notion of origin the dream offers—a "first volume" begat by a reproductively prolific "Dr. Lecher"—mirrors its end in Dr. Freud the reader, who, as the dream's author, is actually the progenitor of Dr. Lecher, whom the dream suggests he would like to resemble. Thus, the example also suggests that the point of the distinction between dream-thoughts and dream-work is to allow the dreamer to marvel at the thoughts in the dream by obscuring the dynamic of thought-production. I'll return to this idea later on.

Second, dream language may also achieve illusory intelligibility through secondary revision, in which the censorship "fills up the gaps in the dream-structure with shreds and patches."[5] "As a result of its efforts," Freud continues, "the dream loses its appearance of absurdity and disconnectedness and approximates to the model of an intelligible [*verständlichen*] experience" (SE V, 490). To extend Mandelstam's metaphor, there are poems that smoothe themselves and people who rumple sheets to make the bed look slept in. Not only does the apparent clarity of language not guarantee the intelligibility of its sense, it can brilliantly obscure. Secondary revision allows Freud to hypothesize that any instance of clear language is only "apparently clear" (SE IV, 331). The problem is that the reverse is then also true. In preserving the possibility of distortion for any instance of language, Freud loses hold of any measure of the dream-work's thoughtlessness. To be strong enough for Freud's theoretical purposes, thoughtless language must be too strong for his interpretive purposes.

Both of Freud's explanations for the faux-intelligibility of dream language—secondary revision and the thesis of imported language—have no formal or empirical dimensions. Thoughtfulness and thoughtlessness prove to be logically distinguishable and formally indistinguishable. There is no way to tell a word from a reproduction of a word: is the painted word "blue" in a Jasper Johns painting a word or a picture of a word?[6] Ironically, *because* the distinction of the dream-work is its dependence on formal expression (SE V, 506–7n), there is no sure formal distinction between a representation of language and language that thinks. We cannot show that dream language thinks, and Freud cannot show that it does not.

INTELLIGIBILITY AND UNDERSTANDING

Words in dream language get their intensity from their received nature, which is one with their cultural density. Freud's examples suggest that the unevenness of the effect comes from selective forgetfulness: I wish the words in the bookstore window were mine, forgetting that I put them there. (These individual forgettings are subsets of the forgotten foundational fact that *I am dreaming*.) As intelligibility depends on access to reproduction in the circular sense of Freud's bookstore dream, insights of understanding may be elations of tautology—moments in which we get to "discover" things we know. At the same time, words are never simply one's own, and in that sense they really are marvelous.

The possibility of tautological insight is raised by "*Asplenium* and the Lizards," a dream recounted by the nineteenth-century philosopher of psychology Joseph Delboeuf and cited by Freud as a heroic feat of oneiric recall. The dream involves the Latin name for a small fern:

> He saw in a dream the courtyard of his own house covered with snow and found two small lizards half-frozen and buried under it. Being an animal-lover, he picked them up, warmed them and carried them back to the little hole in the masonry where they belonged. He further gave them a few leaves of a small fern which grew on the wall and of which, as he knew, they were very fond. In the dream he knew the name of the plant: *Asplenium ruta muralis*. The dream proceeded and, after a digression, came back to the lizards. Delboeuf then saw to his astonishment two new ones which were busy on the remains of the fern. He then looked round him and saw a fifth and then a sixth lizard making their way to the hole in the wall, until the whole roadway was filled with a procession of lizards, all moving in the same direction . . . and so on. (SE IV, 11–12)[7]

Like Freud's dream of reproduced speeches, this Escherian dream is about generation and animation. Delboeuf is taken aback by the Latin name in the dream because "when he was awake, Delboeuf knew the Latin names of very few plants and an *Asplenium* was not among them." "Sixteen years later," Freud writes,

> While the philosopher was on a visit to one of his friends, he saw a little album of pressed flowers of the sort that are sold to foreigners as mementos in some parts of Switzerland. A recollection began to dawn on him—he opened the herbarium, found the *Asplenium* of his dream and saw its Latin name written underneath it in his own handwriting. (SE IV, 12)

The incident combines sensory clarity, intelligibility, and a sense of the marvelous in a recovery of language. The herbarium highlights the objectlike quality of a name: the name identifies the sample flower and the flower exemplifies the name, the noun level with the thing.

The classic notion of thing as name and name as thing occupies the center of a drama of understanding, of obscurity brought to light. What requires explanation is the dream's ability to use a word that the dreamer doesn't know he knows. This name, *Asplenium,* seems unusually memorable. Not only does it stick in a corner of the dreamer's mind without his permission, hence reappearing in the dream; he also remembers that reappearance sixteen years later. *Asplenium* is memorable because of its unaccountability; it had been a "mystery," Freud writes, that remained unsolved. The story of finding the herbarium is presented as a solution to the mystery. It features the phenomenology of understanding, the "dawning" feeling. Delboeuf's understanding is never miraculous; it is his own, in "his own handwriting." It seems miraculous insofar as he forgets what he knows; his having forgotten is what really demands explanation and remains unexplained by the story. We are "driven to admit," writes Freud, that "we knew and remembered something which was beyond the reach of our waking memory" (SE IV, 11). The moment is striking for its simultaneous climax and anticlimax: we begin with a sense of extra insight—which we might be tempted to attribute to superstition, or "overstanding"—and exchange it for a rational explanation, yet every bit of wonder lost to the explanation is replenished by the wonder of our newfound rationality. The circular explanation extends the circular relation between noun and thing, which seems to explain things simply by pairing them ("That fern is an *Asplenium.*" "So that's what it is!")

Freud's point in retelling the dream is not interpretive but theoretical: *Asplenium,* an artifact of photographic memory, embodies the passivity of dream language, which appears very insightful because it is also very received. The temporary occlusion of familiarity is enough to activate a vivacity that belongs all the time to language as such, as the other side of its standardization. "I know this word!" is most of the excitement. The identity of the unthought and the twice-thought cannot be reduced simply to thoughtlessness, however, because that identity just is what it means to have one's own thoughts.

In the dream Freud calls *"Non Vixit,"* the desire to control anxiety about one's capacity for understanding culminates in the relief of access to a prefabricated utterance. In the dream, Freud finds himself conversing with Wilhelm Fliess and his dead friend P. (Josef Paneth, Freud's successor at the Vienna Physiological Institute [SE V, 482n1]).[8] The conversation juxtaposes vague and distinct, flat and intense segments:

> Fl. spoke about his sister and said that in three quarters of an hour she was dead, and added some such words as "that was the threshold." As P. failed to understand him, Fl. turned to me and asked me how much I had told P. about his affairs. Whereupon, overcome by strange emotions, I tried to explain to Fl. that P. (could not understand

anything at all, of course, because he) was not alive. But what I actually said—and I myself noticed the mistake—was, "NON VIXIT" ["He did not live," instead of "Non vivit," "He is not alive"]. (SE V, 421)

Freud goes on,

It was a long time . . . before I succeeded in tracing the origin of the *"Non vixit"* with which I passed judgment in the dream. But at last it occurred to me that these two words possessed their high degree of clarity in the dream, not as words heard or spoken, but as words *seen.* I then knew at once where they came from. On the pedestal of the Kaiser Josef Memorial in the Hofburg [Imperial Palace] in Vienna the following impressive words are inscribed:

Saluti patriae vixit
non diu sed totus.
[For the well-being of his country he lived / not long but wholly.] (SE V, 422–23)

Freud observes elsewhere that clarity and obscurity of presentation can formally express a thematic concern that "arises from the material of the dream thoughts and is a constituent of it" (SE IV, 331). A patient who described "indistinct and muddled" people in her dream, for example, "was obliged to confess that she was expecting a baby but was in doubts as to 'who the (baby's) father really was'" (SE IV, 332). Another dream of Freud's in which Fliess expounds a crystal-clear theory of bisexuality turns out to be wishing that Fliess could be so lucid (SE IV, 331). *"Non Vixit,"* too, is about clarity and obscurity, vivacity and aliveness. Freud's groping, then piercing dream wishes to be clear and satisfies itself with an imported visual memory of language.

In keeping with his own hypothesis that dream language is not thoughtful, Freud invokes the inscription and appropriates its authority. The alien chill of the words lies in their chiseled sharpness against the fumbling three-way conversation in which Freud utters them. Fliess speaks unnamed words about his sister, then "some such words as 'that was the threshold'" when "P. fail[s] to understand him." Fliess then turns rather accusingly to Freud, who "trie[s] to explain" why P. does not understand. Fliess seems to blame the misunderstanding on Freud, who passes the blame on to P. Freud's explanation falls short in turn, and not only because of his error in tense. In parentheses Freud fills in for the reader the reasoning he was trying to give Fliess, but apparently didn't provide: "P. (could not understand anything at all, of course, because he) was not alive" (SE V, 421). While Freud wanted to convey that P. could not understand anything because he was not alive, what he immediately meant to say was "P. is not alive"—which is hardly illuminating, and still not what he claims he really wanted. Discussing the dream's associations, Freud realizes that a verse by Heine hovers over the scene:

Selten habt ihr mich *verstanden,*
Selten auch verstand ich Euch,
Nur wenn wir im *Kot* uns fanden,
So verstanden wir uns gleich.

[Rarely have you *understood* me,
And rarely too have I understood you.
Not until we both found ourselves in the *mud*
Did we promptly understand each other.] (quoted in SE V, 513)

Freud dispels a gathering panic about the treachery of speaking and listening by saying something that has to be distinct because it has been inscribed on a monument. All this seems to be forgotten, however, once the fatal words are out. Upon Freud's death sentence pronounced in a dead language, P.'s "form grew indistinct . . . and finally he melted away" (SE V, 421). "It's not our words that are indistinct, it's you who are indistinct," Freud seems to say to P., and he says it so clearly that P. disappears. Yet this is not a comfortable conclusion: Freud has to speak from the monument to negate his friend; he has to lose the illusion of speech, as he would himself define thinking speech, in order to communicate this well.

The dynamic of "*Non Vixit*" is conventionally uncanny and sublime: the ready-made visual memory of language supplies what appears as new power because its familiarity is veiled. As in "*Asplenium*," thought does not need to be new for the feeling of understanding to dawn: indeed, it needs not to be. Most interesting for my purposes is Freud's satisfaction with the inscription as a *clarification of the clarity* of the words in the dream. The words have "a high degree of clarity" because of the breathtaking efficiency of the mind's access to its own stored ideas—the access of the dream-work to the dream-thoughts. The experience is one of the shortening of obstruction, where "obstruction" means consciousness: Freud becomes a minimal channel through which the lapidary words swiftly and killingly flow. Rapidity of access replaces construction: the access is rapid—and the experience powerful—because the thoughts are already thought. The speed of Freud's utterance, outrunning his ability to know what he's saying, registers the brilliance we feel when we begin processing something we've already processed. Sublime forgetfulness, Freud's dream implies, casts our relief at reaching familiar territory as discovery, and figures as insight the fantastic speed at which we travel over ground already behind us.

Ready-Made Fantasy

These dreams of language hint at a materialist informatics even as Freud's explications explore the sublime feelings of clarity and vivacity they inspire. This is no contradiction: from its origins in Freud's *Project*, psychoanalysis bridges phenomenological depth to quantity. In this, psychoanalysis is the ancestor of the cognitive science that is sometimes perceived as having replaced it. Daniel Dennett's article "Are Dreams Experiences?" (1976), for example, also proposes a theory of information access *en bloc*. Noting that the "received view" of dreaming posits a phase of nocturnal presentation accompanied by recording and a subsequent phase of waking retrieval, Dennett considers problems created for the received view by dreams that know too much—beautifully detailed, elaborately plotted dreams that incorporate the circumstances of waking:

> Perhaps you have had a dream leading logically and coherently up to a climax in which you are shot, whereupon you wake up and are told that a truck has just back-fired outside your open window. Or you are fleeing someone in a building, you climb out a window, walk along the ledge, then fall—and wake up on the floor having fallen out of bed. In a recent dream of mine I searched long and far for a neighbor's goat; when at last I found her she bleated *baa-a-a*—and I awoke to find her bleat merging perfectly with the buzz of an electric alarm clock I had not used or heard for months.[9]

Dennett begins by recognizing that composition within the dream is not an option—obviously not when the prescience of the dream exceeds the capacities of any life. He argues that while these dreams cannot be fathomed within the temporality of presentation and recollection, they are possible if there is no dream presentation (no present-tense experience of dreams). What if, instead, "all dream narratives are composed directly into memory banks," available to be chosen at the moment of waking? "If our memory mechanisms were empty until the moment of waking," Dennett notes, "and then received a whole precomposed dream narrative in one lump, the idea that precognitive dreams are experienced episodes during sleep would have to go by the board"—but the unconsciousness of dreams would be preserved, and the uniqueness of dream life acknowledged, without superstitions of precognition.[10] Further, the attack holds for the received view of all memory and peripheral experience: a "cassette theorist" like himself, "emboldened by the success with dreams, puts forward the *subliminal peripheral recollection-production* theory, the view that the variety of peripheral details . . . are not consciously experienced, but merely unconsciously recorded for subsequent recall."[11]

Freud develops his own "cassette theory" of dreams in his reflection on a "famous" dream in the memoirs of Emile Maury, to which he refers three times in *The Interpretation of Dreams*.[12] "Maury, having been struck in his sleep on the back of his neck by a piece of wood, woke up from a long dream which was like a full-length story set in the days of the French Revolution" (SE V, 495). Freud recounts how the dreamer

> was condemned, and led to the place of execution surrounded by an immense mob. He climbed on to the scaffold and was bound to the plank by the executioner. It was tipped up. The blade of the guillotine fell. He felt his head being separated from his body, woke up in extreme anxiety—and found that the top of the bed had fallen down and had struck his cervical vertebrae just in the way in which the blade of the guillotine would actually have struck them. (SE IV, 27)

Because the blow of the furniture coincides with the blow of guillotine, it seems as though "the whole elaborate dream must have been composed and must have taken place during the short period of time between the contact of the board with Maury's cervical vertebrae and his consequent awakening" (SE V, 495–96). Freud proposes that the dreamer invokes a "long-prepared phantasy" at the moment of waking, much as a "key-phrase" from Mozart's *Figaro* may serve "as a port of entry through which the whole network is simultaneously put in a state of excitation" (*als Einbruchsstation, vor*

der aus ein Ganzes gleichzeitig in Erregung versetzt wird) (SE V, 497). "Nor is it neces-
sary that this long-prepared phantasy should have been gone through during sleep,"
Freud continues, "but only in the recollection of the sleeper after his awakening" (SE
V, 497). If something in the dream-work seems too ingenious to be improvised, it is.

Freud does not assert that all dreams, or even "*all* arousal dreams," "admit of this
explanation" of what he calls "ready-made phantasies" (*fertige Phantasien*) (SE V 498,
496). It would not damage Freud's general dream theory if he did, however, just as it
does not damage his theory that the dreamer's report of the dream is part of the
dream.[13] To the contrary, Freud's description of dream language invites extension into
a general theory of legibility. "If we look closely into a speech that occurs in a dream,"
Freud maintains,

> we shall find that it consists on the one hand of relatively clear and compact portions and
> on the other hand of portions which serve as connecting matter and have probably been
> filled in at a later stage, just as, in reading, we fill in any letters or syllables that may have
> been accidentally omitted. Thus speeches in dreams have a structure similar to that of
> breccia, in which largish blocs of various kinds of stone are cemented together by a bind-
> ing medium. (SE V, 418–19)

Freud's DNA-like vision consists "on the one hand of relatively clear and compact portions" of dream language and "on the other hand of portions which serve as connecting matter." The "connecting matter" sounds subordinate, like grammatical particles,
but the "clear and compact portions," presented as rock fragments, are also static and
inorganic—not the usual associations of language that is clear and compact. Whole
fantasy retrieval and "ready-made" interpolation suggest that the greatest condensation and vivacity, in culture as in dream life, can be found not in the immediate but
in the previously worked, the thing produced "from concentrate": in the cultural sed-
iment of language.

Although Freud proposes that dream language is unthinking and that conscious
language is thinking, the language in his dreams is both and neither of these. By maintaining the unique unthinkingness of dreaming despite its intelligible language, Freud
distances its implications for conscious thought. Over the course of his career, the ambiguity never stabilizes: Freud alternately questions and reinstates the duality of linguistic thoughtfulness and thoughtlessness. Contemplating an especially dazzling example of dream clarity in chapter IV, Freud juxtaposes a "particularly well-constructed"
dream to a sleepy idea about dreaming, and loses and refinds the distinction between
the two:

> Thus I remember a dream of mine which struck me when I woke up as being so par-
> ticularly well-constructed, flawless and clear that, while I was still half-dazed with
> sleep, I thought of introducing a new category of dreams which were not subject to
> the mechanisms of condensation and displacement but were to be described as
> "phantasies during sleep." Closer examination proved that this rarity among dreams

showed the same gaps and flaws in its structure as any other; and for that reason I dropped the category of "dream-phantasies." (SE IV, 331)

The almost sleeping Freud dreamily thinks and thoughtfully dreams of a new category of dreams that would be more like thinking. Disqualifying the new kind of dream from thought, after all, because it has "gaps and flaws in its structure," Freud deflects the equally Freudian thesis that thought itself is structured by gaps and flaws. But he adds in a 1930 footnote: "Whether rightly I am now uncertain" (SE IV, 331n).

NOTES

The epigraph to this chapter is drawn from Osip Mandelstam, "Conversation about Dante," in *The Complete Critical Prose and Letters,* ed. Jane Gary Harris, trans. Jane Gary Harris and Constance Link (Ann Arbor, Mich.: Ardis, 1979), 397.

1. For assessments of the place of dream language in Freud's theory of dreams and language, see Jean-Michel Rey, "Freud's Writing on Writing," *Yale French Studies* 55-56 (1977): 301–28; and J. B. Pontalis, "The Dream as Object," *International Review of Psychoanalysis* 1 (1979): 125–33. Sara van den Berg observes that "several of the dreams in Freud's books hinge on a single word or phrase: trimethylamin, *pelagie, non vixit, afflavit et dissipati sunt"*—and she considers some of these dreams in "Reading the Object: Freud's Dreams," *Psyart: A Hyperlink Journal for Psychological Study of the Arts* (1997), www.clas.ufl.edu/ipsa/journal/articles/psyart77/vanden01.htm.

2. Appendix C, "The Nature of Q," SE I, 392–97.

3. J.-F. Lyotard, "The Dream-Work Does Not Think," trans. Mary Lydon, in *The Lyotard Reader,* ed. Andrew Benjamin (Oxford: Blackwell, 1989), 19–55.

4. This dream is related in many ways to the better-known Dream of the Botanical Monograph.

5. Freud asserts at one point that "only in extreme cases" does dream language think (SE V, 490). Although he does not give an example, his later idea that secondary revision may be a kind of thought may indicate that it is the extreme case he has in mind.

6. Lyotard describes but does not reflect on this problem. He remarks that through condensation, "it could happen that '*Révolution d'Octobre*' might read '*Révons d'Ore*' and be heard as '*rêvons d'or*'" (*Lyotard Reader,* 27). "*Rêvons d'or*" is a perfectly standard phrase unless context marks it as nonsense; nothing reveals that it is actually a crumpled version of "*Révolution d'Octobre.*" A similar problem occurs when Husserl argues that words addressed mentally to oneself are merely a "phantasy" of words, when Austin disqualifies "words spoken in soliloquy" from being performative utterances, and when P. D. Juhl asserts that words uttered by parrots only seem to be words (Edmund Husserl, *Logical Investigations,* trans. J. N. Findlay, 2d ed., 2 vols. [New York: Humanities Press, 1970], First Investigation, sec. 8; J. L. Austin, *How to Do Things with Words,* ed. J. O. Urmson and Marina Sbisà, 2d ed. [Cambridge: Harvard University Press, 1975], 22; P. D. Juhl, *Interpretation: An Essay in the Philosophy of Literary Criticism* [Princeton: Princeton University Press, 1980], 109).

7. According to Freud, the "correct name" of the plant "is *Asplenium ruta muraria,* which had been slightly distorted in the dream" (SE IV, 12).

8. For another dream about Freud's rivalry with Paneth, see SE IV, 229ff.

9. Daniel Dennett, "Are Dreams Experiences?" in *Brainstorms: Philosophical Essays on Mind and Psychology* (Cambridge: MIT Press, 1981), 135.

10. Ibid., 137.

11. Ibid., 143.

12. See Emile Maury, *Mes Souvenirs sur les evénéments des années 1870–1871* (Paris: La Boutique de l'histoire, 1999).

13. See Dennett, "Are Dreams Experiences?" 147.

INTERPRETATIVE ARTS

17. The *Marnie* Color

Raymond Bellour

ONE

When I received a letter from the University of Minnesota inviting me to celebrate, with the end of the century, the publication of *The Interpretation of Dreams*, I felt honored but mainly thrilled. I couldn't help thinking back at that moment to when, very young and in a tiny hotel room in Munich, I read the book, at that time out of print, in the old translation of Ignace Meyerson, *La Science des rêves*, as it was called in French—a copy of which had been lent to me by my friend, the future French philosopher André Glucksmann. This turned out to be one of the most extraordinary episodes of reading in my whole life, and one that has remained inalterable, whatever I may think now, after *Anti-Oedipus* and *A Thousand Plateaus*, about psychoanalysis in general as one of the last romantic gospels of the nineteenth century still shaping our now passed twentieth century.

So, I want to thank all of you who invited me, and particularly John Mowitt, who took care of everything regarding my presentation.[1] As I do usually when I have to speak English in public, I prefer to struggle with my rough personal English, or "French-English," rather than read you a convoluted translation that I'll not be able to phrase properly or even understand terribly well.[2]

TWO

I could not presume, for various reasons but mainly for lack of time, to elaborate anything on Freud's book itself, or even to make some new general statement, for example, about psychoanalysis and cinema. So the organizers and I agreed that I would present some remarks that I had recently elaborated about Alfred Hitchcock's film, *Marnie,* and more precisely about the use of one color in *Marnie,* the "red," which emblematizes compulsively the "coming back" effect of the initial trauma throughout the life of the heroine. When I was asked, some years ago, to contribute to an important book about color in cinema, edited in France by Jacques Aumont, the first and only thing that came immediately to my mind was this "red," this *"Marnie* color" that, years and years after my first interest and work on the film, still retained its immediate and affective violence. [3]

Before getting concretely to the variations of this red throughout the film, this necessitates a few remarks about Freud and Hitchcock. First, we must remember that Hitchcock had directed *Spellbound,* for David Selznick, in 1945, a film that has been considered officially as the first American film explicitly devoted to psychoanalysis. Years later Hitchcock will say to Truffaut: "just another manhunt story wrapped up in pseudo-psychoanalysis."[4] This remark, along with the fact of Hitchcock having specifically been asked to direct *Spellbound,* should be taken in at least two ways. First, that Hitchcock was well aware of the way in which any film, to be a film, could only deal explicitly with psychoanalysis in a "pseudo" way, an inevitable distortion effect of its inner reality and truth. But, also, such facts imply that Hitchcock, through his "manhunt stories," was perhaps the director who has approached instinctively and in the closest way this reality and this truth of the contradiction between film and psychoanalysis.

This means that Hitchcock has been addressing more or less in all of his films since the 1920s the overwhelming question that had been developed by Freud through the discovery of psychoanalysis as well as through its whole history: the question of *trauma* and of its interpretation. Hitchcock's films are all organized around traumatic events, which have to be interpreted by one or several characters through the development of the action and for this reason by the spectator or spectatrix each for him or herself. This is why Deleuze, without reference to psychoanalysis, can make of Hitchcock (in *Cinema I: The Movement-Image*) the hero of the crisis of the action-image, the hero of the mental image as an exemplification of the relation-image, and through this, the transition and the link between classical and modern cinema.

This question of trauma and of its interpretation acquires a particular degree of acuteness when it happens to be inscribed within films in which mental illness and pathological cases are linked explicitly to psychoanalytical theory, and in which the didactic obligation of naming and explaining the symptoms parallels the development of action and more or less inspires it. This is the line through Hitchcock's œuvre that separates, on one side let's say *Shadow of a Doubt* and *Strangers on a Train,* and on the other, *Spellbound, Psycho,* and *Marnie.* And in these last, which are the three Hitchcock films where a psychoanalyst is present (either professional, in *Spellbound* and *Psycho,* or amateur, "pseudo," as in *Marnie*), another distinction must be made. In

Psycho, the last-minute contribution of the psychiatrist to the rationalization of the enigma reinforces the speculative dimension of the film without weakening its uncommon structural and emotional power. For this reason among others, *Psycho* is perhaps Hitchcocks's masterpiece, and is really the film that divides the American cinema between the "old and the new." In *Spellbound* and *Marnie,* in different ways, the imbrication of the drama and of its psychoanalytical interpretation provokes a sort of split, which generates the specific and tormented interest of both films.

In order to be clarified, and, ultimately, resolved, the original trauma has to be conveyed through the whole film by its actual clinical symptoms, and finally to be shown in itself, as a sort of final primal scene. This very need clearly carries its own risk, a mixture of crudeness and intellectual vulgarity, both in the propositions of the scenario and in their elaboration through images. Elsewhere Hitchcock has been perfectly conscious of this, saying to Truffaut about *Marnie:* "I was forced to simplify the whole psychoanalysis aspect of it."[5] But this risk also has its possible reward. Specifically, it challenges one to recreate figuratively the appearances of the symptoms and the final explosion of the primal traumatic scene itself. It is interesting to note that this problem, which—through the various levels of traumatic moments Hitchcock has attempted to depict—has always been fundamental for him. Moreover, it echoes Freud's famous reply to Karl Abraham regarding the proposal for Pabst's film, *Secrets of a Soul,* in 1925: "My chief objection is that I do not believe that satisfactory plastic representations of our abstractions is at all possible."[6]

Here could be the most challenging part of the problem: How can the image, through its figurative and figural choices, express the abstractions with which Freud is concerned; but also, how can the image qualify and carry more fundamentally something of the economical dimension Freud consistently attached to trauma? Recall here his characterization of trauma in the *Introductory Lectures on Psychoanalysis:* "Indeed, the term 'traumatic' has no other sense than an economic one. We apply it to an experience which within a short period of time presents the mind with an increase of stimulus too powerful to be dealt with or worked off in the normal way, and this must result in a permanent disturbance of the manner in which the energy operates" (SE XV, 275).

And this leads us directly to the Marnie color, the red in *Marnie.*

THREE

It is a thematic color, which obeys a very simple principle, and which seems to have been a screenwriter's idea: a child who kills a man, in a scene in which she felt herself to be the victim, and which has since been repressed, cannot now bear the sight of the red, which terrifies her as a vision carrying all the strength of the buried memory of her violent act.

The importance of this red in *Marnie* lies first in its generation of an irreality (*un irréalisme*). It is one about which we don't care because we are carried along by the developing story about this woman the film constantly follows, whose looks fill so many scenes. There is so much red in life—for example at the corners of so many streets—that the image in *Marnie* had to be emptied of all the likely and even possible reds. So, from the point of view of "natural perception," so to speak, a world almost without red had to be conceived so as to save the red for the drama that it embodies. This explains a particular quality of the color in general in *Marnie,* of which it's not easy to evaluate the perceptible result, but which can nevertheless be qualified. On the one side, the effects of contrast and insistence are reserved for other colors (the bright green of the meadow, for example, in the hunting episode, or the enigmatic crudeness of the yellow handbag in the opening shot); on the other side, a very rich scale of inter-mediary tones (in the blues, browns, and greens) avoids any combination with the red, in order not to risk any type of confusion with its symbolism.

A slight but telling exception seems to have been reserved for the character of Lil, Mark Rutland's sister-in-law, who is clearly a bit too jealous of Marnie. She appears twice in tones close to red: a crimson dressing gown for her daily life at home, and a rose-orange dress for the reception given at Rutland's house to introduce Marnie.

Here is the first irreality (*le premiere irréalisme*) of a film that struggles to orches-trate all the ones it has combined: actors (Sean Connery, still too much stuck to the James Bond myth, overwhelmed by this role of intellectual-boss-husband-amateur therapist); screenplay (the roughness of the theory of trauma, of its miraculous reso-lution); this extreme and rare challenge of trying to express through the sudden irrup-tion of a color the intensity of an interior state, further than the actor's performance can bear, further than words can say.

The process is simple: it conveys the color from so-called objective perception toward its subjective counterpart. As a result, the figure created is elaborated so as to increase affect as much as possible, perhaps by means of this excess saving what the coherence of the represented story cannot really deal with.

Rarely will a film have shown so clearly that "cinema, first, is stupid," as the French philosopher Dionys Mascolo has said commenting on Marguerite Duras's *India Song.*[7] He continues: "Stupid two times: on one side as power, on the other as servitude, by its total submission to the reality of things (*force des choses*)." Hitchcock's intelligence, or maybe his instinct—here, where he is confronted more than ever by "stupidity," where he more or less gives up the pure mechanics of the intrigue (else-where, his strength), and confronts himself directly with psychology in the form of a travestied psychoanalysis—here, Hitchcock's instinct has pushed him to organize a chain of instants forged by a color, and thus to balance through a certain intransitive violence—what is then signified about the theme and its symbolism.

So it happens that seven times the red, as purely material but abstract, invades the screen, covers the image and then disappears. To list each of the seven times: first, the vision of the gladioli when Marnie visits her mother in Baltimore; second, her first nightmare (in her mother's house); third, the red ink that spills on her sleeve in her office at Rutland's firm; fourth, the jockey's jersey at the horse races; fifth, the second nightmare (in Rutland's house); sixth, the jacket worn by the "lancer" during the fox hunt; and seventh, in the final scene, when the brightness of the trauma is given back its full memory.

An eighth scene contrasts with the seven others, entering in the series and becoming the fourth in their unfolding. To lure her into the trap into which he himself is falling, Mark Rutland has asked Marnie to come to his office over the weekend and type an article he has written about zoology, his former interest.

This scene, through its capacity to suggest—that is to say, to link—touches on the most "stupid," the most perverse aspect of the symbolic circuit. One finds here the only example of a distinct but minimal red seen by Marnie without the otherwise characteristic reaction of fright, the effect of which will be developed in another way through the scene: the tongue or the throat of a little stuffed animal, "a female jaguarundi," as Mark Rutland specifies, which was part of the collection of his former wife, an anthropologist, recently and suddenly dead. It's between two shots of Marnie's look that this red stain glitters, and that the conversation shifts from animal predators to their human equivalents: men and women. But the storm that erupts, and which is a central element of the original scene of the trauma (not to say the "primal scene"), accelerates the return of the trauma. The importance of the storm in terms of color is that it links gradations of different hues—red, but mauve and blue as well—to the total whiteness of the lightning out of which the colors seem to stream. A terrified Marnie, protecting herself against the wall opposite the main window, and as if struck by the rhythmic flashes of lightning, cries out: "The colors! I can't stand more colors." "But what colors?" answers Mark, as he moves near to her and takes her in his arms. They are then suddenly both deprived of any natural color by the white of the lightning, which bears in itself the entire spectrum of colors, first and foremost the red it implies and carries, a white that illuminates Marnie's and Mark's faces in a close-up. The kiss that follows the last lightning flash and that shows more and more closely Mark's mouth looking for Marnie's lips—this kiss reaches a sort of obscenity, which is underscored by a faded color: Marnie's lips are marked by a pale red. Were she to open them—which, being frigid, she does not do (this being the ultimate stake of the film)— the inside of her mouth would glitter with the same red that had appeared in the jaguarundi's throat. This color terrifies her, because it is the color of her body's interior, real and imaginary (*réel-imaginaire*), and of her sex organs as they are seen and dreamt of (*vus-rêvés*) here by Rutland—and by Hitchcock as well, who himself clearly enjoys a specific *jouissance* in the shooting of this scene.

So each of the eight scenes may be read, depending on its position in the unfolding of the screenplay (*scénarisation*), as an element of a symbolic embroidery, which Hitchcock thus crudely refines. But the strength of the red is not only that of an announced raw symbol, a symbol of the blood linked to sex; the red is also acting with the subtlety of an agent that modifies what surrounds it, chiefly the most physical components of the mise-en-scène: framings, movements, and the actors' expressions. Generally, when Marnie is seized by the red she is framed in a still, close shot, or even a very close shot, and she is either dreaming and groaning, or her look is fixed on the mesmerizing (*médusant*) object (indeed, mixing these two types of scenes is one of the ways through which perception and hallucination make common cause). The color saturating the screen modifies this action, in that it overcharges (*sur-affecte*) the expression and at the same time makes it less visible. It does so by acting as a veil, through its own thickness, one could say. Thus the color becomes the sign of what can't be expressed.

One time, in the episode of the red ink, movement is added: movement of the camera, first, as soon as the red appears on the screen, which leads our look to the close-up, as if the look were stirred by this red through which it enters; and second, the movement of Marnie herself, who rushes, once the color has subsided, to the restroom. She is followed by a camera far slower than her that stops to see her move away (a careful eye may then, in the depths, by chance or by virtue of a perverse sign, see a red seat), before we again find her cleaning the stain on her sleeve, and with it all this red-screen (*écran rouge*), which, as though carried by her movement, remains stuck to our eyes.

A second time, in the final scene, where everything is rebuilt and offered to the spectator or spectatrix, the camera movement absorbs and diffuses (one does not know to what precise point) the excess of the color. After the murder of the sailor-client of the prostitute-mother, two close-ups of the mother and her daughter howling embody the excess of the trauma. Here, however, it is a completely blank screen that is covered with red. In fact, this time the screen is not fully covered, as happens in the other scenes, where the red covers the elements represented in the image. This serves to introduce the idea that, in addition to the excess of the symbol, this shot depicts real blood as it invades the white cloth of the screen. Almost immediately the shot is affected by a brutal and short camera movement, from the bottom to the top, which pulls it at the same time toward an absolute of blood and an absent field—in effect, a memory of the pure movement of the trauma. This, at least, is what one feels after the event, when one has abruptly fallen into the facticity and the present of the following shot.

It would appear that Truffaut remembered this shot in *Les Deux Anglaises et le continent*, when shooting the defloration of Muriel: the camera focuses on the stains of blood on the sheet, which thus extend to invade the whole screen, with an effervescent red on which the camera is fixed, imposing there a sort of abstraction. But there is no other narrative stake. There is simply the insistence on a variation on life, sex, and death, through the two sisters of Henri-Pierre Roché, transformed into Brontë sisters.

What then can one say, finally, about color, about this specific use of color? On one side, the color accentuates the symbol; on the other, it obscures it. How so? Beyond the meaning the color confers on the symbol, it insists as a physical pressure, which has its own value, producing a sort of strictly somatic energy. The music contributes to this effect by means of its brutal thrusts, those scannings of the theme so well liked by Bernard Hermann. At the same time such themes isolate the moments and connect them to the modulation of the whole film, according to a consummate art of the system, which is peculiar to the great classical cinema and especially to Hitchcock. However, as with the expressivity of the color, the expressivity of the music challenges the meanings it also qualifies. The trouble is linked to the fact that, filling the whole frame, the color is itself related to Marnie, the figure who appears within it. Thus, what produces this body, and the space in which it appears, creates an impossible equation between the materiality of this space and the interior sensation posed by it. The body of the actress communicates this, in its pure exteriority, only because the immobile spectator or spectatrix receives it through perception, in the silent but lively intimacy of his or her own body. It is this movement, this migration of the acting body toward the spectator's immobile body, accentuated by the color, which—from an effect of interiorization that is supposed to come from the screen itself—makes color at once perceptible and intelligible. This is why the effect of the last shot of the traumatic scene (from which Marnie is absent) is, paradoxically, so strong: it is the screen as such, that is to say, beyond the character, the technique (*dispositif*) of the projection itself, which is caught in the movement to which it is submitted. This happens because—from the point of view of the fiction, and indeed despite this fact—the scene produces the most absolute psychical instant: the mother and the daughter, simultaneously in the past and in the present, live and relive the scene with, as witness-spectator, the man who sees and hears (*les entend*) them: Mark, the one who has just occupied, under the figure of the bloodied sailor, the place of the dead man (*du mort*) in the drama.

FOUR

As an epilogue, I would like, briefly, to introduce *Spellbound*, in order to clarify as well as elaborate this view about the somatic value of an image devoted to the evocation of an initial trauma. In *Spellbound*, the equivalents of the "red" and of the storm in *Marnie* are also formed by a combination: the phobia of a color, the white—much more difficult to treat in a film in black and white—and of a motive—stripes, different sorts of stripes—which may be produced by a fork drawing a pattern on a tablecloth, or printed on a dressing gown, or even by the image of railway tracks. Those moments, qualified, as in *Marnie*, through the look of the frightened hero, are striking, but they are not as systematically organized as they are in *Marnie* through the chain of "reds."

Two other moments in *Spellbound* deal directly with the traumatic material. The first one is a dream, which has become famous, largely because Hitchcock asked Salvador Dali to design the artwork for it; the second one, near the end, is the "coming back" of the trauma itself. Strangely, the dream images, however impressive, because of the strangeness of their motives, are not really physically disturbing; nor are they, in their connection one to another, truly emotional. The reason for this may be that these images are offered directly for interpretation by the film through the deciphering of the dream's meaning by the psychoanalyst Constance Petersen/Ingrid Bergman and her master Alex Bolow. In contrast to these so-called surrealist—but in a way pretty tame—images, one can oppose the final shots of the return of the original trauma, which present a high degree of perceptual and sensorial disturbance.

We are on the slopes of Gabriel Valley. Gregory Peck—that is to say John Ballantyne, who is pretending to be John Brown—is accused of having murdered Doctor Edwards, whose identity he has borrowed, because of Ballantyne's deep guilt complex. John Ballantyne has been brought to Gabriel Valley by Constance Peterson, his psychoanalyst and lover, to try to overcome his amnesia and to facilitate the revelation of the truth. The dream has been a crucial step toward this end.

Similar to *Marnie*'s ending, but in a situation so completely unrealistic that it actually increases the anxiety of the spectator or spectatrix, John Ballantyne and Constance Peterson are both skiing—indeed in the same way that John is supposed to have done with Dr. Edwards when he was killed.

As we have seen, these shots are very brutal. Their speed so taxes actual perception that even Truffaut missed one of them when, in his book on Hitchcock, he presented a series of photograms, each of which supposedly corresponds to a different shot. (Thus Truffaut prints five photos instead of six, missing the second shot—namely the first occurrence of the fourth shot, which depicts the young John Ballantyne's point of view when he is sliding on the stone balustrade.)

What makes this scene an extraordinary moment of cinema, one capable of achieving a high degree of emotion, able to communicate and imprint in the spectator or spectatrix the strength and the horror of the trauma?

Four elements are at stake: (1) The identity of the framing (a close shot) on John Ballantyne skiing and on him as a little boy, which reinforces the identification, not only with the character, but with the movement itself; (2) the reversibility of the point of view, the boy seeing and being seen, not only by the viewer, but in a sense as seen or at least felt by his younger brother, who, though too late, will look back—a position we ourselves will adopt; (3) the expressivity of the components of the shot—framing, lighting, and, above all, the expression of John, who acts as if in a nightmare; and finally (4) there is the question of speed. In an instant, we have both the descending movement of the boy *and* the division of the space of this action by the time of the succesive shots. This creates an extreme brutality in the transitions among the shots. In effect we have not really seen what we have seen, but for that reason we have seen it too much.

It seems to me that here, as with Marnie's color, we are confronted with the image's high degree of physicality, a physicality that concerns directly the very somatic dimension of the human experience Freud tried all his life to delineate as the *economic.* To speak in Lacanian terms, while this somatic level is never independent, in Hitchcock's films, from the *symbolic* organization of the plot and its elements, neither is it reducible to them. In this sense, the somatic level also escapes the systematicity of what a long time ago I myself called, in my analysis of *North by Northwest,* the "symbolic blockage."[8] Indeed, this level may also escape the hyper-Lacanian logic to which Slavoj Žižek, in the volume he edited, *Everything You Always Wanted to Know about Lacan, But Were Afraid to Ask Hitchcock,* has submitted all of Hitchcock's work.[9]

But how, then, is one to imagine, for those extremely traumatic moments, as well as, in a more general way, for film form and figuration, that is, for the film considered at the level of *the emotions* it carries—how is one to imagine a satisfying regime of conceptual description and an evaluation for the aesthetic experience?

I can see only two ways to grasp this aesthetic dimension of the film body, of the body of cinema. One would be to keep on building a strict and explicit Freudian aesthetics, as is proposed by Jean-François Lyotard in his central book, *Discours/Figure.*[10] The other would be to find a medial way and an articulation between two directions of thought that may be seen as having little to do with one another, but which can be linked in unexpected ways: on one side are Félix Guattari's and Gilles Deleuze's works in general, mainly concerning the concepts of *fluxes* and *intensities,* or of *modulation;* on the other is the work of the American psychoanalyst and experimental psychologist Daniel Stern, in his crucial book, *The Interpersonal World of the Infant.*[11] My preference is clearly for the second way. You will understand that now is not the right moment to elaborate such a point of view. I will only suggest that it could be, even paradoxically, not the least faithful way to echo Freud's obsessive but fundamental concern with the economic dimension of desire that traverses all his work, and mainly in *The Interpretation of Dreams.*

NOTES

1. [This essay was delivered after a screening of Alfred Hitchcock's *Marnie,* organized as a special event at the Walker Art Center, on Friday, November 5, 2000. We wish to thank the Walker Art Center for making this event possible.—Ed.]

2. [It must be acknowledged that the text published here differs slightly from the text read during the conference in October 2000. When discussing this volume, Professor Bellour asked that I blend the French text he had initially submitted and subsequently translated, with the elaborations, written in English, that he had added to the text prior to its delivery, smoothing out the English in the process. Having been provided with the original French text, I did avail myself of it when pondering especially rough passages. This is not then a translator's note per se, but a word to the wise just the same.—Ed.]

3. Jacques Aumont, *Introduction à la couleur: des discours aux images* (Paris: Armand Colin, 1994).

4. François Truffaut, *Hitchcock*, rev. ed. (New York: Touchstone Books, 1985), 165.

5. Ibid., 304.

6. Sigmund Freud, *A Psycho-Analytic Dialogue: The Letters of Sigmund Freud and Karl Abraham*, ed. Hilda Abraham and Ernst Freud, trans. Bernard Marsh and Hilda Abraham (London: Hogarth Press, 1965), 384.

7. Dionys Mascolo, "Naissance de la tragédie, à propos d' *India Song*," in *Marguerite Duras* (Paris: Editions Albatros, 1975).

8. Raymond Bellour, *The Analysis of Film*, ed. Constance Penley (Bloomington: University of Indiana Press, 2000).

9. Slavoj Žižek, ed., *Everything You Always Wanted to Know About Lacan, But Were Afraid to Ask Hitchcock* (London: Verso, 1992).

10. Jean-François Lyotard, *Discours/Figure* (Paris: Klincksieck, 1971).

11. Daniel Stern, *The Interpersonal World of the Infant: A View from Psycho-Analysis and Developmental Psychology* (New York: Basic Books, 2000).

18. "Other Languages"

Testimony, Transference, and Translation in Documentary Film

Jonathan Kahana

The analyst's ear practices precisely on hearing the murmurs and games of these other languages. It makes itself attentive to the poetics which is present in every discourse: these hidden voices, forgotten in the name of pragmatic and ideological interests, introduce into every statement of meaning the "difference" of the act which utters it.

—Michel de Certeau, "Lacan: An Ethics of Speech"

FILM AND THE SCENE OF LISTENING

A staple of documentary cinema from its earliest days, the interview may be the one situation in cinema where vision is redundant. The power of the interview as a documentary technique has primarily to do with the temporal continuity between the event and its cinematic representation embodied in the interview subject's voice. The synchronous recording of sound and sight in the documentary interview presents us, then, with another instance of the confrontation of the look and the gaze in cinema. To the viewer, this gaze takes the form of a question that can never be articulated: if I can hear, why do I need to see?

For a diverse group of contemporary documentary filmmakers, this problem has become critical to the relationship between theory and practice. For these filmmakers, it is no longer possible to regard cinema as a mere instrument of historical knowledge. One prominent example is Claude Lanzmann's epic oral history of the Holocaust, *Shoah,* a film explicitly concerned with the difference between visual and aural memory, and that builds on the observation made by Alain Resnais (in his 1955 film, *Nuit et Brouillard* [Night and Fog]) that the technology of cinema is related to the destruction of the very past it seeks to recover.[1] The role of testimony in Lanzmann's film is, in part, to oppose the efficiency of mechanical vision through which the past can be painlessly apprehended.

In a scene filmed at a town square in Corfu, where the members of the Jewish population were rounded up and loaded onto trains or shot, a survivor tells Lanzmann that while these events were taking place, Christians from the town stood by and watched. Lanzmann isn't present in the shot that frames the survivors who have accompanied him to the site of their deportation, as he is in other interviews, but his voice is heard pressing his subjects on the fine details of their memory, determining exactly where and how events took place. The director and his camera operator are positioned in such a way as to force the main subject of the interview to appear in profile in the frame, so that one looks him in the ear. "Christians heard that Jews were being rounded up," the survivor tells Lanzmann, "so they came." Feigning disbelief, Lanzmann asks, "Why'd they come?" The survivor responds, "To see the show." This last remark appears in the original French of the interview as "Pour voir le cinéma." This irony would not be lost on Lanzmann, who elsewhere challenges the accuracy of his translators on screen, admonishing them for leaving out details in their encounters with non-French-speaking subjects; but it is lost on a monolingual audience that can only *read* the subtitles. Translation in cinema, as *Shoah* demonstrates, is not just from one language to another, but also from the register of the aural to the register of the visual.

Thus the supplementary relation between vision and listening in the documentary interview of this sort can present the cinema with an immanent critique, a confession that follows a Freudian logic. In his prefatory comments to the analysis of the Dream of Irma's Injection, Freud confesses: "I have other difficulties to overcome, which lie within myself," by which he means his "hesitation about revealing so many intimate facts about one's mental life" (SE IV, 105). But the desire to create a public for this new science overcomes his modesty, and before long he has turned this limitation into the condition of his appeal: "my readers," he promises, "will very soon find their initial interest in the indiscretions which I am bound to make replaced by an absorbing immersion in the psychological problems upon which they throw light" (SE IV, 105). Freud thus transfers or displaces the material of the confession from the autobiographical to the clinical realm.

In her discussion of these remarks, Shoshana Felman gives this process the name "testimony." In this way, psychoanalysis theorizes listening as a relationship that is always producing an extra perspective. In the psychoanalytic dialogue, Felman observes, "[T]he doctor's testimony does not substitute itself for the patient's testimony, but *resonates with it,* because, as Freud discovers, *it takes two to witness the unconscious*" (15). In fact, given Freud's concern for the readers looking and listening over his shoulder, we might want to say that it always takes *more than* two.

This extra perspective is familiar to anyone who has seen a conventional documentary interview, of the sort where a subject offers his or her speech in support of the film's argument. Two things are emphatically missing in such encounters: the sound of the question that produces the testimony, and the visible presence of the interviewer,

for whom the unwavering look of the camera is a kind of surrogate, linking or trans-
ferring the effect of the interview to the film's audience. This speech can be said to
have a visual component: to paraphrase Theodor Reik's description of the psychoanalytic dialogue, it is on display insofar as the subject speaks not *to* the listener so
much as *before* him.[2] But this means that, like the speech of the analysand, the testimony of the interview subject is, in effect, blind, because it is addressed to an audience
it cannot see.

As he does throughout the film, Lanzmann initiates a dialogue with unsettling
resonance for documentary cinema itself, particularly the work of documenting a
crime meant to leave no evidence. By relying entirely on interviews for evidence of
events that *Shoah* recounts and eschewing the kind of historical imagery that docu-
mentaries about the Holocaust usually employ, he waives the usual guarantees of the
documentary genre's authority. The effect of familiar images of victims, perpetrators,
and locations is to ground the typical Holocaust documentary in historical actuality.
This traditional use of stock footage advances a more or less implicit claim about
the trustworthiness of cinema, as a medium, against the vicissitudes of memory. It also
allows a particular film to derive some of the broad historical authority of the cinema
archive. Lanzmann's suspension of these relations of trust is vital to his film's ethical
agenda; it answers Resnais's question about how cinema will avoid reducing the Holocaust to a singular event, fixed in the past.

As with the analytic dialogue, the cinematic interview makes the voice of testimony alien or foreign—even to the speaker. The value of a comparison between
documentary and psychoanalysis is in the attention such a comparison focuses on
the rhetoric of testimony. Where disciplines of listening and interrogation tend to
naturalize—often at great pain to the testimonial subject—his or her oral "evidence
of experience,"[3] the form of the interview employed by the filmmakers I will examine
establishes the significance of this voice in the subject's exterior, outside consciousness: in the texts, spaces, and technologies structuring it. In this way documentary
can be used to call into question the currently fashionable distinction between memory and history, a distinction that depends on a particular fantasy of what Walter
Benjamin referred to as the "equipment-free aspect of reality." Demonstrating the
tangency of the concepts of testimony, transference, and translation is one of the ways
the kinds of documentary films I will deal with have effected this critique.

THE DREAMS OF CINEMA

The opposition of the spectator's look on the one hand and the gaze of the cinematic
apparatus on the other, a problematic imported into film studies from Lacanian psychoanalysis, has been a staple of film theory since the 1970s. This problematic, like
film theory in general, has rarely been applied to nonfiction cinema. Until recently, the

exemption from theoretical analysis granted documentary cinema has been related to a certain conception of another oppositional relation: that of the image and reality.

As Jane Gaines has suggested, film theory began, in the 1970s, to regard the issue of realism, which fascinated postwar critics such as André Bazin and Siegfried Kracauer, as something of an embarrassment, if not a scandal.[4] In the early 1950s, Bazin had separated practitioners of cinema into two kinds of filmmakers: those who "put their faith in the image, and those who put their faith in reality."[5] Lacanian and Althusserian positions, which have dominated film theory since the 1970s, turned film away from reality and toward the image. If theorists who took up these positions could not exactly be said to believe in the image, nonetheless they certainly behaved as if spectators did. This criticism, whether psychoanalytically or ideologically inflected, directed itself at the social conditions and consequences of regimes of spectacle, voyeurism, and fetishism that had promulgated certain misrepresentations of the world. (It was as if Bazin's distinction between two kinds of directors, the realists and the imagists, had been collapsed into a suspicion of the image presupposing the existence of reality external to representation.)

One well-known and far-reaching version of this iconophobic position was the critique of the male gaze that objectifies women. As has been pointed out by a number of feminist film theorists seeking to correct a misreading of Lacan, the gaze is not "an idealized point from which the film can be looked at."[6] Rather, the gaze, in psychoanalytic theory, stands precisely for that which is impossible to translate into visual representation. In the translation from the object world to a system of visual representation, the gaze occupies the place of what is lost in translation, that operation by which the human subject surrenders agency to the cinematic apparatus. The translation of the psychoanalytic subject into the language of film theory had, in other words, the effect of making the correspondence between the technology of cinema and what Christian Metz called the "mental machinery" of cinema appear more complete than it is in practice.[7] The problem with this theory of the cinematic apparatus is, as Mary Ann Doane has written, "that the apparatus always works. It never breaks down, is never subject to failure."[8]

A number of recent works of documentary cinema engineer this failure and place it on display. In their attention to what Metz called the "aural object," a sound that resists identification, these works challenge the theory that the technology of cinema models the spectator's activity. Because of their attention to the ethics and aesthetics of listening, these works reflexively raise the question of what it means to be an audience. In such scenes, the theory and practice of cinema come together, as they do in psychoanalysis, where "the encounter between analyst and analysand. . . inevitably produces the surprise, the destabilization of the given theories—the constant shock of otherness we associate with the unconscious."[9] These works might, therefore, renew the question of how psychoanalysis can model the analysis of cinema. They do so precisely by posing again Bazin's question: what kind of irrational desire makes the cinema real? By "real," of course, Bazin meant a collapse of the distinction between theory and practice: the photographic image doesn't just share "the being of the model of which it is the reproduction," he argued, "it *is* the model."[10]

In the example I will focus on, Isaac Julien's psycho-biography of Frantz Fanon, conventional documentary methods are joined with narrative and avant-garde techniques that recall not only the language and grammar of fiction film, but the early history and pre-history of cinema itself. Julien joins other practitioners of a hybrid version of nonfiction cinema, including filmmakers as diverse as Trinh T. Minh-ha, Werner Herzog, and Errol Morris, in challenging the ontology of the documentary form while working in it. Especially in their staging of the documentary interview, these filmmakers demonstrate the resemblance between cinema and the Freudian theater of the unconscious.

Each of these filmmakers has attempted to capture the effects of the "other languages" of the unconscious (to use Michel de Certeau's formulation) in the subjects of their films. In their eliciting of repressed or traumatic speech, these films suggest a simple methodological resemblance between the interview in documentary cinema and the psychoanalytic dialogue. But the more compelling reason to use the model of psychoanalytic dialogue to describe these works of documentary is to capture the character of a particular theoretical gesture that one finds in the work of the aforementioned filmmakers: a reflection on the language of documentary testimony that inhibits or interrupts the film's transmission of evidence from a moment or site of origin.

This thesis builds on Mary Ann Doane's remarks about psychoanalytic dialogue where she writes that

> psychoanalysis itself proposes the fragility of any theoretical construct, its affinity with paranoia and delirium, and hence the problematic status of knowledge and he who purports to know. In other words, psychoanalysis must be contaminated by its own theorized and simultaneously untheorizable object—the unconscious.[11]

Doane makes use of the fundamental impasse in the concept of theory that Freud articulates in *The Interpretation of Dreams*, where the concept of the unconscious must function at once as the foundation of the science of psychoanalysis and as a site of resistance to reason itself. As Freud writes: "To explain a thing means to trace it back to something already known, and there is at the present time no established psychological knowledge under which we could subsume what the psychological explanation of dreams enables us to infer as a basis for their explanation" (SE V, 511). This object—the unconscious—provided an opportunity to devise a new science. And to justify itself, this new science had to maintain the inexplicability of its origin. Theoretical knowledge is, according to Doane, at once the source and the casualty of the destabilizing that psychoanalysis effects on the concept of consciousness.

Dream 1: Nadar

It is perhaps no accident that the interview is so frequently the central explanatory device of films challenging the ontological and epistemological premises of documentary, since the practice of the interview appears in founding statements of both psychoanalysis and cinema theory. In "The Myth of Total Cinema," where he famously concludes that cinema had not yet been invented, André Bazin refers to the "dream" reported by the nineteenth-century French photographer Nadar in 1887, several years before the first publicly exhibited moving pictures: "My dream is to see the photograph register the bodily movements and the facial expressions of a speaker while the phonograph is recording his speech."[12] Nadar did, in fact, publish a prototype of the filmed interview in the *Journal illustré* in 1886, a series of photographs of the chemist Chevreul on the occasion of his hundredth birthday, captioned by statements Chevreul was apparently speaking at the moment each image was taken. Nadar had intended to accompany the photographs with recordings made with an invention called a photophone, but because of technical difficulties with the apparatus, he was forced to resort to approximate transcriptions of Chevreul's speech. Since his failed invention only forestalls the future realization of cinema in its pure state, it functions, for Bazin, as a more authentic site of origin than the ephemeral—and profit-driven—industrial experiments of Edison and the Lumière brothers.

If the return to this pure origin—the first moment at which cinema was *conceptually* rather than *technically* possible—eludes the cinema, then each subsequent practice of the filmed interview also replays, on a transferential stage, this frustrated return to the origin. The filmed image connects viewers to history only by an act of magic (or, as Bazin would prefer, faith) that permits them to take the present moment of moving pictures for the past instant of recording. In the scene of recording we are presented with in the interview, the equipment of sound filmmaking is seemingly made to disappear, and cinema effects the return to a primitive depiction of movement, the movement back in time through a voice inspired by memory.

Dream 2: Little Dieter

This fantasy is on display in Werner Herzog's 1997 film, *Little Dieter Needs to Fly*, a film that consists essentially of one long interview with the full-grown Dieter of the title, who became obsessed with a childhood dream of flight during the Second World War, when his German town was bombed by American planes.[13] To pursue his dream, Dieter emigrated to the United States, eventually joining the Navy and flying military missions during the Vietnam War. He was shot down over Laos and spent several months as a prisoner of war in Laos and North Vietnam. During these months of captivity, Dieter endured unspeakable cruelties, and finally made a miraculous escape. The film recreates these experiences through a combination of archival footage and present-day interviews with Dieter, who has a remarkable capacity to narrate: he speaks almost continuously throughout the film, recalling his experiences in vivid detail, and almost without a trace of emotion. The presence of cinema in the locations Dieter speaks about is incongruous, because documentary cinema is logically opposed to the kinds of "visions" the film revisits and restages. If the film is to demonstrate that his stories are true, grounding them in experience and historical reality (and thus liberating both Dieter and the audience from what Deleuze called *the dream of the other*), it must differentiate Dieter's visions (dreams, fantasies, hallucinations) from those of the documentary apparatus, from the evidence gathered by the mechanical eye and ear. In this way, the film establishes the trustworthy character of its encounters: with this traumatized individual, and with the past that produced him.

But Herzog refuses to distinguish the reality of Dieter's visions from the reality produced by cinema, thus demonstrating the Bazinian dictum that "despite the promptings of our critical intelligence," the photographic image has an "irrational power" that "bear[s] away our faith" in reality.[14] The incredible story Herzog coaxes out of this material suggests that Dieter was doomed to play out, and suffer the consequences of, his childhood fantasy. The film's exposition stresses the tension between these mental visions and the vision of the film itself, as when archival images of devastation and privation are accompanied by the words, spoken by Herzog himself, "as a child, Dieter saw things around him that just made no earthly sense at all. Germany had been transformed into a dreamscape of the surreal." Indeed, Dieter's life story is one in which the imaginary makes a regular appearance. In a manner that stretches credibility, Dieter's history is measured according to the recollection of hallucinatory images: on a street just like this one, Dieter remembers seeing a shop window displaying the first sausage anyone had seen in years; here is the place where Dieter, escaping from his North Vietnamese captors, had a vision of his dead father, pointing out an escape route. (Sausages, a dead father: are objects like these not the very reason Freud invented the unconscious?)

To underscore the force of Dieter's original dream of flight in the subsequent events that make up his biography, the interviews with him are more mobile than usual. The interview-based documentary tends to frame its subjects in a single, evocative or emblematic location: in front of the factory where they once worked; next to a ravine where a terrible event occurred; in the office where they conduct their research. This technique accentuates the magical power of the testimonial voice, its capacity to (re)cover great distances in space and time, and to spirit the viewer to another place and time than the one seen in the present image. The frame of the image is often static during these interviews: the mobility of the apparatus is muted, so the agency of the voice can be brought into relief. Herzog, in contrast, replaces Dieter in the authentic settings of his story, using editing to transport him back and forth between locations identified with the more distant or more recent past. If this visual displacement is meant to illustrate the power of the voice to evoke images of the past, these literal demonstrations—as when Dieter is made to narrate, while bound and running through the jungle, the story of his forced march from Laos to North Vietnam—have the opposite effect: they undermine the voice's agency and aura, placing the documentary power of the image in conflict with that of the voice. The Freudian character of this reversal consists in its destabilization of the origin: Dieter and Herzog return to the original locations of Dieter's dreams and nightmares and find, of course, that the perpetrators of his torture are no longer there, that the sites themselves are transformed. In staging a cinematic version of the dialogue in the analyst's office, and pursuing the same therapeutic effects, Herzog's film demonstrates the incomplete or frustrated character of the transference between cinema and psychoanalysis.

FANON'S OTOBIOGRAPHY

In *Black Skin, White Masks*—a text written within earshot, we might say, of Lacan's influential lectures—Frantz Fanon captures precisely the difference between the gaze and ordinary human vision when he writes that

> [t]he *eye* is not merely a mirror but a correcting mirror. The *eye* should make it possible for us to correct cultural errors. I do not say the *eyes,* I say the *eye,* and there is no mystery about what the eye refers to; not to the crevice in the skull but to that very uniform light that wells out of the reds of Van Gogh, that glides through a concerto of Tschaikowsky, that fastens itself desperately to Schiller's *Ode to Joy,* that allows itself to be conveyed by the worm-ridden bawling of Césaire.[15]

Fanon describes a fantastic confusion of the senses: great works of art force on us a synesthesia, wherein music or literature may speak to us in light. But how does the vertigo precipitated by this derangement of the senses amount to a correcting experience?

Fanon's reflections on Western art appear in the chapter of *Black Skin, White Masks* on "The Negro and Psychopathology," in which he argues that racism is directly related to the language of vision. Like the Jew, Fanon says, the Negro is a symbol of Evil, "[t]he black man more so, for the good reason that he is black. Is not whiteness in symbols always ascribed in French to Justice, Truth, Virginity?" (180). If Fanon's humanism obligates him, at this stage in his political development, to value citizenship over nation or ethnicity ("What is all this talk of a black people, of a Negro nationality? I am a Frenchman. I am interested in French culture, French civilization, the French people" [203]), then undoing the peculiar cultural logic of perception that ties skin color to "French" is nonetheless one of his central goals. In his later writings on the Algerian revolution, Fanon stresses the place of listening in both colonial and anticolonial strategy, from the use of radio for propaganda and counterpropaganda to police practices of interrogation and the variations on psychotherapeutic dialogue applied by both the French and the Algerian liberation movement, which eventually included, of course, Fanon himself. These writings on listening practices can be read as a continuation of the theme Fanon introduces in the above passage: the separation of signification from the evidence of the senses, for the purposes of "correcting cultural errors."

In his writing on "Aural Objects," Christian Metz suggests that aurality provides an opportunity to reverse the "primitive substantialism" of visual culture, the primacy accorded to classes of objects that confirm the independence and integrity of the subject sensing them.[16] In the language of cinema, Metz shows, the image is encoded with "tactility": we experience images as either "there" or not. Within the boundaries of the frame and screen, images are fully present and fully separate from the spectator. Metz argues that a description of cinema that restricts itself to the objects of screen and image is fated to explain the experience of cinema in terms drawn from the Enlightenment conception of the subject, and to perpetuate the "world view" that maintains this subject's privilege.[17] By making use of what Metz calls the "infra-objects" of sound in cinema, Julien and the other filmmakers I have mentioned challenge this "primitive substantialism" and, in doing so, the premise that distinguishes documentary from fiction filmmaking and that has exempted documentary from theoretical analysis: the idea that recording is essentially *physical,* not social.

The analysis of a gaze in listening is one of the central themes of Julien's 1996 film, *Frantz Fanon: Black Skin, White Mask.*[18] Like some of Julien's previous works, including the 1991 feature *Young Soul Rebels,* and the semi-documentary "meditation" on Langston Hughes, *Looking for Langston, Frantz Fanon* uses a complicated sound design to underscore a politics of group identity.[19] As in those previous works, listening—as both diegetic content and as dimension of the spectator's experience—is central to the film's efforts to challenge the separation of media and cultures into original and authentic domains. *Frantz Fanon* recounts Fanon's biography using various forms of documentary exposition, including archival footage, interviews, dramatic reenactments of Fanon's life and writings, and the social and political consequences of his work on behalf of the Algerian nationalist cause. Fanon himself appears in both documentary and fictionalized scenes; the latter include a series of choreographed, mute tableaux of his family life. These recreations illustrate one of the film's central questions: how is the vexed status of the Oedipus complex in Fanon's notion of the alienated black male, and thus for colonial society itself, related in a decisive way to his biography? In an early tableau that will be revisited again and again, young Fanon is listening to Caribbean dance music on the radio when his mother enters and turns the music off. This scene reverberates through the rest of the film. Before describing its organization in detail, I will explain how the film arrives at its basic set of topics.

The film's narration is suspended between two authoritative kinds of interviews distributed throughout its length: on the one hand, there are interviews with Fanon's interpreters, scholars such as Stuart Hall and Françoise Vergès; and on the other, with figures who stand for the historical origins of Fanon's work, including co-workers and relatives, such as Joby Fanon, Frantz's brother, and Olivier Fanon, Frantz's son. Although the two types of interviews are distinguished from each other in overtly formal ways, both respect the cardinal rule of the documentary interview: that the subject does not address the camera directly, but appears to be engaged in conversation with an interlocutor slightly off-axis from the camera. (This adherence to documentary tradition is one of the film's many ambivalences, since Julien breaks the taboo against actors looking into the camera—which applies in documentary as strictly as it does in narrative cinema—almost every time the actors playing Fanon appear on screen.)

What comes to look like the film's "primal scene," the family conflict over the radio, is prefaced by a portion of the interview with Stuart Hall, in which Hall outlines the Hegelian contract of identity on which Fanon's theory of the look relies (and which, at the same time, it revises[20]), the so-called Master-Slave Dialectic. As Hall's explanation is presented on the soundtrack, the screen displays newsreel footage of a colonial ceremony of recognition. Hall's description of colonial relations interprets this newsreel footage theoretically, making it clear that by "look," the film is not referring to purely perceptual relations. In the newsreel image, a formally dressed official is shaking the hands of a line of colonial subjects, recognizing them for service to the empire. In this image there are at least four possible looks: that of the colonial administrator and his ceremony of recognition, the look of the colonized back at the official, the look of the newsreel camera recording the event, and of the camera rephotographing the newsreel for inclusion in the film we are watching. The look with which the film is ultimately concerned, then, is not that face-to-face relation that takes place within the physical relations of colonialism, but the sense of overlooking that the entire ceremony represents. The newsreel apparatus can be seen as complicit with the gaze of colonialism, insofar as the techniques convey the deeds of a benevolent administration back to the nation. There is a kind of slippage, it is suggested, between acts of face-to-face looking, acts of official recognition, and the cinematic apparatus. One of the goals of Julien's film is to deconstruct this sense of visuality, even as he claims to be using the medium to "visualize theory," a contradiction that leads to the film's most interesting problems.[21]

As this rhythm of document and analysis unfolds, the film continues to explore the construction of perceptual space. When we return to the shot of Hall's interview, the critic explains that the colonial situation is an extreme version of the Master-Slave Dialectic, which stretches it to its limit: "[I]t is the master saying, 'I do not see you at all.'" This statement is accompanied by a cut to a black-and-white ethnographic photograph of an unidentified group of natives facing the camera. Julien's camera pans over this photograph and then passes into the setting of Fanon's memory, a tableau vivant of the traumatic family scene at the radio. Aided by a musical cue, a Caribbean dance tune, which rises in volume as we leave the field of the photograph and enter the mise-en-scène of the familial space, the camera here articulates an aural logic of space, an architecture of listening derived from the associations that occur, among other places, in the analytic dialogue. Passing from one space and time to another, the film here subordinates the logic of the image—which governs the structure in place since Griffith, of spaces abutted on the order of discrete shots—to the logic of sound, which, as we shall see, is a logic not of parallelism or metaphor, but of contamination and overdetermination. In the sequence of seven shots that follows, the sounds of the radio at which the young Fanon sits move us back and forth between two different physical spaces: the interior of the home and a dance taking place in an "outside" as it is represented by newsreel footage. When Fanon's mother reaches down to shut off the radio, the camera moves in, framing young Frantz against a black background, staring defiantly into the camera.

As this final image is composed, two sounds come up in the mix: the beginning of the next interview and the musical signature of this event—a few brooding notes from a chamber orchestra and a brief aria sung by a woman's voice. Each time a crisis of identity strikes Fanon in the film this voice is heard, linking the crisis to its source in this scene. In the following sequence, Françoise Vergès explains the significance of the previous scene: Fanon's mother was a very light-skinned Alsatian, and his father was very dark. One day Frantz was listening to his mother singing a French song. When he interrupted and asked her for a Creole song, his mother told him to "stop being like a nigger." Finally, the camera movement linking the discourse on the look and the following discourse on sound from the beginning of this sequence—a movement that appeared to function in a purely grammatical, copulative manner—is grounded in a biographical source: it becomes the signifier of Fanon's mother's racism, which the film diagnoses as a phobia of contamination.

Julien's staging of this moment of castration refers to and, in a clever way, resists one conventional explanation for the acoustic "mirroring" that hearing is supposed to effect in the subject. The subject's voice has the property, according to Guy Rosolato (from whom Kaja Silverman takes the notion of the "acoustic mirror"), of "being at the same time emitted and heard, sent and received," internalized at the same time that it is externalized. This relationship to one's own voice extends the experience of sound presumed to take place in the womb, where hearing is a primary and *omnidirectional* sense.[22] The "subtle" and "archaic" sense that Michel Chion describes in *The Voice in Cinema* develops from the primitive situation of the fetus and the infant: "In the infant's experience, the mother ceaselessly plays hide-and-seek with his visual field. . . . But the olfactory and vocal continuum. . . maintain the mother's presence when she can no longer be seen (in fact, *seeing* her implies at least some distance and separation)."[23] Julien makes reference to these ontogenic arguments by making this scene of listening into a primary source of identity for Fanon. This nostalgic structure is seemingly reinforced by Julien's use of the tableau vivant to stage this and other emblematic scenes, since the frontal, exhibitionist image created by this framing recalls the shot favored in early or so-called "primitive" cinema: the wide, static shot that allowed an entire narrative to be played out in a single take.

But Julien also undercuts this psycho-biological premise by making the *radio* the source of the racially and spatially undifferentiated sounds that inspire Fanon's pleasure and later his political energy. The mother is here identified with the incisive injunction *against* listening to "nigger" music, a command that separates "inside" from "outside" and "you" from "that" or "them." (The betrayal of the "son" by the "mother" is already one of the film's tropes: the story about the mother reminds us of the story we have just heard about how the Empress Josephine convinced Napoleon to reinstitute slavery in the colonies—a story accompanied by an image of a decapitated and bloodied statue of the Empress.) Julien is probably closer here to the conceptions of listening offered by Metz, who emphasizes the indeterminacy of a sound's origin, or by Paul Willemen, whose theory of cinematic enunciation insists upon an "unceasing . . . oscillatory dialogue" between "the subject's sense of identity" and the "image of another."[24] The presence of a technological apparatus, the radio, in Fanon's fantasmatic scene echoes Willemen's suggestion that the subject spoken by cinema is the product of a "filling-in operation reconstituting the fantasy of pre-oedipal plenitude, a fantasy always marked by the symbolic incision of the frame."[25] As is the case with the Freudian concept of testimony, where the metaphor of the technical apparatus is present from the beginning, it is impossible to separate the textual operation from its subject-effects.[26]

In fact, the distance between this scene of listening and a bio-historical point of origin is further increased by the recognition that its construction strongly resembles other scenes of listening in Julien's work, scenes in which forms of identity and community unspeakable in the historical situations depicted are "spoken" by the film. In *Young Soul Rebels*, for instance, the mixing of records in a dance club scene brings together two distinct subcultures—white punks and gay black disco dancers—who had been presented in the diegesis as antagonists. *Looking for Langston* constructs an imaginary world of gay life during the Harlem Renaissance from a combination of fictional period scenes and archival images, including footage from films by Oscar Micheaux, newsreels, and a television appearance by Hughes. The collage of images, which moves around freely in time and history, is mirrored in the soundtrack, which blends the poetry of Hughes, James Baldwin, Bruce Nugent, and Essex Hemphill with Bessie Smith's blues and contemporary dance music. One is tempted to read Julien's habitual use of sound mixing to bridge past and present as an authorial signature: he encourages such an interpretation by frequently appearing in his films, as in the opening sequence of *Looking for Langston*, in which Julien appears as the corpse in a coffin, while Toni Morrison reads James Baldwin's poetry (at Baldwin's funeral) on the soundtrack.

But such an autobiographical reading is, at the same time, discouraged by the recognition that scenes of listening appear as frequently in Fanon's own writings. These writings are the other significant point of reference for Julien's use of sound in *Frantz Fanon*.

We noted that in *Black Skin, White Masks* Fanon uses an image of synaesthesia—sounds and words that can be seen—to describe the gaze, which he charges with the task of "correcting cultural errors." When Fanon takes up the cause of Algerian nationalism, this critique of perceived truth—particularly spoken truth—remains an important tactic. In his discussion in *The Wretched of the Earth* of the mental disorders produced on both sides by the colonial war in Algeria, Fanon notes the variety of devices developed by French medical personnel to compel speech and break down resistance. These devices include a variety of psycho-sociological and pharmacological "treatments" for the "pathology" of political resistance that French psychiatrists found among the Algerians. Echoing Freud's description of the unconscious as the "internal foreigner" in consciousness, the term used for this resistance is a "*corps étranger*," or "foreign body." A variety of methods of torture, mockeries of free speech, were intended to "liberate" the victim from the foreign body of politics that had invaded his consciousness. These methods included injections of pentothal, or "truth serum," and the play-acting of intellectual communities, in which torturers would engage in debate with suspected members of the Front de Libération Nationale (FLN) to convince them of their errors in judgment. According to Fanon, these tortures had the effect of leaving the victim with the feeling that he could no longer trust himself to keep confidences or engage in properly private conversation.

The induction of truth into the body of the prisoner and its consequent extraction by force is, according to classicist Page du Bois, a time-honored practice at the heart of the Western concept of truth.[27] Long before the Algerian war—or, for that matter, psychoanalysis—the Greek practice of slave torture established the powerful fiction of the body of the testimonial subject as the origin and container of a truth unknown to that subject. Torture appeared to press this truth out of the body through the mouth, in speech. The fiction of a physiological location of unconscious truth is engaged by Freud when he decides that, rather than treating the "mind" for which the patient's testimony serves as evidence, he will work on the patient's words themselves (the event of the dream, for instance, is fabricated in a conversation about it). With rueful sarcasm, Fanon captures the cynical force of this obvious fiction when he observes that there are two categories of people who undergo torture in Algeria, "those who know something" and "those who know nothing."[28] In both cases, torture is intended to turn the victim's own voice against him: the confession beaten out of him demonstrates to him—and to those among whom his treatment will be broadcast—that one's own statements ("I know nothing," "I will never tell what I know") must not be trusted.

The brilliance of Fanon's analysis of Algerian radio is in his noticing how indigenous practices of listening not only resist this violence, but also submit the concepts of "native" and "traditional" culture to a deconstructive reversal. In *A Dying Colonialism*, in the chapter called, in the English translation, "This Is the Voice of Algeria,"[29] Fanon describes how the opposition, set in place by the European bourgeoisie in

Algeria between the modern and the traditional, the civilized and the primitive, plays out along the lines of a linkage of property and cultural value specific to the colonial situation:

> For a European to own a radio is of course to participate in the eternal round of Western petty-bourgeois ownership, which extends from the radio to the villa, including the car and the refrigerator. It also gives him the feeling that colonial society is a living and palpitating reality, with its festivities, its traditions eager to establish themselves, its progress, its taking root. But especially, in the hinterland, in the so-called colonization centers, [radio] is the only link with the cities, with Algiers, with the metropolis, with the world of the civilized. It is one of the means of escaping the inert, passive, and sterilizing pressure of the "native" environment. (71)

The counterpart to this colonial fear of contamination by native language and culture is the indigene's "traditional" modesty, which compels him to avoid listening to or even owning a radio so as to avoid "sex allusions, or even the clownish situations meant to make people laugh," elements of French broadcasts that might "cause an unendurable strain in a family listening to these programs" (70). This concern for respectability is, according to Fanon, a tactic of resistance; when the FLN began broadcasting news of the revolution with its own transmitters, Fanon observes, sales of radios among the native population soared. Similarly, the ability of the colonized to resist the official truths broadcast over Radio-Alger, the organ of the occupying force, with news broadcasts on the Voice of Fighting Algeria had the effect of contaminating this singular truth: "The 'truth' of the oppressor," writes Fanon, "formerly rejected as an absolute lie, was now countered by another, an acted truth. . . . *Because it avowed its own uneasiness, the occupier's lie became a positive aspect of the nation's new truth*" (76). This contamination or hybridization of the official truth extended even to the phenomenology of listening. Since the French jammed and distorted the Algerian broadcasts, groups of listeners relied on a single "interpreter" sitting close to the receiver to tell them what the broadcasts said. These listeners were often forced to *imagine* they had heard the news they wanted to hear: "Under these conditions, claiming to have heard the *Voice of Algeria* was, in a certain sense, distorting the truth" (87).[30]

    This critique of the originality or authenticity of the voice, or of audible truths more generally, is echoed in Julien's own use of sources, both testimonial and textual. Both Fanon's writing and Julien's film rework metaphors of the voice—the "voice of the people," authorship—to reduce the phenomenal character of speech. The acts of speech and listening that Fanon describes are beset by what Jacques Derrida, describing the "writing machines" in Freud, calls *différance:* a way of recording "living, full speech, master of itself and self-present" that is less a transcription than a translation.[31] The metaphors Freud has to reach for to describe the unconscious introduce into this "full speech" a delay or discrepancy that makes speech into writing, a "non-origin which is originary."[32] If scenes of listening (to torture, to the radio) are Fanon's versions of these "writing machines," their echoes in Julien are less the literal *transcriptions* of these scenes than the air of fantasy, simulation, misrecognition, and error that makes us question their accuracy. Julien's way of responding to Fanon's call for an art that corrects cultural errors is, in other words, to make his own.

To borrow the term Olivier Fanon uses in the film to describe his father, I am suggesting, in other words, that we are compelled to read the film's depictions of oral testimony, both documentary and fictive, as attempts to *derange* cinema.[33] Julien's attempt to be faithful to his subject while obeying that subject's revolutionary appeal results in a curious mixture of aural and visual figures. Rather than viewing these instances as errors, however, I suggest that they should be regarded as attempts, consistent with Fanon's dialectical analysis of technological culture, to jam the apparatus of visually based film theory, and to replace the "delirium of clinical perfection" in apparatus theory with the *transferential*, intermittently successful model that Mary Ann Doane discovers in Freud.[34]

As the story of Fanon's work on behalf of the Algerian cause unfolds, the film's own voice becomes less and less coherent: contradictions in Fanon's theory and character are expressed in offsetting interviews with followers and critics. But rather than pursuing a purely characterological explanation for these contradictions, *Frantz Fanon* uses them as an opportunity to examine the relation between film theory and film practice. The mirror-stage thesis, for instance, becomes a visual trope in the film, sometimes quite literally (as when a mirror appears in the background of the interview with Françoise Vergès about Fanon's interpretation of the mirror-stage: when Vergès explains that misrecognition prevents the white subject from seeing his black other, Julien places himself, out of focus, in the mirror behind her). Although Julien is clearly indebted to Laura Mulvey's use of the Freudian lexicon of vision in her foundational essay, "Visual Pleasure and Narrative Cinema," the film is at least ambivalent about Mulvey's assertion that cinema is defined by the question of "the look," its narrative structure, and its psychic function.[35]

Julien is occasionally so insistent on "visualizing" Fanon that he overstates Fanon's relation to the theory of the look. One of these moments is the film's interpretation of Fanon's "phobia" of male homosexuality. Fanon's attitude to homosexuality, as Diana Fuss observes, conforms to his own definition of phobia: "When Fanon confesses, 'I have never been able, without revulsion, to hear a *man* say of another man: "He is so sensual!" the very form of the enunciation obeys the terms of Fanon's own earlier definition of phobia as 'terror mixed with sexual revulsion.'"[36] When this scene is presented in *Frantz Fanon*, however, this expression of desire is mute and visual, and the aural formulation of the phobia's etiology—"I have never been able to *hear* a man say of another man"—is lost. Fanon is in the foreground watching a male couple kissing, returning his look.

This staging misses the opportunity to link it to Fanon's anxiety about another community from which he was excluded: speakers of Arabic. As Fanon did not speak Arabic well enough to conduct his psychiatric interviews in that language, he was forced to converse with his patients through translators. The film renders this relationship in ways that again suggest that this trauma of hearing has effects that make sense only in visual terms. A later series of dramatizations of case studies from *The Wretched of the Earth* shows Fanon listening to the dreams and symptoms of the French torturers. Julien stages some of these interviews as relations between three bodies, with the Arabic-speaking male nurse present at the rear of the shot and Fanon and his patient arranged in the foreground and middle distance of the shot, Fanon listening to testimony entirely in English (which stands in for French). By rendering Fanon's response to this testimony as a horrified stare back into the camera, Julien forces these moments to resonate with the traumatic scene in Fanon's biography, rather than exploring more fully the comparison between the violence of torture and the violence of testimony.[37]

But what appears to be a simple mistranslation of the text (of Fanon's life and theory) into visual language can be regarded, from another perspective, as an attempt to remind the viewer of the capacity of the apparatus to break down. (It is not enough, after all, to notice that Julien has translated a scene of listening into an illustration of the mirror-stage thesis central to psychoanalytic film theory; the viewer has to recall as well that earlier in the film Stuart Hall has interpreted Fanon's rendering of this theory as critical of its Hegelian and Lacanian sources.) If it seems that Julien has, at times, simply displaced the question of listening onto stock figures of "the gaze," he seems at other times to take seriously Mulvey's challenge to construct a material, dialectical cinema.[38] For Mulvey this radical act consists in materializing two looks denied or subordinated by the fantasy structure of classic narrative cinema: the camera's and the spectator's. For documentary filmmakers, the radical act consists of just the opposite: shattering the illusion that the spectator's perception and the recording capacity of the apparatus are engaged, and turning evidentiary or indexical signs (particularly the signs of the voice) into textual figures. One of the film's final interviews is a good example of Julien's attempt to effect this documentary unpleasure.

The uncanny assonance between the issue of translation in Fanon's practice, as a problem of colonial relations, and the film's effort to find an appropriate audio-visual expression for this problem, is amplified in the climactic interview with Joby Fanon, close to the end of the film, where testimonial speech is given the form of a visual fetish. In this densely textured scene, Julien evokes the difference between the subject of film's speech and its speaking subject.[39] Sitting at a table covered with photographs of Fanon, Joby is being interviewed about Fanon's death. He introduces an object, which turns out to be Frantz's last letter, written as he was receiving treatment for leukemia in Washington, D.C. As the camera pans from Joby's face to his hands and the letter, he fiddles with the letter, which is in a clear plastic cover, and explains its significance in a voice-over delivered from just outside the frame: "When I received it he was already dead." Joby then speaks of the letter in terms that describe it simultaneously as a lens and a voice: "In it you see the very lucid side of Frantz," and "It is almost an appeal." In close-up, Joby's hands withdraw the letter from its cover, and he lays his glasses on the table. Finally he begins to read: "I'm writing to give you some news"—and then he can go no further. Overcome with the memory produced by this act of ventriloquism, Joby experiences the rush of visible emotion that documentary filmmakers value so highly, the reason that they bother at all to accompany speech in the interview with a visual record. He waves off the camera, and the scene fades to white.

The film could be understood here simply to return the aural and visual signifiers to their proper places in the cinematic hierarchy, relegating speech to a lifeless corporeality. After all, Julien is making use of a cliché of documentary: crying, and the interruption of "lucidity" that accompanies it. The performance conventionally accompanying the emotional display of this effort to remember posits the source of the interviewee's speech in the closet of the body, returning to it an interior cavity that the scopic drive can then appear to unfold. Is Julien aware that he restages here one of the pernicious traditions of documentary, a trope that connects the form to a very ancient justification for torture? Perhaps it is in response to this question that, after the fade to white, the film turns from authentic speech to the idiom of the revolutionary martyr. Fanon's death is signified by a series of highly conventional images: first, a staged sequence of funereal clichés (the single tear on the face of an FLN soldier bearing a flag-draped coffin, lilies, mist), and then a newsreel sequence of Algerians casting votes, indicating the passage of the leader into the popular will.

This recourse to a commonplace, exhausted iconography of martyrdom seems designed to highlight, by comparison, the power of the interview as a cinematic device that invents its own iconography. When we return to Joby, after the funereal interlude, he has composed himself and continues to read from the letter. Joby's emphasis on the letter's *transparency* as a record of Fanon's final words—a transparency described in terms both visual ("lucid") and aural ("appeal")—makes this scene especially difficult to read, since it gives to a document *within* the scene the transcendent capacity of film itself. Indeed, the final words Joby reads are "I was between life and death. . . . " Does cinema here confront a mirror of its own, the image of a voice, a call, with the power to bring the past—and the dead—to life?

When Roland Barthes describes psychoanalysis as the auditorium in which "listening speaks," he means to capture its intersubjectivity, the reversibility of the unconscious "structured like a language": "The psychoanalyst, attempting to grasp the signifiers," Barthes writes, "learns to 'speak' the language which is his patient's unconscious. . . . Listening is this means of trapping signifiers."[40] Under these conditions, "I am listening" can be translated as "listen to me." If its technological character prevents cinema—even a film practice based, as documentary is today, on acts of listening—from fully effecting this reversal, this very failure nonetheless provides a language for Julien's portrait of Fanon: a theorist, as the film reminds at its close, of the irreducible corporeality of "questions," and questions, above all, of the symbolic function of bodies. The various errors, displacements, reversals, and infidelities the film commits with respect to its sources are the marks of Julien's commitment to a dialectical art of documentary, and to the oscillatory dialogue between film theory and practice.

Notes

1. *Shoah,* directed by Claude Lanzmann, Aleph/Historia, 1985; *Nuit et Brouillard* [Night and Fog], directed by Alain Resnais, Argos/Como, 1955.

2. Theodor Reik, *Listening with the Third Ear: The Inner Experience of a Psychoanalyst* (New York: Farrar, Straus and Company, 1948), 108.

3. The phrase is from Joan W. Scott's essay, "The Evidence of Experience," *Critical Inquiry* 17 (Summer 1991): 773–97.

4. See Gaines's "Introduction: 'The Real Returns,'" in *Collecting Visible Evidence,* ed. Jane M. Gaines and Michael Renov (Minneapolis: University of Minnesota Press, 1999), 1–18.

5. André Bazin, "The Evolution of the Language of Cinema," in *What Is Cinema?* trans. Hugh Gray (Berkeley and Los Angeles: University of California Press, 1967), 1: 23–40.

6. The quotation is from Joan Copjec's 1986 essay, "The Delirium of Clinical Perfection," quoted in Mary Ann Doane's essay, "Remembering Women: Psychical and Historical Constructions in Film Theory" (in *Femmes Fatales: Feminism, Film Theory, and Psychoanalysis* [New York: Routledge, 1991]), 82. Doane generously points out that it is she herself, along with Patricia Mellencamp and Linda Williams, her co-editors of *Re-Vision: Essays in Feminist Film Criticism* (Frederick, Md.: University Publications of America, 1994), who are being corrected by Copjec.

7. Christian Metz, *The Imaginary Signifier: Psychoanalysis in the Cinema,* trans. Celia Britton et al. (Bloomington: Indiana University Press, 1982), 7.

8. Doane, "Remembering Women," 83.

9. Ibid., 88.

10. André Bazin, "The Ontology of the Photographic Image," in *What Is Cinema?* 1: 9–16.

11. Doane, "Remembering Women," 87.

12. André Bazin, "The Myth of Total Cinema," in *What Is Cinema?* 1: 17–22.

13. *Little Dieter Needs to Fly,* dir. Werner Herzog, Werner Herzog Filmproducktion, 1997.

14. Bazin, "Ontology," 14.

15. Frantz Fanon, *Black Skin, White Masks,* trans. Christian Lam Markmann (New York: Grove Press, 1967), 202.

16. Christian Metz, "Aural Objects," trans. Georgia Gurrieri, in *Film Sound: Theory and Practice,* ed. Elisabeth Weis and John Belton (New York: Columbia University Press, 1985), 154–61.

17. Ibid., 157.

18. It should be noted that I will be referring here to the 52-minute version of *Frantz Fanon: Black Skin, White Mask* (dir. Isaac Julien, 1996) and not to the 71-minute, 35mm version of the film.

19. *Young Soul Rebels,* dir. Isaac Julien, BFI/Film Four/Sankofa Film and Video, 1991; *Looking for Langston: A Meditation on Langston Hughes (1902–1967) and the Harlem Renaissance,* dir. Isaac Julien, Third World Newsreel, 1989.

20. In "The After-life of Frantz Fanon: Why Fanon? Why Now? Why *Black Skin, White Masks?*" in *The Fact of Blackness: Frantz Fanon and Visual Representation*, ed. Alan Read (Seattle: Bay Press, 1996), 12–37. Hall asserts, somewhat more strongly than he does in his interview in Julien's film, that he considers Fanon to be distancing himself from Lacan, even as Lacan distinguishes his concept of mirror-identification from Hegel's notion of "recognition." See "The After-life of Frantz Fanon," 26–27.

21. Julien makes this claim in an interview with Coco Fusco ("Visualizing Theory: an Interview with Isaac Julien," *NKA: Journal of Contemporary African Art* 6–7 [Summer/Fall 1997]: 54–57) and repeats it in a later essay co-written with the film's producer, Mark Nash, "Frantz Fanon as Film," published in *The Film Art of Isaac Julian* (Annandale-on-Hudson, N.Y.: Center for Curatorial Studies, Bard College, 2000), 103–10. Although Julien claims to be visualizing Fanon's theory, the sequence of images just described can be read as an illustration of classic statements in film theory on the construction of the spectator's position, such as Jean-Louis Baudry's "The Ideological Effects of the Basic Cinematic Apparatus" (*Film Quarterly* 28.2 [Winter 1974–75]: 39–47) or Nick Browne's "The Spectator-in-the-Text: The Rhetoric of *Stagecoach*" (*Film Quarterly* 29.9 [Winter 1975–76]: 26–38).

22. Rosolato is quoted by Kaja Silverman in *The Acoustic Mirror: The Female Voice in Psychoanalysis and Cinema* (Bloomington: Indiana University Press, 1988), 80.

23. Michel Chion, *The Voice in Cinema*, ed. and trans. Claudia Gorbman (New York: Columbia University Press, 1999), 17.

24. Paul Willemen, "Cinematic Discourse: The Problem of Inner Speech," in *Looks and Frictions: Essays in Cultural Studies and Film Theory* (New York and London: Routledge, 1994), 27–55.

25. Ibid., 49.

26. As has been frequently noted, a number of references to optical technologies appear in *The Interpretation of Dreams.* One of Freud's references to aural technologies appears in his 1912 observations on analytic technique, where he suggests that the analyst "turn his own unconscious like a receptive organ towards the transmitting unconscious of the patient. He must adjust himself to the patient as a telephone receiver is adjusted to the transmitting microphone. Just as the receiver converts back into sound waves the electric oscillations in the telephone line which were set up by sound waves, so the doctor's unconscious is able, from the derivatives of the unconscious which are communicated to him, to reconstruct that unconscious, which has determined the patient's free associations" (SE XII, 115–16).

27. See duBois's remarkable book, *Torture and Truth* (New York and London: Routledge, 1991), which begins with a description of torture devices—"*macchine atroci*"—at an exhibition duBois visited in Rome. One of these devices stands out from the rest by its "graceless, banal, ugly" modernity. Unlike the others, its function is not immediately apparent, though it appears to have some connection to listening, since it looks "something like a microphone, with electrodes dangling from it" (3). Although she recognizes the device from accounts of torture in the Americas and "films of the Algerian war" (3), duBois purposely leaves its identity obscure, in part to allow it to function as an emblem for her entire study of the Greek concept of *basanos*, a term which meant "a test or trial to determine whether something or someone is real or genuine" and then, some time later, "comes to mean also inquiry by torture, 'the question'" (7).

28. Fanon, *The Wretched of the Earth*, trans. Constance Farrington (New York: Grove Press, 1968), 281.

29. John Mowitt ("Breaking Up Fanon's Voice," in *Frantz Fanon: Critical Perspectives*, ed.

Anthony C. Alessandrini [London and New York: Routledge, 1999]) notes that the translation of this chapter title, which appears in *A Dying Colonialism* (trans. Haakon Chevalier [New York: Grove Press, 1967]) without the quotation marks that accompany it in the original French, where it appears as "*Ici la voix de l'Algérie,*" loses the "conspicuously cited character" of the phrase (95). My reading of Fanon's chapter is indebted to Mowitt's own.

30. Fanon also notes changes in the psychotic reception of voices, changes he links to the use of radio by the revolutionary forces: "Before 1954, in the psychopathological realm, the radio was an evil object, anxiogenic, accursed. After 1954, the radio assumed totally new meanings. The phenomenon of the wireless and the receiver set lost their coefficient of hostility, were stripped of their character of extraneousness, and became part of the coherent order of the nation. In hallucinatory psychoses after 1956, the radio voice became protective, friendly. Insults and accusations disappeared and gave way to words of encouragement" (*Dying Colonialism*, 89).

31. Jacques Derrida, "Freud and the Scene of Writing," in *Writing and Difference*, trans. Alan Bass (Chicago: University of Chicago Press, 1978), 196–231. In "Me-Psychoanalysis: An Introduction to the Translation of 'The Shell and the Kernel' by Nicolas Abraham" (trans. Richard Klein, *Diacritics* 9, no.1 [Spring 1979]: 4–12), Derrida uses the concept of translation to describe psychoanalysis. "Psychoanalysis," Derrida writes, "stakes out its domain precisely on the *unthought* ground of phenomenology" (19). In doing so, psychoanalysis raises a question about discourse itself: "[H]ow to include in a discourse—in any one whatever—that very thing which in essence, by dint of being the precondition of discourse, escapes it? If non-presence, the kernel and ultimate ground of all discourse, is made to speak, can it—must it—make itself heard in and through presence to self?" (19).

32. Derrida, *Writing and Difference*, 203.

33. *Déranger* is usually translated as "to disturb," but can also mean *mixing* or *disordering,* terms with a particular relevance to Julien's own cinematic craft.

34. On the technological character of Fanon's revolutionary persona, see Mowitt, "Breaking Up," especially 92–95. My analysis of the contradictions in *Frantz Fanon*'s "voice" applies some of the arguments that Bill Nichols makes about interview-based documentary in his useful essay, "The Voice of Documentary" (in *Movies and Methods,* ed. Bill Nichols, vol. 2 [Berkeley and Los Angeles: University of California Press, 1985]: 258–73), where Nichols deals at length with the work of Emile de Antonio, a filmmaker from whose style Julien's editing draws, even if the citation remains unconscious in Julien's work.

35. Laura Mulvey, "Visual Pleasure and Narrative Cinema," in *Visual and Other Pleasures* (Bloomington: Indiana University Press, 1989): 14–26.

36. Diana Fuss, "Interior Colonies: Frantz Fanon and the Politics of Identification," *Diacritics* 24, no. 2–3 (Summer-Autumn 1994): 20–42.

37. The longer 35mm version of the film does make an emblematic reference to torture, according to Julien and Nash's essay "Frantz Fanon as Film," by ending with a passage from *Black Skin, White Mask* on the resistance that the body of the interrogated subject offers the torturer (110).

38. Mulvey, "Visual Pleasure," 25.

39. Or, in the terms Paul Willemen uses in his essay on cinematic "inner speech," "the difference between the subject-image produced by a text and the historical, biological subject which presided over its manufacture" ("Cinematic Discourse," 41).

40. Roland Barthes, *The Responsibility of Forms: Critical Essays on Music, Art, and Representation,* trans. Richard Howard (New York: Hill and Wang, 1985), 245–60, 256, 246.

19. Wondrous Objectivity

ART HISTORY, FREUD, AND DETECTION

Andrew McNamara

THE "TWO-SIDEDNESS" OF ART HISTORY: HEGEL, PODRO, AND BOIS

While outlining a philosophy of "fine art," Hegel offered some advice to the nascent discipline of art history. It could be summed up, more or less, as "stick to the facts." Of course philosophy would forge the aesthetic-theoretical hardwiring of the field. If there had been a sufficient number of art historians at that time to constitute a discipline, this intellectual division of labor might have been understood as a grievous insult. The subsequent formation of the discipline shows that many art historians have indeed treated this as exemplary advice, and thus an extensive arm of art history has concerned itself exclusively with what has been termed its "archaeological inquiry." Yet this focus upon realia, document, and data collection only served to reveal a schism at the core of art-historical investigation. Another arm of the discipline, in contrast, has encroached on the philosophical terrain of aesthetics to develop its critical credentials. That this aesthetic inquiry today forms an integral feature of the tradition of art-historical investigation is evidenced by the fact that Michael Podro could produce a study exclusively devoted to a *critical* art history. While the archaeological inquiry delves into "historical facts, into sources, patronage, purposes, techniques, contemporaneous responses and ideals," the critical history, as Podro shows, remains at odds with the seemingly tangible criteria of the archaeological inquiry because it "requires us to see how the products of art sustain purposes and interests which are both *irreducible* to the conditions of their emergence as well as *inextricable* from them."[1]

The very existence of a critical art history reveals that Hegel's good counsel did not fully guide the development of the modern discipline of art history. What art history ended up with, thus, was a dichotomy in its inquiry. As Podro outlines in his study, a cleft appears in art history between its archaeological and its critical inquiry—they are related, even intrinsically linked, but nonetheless irreducible to one another. Increasingly what has become an issue is the ambivalence of its inquiry, and to compound this, the fraught, elusive nature of its object. Already, in his "Lectures on Fine Art," Hegel noted the conflictual pattern in the "scientific" treatments of art and beauty. If the empirical is, as he suggests, the "indispensable route for anyone who thinks of becoming a *scholar* in the field of art," this scholarship nonetheless produces opposing treatments:

> On the one hand we see the science of art only busying itself with actual works of art from the outside, arranging them into a history of art, setting up discussions about existing works or outlining theories which are yet to yield general considerations for both criticizing and producing works of art.
>
> On the other hand, we see science abandoning itself on its own account to reflections on the beautiful and producing only something universal, irrelevant to the work of art in its peculiarity, in short, an abstract philosophy of the beautiful.

A genuine scholarship, of course, "must be of many kinds and of wide range," he continues, but the difficulty occurs when the characteristics observed "in their *universality* make no advance toward establishing the *particular*." The ensuing prescriptions that the "art-doctors wrote to cure art," Hegel notes wryly, "were even less reliable than those of ordinary doctors for restoring human health."[2]

The good health of art scholarship seems just as fraught today—Hegel's remedies notwithstanding—and the issue of art-historical objectivity remains a contentious and thus perilously elusive terrain. Hegel thus bequeaths to art history not a prescription for the good health of the discipline, but an enduring analysis of the fraught condition of art-historical objectivity. Take the protests on behalf of art history and its disciplinary objectivity. What would unhinge an art history forged on such contrary principles? Well, surprisingly enough, art history is unhinged, if we are to believe David Carrier, by a lack of footnotes—footnotes, that is, containing relevant references testifying to the history of art-historical inquiry. What would an art history without footnotes be? An unhinged art history? One without anchor, it appears. David Carrier once suggested that the lack of footnotes signals the province of the amateur art historian: "The amateur believes that the artwork can be adequately described without exploring all of the earlier attempts to contextualize it."[3] These "amateurs" are writers, critics, or philosophers who project indiscriminately onto the artwork in an effort to display their critical self-sufficiency, as well as their intellectual-cultural scope, and thus they happily ignore the history of art-historical interpretation. Art historians, in contrast, are more meager souls, and they studiously make reference to a history of prior interpretation and deeds of fact finding. "Amateur" readings are impertinent, devoid as they are of any art-historical reference. No footnotes can be found in such texts—hence, no prior interpretations, no acknowledgments, no debts, no constraints at all. Carrier is not an art historian, either. He, too, speaks on behalf of art history, and of its disciplinary objectivity displayed in and by footnotes; more properly, he defends his own definition of art history as a relative field of interpretations that more or less subsume one another. There seems something roundabout here: we have Hegel, who would commit art history to fact finding, despite the confused sense of objectivity that ensues from this limitation, and the philosopher who would speak on behalf of the value and merit of art-historical objectivity in somewhat Hegelian tones.

Is this the type of surrogate advocacy that drove Yves-Alain Bois to his intemperate outbursts in *Painting as Model* of 1993? Bois's complaint also lies with the text *about* art by a literary writer or philosopher. He pulls no punches: each example, he chides, does "his little number" (reading art) as an obligatory step to "reach the pantheon of letters or of thought."[4] It is not a question of merely being *about* a work, but more an issue of a certain appropriative violence, an a priori subjection that knows no bounds. The artwork becomes simply the screen for the projection of an unsubstantiated theoretical speculation. So Bois, in turn, asks: "[C]an one designate the place of the theoretical in painting without doing violence to it . . . ?"

The pacific alternative that Bois annunciates in *Painting as Model* is a "materialist formalism," grasping the "means of production in its slightest detail" (xix). A *materialist* formalism would never amount to instrumental theory, because it will never foreclose what remains (citing Hubert Damisch) "without assignable end" (248). To adhere to the requirements of this fastidiously detailed and endless inquiry, "concepts must be forged from the object of one's inquiry or imported according to that object's specific exigency" (xii). This endeavor would sidestep two major impediments: "the stamp collecting approach of traditional art historians" (that is, "the gibberish of documentalists and antiquarians") and "the ineptitude of art criticism" (245–46). Its course of inquiry becomes evident in the passage from reading *about* an artwork to reading *from* or *according to* an artwork. Hence Bois refuses Hegel's advice too; he would somehow like to revive the archaeological endeavor—with its vigorous, but ultimately myopic, attention to detail—by linking it to a critical inquiry.

But how does one know when the "means of production in its slightest detail" has been grasped, especially when it occurs in a process without an "assignable end"? In Bois's own excruciatingly long and detailed readings—hence extremely thorough, rigorous, and highly illuminating readings—a question always niggles away in the background of these fine elaborations: when is this "slightest detail" granted its due? The reading of the slightest detail without assignable end is the antithesis of the archaeological reading, with its limited antiquarian zeal for the accumulation of facts; everything is kept open by a materialist formalism as compared with the finitude of closure and exhaustion. Perhaps for this very reason the very materiality of art history seems a foreign intrusion within such a critically attentive material formalism. Art history remains without end because this "means of production in its slightest detail" inhabits a parallel realm—always approximated but never quite grasped, as though the art historian runs along a glass barrier, seeing his or her object in proximity but never quite able to broach that other realm without violence. Yet the situation is more complicated than this: as Bois acknowledges, every new interpretation that has critical force "re-shuffles the cards, discovers new aspects that previously had been left unnoticed." Artists, too, contribute to these reshufflings, because they "often provide extremely precise analyses of works of other artists, past or contemporaneous, in their works."[5] Yet what remains critically untenable is the fact that the specificity of reading unique to art history operates within a critical economy stretched between immanence and violence—in which the value of each is unstable and inconsistent as they differ according to circumstance—as well as between what stems from a given context and that which defies all efforts to determine the work as part of that same context.

In this regard Bois touches on something intriguing: that the fate of a critical inquiry within art history lies with its attentiveness to production in its slightest detail. With this attentiveness to detail, Bois seeks to evade both the idle details of the antiquarian as well as the reading *about* an artwork (whether proposed by the literary writer, the philosopher or, in more recent times, cultural studies).[6] This materialist formalism grapples with the "object's specific exigency," but the exigency that propels this critical inquiry is, Bois concedes, a singular event that bursts forth like some unfathomable explosion from a particular set of circumstances (whether they be social, biographical, artistic, or political), which no longer account for this eruptive event.[7] This admission about the exigency of the "event" brings the discussion back to where it began: to Podro's dichotomy between work and a critical "event" simultaneously inextricable from and irreducible to a critical context—a volatile combination that constitutes the unstable foundation of art-historical inquiry.

A few years further on, Bois's fellow author at *October*, Hal Foster, admits he has come to champion the disciplinary specificity of art-historical inquiry because he now realizes that "to move beyond these disciplines in a truly interdisciplinary way, it has become clear that one has to know them, to be grounded there first." Disciplinary grounding, he makes clear, does not mean upholding the specificity of "painting or sculpture or an orthodoxy of Marx or Freud," but more an "attention to the historicity of artistic practices and critical discourses—how they develop, under what pressures, into what forms."[8] In making this important point, Foster reiterates Bois's strong statement on behalf of the critical capacities of art-historical inquiry. At the same time, must one not ask more about these orthodoxies that have the potential to become disciplinary fortresses?

As we have seen, disciplinary grounding within art history necessitates being attuned to a fraught structure of specificity—one that is forever subject to erosion, to the impertinent violence of outside or "amateur" readings, to an identity forever compromised as it pursues specificity down to the slightest detail. Its greatest critical challenges may well be found, as Foster now claims, within its own, grounded critical discourse; but that grounding is constantly prone to being lost outside of itself, that is, outside of this grounding. Yet the issue of art history's grounding is more unsettling than even this suggests. The presumption of art history is that its critical inquiry constitutes a harmonious rendezvous with its objects, which, in turn, compose the self-validation of its grounding and its inquiry. What critical art history attempts to fathom is an analytic scene in which a wondrous object appears that is inextricable from this grounding, yet at once is such that it always takes leave of this scene. Bois's own forceful argument declares nothing less: a "materialist formalism" grasps "the means of production in its slightest detail," but that production is a singular, irruptive event that unhinges its very grounding. To be true to the adventure of its disciplinary grounding, art history then must remain attentive to that which constantly leaves its ground. One of those "orthodoxies" Foster lists shares a common fascination with this wild analytic scene that elicits so much "by never being itself, by always being the promise (the bud or the echo) of some other scene"—and that is the scene of the Freudian circuit of analysis, which has much to say about this critical undertaking.[9]

WALLOWING IN DETAILS: FREUD, CONNOISSEURSHIP, AND THE PURSUANCE OF ANALYTIC CLUES

Long before he had heard of psychoanalysis, as Freud remarks at the outset of section 2 of "The Moses of Michelangelo," his attention had been drawn to the odd aspects of the analysis of art history. What had caught Freud's attention was an outpost of art-historical connoisseurship promoted by the Italian physician, Giovanni Morelli. Freud's interest was sparked by the manner in which Morelli's method of identifying paintings directed attention away from the general impression of the work to incidental features. One could distinguish a forgery from the genuine article, according to Morelli's method, "by laying stress on the significance of minor details, of things like the drawing of the finger-nails, of the lobe of the ear, of halos and such unconsidered trifles which the copyist neglects to imitate." For Freud, the correlation of this method of inquiry with psychoanalysis was readily evident: "It seems to me that this method of inquiry is closely related to the technique of psychoanalysis. It, too, is accustomed to divine secret and concealed things from despised or unnoticed details, from the rubbish heap, as it were, of our observations" (SE XIII, 222).

Freud's account of the significance of Morelli's method recalls Walter Benjamin's espousal of Karl Kraus's dictum: "The more closely you look at a word, the more distantly it looks back." Benjamin ruminates on the distance posed and assumed by intense scrutiny, noting to himself: "How things withstand the gaze."[10] Freud, oriented in a different direction, peers intently to find what is unnoticed in the most intent observations and reflections. In such remarkable formulations, intense observing elicits something—but not quite what was observed. The unnoticed reveals the despised, and the genuinely revealing is discovered only in the rubbish heap of observation.

If credit should go to anyone for installing in him the value of observation, then Freud states it should go to Charcot, because it was Charcot—his "master"—who sees, a *"visuel."* In an upright scientific manner, Charcot defended the importance of clinical observation, which, as Freud notes, "consists in seeing and ordering things, against the encroachments of theoretical medicine." Against the latter encroachment, Charcot advised that one should "look at the same things again and again until they themselves begin to speak."[11] Long before he came across psychoanalysis, as Freud puts it—as if to suggest he himself had just stumbled across it—Freud found something uncannily familiar in Morelli's distinctive version of art-historical detection. The affinity was due to the manner in which both paid attention to a detailed observation touching upon the disguised or untoward. While Charcot's example may have been pivotal to Freud, what became most significant for Freud the pupil is an attentiveness not only to the point where things speak, but where things speak, almost in the vein of Kraus, of what is not discernible—even of the genuinely revealing as indiscernible.

How does one divine what is unobservable, secret, and concealed? These questions touch upon Bois's concern for an art-historical practice that uncovers the "object's specific exigency." What a detour to Freud provides is an insight into managing an untenable situation: how one must attend to what is both (necessarily and simultaneously) graspable and ungraspable in pursuing singular exigency. Freud starts out by dismissing two interpretative methods (in regard to dream analysis) that share much in common with the methods Bois opposes. These methods are the cipher and the symbolic methods of interpretation, which both search for an assignable meaning that might situate itself in a chain linking interpretation and meaning, the part with the whole.[12] The "symbolic method" of interpretation "considers the content of a dream as a whole and seeks to replace it by another content which is intelligible and in certain respects analogous to the original one" (SE IV, 96–97). Art historians would recognize an affinity between this method and the footnote-less, "amateur" reading of art, which ignores a history of interpretation in order to transpose another hypothesis, often viewed as a completely fanciful projection. Yet, at the same time, the symbolic mode presumes a certain intuitive knack essential to the connoisseur: "Success must be a question of hitting on a clever idea, of direct intuition, and for that reason it was possible for dream-interpretation by means of symbolism to be exalted into an artistic activity dependent on the possession of peculiar gifts" (SE IV, 97).

The second method, the cipher or "decoding" method, "treats dreams as a kind of cryptography in which each sign can be translated into another sign having a known meaning, in accordance with a fixed key." But this relies on the supposition that such a "key" is reliable or trustworthy, and, for Freud, all guarantees for this are lacking (SE IV, 97). The essential point is that the work of interpretation is applied not to the entirety of dream, "but on each portion of the dream's content independently, as though the dream were a geological conglomerate in which each fragment of rock required a separate assessment" (SE IV, 99). This complaint about the limitations of the cipher method accords with the argument raised most frequently against the archaeological inquiry: its critical myopia. The cipher method in art scholarship merely amounts to a piecemeal conglomeration of factual details without the benefit of a guidebook.[13] The symbolic method proves equally limited insofar as it is unable to be "laid down on general lines" (SE IV, 99–100).

If there is a Freudian orthodoxy lurking within art history, as Foster suggests, then it is ironic that a "Freudian reading" has come to be associated with either a symbolic or a cipher method of analysis. Art history fails to heed Freud's challenge to interpretation just as it remains reticent about what is truly radical and disturbing within art-historical interpretation. This misconstruing of the Freudian challenge is odd, given that the expressed value of the artwork as an object of inquiry is that it simultaneously sustains and eludes reading. Bois's formulation of a materialist formalism is crucial to a disciplinary grasp of this precarious situation; yet, as we have seen, Bois himself focuses his considerations upon whether art history can produce a nonviolent critical speculation. What is at stake is a certain connoisseur-like knack or intuition that depends on different ways of considering its actions as "divining." The challenge of a psychoanalytic "divining" is that it undermines the distance one seeks to establish between a detached, clinical observation and an object to be uncovered more or less untouched and intact. Freud, of course, is personally preoccupied with the recognition and eliciting of something new, but uncovering something "new" relates precisely to the "unseen" and the frequently passed over, often leading to the uncovering of something unsavory.[14] As Carlo Ginzburg aptly suggests, what would have attracted Freud to Morelli's work is the "identification of the essence of artistic individuality with elements outside conscious control." Ginzburg goes on to link this intriguing element with the significance of discarded information or marginal data to an evidential paradigm that emerged in the nineteenth century and which encompassed many newly emerging disciplines. "In each case," he writes, "infinitesimal traces permit the comprehension of a deeper, otherwise unattainable reality: trace—more precisely, symptoms (in the case of Freud), clues (in the case of Sherlock Holmes), pictorial marks (in the case of Morelli)."[15]

Ginzburg notes that with time, Morelli's system fell into disrepute because "it came to be judged mechanical, crudely positivistic."[16] The latter rebuke still echoes today: it is readily evident in Bois's jibe about "the stamp collecting approach," "the gibberish of documentalists and antiquarians," or even in Benjamin's dismissal of the archaeological art history because it provided merely a "patchwork diagnosis of data" or a positivist amalgamation of odds and ends (*die positivistische Kunstklitterung*).[17] Archaeological inquiry accumulates data for which there is no comprehensive grasp, only an intuitive knack for yielding analogies here and there or, alternatively, for discovering some fanciful meaning for the agglomeration of details built up like a jigsaw puzzle (albeit a puzzle without a handy guidebook to decipher it). Above all, its limitation is its lack of willingness to confront what withstands critical scrutiny—it has no knack for the indiscernible. The critical inquiry faces similar difficulties; but on the other hand, like psychoanalysis it pursues a wondrous objectivity that is propelled by, and propels, interpretation, all the while defying these efforts to reach a settled meaning. In this sense, the work of art operates in a way suggestively similar to Freud's description of the neurotic's dream. In dreams of motion, Freud contends, sensations of flight or of descent do not derive from tactile feelings while asleep. They are more apt to derive from the memory of such events. Even so, he declares himself unable "to produce any complete explanation of this class of typical dreams," a conclusion that leads Freud both to emphasize the importance of detailed individual analysis and to stress the utter futility of this endeavor when it comes to unpacking the neurotic's dream:

> I am not be able to say, however, what other meanings may become attached to the recollection of such sensations in the course of later life—different meanings, perhaps, in every individual case, in spite of the typical appearance of the dreams; and I should be glad to be able to fill up the gap by a careful analysis of clear instances. . . . The dreams of neurotics, moreover, of which I might otherwise avail myself, cannot always be interpreted—not, at least, in many cases, so as to reveal the whole of their concealed meaning; a particular psychical force, which was concerned with the original constructing of the neurosis and is brought into operation once again when attempts are made at resolving it, prevents us from interpreting such dreams down to their last secret. (SE IV, 273)

The dream of the neurotic defies detailed analysis right down to their last secret. Yet divining secrets from "despised or unnoticed details" is an activity psychoanalysis shares with Morelli's art history. A work of art is not exactly a neurotic's dream, yet the genuine artwork, as Bois suggests, is at once like the wild flight of singularity. Art history and psychoanalysis do share a fascination for this radical exigency. It is just that psychoanalysis finds its provocation in the more disturbing aspects of such a pursuit—and what disturbs most is this neurotic trajectory of interpretation, which lacks a chain of fully assignable meaning.

The uncanny wonder that provokes Freud's attention takes critical analysis far from the affirmative wonder of aesthetics. The aesthetic treatise, as he suggests, is concerned with feelings of a positive kind—that which can be considered beautiful, sublime, or attractive—whereas topics such as the "uncanny" provoke repulsive or embarrassing preoccupations (*abstoßenden, peinlichen beschäftigen*) (SE XVII, 219). It is perhaps for this reason that from time to time Freud expressed reticence about the tenor of his discovery, and even "longed to be away from all this grubbing about in human dirt."[18] Who would lay claim to these tawdry "new" discoveries unearthed in repulsive, embarrassing preoccupations? As Lacan suggests, transgressing the limits of expectation entails guilt.[19] The question is not just one of guilt, but also the thrill of transgression, a guilty thrill that prompts a sequence of authorial elisions and scenes of subterfuge. Thus, for example, we find that Morelli covertly publishes his findings on art-historical scholarship under the Russian pseudonym of Ivan Lermolieff. Freud is fascinated to discover that the Italian physician Morelli is the real author. Yet in turn Freud himself felt compelled to deflect his authorship of the essay on Michelangelo. Assuming a veil of anonymity meant that Freud, while unearthing a precursor "closely related to the technique of psychoanalysis" within backwaters of art-historical inquiry, sidesteps acknowledgment for his essay in referring to an author whose "mode of thought has in fact a certain resemblance to the methodology of psychoanalysis."[20]

And yet, as John Forrester has shown, Freud also took recourse to such deflection of the discovery of psychoanalysis on other occasions. He suggested that Breuer found the key to psychoanalysis when Anna O. (Bertha Pappenheim) exclaimed that she had become pregnant by him—Breuer, the physician treating her—except that Breuer took fright at her declaration and fled the scene. Freud was left holding the baby, as it were, and was thus left to work out the knot of transference-countertransference. But Freud, obsessed as he was with discovery, also felt obliged to sidestep acknowledgment for opening this can of worms. Breuer discovered it, it's just that he did not recognize it. There are many such instances of the repetition of the "founding scene of psychoanalysis," as Forrester notes (the Dream of Irma's injection, Breuer's treatment of Anna O.) and these constitute "an attempt to avoid repeating Breuer's flight in the face of the anxiety of responsibility, medical, marital and otherwise." But psychoanalysis avoids that repetition—that flight of fright—by placing the onus of responsibility for founding psychoanalysis elsewhere. In avoiding that responsibility, Freud could thus discover the sexual transference: "[H]e could rename the moment when a patient (or his wife) said 'Dr. Freud's baby is coming!' as nothing to do with him. Someone else's responsibility. Whose?"[21]

The trajectory of psychoanalysis is discovered in the realization that things observed intently do not simply look back more distantly; indeed they can "speak" with malevolent effect. Such discoveries perplex the discoverer precisely because one expects a good return from one's critical endeavors. That this may not be the case is shocking, because one hopes to have one's pursuits, one's efforts, and one's gifts of analysis confirmed in some way. The Freudian scene is disturbing because critical observation is not necessarily validated; things look back malevolently because they did not verify one's starting position. Here the anxiety of critical responsibility arises— but responsibility for what? For something that defies one's grasp? This is an untenable breach and it must be compensated for—even overcompensated for. This is precisely what the art historian does. If the work of art bears an affinity with the neurotic's dream, then the art historian, fueled by aesthetic wonder, possesses affinities with the neurotic, insofar as the critical trajectory is plotted in advance to coordinate with its objects, but also with the paranoid: nothing is irrelevant, nothing evades one's grasp, nothing remains too inconsequential.

Together the paranoid and the neurotic, as Freud hints, suggest the epitome of interpretative zeal. Nothing is indifferent or can be left out, and in the end everything is accounted for in advance. Why? The affinity with both these predispositions in art-historical scholarship rests with their shared orientation to the future: "The idea of dreams being chiefly concerned with the future and being able to foretell it—a remnant of the old prophetic significance of dreams—provides a reason for transposing the meaning of the dream, when it has been arrived at by symbolic interpretation, into the future tense" (SE IV, 97). A similar transposition occurs in books offering to decode dreams: "If I consult a 'dream-book', I find that 'letter' must be translated by 'trouble' and 'funeral' by 'betrothal'. It then remains for me to link together the key-words which I have deciphered in this way and, once more, to transpose the result into the future tense" (SE IV, 97). Art history might seek to avoid the pitfalls of the symbolic mode of interpretation—which it might equate with a reading oblivious to the specific exigencies of the work—but most forms of interpretation tend to surmise an imminent future in which the coincidence of interpretation and of its object are realized in harmonious resolution: a transposition that leaves each intact but unified together. The rendezvous of art history with its elusive objects sustains itself as a vision of a fulfilled inquiry. In concluding *The Interpretation of Dreams*, Freud rounds in on this very issue of a rendezvous with the future:

> [T]he ancient belief that dreams foretell the future is not wholly devoid of truth. By picturing our wishes as fulfilled, dreams are after all leading us into the future. But this future, which the dreamer pictures as the present, has been moulded by his indestructible wish into a perfect likeness of the past. (SE V, 621)

Only the paranoid disposition finds everything has significance right down to the last detail. It is also a feature of paranoia that nothing lacks relevance to the subject of it. Nothing remains indifferent. For Freud it is in fact essential to compare everything with oneself, but this is in order to understand "something other than oneself." For the paranoid there is no distance, no irrelevance, nothing that escapes being plotted into the big picture. But it is the neurotic who lives life as mapped out in advance. Our most cherished modes of interpretation follow a similar path—though not always, we might hope, in such a delirious fashion—as Freud suggests: "There is an intellectual function in us which demands unity, connection and intelligibility from any material, whether of perception or thought, that comes within its grasp; and if, as a result of special circumstances, it is unable to establish a true connection, it does not hesitate to fabricate a false one" (SE XIII, 95).

Where every detail is relevant, nothing is left to chance. Everything must be allocated meaning. But what becomes of that which one fails to grasp? The greatest tragedy is the situation in which we find that everything speaks to us and tells us everything there is to know, already in advance. "The aim of psychoanalysis," as Forrester asserts, "is to undo such identifications. In this sense, its aim is to *un*write the future, which the neurotic lives as already written, structured by the words and deeds of those he or she has identified with." It is precisely the determination of this already ordained future that is unwritten. Hence psychoanalysis will seek to deliver one into an unscripted realm "in which there are no *rendez-vous,* planned or unplanned, in which there is no diary by which the future is arranged. The aim of analysis, basing itself on premonitions, prophecies and whatever, is to unwrite the future, to erase the future."[22]

TWO UNHINGED EXAMPLES

If the paranoid and the neurotic dispositions form aberrant but nonetheless ideal models of interpretation, then it is because the paranoid-neurotic interpretive zeal fills all gaps in knowledge—any and every gap. If something cannot be grasped, then a link will be fabricated and the script scripted in advance. Concern only arises when deliberations touch on something that cannot be contained and incorporated, "something other than oneself." Grasping not only becomes apprehensive, it unleashes a volatile engagement. Persecutory paranoids, as Freud notes, "take up minute indications with which these other, unknown, people present them, and use them in their delusions of reference. The meaning of their delusion of reference is that they expect from all strangers something like love." But the "enmity which the persecuted paranoid" observes constitutes the "reflection of his own hostile impulses against them."[23]

If "things" remain capable of "speaking" with malevolent effect, of "speaking" otherwise, and perhaps never ever fully down to the last detail, then why pursue them so vigorously? Two concluding examples might help tease these issues out further. The first is drawn from a James Ellroy novel, *Clandestine,* which deals with the malevolence of fascination—a close scrutiny that bites! This work explores a theme that is elaborated more explicitly in his subsequent nonfiction account, *My Dark Places,* which deals with the murder of his mother, which happened when the author was a young boy in Los Angeles. In this subsequent account, Ellroy and a detective reopen the long-distant murder case, only to finish with inconclusive findings and a still unsolved murder. During the course of the investigation, Ellroy frankly depicts his Oedipal delirium in relating his dream of having sex with his mother, now long dead. Possession in this case is a fraught exercise that serves to highlight the chasm—but also the nexus—between knowing, desire, loss, and longing. Other than in this dream, Ellroy can only engage with his mother by means of the remnants of forensic evidence: samples of fingernails, hair and pubic hair, a dress and a bra. "I held them and put them to my face. I couldn't smell her. I couldn't feel her body in them. I wanted to. I wanted to recognize her scent and touch her contours."[24]

Clandestine, the novel in which Ellroy first rehearses these issues, revolves around a young cop, Underhill, who is compelled by "wonder," which is described as a desire to know fuelled "on the track of the immutable yet ever-changing."[25] As a raw recruit, Underhill differentiates himself from all the other cops solely on the basis of a capacity for wonder: "Physically, they were splendidly equipped for fighting crime,

what with their great size and illegal dumdum bullets, but there their efficacy ended. . .
They had no capacity for wonder, only a mania for order" (68). These are men attuned
only to physical discipline; they are not prone to speculative flights of reason. Yet
Underhill is no bastion of Enlightenment reflection, either. An imposing physical
distinction similarly differentiates the tall, athletic Underhill from his love interest,
Lorna, "a crippled Jewish attorney" (133). More important, extending this difference
further, Underhill is willing to indulge in the unseemly in order to pursue "wonder":
he'll let it take him anywhere, he'll follow it wherever. The entire novel portrays a
moral universe in which there are no ordering principles of justice, only wonder. Wonder propels people, but it is not a neutral, aloof mix of observation and interpretative
skill. It contains these elements, but it also contains something obsessive, even illusory. The contrast between the policeman fueled by wonder and the lawyer is further
delineated in terms of their attitudes to law and justice. When told that the wonder is
"just the wonderful elliptical, mysterious stuff that we're never going to know completely," the lawyer, Lorna, is exasperated; she wants something more concrete, she
wants justice:

> The wonder is for artists and writers and other creative people. Their vision gives
> us the compassion to face our own lives and treat other people decently, because we
> know how imperfect the world is. But I want justice. I want specifics. . . . I want to be
> able to see results, not wonder.[26]

Underhill's aesthetic sense, if he has one, is less affirmative. Instead he avers that
wonder underpins and undermines everything: "the grand jury system is predicated
on people, and people are imperfect and wonder-driven; so justice is no kind of absolute—it's subservient to wonder" (139).

Like many of Ellroy's tales, *Clandestine* is a squalid account of confused cross-
roads of frantic ambition, desire, and knowledge—a world of "lonely juiceheads" (222).
Ambition is always contaminated. Wonder, much like Freud's disclosures, produces
embarrassing disclosures all along the way. In *Clandestine,* the protagonist, propelled
by wonder, explores the wastelands of aspirations, which involves a string of furtive
sexual encounters with women picked up at bars around L.A.—among them one who
is murdered soon afterward. In rapid succession, the narrative speeds up to run through
a succession of colliding, related events: Underhill rockets to promotion in the police
force by helping frame a purportedly homosexual suspect for this murder; the suspect commits suicide in his cell; the now dead suspect is soon shown to have been
framed for the crime; Underhill, the boy-wonder, is then kicked off the force for reasons that relate both to the frame-up and certain Communist links going back to an
earlier "pick-up." Only long after this expulsion from the police does the sense of
"wonder" propel Underhill to return to this still unsolved murder—this time outside
his former framework within the legal system. His delving into the case of the second
murder victim, Marcella de Vries, exposes a complex web of tormented family and

sexual relationships that had been concealed by the opportunistic, careerist-inspired framing of the initial suspect many years earlier.

Given the obsessions of *My Dark Places* and Ellroy's contorted emotions in first despising his murdered mother and then wishing to be reunited with her, *Clandestine* presents a virtuoso case of wish fulfillment, as the fictional cop, Underhill, adopts the troubled son of this second murder victim (after contributing to the death of the boy's fascist, homicidal father). Underhill feels redeemed; he finds happiness again, reconciles with his wife (the crippled Jewish lawyer), solves a murder, and finds "closure" by operating outside the law (and participating in the murder of a murderer). In the first case, the mode of resolution is akin to the symbolic method of inquiry discussed above: the crime is "solved" by transposing a plausible meaning, even if fabricated, and Underhill rockets to promotion. Wonder propels inquiry, even if it is not containable within a satisfied meaning. It elicits the requirement for a knack, or intuition, in analysis, and it can do so without foreclosing on the possibilities of meaning. This is at least one side of the unseemly or embarrassing side of our reflections, the side that fails to grant any distance from what the inquiry pursues. Nothing withstands the gaze, nothing remains indiscernible—for this admission alone, one may soar through the ranks.

But what does compel inquiry after all? A driven fascination. In comparison, the archaeological side of detection is too reticent. True inquiry emerges from the wanton pursuit of that which permits no fully discernible chain of meaning to the last detail. It is a wanton responsibility because, just as in Breuer's case, one must claim responsibility where recognition is not quite adequate. Is "justice" achieved in grasping something pristine or in coming full circle to verify one's initial presumptions? Justice of the singular is always to be achieved, and that may only be possible if one admits that one seeks to annihilate both that wondrous objectivity that triggers fascination and that sense of self-justification and self-knowledge in pursuit of it. Only by holding these two incompatible possibilities together can one further critical interpretation. It is triggered by the fascination that involves both love and enmity; fascination incites an inquiry that amounts to an apprehensive grasping. Connoisseurs, like Ellroy's detective, find themselves already driven amidst their objects of inquiry—driven by their fascination for them. They are both obligated in advance and tarnished by that obligation. The connoisseur pursues an object that will never submit; but it is only in that pursuance that one gauges that this will ever be so and that anything ever happens.

But what has all this to do with art history, where this discussion began? It would be remiss not to return to what triggered these thoughts in the first place. Let's finish with Bois, who furnishes us not with a complaint about the violence of critical interlopers, but with a counter-example garnered from within modern art practice. If the tenor of art-historical method is strife caused by irresolute outcomes, then the relation of opposites is where *de Stijl*, the Dutch avant-garde idea, begins its deliberations. And it is in fact primarily an idea—de Stijl—Bois tell us, an idea that engaged with the two contradictory principles informing both art-historical method and modernist avant-garde practice. These principles invoked both a quest for ontology—the attempt to secure the specificity of each medium—and they foresaw an eventual universal unfolding of monumental art, couched in a quasi-Hegelian historicism, which "prophesied . . . the inevitable dissolution of art into an all-encompassing sphere ('life' or 'environment')." This two-sidedness is summed up in the guise of the grid—an ambivalent site of action that suggests a centripetal and a centrifugal movement. Mondrian eventually rejects the centrifugal grid because it is too static—it only engenders "univocal rendering"—and he gives up on attempting to yield the specificity of painting as the ambivalent site of the centrifugal and centripetal. Instead he employs a centripetal grid format that aims to secure painting by means of a "dynamic equilibrium"—a dynamic display that is not prone to stasis, but still remains within the frame.

Van Doesburg's deployment of the oblique, which runs right out of the frame (and so triggered an irredeemable dispute with Mondrian) touches on one of those great modernist controversies that seems to hinge on the most finicky distinctions and propositions. Transferred into another context, the oblique underwrites the presumption of specificity—that is, it strives to uphold the specificity of painting in the painting-architecture nexus by ensuring that painting is not subordinated to a decorative role. Painting gains a more active role in this interrelation, but its role is that of camouflage. Van Doesburg's device aimed to work against the stasis of symmetry and repetition in architecture (Oud's in particular). Furthermore, to this development Huszar and Rietveld began to explore the corner as a "visual agent of spatial continuity" in their Berlin Pavilion of 1923. The final feature stemming from de Stijl's idea was that of the screen—an axiomatic hinge in the exploration of planarity. The screen resides on an undecidable relation between two contradictory functions, as Bois testifies: "[I]n profile it appears like a vanishing line, frontally it is a plane that blocks spatial recession."[27] With this employment of the screen, the nexus between painting and architecture is unfathomably tight. Volumes become more dynamic and intersperse with one another, confronting each other and interjecting into one another. Rietveld again developed this particular feature to explore the relevance of this insight regarding the screen to that last solid bastion of architecture, its frame.

Bois concludes his incisive discussion of the de Stijl idea by arguing that Rietveld shifts the parameters here from a functionalist ethic to something akin to Baudelaire's "Ethic of Toys." What he draws out from this conclusion is that this procedure elicits a thought more akin to a child's desire to pull a toy apart in order to find what makes it tick—in other words, to discover its "soul." However, according to Bois, Rietveld's architectural operations uncover nothing essential, nothing like a soul. Dismantling the components proves fruitless; for the "soul" instead resides, in Rietveld's case (to quote Bois's conclusion) "in the articulation of these elements, in their integration."[28] Hence, Rietveld provides the best insight into and articulation of the de Stijl idea. Yet even this very intriguing conclusion remains somewhat tentative because, while clearly we can agree with Bois, this purported integration articulates elements that camouflage and unhinge other elements. There is, therefore, no question of resorting to an entity that might be reassembled and secured, for this very integration brings together two forms that were once distinctive but which, in their combination, operate to blur the boundaries of one another so that it becomes difficult to distinguish them. De Stijl articulates a new relation of painting-architecture: one in which painting camouflages architecture. Rietveld develops this initially by playing off one specified medium against another to unhinge what is hinged within architecture by means of an unsettling articulation of the supporting-supported relation. The result? An unhinged hinging—or the hinging of what is unhinged. De Stijl formulates a practice in which the end result is not the ontological specificity of each medium as such, but the specific capacity of each medium to transform the other. It integrates in order to propel a whole series of transformations.

De Stijl deploys elements in tension, but does not fabricate a connection, a "soul." Art history arises from the deployment of conflictual features, but it cannot envisage itself as such. Instead it always seeks to remain on the positive side of discourse away from the more sordid, conflictual, and even destructive forces of interpretation. The tawdry example might suggest to us another art history: an apprehensive art history that is always committed to grasping the individual case, but one that will unwrite its goal of a history with the perfect end, culminating in an attained, perfect, subsumed fulfillment. Its history is always yet to come in the script that unravels that history already written—and written in advance—in order for it to be pursued again ever so rigorously.

NOTES

1. Michael Podro, *The Critical Historians of Art* (New Haven and London: Yale University Press, 1986), xvi.

2. G. W. F. Hegel, *Aesthetics: Lectures on Fine Art*, trans. T. M. Knox (Oxford: Clarendon Press, 1973), 1:14–15.

3. David Carrier, "Review of Norman Bryson, ed., *Calligram: Essays in New Art History from France*," *The Journal of Aesthetics and Art Criticism* 47, no. 3 (Summer 1989): 286.

4. Yves-Alain Bois, *Painting as Model* (Cambridge and London: The MIT Press–October Books, 1993), 246.

5. Yves-Alain Bois, quoted in A. McNamara and R. Butler, "All about Yves: An Interview with Yves-Alain Bois," *Eyeline* 27 (Autumn/Winter 1995): 21.

6. "I think that if you want to write something about works of art then you better see the ways they have been made and the way they function *in themselves first*. . . . What I'm criticizing in a lot of cultural studies is the lack of mediation. It's a model that says 'go from here to there'! It doesn't work like that for any of us, why should it be sufficient for an artwork? We don't start doing something bizarre because of what we have just read in the newspaper. No, there are mediations. Things are filtered in a very strange way. An artist is never a polygraph test" (ibid., 18).

7. "I believe that there are such things as 'events' and that things emerge, which are singular, out of a larger context. This is not to say that these are transcendent or that they break away easily in any way. I do think that, out of a field of possibilities, things emerge and even violently burst out. To try to understand the singularity of such an emergence, once it has struck me, once it has caught me (more than not, unawares) is what excites me" (ibid., 21).

8. Miwon Kwon, "The Return of the Real: An Interview with Hal Foster," *Flash Art*, March–April 1996, 62.

9. John Forrester, "Who Is in Analysis with Whom? Freud, Lacan, Derrida," in *The Seductions of Psychoanalysis: Freud, Lacan, and Derrida* (Cambridge: Cambridge University Press, 1992), 235.

10. Benjamin himself returns to this reference on more than one occasion. See Walter Benjamin, "On Some Motifs in Baudelaire," in *Charles Baudelaire: A Lyric Poet in the Era of High Capitalism*, trans. Harry Zohn (London: Verso, 1985), 148n90; and "Hashish in Marseilles," in *One-Way Street and Other Writings*, trans. Edmund Jephcott (London: Verso, 1985), 222.

11. Cited in Paul Roazen, *Freud and his Followers* (London: Allen Lane, 1976), 91.

12. "My presumption that dreams can be interpreted at once puts me in opposition to the ruling theory of dreams and in fact to every theory of dreams with the single exception of Scherner's; for 'interpreting' a dream implies assigning a 'meaning' to it—that is, replacing it by something which fits into the chain of our mental acts as a link having a validity and importance to the rest. As we have seen, the scientific theories of dreams leave no room for any problem of interpreting them, since in their view a dream is not a mental act at all, but a somatic process signalling its occurrence by indications registered in the mental apparatus" (SE IV, 96).

13. Hegel, too, suggested this might be the case. For him, such connoisseurial ambition has a positive side insofar as it "concerns a thorough acquaintance with the whole sweep of the individual character of a work of art." It has the defect, however, of having little concept of what is actually art, and so it can only compile information: "For connoisseurship, and this is its defective side, may stick at acquaintance with purely external aspects, the technical, historical, etc., and perhaps have little notion of the true nature of the work of art, or even know nothing of it at all; indeed it can even disesteem the value of deeper studies in comparison with purely positive, technical, and historical information" (Hegel, *Aesthetics*, 34–35).

14. Freud candidly notes his trepidation after coming across an earlier account of Michelangelo's *Moses*: "My first feeling was one of regret that the author should have anticipated so much of my thought, which seemed precious to me because it was the result of my own efforts; and it was only in the second instance that I was able to get pleasure from its unexpected confirmation of my opinion" (SE XIII, 234).

15. Carlo Ginzburg, *Clues, Myths, and the Historical Method*, trans. John and Anne C. Tedeschi (Baltimore: The Johns Hopkins University Press, 1992), 101.

16. Ibid., 97.

17. Walter Benjamin, "Strenge Kunstwissenschaft: Zum ersten Bande der *Kunstwissenschaftlichen Forschungen* (Erste Fassung)" (1933), in *Gesammelte Schriften* (Frankfurt am Main: Suhrkamp Verlag, 1972), 3:367. Thomas Y. Levin translates this term as "positivist art chatter." See also Benjamin, "Rigorous Study of Art: On the First Volume of the *Kunstwissenschaftliche Forschungen*," *October* 47 (Winter 1988): 88.

18. Cited in Roazen, *Freud and His Followers*, 116.

19. Lacan makes this point while hypothesizing about Freud's dream-wish regarding Irma's injection: "I am he who wants to be forgiven for having dared to begin to cure these

patients, who until now no one wanted to understand and whose cure was forbidden. I am he who wants to be guilty of it, for to transgress any limit imposed up to now on human activity is always to be guilty." Jacques Lacan, *The Seminar,* vol. 2, *The Ego in Freud's Theory and in the Technique of Psycho-Analysis, 1954–55* (Cambridge: Cambridge University Press, 1988), 170–71.

20. Note accompanying the anonymously written essay (SE XIII, 211).

21. Forrester is also precise in allocating responsibility: "[I]t is only because Freud could convert this question of personal and medical ethics into one of theoretical significance that he was able to found psychoanalysis, through separating out the dimension of transference-countertransference" (Forrester, "The True Story of Anna O.," in Forrester, *Seductions,* 29, 27).

22. Ibid., 95–96.

23. Roazen, *Freud and His Followers,* 104.

24. James Ellroy, *My Dark Places* (London: Arrow Books, 1997), 222.

25. James Ellroy, *Clandestine* (London: Arrow Books, 1996), 237.

26. Ibid., 139.

27. Bois, *Painting as Model,* 116.

28. Ibid., 121.

THOUGHTFUL
ARTICULATIONS

20. Marx, Condensed and Displaced

A. Kiarina Kordela

In this essay I advance the thesis that there is a structural homology between economic and semantic systems of exchange—two systems that in the secular capitalist era cover nothing less than the fields of capital, sign, and subject. By claiming a structural homology among these three fields I also mean to place them on the same epistemological level, whereby none of these fields can be considered to be the cause of the other fields. Rather, all three are caused and determined by a function of different ontological and epistemological status: surplus.

This surplus is ontologically different from capital, sign, and subject identity insofar as it does not manifest itself empirically as such and, hence, pertains in Lacanian terms to the status of the real. Though in itself empirically transcendent, the surplus gives signs of its existence through its two empirical effects. In the field of economy, where surplus coincides with what Marx called "surplus-value," the two manifest effects of surplus are "exchange-value" and "use-value." In the fields of semantic exchange as well, the surplus makes itself manifest within experience in two forms, respectively: metaphor and metonymy within the field of the signifier, condensation and displacement within the field of the Freudian subject; and enjoyment of meaning *(jouis-sens)* and enjoyment *(jouissance)* within the field of the Lacanian subject. Though linguistics and Freudian psychoanalysis have always observed the distinction between these two empirical forms of surplus, they have largely neglected surplus in itself, as the empirically nonmanifest real. The importance of the Lacanian intervention largely lies in his introduction of surplus enjoyment *(plus-de-jouir)*, that is, the introduction of the function of the real or surplus into the field of psychoanalysis—a function hitherto acknowledged only within the field of economy, as surplus-value.

Thus the epistemological significance of my argument is threefold. First, it attempts to overcome the impasse of the two dominant alternatives offered since Marx regarding causal relations between material and economic conditions (base) and culture (superstructure), namely traditional Marxism itself, in which the base determines the superstructure, and the bourgeois inversion of this causal relation. Crucially, my argument differs from the contemporary reevaluations of Marxism in the aftermath of Croce's and Gramsci's theories of hegemony and Althusser's theory of ideology. I do not wish simply to argue that the distinction between base and superstructure is untenable since they are overdetermined or, to put it in Spinozian terms, they relate to one another in terms not of transitive, but of immanent causality (with the cause indwelling, and existing but in its effects). Rather, I argue that if this position of much contemporary Marxism (a position to which the field of contemporary cultural studies owes its emergence) is true, this is due to the fact that both material-economic conditions and culture (including both artifacts and subject identities) are caused and determined by their surplus, which is a third function that transcends them and is simultaneously their effect and cause.

Second, my argument attempts to offer a long-awaited justification of a central assumption underlying the theories of thinkers whose work has contributed to the constitution of cultural studies, such as Roland Barthes, Michel Foucault, and Jacques Lacan, and which, consequently, informs the theory and practice of cultural studies itself. Though never systematized into a coherent theory, the assumption that, their ontological differences notwithstanding, the structures and functions of capital and the sign epistemologically coincide, underlies the work of these thinkers. In Barthes's words:

> In the past . . . money "revealed"; it was an index, it furnished a fact, a cause, it had a nature; today it "represents" (everything): it is an equivalent, an exchange, a representation, a sign. . . . Shifting from a monarchy based on land to an industrial monarchy, society changed the Book, it passed from the Letter (of nobility) to the Figure (of fortune). . . . The difference between feudal society and bourgeois society, index and sign, is this: the index has an origin, the sign does not.[1]

Barthes's statement, which can be read as a paraphrase of Marx's notorious citation of the two French proverbs—"Nulle terre sans seigneur" (no land without a lord)— and "L'argent n'a pas de maître" (money does not have master) —testifies not only to Barthes's own conception of the structural parallelism between capital and signifier, but also to the fact that this parallelism is already entailed in Marx's account of capital.[2] In fact, we could say that Marx defined capital as a signifier *avant la lettre*, that is, prior to the moment at which linguistics defined the signifier as such (that is as having no other value than the one differentially defined in relation to other signifiers).

Similarly, Foucault's work presupposes this Marxian homology between capital and signifier. In *The Order of Things*, the economic shift from feudal to capitalist economy and the corollary shift from money of precious metal to money of symbolic value (paper money) parallels the discursive shift from the ternary, representational sign—the authority of which derives from the assumption that, in whatever distorted ways, it ultimately represents both the world and God's Word—to the binary, differential, and arbitrary sign of the secular modern era.[3] Thus Foucault can refer to both money and the sign as the manifestations of one and the same epistemic configuration:

> Money does [no longer] draw its value from the material of which it is composed . . . money (and even the metal of which it is made) receives its value from its pure function as sign. . . . . Things take on value, then, in relation to one another . . . but the true estimation of that value has its source in human judgment. . . . Wealth is wealth because we estimate it, just as our ideas are what they are because we represent them. Monetary or verbal signs are additional to this. (175–76)

Finally, with Lacan and his definition of the subject as the subject of the signifier, the homology between capital and sign presupposed by Barthes and Foucault extends to comprise the constitution of subjectivity. Hence, when we speak of a structural and functional homology between economic and semantic exchange, we are effectively speaking of a homology among three fields: economy, linguistics, and the constitution of the subject.

Turning now to cultural studies: Its fundamental assumption—that discursive practices are effectively political practices, being effected by and effecting power dynamics—also presupposes a homology among the fields of capital, sign, and subject. This assumption allows for the interdisciplinary approaches that characterize such studies. However, cultural studies does not provide an epistemological theory that justifies its reliance on this homology. Is this homology due to some causal hierarchy among these fields—that capital determines the sign, and the latter the subject, or that the sign is the determinant factor for both capital and subject, and so on? Or is such a homology to be conceived in an entirely different way? This question is crucial, for, if the response to the above question is the former, then cultural studies (whatever causal hierarchy among these three elements it may opt for) inevitably reverts to either classical Marxism (economy determines the world) or to bourgeois explanatory models, whether of the classical type (the subject determines the world) or of the postlinguistic type (the sign determines the world). Thus the third upshot of my argument concerns the possibility of grounding cultural studies epistemologically.

In addition, I address a core opposition between, on the one hand, deconstruction and the epistemological assumptions shared by both mainstream and much academic postmodern discourse —notably the trend under the rubric of "postideology"—and, on the other hand, Lacanian psychoanalysis: the acknowledgment of a real, which, being a surplus effect of signification, transcends and determines it. A recurrent strategy by which deconstruction has argued against the Lacanian concept of the real is its challenge to the epistemological tenability of the distinction between metaphor and metonymy (and their linguistic or rhetorical cognates)—a distinction that, as I will show, amounts, in Freud, to that between condensation and displacement, and in Marx, to that between exchange value and use-value.[4] The obliteration of these distinctions prevents any possibility of even approaching the function of the real or surplus. My argument will foreground the difference between the political and ideological implications of the postmodern and deconstructive resistance to the real, and the Lacanian insistence on it and persistence with it.

THE FUTURE REVISION OF *THE INTERPRETATION OF DREAMS* (FREUD AND JAKOBSON)

To trace the discursive articulation of the aforementioned homology between the fields of economic and semantic exchange, I will map the itinerary of certain major concepts and structures common to the fields of economy, linguistics, and psychoanalysis. Specifically, I will focus on the conceptual vicissitudes that lead from Marx's tripartite distinction—use value, exchange value, and surplus value—through Freud's binary distinction between displacement and condensation in *The Interpretation of Dreams* to Jakobson's binary distinction between metonymy and metaphor, and finally back to Lacan's tripartite distinction—enjoyment, enjoyment of meaning, and surplus enjoyment.[5] I argue that Lacan's ternary scheme can be thought of as a properly Marxian corrective to Freud's and Jakobson's binary formulas, and thus as a Marxian intervention within psychoanalysis and linguistics.

In keeping with Freud's principle of belatedness or deferred action (*Nachträglichkeit*), we can narrate the development of his theory of the interpretation of dreams as follows. At the time *The Interpretation of Dreams* is first published, Freud overlooks *two* decisive obstacles to his theory, which would retroactively ascribe a pathogenic (i.e., false or untenable) meaning to certain of its concepts, and lead him to rework the theory over many years.

First, in maintaining his thesis that all dreams function as wish fulfillments, Freud was limited to the insight that anxiety dreams "form a marginal case [*Grenzfall*] in the function of dreaming" (GW II/III, 492; 1998, 525; 1985, 398).[6] After World War I, however, Freud could not ignore the apparent anomaly to his theory presented by the recurrent anxiety dreams experienced by shell-shocked soldiers. It was not until *Beyond the Pleasure Principle* (1920) that Freud would overcome the apparent contradiction between his theory and his experiences treating traumatized soldiers by developing the concepts of repetition compulsion and the death drive as supplements to the pleasure principle, which dreams, now as then, satisfy by remaining wish-fulfilling.[7] Misunderstandings of the relation between the death drive and the pleasure principle persisted until Daniel Lagache and, more effecively, Lacan and Deleuze, helped clarify things by stressing that the death drive and repetition compulsion are not the disobedient exception to the pleasure principle, but rather its logically necessary precondition.[8]

To recapitulate the debate over these psychoanalytic concepts, the relevant question is not, as Edward Bibring asks, whether repetition compulsion, albeit disobedient to the pleasure principle, is nevertheless used by the restitutive tendency of the latter in the service and benefit of the I. As Daniel Lagache argues, alongside the repetition of needs triggered by the pleasure principle, we should assume the existence of another, more fundamental need: a need to repeat. Lagache, however, does not go far enough. Like Bibring, he assumes that this transcendental need does not obey the rules of the pleasure principle. We must assume that repetition compulsion and the death drive are of an order transcendental to that of the pleasure principle, but not because they defy its rules; rather, these two principles must be considered the very instance that determines these rules and renders the pleasure principle possible in the first place. For to say that a dream induces pleasure by fulfilling a wish presupposes knowledge of what is pleasurable for the subject. But what is perceived as pleasurable is itself something mediated by several layers of ideological assumptions. A quasi-hedonistic biological and procreational pragmatism, for instance, perceives as pleasurable that which both offers sexual pleasure and leads, according to what Freud called the "principle of constancy," to the release of tension, as well as to the propagation of the species (GW XIII, 5; 1961, 6). On the other hand, the retributive and redemptive justice that equally marks Western Christianity, any economy of exchange, and the notorious will to power, perceives as pleasurable any sacrifice (sexual, personal, or material) that promises future redemption (metaphysical or economic) or proximity to power (such as potlatch, exhibitionism of disposable wealth in media). Sometimes it takes millions of dollars or lives to fulfill a wish; and much of the time, the repetition of what can be perceived as destruction, waste, and sacrifice can be as pleasurable and as *natural* as sex is for biological pragmatism. It was because of this insight, made so glaringly evident in the wake of the carnage of World War I, that Freud was forced to write, in *Beyond the Pleasure Principle,* that "[m]ost of the unpleasure that we experience is *perceptual* unpleasure" (GW XIII, 7; 1961, 9). Death drive is that which determines what is pleasure and what is "unpleasure" for the subject. In other words, "by the 'beyond' of the title," as Deleuze writes, Freud does not mean "the exceptions to that principle," but "a residue that is irreducible to [the pleasure principle]" *without* "contradict[ing] the principle—in short, "a second-order," "transcendental" principle, which is epistemologically presupposed in order to "account . . . for the necessary compliance of the field [of life] with the empirical [pleasure] principle."[9] It is therefore qua transcendental critique, in the Kantian sense, that the deferred action of *Beyond the Pleasure Principle* supplements *The Interpretation of Dreams.*

A second obstacle that would have ramifications for Freud's theory of dreams came in the form of his own theories of the Oedipus complex and the hysteric's resistance. These theories forced Freud to supplement his psychoanalytic edifice with the concepts of transference and transferential resistance, which are in evidence from their initial, unpolished manifestation in the 1895 *Studies in Hysteria* through his final writings. This particular amendment of Freud's runs as follows: Even if no conceivable interpretation can explain the dream as fulfilling one of the analysand's wishes, it nonetheless fulfills the hysteric's wish (emerging in the process of her transferential resistance to the analyst) to repudiate Freud's theory of dreams. As Freud writes in "Analysis Terminable and Interminable" (1937), "the defensive mechanisms directed against former danger return in the treatment as *resistances* against recovery. It follows from this that the ego treats recovery itself as a new danger" (*Gesammelte Werke* XVI, 84; SE XXIII, 238). Of course, in terms of countertransference, as Lacan says, "the patient's resistance is always your own, and when a resistance succeeds it is because you are in it up to your neck, because you understand. You understand, you are wrong."[10] But by supplementing the theory of the interpretation of dreams with a transference, which authorizes the emergence of wishes regarding the analytic theory *itself,* you wipe out the chances that you'll ever be wrong again. Transference is therefore the deferred supplement, which, among other things, guarantees that, one way or the other, at the end of the day, the theory of the interpretation of dreams is irrefutable (as many a critic of psychoanalysis has argued).

Keeping these two deferred supplements (death drive or repetition compulsion and transference) in mind, we can now return to *The Interpretation of Dreams* to see how they effect the theory there advanced. In 1900 Freud had already identified condensation (*Verdichtung*) and displacement (*Verschiebung*) as the major, complementary processes through which the unconscious manifests itself in dreams, albeit only in a disguised and distorted way. Condensation is an image or concept (*Vorstellung*) in which various associative chains intersect, so that the image or concept is in fact overdetermined by all these chains, just as these chains may also intersect at other images and concepts manifest in the dream. In other words, as has been pointed out, condensation is the psychoanalytic equivalent of the linguistic metaphor, postulating that there is no one-to-one correspondence between signifier and signified, since both slide in theoretically infinite chains of substitution. Because they are exclusively motivated by the sliding of signifiers and signifieds, it follows that metaphor and condensation are always motivated semantically, independent from physical or pragmatically determined experience. Displacement, by contrast, is the sliding or transfer, not of meaning, but of affects and intensities, from the initial concept or image that produced them to other images or concepts that are less invested emotionally and are in some way associatively linked to the initial, overinvested concept or image. It follows that, while metaphor and condensation are always motivated semantically, and hence independently from actual, pragmatically determined experience, metonymy and displacement are also determined by pragmatic and affective factors. This is a crucial point to which we shall return shortly.

To complete this brief recapitulation of Freud's account of condensation and displacement, these two functions are complementary mechanisms of the dream-work process, whereby displacement facilitates condensation by producing, through the transfer of affect from one associative chain to another, the intersections required for condensation to take over. As functions of the primary processes of dream-work, condensation and displacement are the precondition for the constitution in the first place of latent dream thoughts out of free, unbounded energy. As functions of the secondary process, on the other hand, condensation and displacement, in Freud's words, "censor" and "interpret" the "absurdity and disconnectedness" of the raw, latent, dream thoughts, so that they become a manifest dream content that already "approximates to the model of an intelligible experience" much "before being submitted to waking interpretation" (GW II/III, 494; 1998, 528). Condensation and displacement unveil truth only inasmuch as they veil it.

Crucially, it is clear in Freud's rhetoric that condensation and displacement qua processes of the dream-work extend in awakened life to the transference qua process in the analytic experience. By allowing repressed affects to bind themselves to less disturbing images, displacement qua dream-work contributes as much to their manifestation as it conceals their meaning by causing, in Freud's words, confusing "reevaluations of the psychic valence" that ultimately derail us out of the path of the dream's truth (*Über den Traum*, GW II–III, 667; SE V, 655). Similarly, transference with the analyst can be positive, allowing the analysand to revive repressed affects by displacing them onto the analyst, or can be negative, as in transferential resistance, impeding the analyst's discovery of truth. In *The Interpretation of Dreams* it is not an accident that Freud often calls the former function of displacement *transference* (*Übertragung*), just as he defines transference in the analytic situation as the *displacement* of affects from one's past experiences onto the analytic experience (*Affektverschiebung*). Condensation, too, is similarly constitutive of transference, insofar as the revived experience is not repeated literally, but as a metaphorical equivalent of what is supposed to be revived. The fact that the revival of affects in transference is triggered by the mere verbalization of one's past experiences makes its metaphorical nature particularly conspicuous. As Freud writes in the *Studies on Hysteria*, "language serves as a *substitute* for action; by its help, an affect can be 'abreacted' almost as effectively" (emphasis mine).[11]

Let us now return to the crucial distinction between condensation, which is motivated purely semantically, and displacement, which is always motivated by a *real* affective analogy between the substitute and the real, empirical cause of the repressed affect, so that the analogy cannot be explained purely semantically. Linguistic metonymy, too, is motivated by cultural knowledge of pragmatic relations—power, convention, possession, etc.—that also cannot be explained purely semantically.[12] When somebody is metaphorically called a "swine," and when we metonymically refer to the cautiousness of the U.S. government by saying, "the White House is cautious," the referent of the metaphor "swine" is free to be me as much as the U.S. government is; but it's safe to say that *I* will not be the referent of the metonymy "White House" unless certain pragmatic relations change rather drastically. In accord, therefore, with Lacan's argument in "The Agency of the Letter in the Unconscious, or Reason since Freud," and against Derrida's and de Man's systematic attempts to render metaphor and metonymy conceptually indistinguishable, I would insist that only metaphor and condensation (*Verdichtung*) enjoy the arbitrary licenses of poetry (*Dichtung*). Far from indulging in this free play of metaphor and condensation, metonymy and displacement, on the other hand, are restrained by pragmatic limitations.

If this distinction is true, then, contrary to the prevailing postmodern conviction, neither the constitution of meaning and truth, nor the constitution of subjectivity and identity—phenomena involving both metaphor and metonymy or condensation and displacement—can be reducible solely to a "free play" of signifiers. Finally, if the homology among the fields of the signifier and subjectivity, on the one hand, and that of economy, on the other, is also true, then economy must also involve both metaphor- and metonymy-like aspects, so that it, too, could not be legitimately reduced solely to a "free play" of exchange values. We shall return to this point in the last section.

Ethical Arbitrariness against Cognitive Commodities

To return momentarily to the status of the psychoanalytic interpretation of dreams, Freud's future revision of the theory of dream interpretation belatedly affirms that the process of dream interpretation operates by means of displacement and condensation, and that, like the dream itself, analysis can approach the truth of the dream only inasmuch as it moves away from it. In fact, as is known, the reason that deconstruction so consistently targets the distinction between condensation or metaphor and displacement or metonymy is not its concern with dreams and their interpretation; rather, it is precisely that these pairs of concepts function well beyond dream-work, permeating—through transference, which, as we know, is experienced not only in analysis—waking life, including, not least, the activity of analyzing texts, whether these texts are dreams, literature proper, or any other cultural artifact. To be sure, there is one point of agreement between the deconstructionist and the psychoanalytic approaches to this issue. Both assert that, far from being a progressive, enlightening process moving unidirectionally toward truth, textual interpretation is nothing more or less than another dream that reveals only as much as it conceals. Thus the oneirically radical arbitrariness that extends beyond the constitution of the text itself so as also to be involved in the process that interprets it, far from containing the text's limits of disguise and distortion, extends them infinitely. This also reconfirms Freud's thesis in *Totem and Taboo* that there is an inherent "intellectual function in us which demands unity, connection and intelligibility from any material" and which, "if . . . it is unable to establish a true connection . . . does not hesitate to fabricate a false one" (SE XIII, 95). Falsity and arbitrariness pertain equally to the text and to its interpretation. Taken to its logical climax,

then, even the founding thesis that dreams are manifest, distorted contents of unconscious thoughts will—by dint of its own logic, once it has been retroactively supplemented by its future revision—always already have become no less arbitrary and
ungrounded than any other wish-fulfilling interpretation of dreams, including the increasingly popular behaviorist assumption that dreams are meaningless, mechanically
and chemically determined biological reactions to environmental stimuli.

If we want to play according to the rules of what is often called "postmodern"
epistemology—an epistemology largely articulated through the insights brought about
by linguistics and psychoanalysis—we have to admit that the psychoanalytic and the
biologistic takes on dreams are equally arbitrary and ungrounded. But, as is always the
case with arbitrary and ungrounded hypotheses, each serves a distinct political purpose. However arbitrary the truths of the psychoanalytic interpretation of dreams may
be, by turning dreams into a signifier of the subject's truth about its relation to itself,
others, and society, interpretation is inherently forced (that is, it is inherently free)
to offer either a social reconfirmation or a critique. By contrast, the biologistic reduction of dreams to chemistry and mechanics deprives dreams of all semantic function—
except, of course, that of repetitively signifying the steady progress of science, which
can reduce ever more dreamt images to mechanical and chemical reactions, thus
invariably reconfirming a technocratic society and its status quo.

It follows (and this has implications extending far beyond Freud's work and
beyond psychoanalysis itself) that, at the present, post-Freudian epistemological juncture, social critique can emerge only where arbitrariness is admitted and interpretative
choice is openly relegated to an extra-rational, and hence nondeconstructible, ethical
and political certainty. In other words, for social critique to be possible, some form of
interpretation and certainty must be recognized as both irrational and necessary.

Leaving aside the current dominance of technocracy and positivism, both of
which deny arbitrariness, I focus here on the interpretative line within the nonpositivist, post-Freudian field of psychoanalytic or literary and cultural analysis that, on
the contrary, admits to the arbitrariness of interpretation, but denies this necessary
moment of an interpretative certainty that is not rational, but ethical. It is this trend of
thought that I call deconstruction and "postideology."

For I wish to argue that, by reducing interpretative arbitrariness to yet another
reason why we should deem all truths to be merely equal, potentially exchangeable
and marketable, like any other market commodity, this nonpositivist but radically rel-
ativist, "postideological" line of thought empties arbitrariness of its political potential.
It reduces the function of all discourse to that of technology—the latter producing and
circulating technological commodities, and the former interpretative and cognitive
commodities—and in the process the possibility of challenging this global economy of
truths and other commodities rapidly disappears. Freud's epistemological contumacy
enables effective social critique and political intervention only if the ungroundedness,
arbitrariness, and exchangeability of deconstructible truths necessarily presupposes

some other, nondeconstructible, and hence nonexchangeable truth, which, though equally arbitrary, functions as absolute. After all, while semantic condensation allows pain to displace its cause onto some arbitrary concept, leaving this cause unknown and subject to arbitrary interpretation, the pain itself reconfirms that some real, albeit elusive, cause must nevertheless have induced it in the first place. Similarly, in capitalism, labor-power qua objectified *exchange-value* freely circulates and substitutes for any other commodity within the force of self-propelling and self-generating capital—but only under the precondition that labor-power is also a value of a radically different kind, a unique and nonexchangeable *use-value*, which does not profit from the surplus value produced by its aspect as exchange-value. In Marx's words, although value is a "self-moving substance" that "throws off surplus-value from itself," nevertheless value "must have its origin both in circulation and not in circulation," both in exchange-value and in use-value.[13] The same principle applies to semantic value: even though the signifier is also a self-moving, self-referential and differential substance, content in its own free play (the aspect of the signifier foregrounded by deconstruction), semantic value must have its origin both within this free circulation of exchangeable signifiers and, at the same time, outside of it: in the realm of affect and pragmatic relations.

Two major denials on the part of deconstruction, therefore, prevent any possibility of it challenging the order of late capitalism. First, there is the denial of two homologies: one among use-value, displacement, and metonymy, and the other among exchange-value, condensation, and metaphor. Second, there is the denial of the conceptual distinction between the above two aspects of capital (use as opposed to exchange), signifier (metonymy as opposed to metaphor), and subject (displacement as opposed to condensation). The vehement repudiation of this homology among these three fields and of this distinction within each of these fields is a forceful political act, intended to sustain a capitalist circulation, economic and semantic, that does not want to know anything about use-value and metonymic relations. To deny the conceptual distinction between metaphor and metonymy or condensation and displacement amounts to denying that exchange- and use-value are conceptually distinguishable—just as they are not distinguishable in liberal economic ideology, where every concrete social ill can be solved by the introduction of increased commodification. Finally, the combination of these denials amounts to abandoning both Marxism *and* psychoanalysis.

THE FUTURE AND PAST REVISION OF *THE INTERPRETATION OF DREAMS* (FREUD, LACAN, MARX, HEGEL)

I now argue—against the aforementioned anti-Marxian and anti-psychoanalytic trend of denying the conceptual distinctions between metaphor and metonymy, condensation and displacement, and exchange-value and use-value—that Lacan's concept of enjoyment (*jouissance*) signals an attempt, at once within and against postmodernism, to perform a restitution of absolute truth or certainty, affect, and use-value (in one word, the *real*) in their (its) proper field: the field of the subject as a subject of the signifier, and hence of capital. In this context it is helpful to conceive of the signifier as something that, as Paul Ricoeur puts it, has a "split reference," referring both to other signifiers and to the realm beyond signification.[14] To sustain both affect and pragmatic relations within the field of signification as one aspect of its split reference, and to bring them to bear on the constitution of the subject as the subject of the signifier, Lacan introduces and distinguishes between enjoyment of meaning (*jouis-sens*) and enjoyment (*jouissance*).[15] Enjoyment of meaning, like Freud's condensation and Jakobson's metaphor, is motivated by the semantic aspect of signification. Enjoyment (*jouissance*), as we shall presently see, extends beyond this aspect to involve and be motivated both by affects (like Freud's displacement) *and* pragmatic relations (like Jakobson's metonymy).

Set against the pleasure principle, as the tendency to go *beyond* it and its prohibition of enjoying, enjoyment, in Lacan's 1969 words, is "the path to death" and its anticipated pain.[16] By this assertion, enjoyment points not only to the mortal body, as opposed to the immortal signifier, but also to pragmatic and power relations. For when Lacan refers to death in the context of enjoyment, he means it precisely in the Hegelian sense, as that which one must defy to become a master. To renounce death or enjoyment amounts to becoming master. In Lacan's words from the same seminar: "[T]he master . . has renounced everything, and above all enjoyment, since he has exposed himself to death, and . . . he stays well fixed in that position, of which the Hegelian articulation is clear. No doubt, he has deprived the slave of the disposition of his body, but this is nothing, [the master] has conceded to him enjoyment."[17] The slave cannot dispose of his body as he wishes, nor has he any control over it, but he, unlike the master, feels its pain and fear in the face of death. By contrast, the master has no access to enjoyment, since enjoyment is conceded to the slave. This state of affairs seems to entail that any speaking subject is in the position of the master insofar as "*jouissance* is forbidden to him who speaks, as such."[18] Castration and the entry into the symbolic order, as Lacan writes, "means that *jouissance* must be refused." But this is not the end of the story: *jouissance* must be refused initially, Lacan continues, "so that it can be reached on the inverted ladder . . . of the Law of desire."[19] It is due to the mechanisms of this level that every speaking subject is in fact in the position of the slave. The impossibility of language to encounter *jouissance* or death initially allows the subject to identify with the immortal signifier and thus to become the master. Subsequently, however, the "Law of desire" in language transforms the impossibility of encountering death into a prohibition, that is, into the illusion that, were it not forbidden, *jouissance*, or the encounter with death, would be accessible to the speaking subject. Thus the speaking subject is trapped between language's masterful and psychotic impossibility to access *jouissance* and the docile, neurotic illusion that *jouissance* is accessible—an illusion that forces the subject into the position of the slave. This is the split reference of the signifier, which, by prohibiting death, points to death and makes it desirable, as the prerequisite encounter through which the subject can defy it, and thus cease to be a slave.

This promise or hope, however, is doomed to remain an asymptotically remote limit. The speaking subject, so long as it lives, can encounter death only through the signifier, that is, in the mundane world of promise and prohibition, and hence as something always mediated through desire. The speaking, living subject never encounters death on the level of the real, but only as a cultural, mythic and imaginary construction—something that now links enjoyment and death to meaning and its enjoyment [*jouis-sens*]. While the subject is on the one hand drawn by bodily and pragmatic enjoyment toward its own inevitable demise, it is, on the other hand, also pulled by the signifier toward the heavens of immortality. There, far from being the end, death becomes the source of immortal fables, it is woven together with all other collective fables that have existed since eternity, and it binds together the entire community and all time—past, present, and future. In commemoration and mourning—the realm of the signifier and culture—the subject enjoys death qua immortality. Thus the split reference of the signifier corresponds to the central split of the speaking subject: on the one hand, the speaking subject is the master—insofar as it speaks and identifies itself with the signifier—and, on the other hand, it is also the slave—insofar as it is something more than the signifier, a surplus that exceeds the determinations of the signifier: a body, death, the real.

In the above relation of the subject to the signifier, the paradoxes of the Hegelian dialectic between master and slave are particularly pronounced. The speaking subject is master (immortal) only insofar as it is subject to the signifier; and it is slave (mortal) only insofar as it evades and transcends the signifier's determinism.

Thus, having passed through enjoyment and the enjoyment of meaning, we arrive at the third concept of the ternary cluster of enjoyment: surplus enjoyment (*plus-de-jouir*). This emerges out of the paradoxical fact that even though enjoyment belongs to the slave and enjoyment of meaning to the master, both death and the immortal signifier, Lacan argues, in the last analysis fulfill the function of the master in the field of speech. This function consists in having something owed to the master in return for having conceded enjoyment to the slave. In Lacan's words, "The master, in all this, makes a small effort so that everything works, that is, he gives the command. Simply in order to fulfill his function as a master, he loses something. It is at least due to this lost something that something of *jouissance* must be returned to him—specifically, surplus enjoyment (*plus-de-jouir*)."[20] By his reference to surplus enjoyment, Lacan makes explicit that his sources for the cluster of concepts pertaining to enjoyment extend beyond Hegel and Kojève to Marx. Lacan's argument in his seventeenth seminar implies that surplus is a function that marks not only economy, but all aspects of society, because of the simultaneous emergence of capitalism and secular modernity, including discourse, truth, and the subject. The shift to secular capitalism is the shift to an economy *and* a discourse, in which, again citing Lacan, "the impotence of adjoining the surplus enjoyment to the truth of the master . . . is suddenly cancelled," becoming the potency by means of which "surplus value adjoins capital—no problem, everything is homogeneous, we are in the realm of values."[21] The transformation of everything—means of economic exchange (commodities and money) and signs—into "value" is the decisive moment that marks the passage into capitalist, secular modernity. Henceforth, since both capital and sign are values, their respective fields become porous, and intercourse between them is free: surplus value can be adjoined to the signifier, just as surplus enjoyment can be adjoined "to the truth of the master," capital. Thus begins the era of ideology, an era in which mastery and authority can support themselves not only through actual power, but through making use of the signifier. From now on, it is not only actual power (Spinoza's *potentia*) that makes power *power,* but also its imaginarily mediated, distorted representations (Spinoza's *potestas*).[22] We are in the era of capitalism and hegemony.

As far as the circulation of exchange value and signifiers is concerned, neither labor qua use-value, nor pragmatic power relations, nor the mortal body and its affects, nor enjoyment exists. The phenomenologically given chain of exchange-value consists of and recognizes only exchange-value on the economic level, or enjoyment of meaning on the semantic level. It is pure differentiality, totally oblivious to the commodity's use-value or the body's affects and mortality, and, hence, to linear, historical and finite time, including all historically determined pragmatic limitations. As Marx himself argued, the "tendency of capital is *circulation without circulation time.*"[23] Nevertheless, as Marx, Freud, and Lacan all argue, although use-value, affect, and enjoyment do not exist as such within the chain of circulation of exchange and semantic values, they exist *in their effects* upon this circulation—in fact, they are its very precondition. To repeat: although value is a "self-moving substance" that "throws off surplus-value from itself," value, nevertheless, "must have its origin both in circulation and not in circulation," both in exchange- and in use-value.[24] And the same applies to semantic value: even as it also is a self-moving, self-referential and differential substance, it nevertheless "must have its origin both in circulation and not in circulation," that is, also in affect and enjoyment.

To say that use-value, affects, and enjoyment do not exist within the phenomenologically given chains of circulation of capital and the signifier, respectively, is not to say that use value or affects and enjoyment are not part of human experience. Rather it is to say they are not part of the phenomenologically given mechanisms of capital or of human experience as represented by the signifier. Just as use-value is not part of the representable aspect of the circulation of capital (M—M′), affects and enjoyment are not part of the circulation of the signifier. It is the perspectives of capital and the signifier themselves that are blind to use-value and affects or enjoyment. In contrast, the perspective of production and consumption, as well as that of finite human history—as opposed to the *"circulation without circulation time"* of the chain of capital—

are blind to the infinite or synchronic circulation of both capital and signifiers, having eyes only for use value and affects or enjoyment. In other words, the empirical world consists of two distinct phenomenological universes corresponding to two distinct modes of temporality: the one comprises production and use-value, and the affects and enjoyment of the subject that transcend discursive determinations, and operate according to a linear and finite time; the other comprises exchange-value, signifiers, and discursively constituted subject identities, and operates according to a temporality in which infinity and absolute synchronicity or instantaneity coincide. Finally, the sole function that transcends both universes is in itself manifest in neither, and is the cause and effect of both: surplus.

To ignore, therefore, that use-value, pragmatic or metonymic relations, and absolute truth behind displaced affect are the very presupposition of the arbitrary circulation of capital, the signifier, and unfixed subject identities is to remain blind to one of the two universes comprising the modern, secular, capitalist world and subject. To repeat: this self-imposed blindness, in turn, amounts to abandoning both Marxism and psychoanalysis. What is worse, to abandon both is to give up *not* the possibility for the slave, in Lacan's words, to "show in time his truth to the master," as "Hegel *dixit*"—this truth being, in Hegel's scheme, that the slave is actually the real master because it is only he who labors, and through the "formative activity" of this labor, through "fashioning the thing" or product of his labor, "he becomes aware that being-for-self belongs to *him,* that he himself exists essentially and actually in his own right."[25] Such possibility does not exist from the outset, for Hegel's argument rests on a tricky slippage of concepts. The precondition for attaining self-consciousness, according to Hegel's own argument, is the incorporation of the other and its consciousness. *"Self-consciousness achieves its satisfaction only in another self-consciousness"*—but one that is of a dead subject, so that this external consciousness can be internalized by the surviving subject (master) as its own self-consciousness.[26] In Hegel's own words: "[J]ust as each [subject] stakes his own life, so each must seek the other's death, for it values the other no more than itself; its essential being is present to it in the form of an 'other,' it is outside of itself and must rid itself of its self-externality."[27] Only when this occurs is consciousness complete, Hegel continues, for only then does consciousness have

> the experience of what Spirit is—this absolute substance which is the unity of the different independent self-consciousnesses which, in their opposition, enjoy perfect freedom and independence: "I" that is "We" and "We" that is "I."[28]

When, however, the slave attains self-consciousness by means of the otherness of the fashioned thing, the product of his labor—as opposed to by means of the otherness of the master—it can at most be argued that the thereby produced I-We is one shared by the laborer and the product of his labor, but *not* by the master, who is entirely left out. Hence this I-We is not truly universal, nor can it, consequently, be "Spirit." Which is why, as Lacan concludes and as "Marx *dixit,*" in opposition to Hegel, the laborer's alleged self-consciousness is rather the very precondition for the laborer to be "during all this time occupied with fomenting [the master's] surplus enjoyment."[29] And it is the possibility of interrupting this perpetual fomentation of the master's surplus value, I argue, that is abandoned when we ignore the very preconditions of the arbitrary circulation of capital and the "free play" of the signifier.

NOTES

1. Roland Barthes, *S/Z*, trans. Richard Miller (New York: Hill and Wang, 1993), 39–40.

2. Karl Marx, *Capital: A Critique of Political Economy*, trans. Ben Fowke (London: Penguin Classics, 1990), 1:247.

3. Michel Foucault, *The Order of Things: An Archaeology of the Human Sciences* (New York: Vintage Books, 1970). See, in particular, chapter 2, "The Prose of the World," 17–45.

4. The most notable of such attacks include Derrida's critique of Lévi-Strauss's distinction between third term and real opposition—a distinction already intimated in Kant by the pair contrary versus opposite—first presented in 1966 as a lecture at The Johns Hopkins University, and subsequently published as "Structure, Sign, and Play in the Discourse of the Human Sciences" in *Writing and Difference,* trans. Alan Bass (1967; Chicago: The University of Chicago Press, 1978) (see chapter 10, 278–93, and for Lévi-Strauss's argument, see *Structural Anthropology,* trans. Claire Jacobson and Brooke Schoepf [New York: Basic Books, 1963]). Derrida's critique of Austin's distinction between serious and nonserious performative speech acts was presented in "Signature Event Context" (first published in French in 1972 and subsequently in English in *Glyph* 1 [1977]: 172–98), then in *Margins of Philosophy* (trans. Alan Bass [Chicago: University of Chicago Press, 307–30) in 1982, and then in *Limited Inc.* in 1988 (trans. Alan Bass [Evanston, Ill.: Northwestern University Press, 1988], 1–23); and Paul de Man's attempt, at the first *diacritics* symposium at Cornell University, to render indistinguishable metaphor and metonymy or rhetoric and grammar (published in *diacritics* 3, no. 3: [1973]: 27–33) as "Semiology and Rhetoric."

5. Lacan offers an explicit account of the genealogy of surplus enjoyment out of Marx's surplus value in his seventeenth seminar (*Le Séminaire. Livre XVII. L'envers de la psychanalyse, 1969–1970,* ed. Jacques-Alain Miller [Paris: Seuil, 1991]). Žižek has placed all due emphasis on the derivation of Lacanian surplus enjoyment from Marx's surplus value (see, for example, "How Did Marx Invent the Symptom?" in Slavoj Žižek, *The Sublime Object of Ideology* [London: Verso, 1989], 11–53). My argument, however, goes beyond this genealogy into the broader structural homologies among semantics, psychoanalysis (as the field of the constitution of the subject as the subject of the signifier), and economics.

6. Sigmund Freud, *Standard Edition* (London: Hogarth Press, 1940–68).

7. In spite of my critique of deconstruction, I use the Derridean concept of the supplement in the context of Freud's retroactive articulation of the theory of dream interpretation because it accurately describes the constitution of what appears to come first (or to be the cause of a further effect), by what appears to come second (or to be the effect of this cause). This mode of causality characterizes any system of differential and retroactive constitution of meaning or values, and hence is appropriate for describing the chain of circulation of exchange values or signifiers. My critique of deconstruction concerns its nonacknowledgment of another aspect

always presupposed by such systems, whose mode of causality, as I argue, cannot be subsumed under the concept of supplementation. In economy, as we shall see, this is the aspect of production, and, in the fields of the sign and the subject, it is the aspect of pragmatic determinations, affects, and mortality. This aspect operates according to a linear and finite mode of causality. I return to this point toward the end of this paper. Note that the distinction between these two modes of causality converges with Spinoza's distinction between immanent and transitive causality (see Benedict de Spinoza, *Ethics*, in *The Collected Works of Spinoza*, ed. and trans. Edwin Curley (Princeton: Princeton University Press, 1985).

8. Gilles Deleuze, *Masochism, Coldness, and Cruelty* (New York: Zone Books, 1994). See particularly the chapter "The Death Instinct," 111–21.

9. Ibid., 112.

10. Jacques Lacan, *Book III. The Psychoses, 1955–56*, ed. Jacques-Alain Miller, trans. Russell Grigg (New York: W. W. Norton, 1993), 48.

11. Josef Breuer and Sigmund Freud, *Studies on Hysteria*, trans. James Strachey (New York: Basic Books, 2000), 8.

12. See Roman Jakobson, "Linguistics and Poetics," in *Ha-Sifrut Literature: Theory-Poetics-Hebrew and Comparative-Literature* 2 (1970): 274–85; and *Fundamentals of Language*, 4th ed. (The Hague: Mouton, 1980).

13. Marx, *Capital*, 256, 255, and 268.

14. Paul Ricoeur, "The Metaphorical Process as Cognition, Imagination, and Feeling," *Critical Inquiry* 5:1 (Autumn 1978): 142–59, cited in *Critical Theory Since 1965*, ed. Hazard Adams and Leroy Searle (Tallahassee: University Presses of Florida, 1986), 424–34. By this remark I do not mean to construe either affect or truth as what Paul Ricoeur called a "new kind of intuitionism—and the worst kind!—in the form of a new emotional realism." The invocation of something that transcends representation makes sense, to continue with Ricoeur's words, "only to the extent that it is paired with [an analysis] of split reference both in verbal and imaginative structures." In other words, it makes sense only to the extent that imagination and affect, far from being severed from verbalization and cognition, are considered as one of their constituents and references. In his attempt to link not only metonymy but metaphor to feelings, Paul Ricoeur made this self-reflective caveat when he invoked Heidegger's "being-there" (under its mode of *Befindlichkeit*) to argue as follows: "Because of feelings we are 'attuned to' aspects of reality which cannot be expressed in terms of the objects referred to in ordinary language" (433). I leave aside Ricoeur's argument that metaphor refers to affects, since this is effectively always the case insofar as metaphor and metonymy, like condensation and displacement, are always mutually implicated. My emphasis lies rather in maintaining the conceptual distinction between metaphor and metonymy.

15. Lacan fashioned *jouissance* by drawing heavily on Kojève's rereading of Hegel's dialectic of master and slave, on Marx's labor-power as use-value, Freud's displacement of affect, and Roman Jakobson's metonymy.

16. "[L]e chemin vers la mort" (translation mine).

17. "[L]e maître . . . a renoncé à tout, et à la jouissance d'abord, puisqu'il s'est exposé à la mort, et . . . il reste bien fixé dans cette position don't l'articulation hégélienne est claire. Sans doute a-t-il privé l'esclave de la disposition de son corps, mais, c'est un rien, il lui a laissé la jouissance" (translation mine). Lacan, *Le Séminaire*, 123.

18. Jacques Lacan, *Écrits: A Selection*, trans. Alan Sheridan (New York: W. W. Norton & Co., 1977), 319.

19. Ibid., 324.

20. "Le maître, dans tout ça, fait un petit effort pour que tout marche, c'est-à-dire donne l'ordre. A simplement remplir sa fonction de maître, il y perd quelque chose. Ce quelque chose de perdu, c'est par là au moins que quelque chose de la jouissance doit lui être rendu— précisément le plus-de-jouir" (translation mine). Lacan, *Le Séminaire*, 123.

21. "[L]'impuissance à faire le joint du plus-de-jouir à la vérité du maître . . . est tout d'un coup vidée. La plus-value s'adjoint au capital — pas de problème, c'est homogène, nous sommes dans les valeurs" (translation mine, ibid., 207).

If (Lacan continues in order to stress further the homology between surplus value and surplus enjoyment) Marx "had not made surplus enjoyment a matter of accountancy, if he had not made out of it the surplus value, in other words, if he had not laid the ground of capitalism, Marx would have realized that surplus value is surplus enjoyment" (ibid., 123). To clarify further the homology among Marx's account of capital, the linguistic account of the signifier, and the psychoanalytic account of subjectivity, let me briefly recapitulate the relevant part of my argument. For all three systems—economy, language, and the speaking subject—to sustain themselves, each must give the appearance that there is nothing outside the chain of circulation of capital or signifiers. Enjoyment—like metonymic, pragmatic relations, and the real cause of displaced pain—must be denied for the circulation of metaphors or condensed images to appear free, and for truth to become the truth of the master, that is, yet another commodity so that "everything goes" and is equally deconstructible. Similarly, in economy, to recall Marx, the formula of the circulation of capital, M—C—M´ (money—commodity—more money) must appear as M—M´ (with the moment of the exchange between commodity and money effaced) for capitalism to sustain itself. The denial of the moment of the exchange between capital and commodity is analogous to the denial of enjoyment, metonymy, pragmatic relations, and the existence of a real cause for one's affect within displacement. All that remains visible, by analogy to Marx's free play of exchange values (M—M´), is the free play of metaphors, condensations, and enjoyment of meaning.

22. For the distinction between *potestas* and *potentia,* as deriving from Spinoza's distinction, in his *Ethics,* between God's *potestas* and God's *potentia* (prop. 34-6), see Michael Hardt, "Translator's Foreward: The Anatomy of Power," in Antonio Negri, *The Savage Anomaly: The Power of Spinoza's Metaphysics and Politics,* trans. Michael Hardt (Minneapolis: University of Minnesota Press, 1991), xi–xvi.

23. Karl Marx, *Grundrisse: Foundations of the Critique of Political Economy (Rough Draft),* trans. Martin Nicolaus (London: Penguin Books, 1973), 671. For Marx's argument that capitalism annihilates historical time by producing the illusory coincidence of infinity and no time, see the section "Difference between Production Time and Labor Time—Storch. Money. Mercantile Estate. Credit. Circulation," 668–73.

24. Marx, *Capital,* 256, 255, and 268.

25. "Hegel *dixit,* l'esclave avec le temps lui démontrera sa vérité . . ." (translation mine). G. W. F. Hegel, *Phenomenology of Spirit,* trans. A. V. Miller (Oxford: Oxford University Press, 1977), 118.

26. Ibid., 110.

27. Ibid., 114.

28. Ibid., 110.

29. "Marx *dixit,* il sera occupé tout ce temps á fomenter son plus-de-jouir" (translation mine). Lacan, *Le Seminaire,* 123.

21. The Substance of Psychic Life

Karyn Ball

Over the years, the perceived impropriety of Freud's emphasis on the sexual dimension of the unconscious has, in the United States at least, sometimes led to a complete negation of the value of his thought. The controversy in 1995–96 over plans for a national exhibit devoted to Freud's work and influence is a telling instance of this suppression in the public sphere both within and beyond academia. To be sure, Freud himself sometimes felt compelled to qualify a few of the more scandalous aspects of his own thinking on sexuality, such as his initial belief in his patients' statements that they had been seduced into sexual acts as children by adults, including family members. As is well known, he later relinquished this hypothesis in favor of the theory that these confessions reflected fantasies about incest and seduction.[1] In addition, his 1914 rejoinder to C. G. Jung in the "Introduction: On Narcissism" awkwardly guards an increasingly untenable distinction between the "nonsexual" ego-drives and the sexual drives proper in an attempt to separate his theory of the libido from his former disciple's more generalized understanding of its primal character. It is, of course, significant that despite his various protests to the contrary, Freud's subsequent descriptions of the libidinal economy in 1915, 1920, and 1923 will tend rather to confirm than to undermine Jung's revised concept.[2]

In *Life and Death in Psychoanalysis* (1970), Jean Laplanche observes that "*it is sexuality which represents the model of every drive and probably constitutes the only drive in the strict sense of the term.*"[3] Laplanche's *New Foundations for Psychoanalysis* (1987) is partly devoted to retrieving the significance of the libidinal economy as the disavowed foundation of psychoanalytic discourse.[4] From Laplanche I take the lesson that to ignore the drives is to disavow the status of the sexual and the biological valences of Freud's thought and to attenuate the specificity of psychoanalytic inquiry. My affinity for Laplanche is not merely polemical and conceptual; with an eye to Freud's later theory of the libido, I also want to follow through on the strategic direction of Laplanche's return to Freud, which reclaims the radicality of his concepts from and against Freud himself for a post-Freudian intellectual milieu distinguished by the confluence of structuralism, Lacanian psychoanalysis, and antifoundationalist philosophy. In adopting this strategy, my intention is to retrieve the speculative scientism that saturates Freud's theory of the libidinal economy in order to recover a foundation more radical still: his metaphysics of the drives in *Beyond the Pleasure Principle* as metapsychological and economic mediations of biological forces that emanate from the primordial "substance" of psycho-physical life.

It is significant that this centuries-old metaphysical figure of substance "persists" (as substance is prone to do) in Freud's revised theory of the drives in *Beyond the Pleasure Principle* (1920). Substance is a phylogenetic figure in a work that is prone to flights of speculative fancy, drawing on late nineteenth- and early twentieth-century theories about the evolution of basic organisms. To the extent that Freud seeks a corporeal, biochemical, and scientifically "substantive" basis for neurotic and pathological behavior, his recourse to this figure provides him with a metaphysical foundation for an evolutionist staging of the emergence of conscious life.

In what follows, I shall consider Freud's recourse to the figure of *vital substance* (*lebende Substanz*) as a biological origin and foundation for his account of organic and psychic evolution. One dimension of this figure is manifestly phylogenetic, but implicitly metaphysical in narrating the development of a split psyche. Another dimension is metaphysical and topological insofar as it delineates a transcendental basis for the split between conscious and unconscious contents and functions. These phylogenetic and metaphysical formulations of substance attest to the strength of Freud's investment in pinpointing the origins of psychic life. What is more, they indicate the rhetorical value of this figure for Freud, in his schematism of the interrelations among biological, economic, and structural determinisms. My analysis of this trope will seek to demonstrate how the metaphysics of substance informing psychoanalytic praxis constitutes a condition and limit of the process of working through neurotic repression and traumatic fixation.

Laplanche's perspective is borne out by Freud's recurrent speculations about the status of sexuality for his theory of the unconscious, speculations that show how the overdetermined functioning of the libido remains a focal object of Freudian psychoanalysis. According to a 1923 essay, *libido* "is a term used in the [theory of drives] for describing the dynamic manifestation of sexuality."[5] Freud places the emergence of the libido with the discovery of hysteria and obsessional neuroses. He notes that the symptoms of these "transferential neuroses" result from the ego's rejection or repression of the drives, which "then find circuitous paths through the unconscious."[6] The concept of *sublimation* will then allow Freud to account for drives the aims of which do not appear to be sexual.[7]

Freud proposes various versions of the libidinal economy, in which ego or narcissistic drives are opposed to sexual or object drives before arriving at the duality of the life and death drives in *Beyond the Pleasure Principle* (1920). Prior to 1920, "[Drives] and Their Vicissitudes" (1915) maps the "destinies" of the drives as the paths that interrelate four essential components. According to this map, each drive is differentially determined by its respective *source* (*Quelle*) as the "region or zone of the body from which it derives." In addition, every drive is theoretically distinguishable on the basis of its *pressure* (*Drang*), *aim* (*Ziel*), and *object* (*Objekt*).

Reading the 1915 article in light of Freud's *Three Essays on Sexuality* (1905), Laplanche delineates different definitions for the *Quelle*, or source, in Freud's theory of the drives. In its concrete, local, and "strictly physiological" sense, the source is an "erotogenic zone" understood as a privileged site of sexual stimulation. The implication here is that sexual tension is exclusively a property of the oral, anal, urethral, and genital *loca*. In a broader sense, however, the source may refer to any organ or body part that becomes the vehicle of stimulation. This is to suggest that the term *erotogenic* may alternately describe corporeal tension in general.[8]

In *Life and Death in Psychoanalysis*, Laplanche's identification of the progressively diffuse character of the source has significant implications for Freud's economic theory of the psychic apparatus. For it suggests that the source "is nothing but the transcription of the sexual repercussions of anything occurring in the body beyond a certain quantitative threshold" (22). This is to attribute a polymorphous autoeroticism to the body and its organs, a condition that the privileging of genital sexuality both inhibits and aggravates. In addition, because autoerotic sexuality is generalized through the whole of the body, it encourages a more abstract understanding of sexual energy, which must therefore be said to precede object orientations.[9]

Laplanche's reading of the source of the drives invites us to understand autoeroticism in Freud's work as both a dynamic nexus of tensions and as an impetus of libidinal investment. Libidinal investment, or *cathexis* (*Besetzung*), is a term that would then describe a subject's sexually charged captivation with an object that thus provides an orientation for generalized sexual tensions. To the extent that the quantity of tension determines the intensity of investment, the libidinal economy can be viewed as a figuration of a systematic interrelation among differential degrees of cathexis along with shifts in the measure of stimulation that must be regulated and/or released by the psychic apparatus.

Laplanche notes that "the most frequent model used by Freud to account for the relation between the somatic and the psychical employs the metaphor of a kind of 'delegation' provided with a mandate that need not be absolutely imperative. Thus a local biological stimulus finds its delegation, its 'representation' in psychical life as a drive" (12–13).[10] This characterization of the drive emphasizes its status as a metapsychological figure for an autoerotically charged compulsion to obtain satisfaction in relation to an object; yet the object is, significantly, a figure in its own right, insofar as it is a displacement or condensation of sexual and/or sublimated tensions. This double figuration is manifest in fantasy, which visually dramatizes the otherwise obscure trajectory of the drive as an economic and mechanical motility of unbound energy. This is to suggest that the drives are interwoven with fantasy as an imaginary elaboration of the path between a drive's object and its aim.

In the last instance, however, Laplanche identifies the instinct as the ultimate source of the drive, which "mimics, displaces, and denatures it" (22). The instinct is a trace of primal forces, which persist throughout evolution. The source of the drive so conceived exceeds psychology insofar as it incorporates the history of organic life (21).[11] It therefore comprises the biological substrate of the human organism as a psycho-physical system. This is confirmed by a reading of Freud's *Beyond the Pleasure Principle*, where he defines a drive as a derivative of a repressed instinctual urge (*Drang*) that has been refracted through socializing constraints. In that context, he argues that drives are essentially conservative in nature, because they aim to return the organism to a "prior" state. In Freud's words: "*[A] [drive] is an urge inherent in organic life to restore an earlier state of things* which the living entity has been obliged to abandon under the pressure of external disturbing forces; that is, it is a kind of organic elasticity, or, to put it another way, the expression of the inertia inherent in organic life" (SE XVII, 36).[12] This prior state expresses itself in the so-called return of the repressed as an uncanny resurgence of earlier phases of organic and psychic development—those repudiated primal instincts and infantile beliefs or fears that could be said to lie at the root of "irrational" behaviors and that seem "mechanical" in their non-voluntary relentlessness when they reemerge in a "rational" and thus unhomelike space.

Though Laplanche is committed to reinstating the foundational status of the sexual drives for psychoanalytic praxis, he nevertheless retains a critical distance in relation to Freud's account on the grounds that Freud remains captive to biological and phylogenetic determinisms. Indeed, Laplanche seems to feel compelled to attenuate Freud's scientism by reading his theory of the drives as a poetics of the psychic apparatus. In drawing from various discourses and models, this poetics offers an interdisciplinary topography and an explicit tropology for the biological, economic, and structural mechanisms that distinguish Freud's metaphysics of the drives.

In this context, when Laplanche speaks of Freud's *biologism,* he is not only underscoring the ways in which biological motifs provide a poetic means for Freud to conceptualize the physical bases of human behavior. He is also emphasizing the "impurity" of Freud's speculations, which typically draw on late nineteenth- and early twentieth-century pre-quantum-theory, pre-relativity-theory, and macroscopic scientific hypotheses.[13] Laplanche notes that Freud tended to favor the hypothetical formulations of figures identified with the Physicalist school, whose members were committed to bracketing out "everything in psychology that cannot be reduced to the sciences of physics and chemistry."[14] Yet this principle was attenuated by their acknowledgment that there were phenomena that exceeded the physical-chemical level. In these instances, it would become necessary to introduce a Physicalist *model* "into psychology." Such an importation would entail treating the new phenomena with a "dignity" equal to the chemical-physical energies inherent in matter, energies the Physicalists believed were "reducible to the forces of attraction and repulsion."[15]

My own analysis follows Laplanche's with one difference. To understand Freud's rethinking of the libidinal economy and the unconscious in *Beyond the Pleasure Principle*, I want to take the profound implications of Freud's scientism and metaphysics seriously—to believe in them at least provisionally, rather than to dismiss them out of turn because "we know better now." Freud's borrowings from various disciplines, coupled with his faith in science, allow him systematically and poetically to represent inner experiences that would otherwise lack intelligibility. The rhetorical efficacy and radical openness of this contradictory effort, which hinges on the honesty of the speculative *as if*, will only become evident from a standpoint that embraces the same spirit of openness, but that nevertheless acknowledges the limits placed on psychoanalytic praxis by Freud's peculiar assimilation of his scientific and philosophical references.

In their various conjunctures, the biologist and economic motifs that organize *Beyond the Pleasure Principle* portray the psyche as a thermodynamic system, which binds self-preservation and sexual reproduction with death. These motifs emerge through Freud's recourse to an interdisciplinary vocabulary that draws on models taken from the physical and life sciences. Mixed in with speculations on the evolution of protista are metaphors of an overtly metaphysical—and perhaps even cosmological, inasmuch as they map the "universe" of the mental apparatus—character. This universe remains, invariably, a Manichean battleground for libidinal agencies and forces linking the economic with the biological, and the biological with the primal. The split between unconscious (primary) processes and conscious (secondary) processes is just one of several divisions organizing the psyche as a functionally differentiated homeostatic system.

The term *living substance* provides Freud with a metaphysical symbol on which to base his narrative about the psyche's functional differentiation. Vital substance obtains an originary status in Freud's phylogenetic narrative, which constructs it as the most basic component of organic existence. Consequently it serves as the figurative locus of what is, developmentally speaking, "primal" and "primordial" in humans. This primordial living substance predates and founds the possibility of species life in general. It not only precedes the genesis of humans, but also furnishes a departure point for Freud's speculations about sexual differentiation in higher animals. Freud comes to perceive the fundamental capacity for protista to reproduce themselves through mitosis as a phylogenetic antecedent for the development of separate sexes. The sexual tension that spurs the drives is hereby posited as an evolved form of this basic cellular impetus to divide.

It is no coincidence that these observations arise in the midst of Freud's speculations about the role of death in the evolution of organic life forms in the sixth chapter of *Beyond the Pleasure Principle.* Drawing here principally on the writings of
A. Weismann, Freud synthesizes the implications of various theories of his day, which
tie the impetus for cell division to the senescence of protista.[16] The implication of his
synthesis is that reproduction and death converge at the most fundamental level of
organic life. On the one hand, vital processes are conceived as exhausting the organism, which divides in order to replenish its energies and thus to escape death. On the
other hand, death is figured as a determinism that is built into every living organism.

Vital substance is the paradoxical source of this determinism, which prefigures
Freud's theory of the death drive as an extimate as well as a dystopic figure in his
thermodynamics of the psyche. In its initial formulation, the death drive serves the
principle of constancy by defusing excess stimulation. In its radical register, however,
the drive represents a fundamental urge to return the psycho-physical organism to a
state of inorganic calm. This destructive modality of the death drive aims to neutralize the tensions affected by the life drives. It is this primal longing for death, inherent
in and spurred by vital substance, that goes "beyond" the pleasure principle.

Within Freud's topography of the psychic apparatus, the conflicting demands
of life and death also determine the parameters of consciousness as a system geared
toward filtering perceptions. This perceptual-consciousness system (*Pcpt.-Cs.*) lies
"on the borderline between outside and inside" and is "turned towards the external
world" (SE XVII, 24). In contrast, "all excitatory processes that occur in the *other* systems leave permanent traces behind in them which form the foundation of memory"
(SE XVII, 24–25). Freud notes that such memory traces might never be involved in
the process of becoming conscious; indeed, "they are often most powerful and most
enduring when the process which left them behind was one which never entered
consciousness" (SE XVII, 25). The implication of these speculations is that memory
traces cannot remain constantly conscious because they would then curtail the system's ability to receive fresh excitations. This leads Freud to suspect that "becoming
conscious and leaving behind a memory trace are processes incompatible with each
other within one and the same system" (SE XVII, 25). In other words, memory traces
persist, but in another system, where they cannot interfere with the functions of the
perceptual-conscious.

To explain the "division of labor" suggested by this topography, Freud looks
toward the discipline of biology to plot the phylogenesis of a split consciousness. His
speculations focus on the development of a basic living organism "in its most simplified possible form" (SE XVII, 26).[17] This organism consists of an "undifferentiated vesicle of a substance that is susceptible to stimulation." The outer surface of this vesicle
serves as an organ for receiving stimuli; it is thereby differentiated from the "deeper
layers" wherein excitatory processes would "run a different course" (SE XVII, 26). Freud
suggests that the "ceaseless impact of external stimuli on the surface of the vesicle"

produces a protective "crust" (*Rinde*). This crust, in its turn, "would at last have been so thoroughly 'burned through' [*durchgebrannt*] by stimulation that it would present the most favourable possible conditions for the reception of stimuli and become incapable of any further modification" (SE XVII, 27).[18]

It is this hardened and unalterable protective crust that represents Freud's phylogenetic precursor for the perceptual-conscious system. This analogy has significant repercussions for his understanding of the mental apparatus: for it suggests that the elements of the conscious system "could undergo no further permanent modification from the passage of excitation" because they had already been modified in this respect to the fullest possible extent. Furthermore, Freud's description of the "burned through" layer of the cortex implies an additional function for the perceptual-conscious system, that of protecting the "inner layers" of the psyche as a fragment of vital substance:

> This little fragment of living substance is suspended in the middle of an external world charged with the most powerful energies; and it would be killed by the stimulation emanating from these if it were not provided with a *protective shield* against stimuli. It acquires the shield in this way: its outermost surface ceases to have the structure proper to living matter, becomes to some degree inorganic and thence forward functions as a special envelop or membrane resistant to stimuli. In consequence, the energies of the external world are able to pass into the next underlying layers, which have remained living, with only a fragment of their original intensity; and these layers can devote themselves, behind the protective shield, to the reception of the amounts of stimulus which have been allowed through it. By its death, the outer layer has saved all the deeper ones from a similar fate—unless, that is to say, stimuli reach it which are so strong that they break through the protective shield. Protection against stimuli is an almost more important function for the living organism than reception of stimuli. (SE XVII, 27)[19]

It is worth noting that Freud assumes the existence of a deadened inorganic protective layer that is "proper to living matter" (*die dem Lebenden zukommende Struktur*). By the same token, the subsequent metamorphosis of the receptive cortex into a protective layer represents a transformation of a properly living substance into a semi-inorganic shield. On the one hand, Freud describes the result of this petrification as a "death" of the living external layer. On the other hand, this death is also a systemic sacrifice for the sake of the greater good. In effect, the "living death" of the cortical membrane is crucial to the organism's survival, which is to say that this "death-in-life" is essential to the continuity of organic existence.

Freud's narrative about the "death" of the outer layer has far-reaching implications, for it compels him to speculate on the necessary role of destructive elements in the economic balance and health of the psycho-physical system. His speculations ascribe to this desensitized membrane the task of maintaining the resiliency of the receptive system, which must remain open to the flow of energies. Freud thereby implies that, because it is deadened, the surface crust of the receptive layer acts as a buffer zone between external stimuli and the vital interior layers, thus palliating the impact of the world on the organism's inner core.

Freud revises Breuer's distinction between quiescent or bound energy and mobile or cathecting energy to propose that the perceptual-conscious system is limited to the function of mediating the flow of mobile energies. In contrast, bound energies will need to be "stored" in the unconscious, where they subsist in the form of memory traces. This is to suggest that the stimuli that pass through the first system undergo a transformation whereby their mobile energies are translated into bound or quiescent contents. The question is how to understand the character of this transformation in light of Freud's metaphysics of substance.

Freud notes that the main purpose of receiving stimuli is to discover their "direction and nature." It suffices, then, for the sense organs to "sample" the world in small quantities or specimens to determine their character. In addition, these organs include "special arrangements" for protecting the organism against excessive exposures or "unsuitable kinds of stimuli" (*unangemessener Reizarten*). In other words, reception is circumscribed by protective reactions against overpowerful external pressures.

Freud's description of the protective shield implies that the selective function it performs for the basic organism is at once natural and necessary to its survival. As the psychic analog for this shield, the perceptual-conscious system would also carry out this filtering process; however, the limits of this system necessitate the existence of a contiguous psychic dimension, which serves a different function from the conscious realm. This unconscious dimension would fulfill the psychic need to store the residues and excesses of the perceptual material, which is either received and processed, or bypassed by the *Pcpt.-Cs.* By virtue of this division, the traces of events that bypass perception are removed to this indeterminate, internal locus wherein they persist in a potential state. A further implication is that perceptions leave traces that become permanent once they enter the "timeless" unconscious.

In pursuing this claim, it is perhaps not surprising that Freud invokes a revised version of Immanuel Kant's theorem respecting time and space as "necessary forms of intuition" in order to reformulate his own distinction between unconscious and conscious functions:

> As a result of certain psycho-analytic discoveries, we are to-day in a position to embark on a discussion of the Kantian theorem that time and space are "necessary forms of thought." We have learnt that unconscious mental processes are in themselves "timeless." This means in the first place that they are not ordered temporally, that time does not change them in any way and that the idea of time cannot be applied to them. These are negative characteristics which can only be clearly understood if a comparison is made with conscious mental processes. On the other hand, our abstract idea of time seems to be wholly derived from the method of working of the system *Pcpt.-Cs.* and to correspond to a perception on its own part [*Selbstwahrnehmung*] of that method of working. This mode of functioning may perhaps constitute another way of providing a shield against stimuli. (SE XVII, 28)[20]

Freud vigorously insists here on the atemporality of unconscious contents to the extent that "the idea of time cannot be applied to them" (*dass man die Vorstellung nicht an sie heranbringen kann*). He nonetheless goes on to allude to the prospect that such an abstraction is itself potentially a defense mechanism that derives from the perceptual-conscious, whose selective "mode of working" by extension also encompasses Freud's own in this instance. This honest admission appears to undermine the statement about the atemporal unconscious as a whole by calling it a "perception" and perhaps, more precisely, an introspection or self-perception (*Selbstwahrnehmung*) produced by the perceptual-conscious system. He ends this line of discussion with a caveat: "I know that these claims must sound very obscure, but I must limit myself to these hints" (*Ich weiß, daß diese Behauptungen sehr dunkel klingen muß, muß mich aber auf solche Andeutungen beschränken*) (SE XVIII, 28; GW XIII, 28).

What is particularly evocative about the qualifying gesture that jumps from *Selbstwahrnehmung* to *Beschränkung*, from self-perception to self-limitation, restriction, or confinement, is that it echoes and deepens the implications of Kant's own fluctuations on the spatio-temporal relativity of determinations of change. This relativity emerges in Kant's delineation of a transcendental need to construct a figure of substance that abides in space and time as a vehicle of temporal-inner orientation. It is important that the subject's recourse to this figure is itself bound to the structure of intuition, a point mirrored by the self-consciousness of Freud's move to question the unconscious motivations informing his abstract idea of time. To understand the "obscurity" that nevertheless troubles Freud, it is worth briefly revisiting Kant's references to substance in his explanation of the ineluctably spatial and temporal forms of intuition (for which Freud substitutes "thought" or *Denken,* thereby stipulating a conscious perception).

For Immanuel Kant, time is the condition of all empirical and immanent determinations (as opposed to space, which is initially identified as a condition of outer experience).[21] In the *Critique of Pure Reason,* he elaborates on this thesis in the context of a discussion about the relation between substance and appearance. Substance is, in the "Analogies of Experience," "the substratum of all that belongs to the existence of things" (213). This definition of substance supports Kant's commitment to investigating the prospect of ascertaining the transcendental conditions for a unified consciousness. He requires this transcendental schematism to address the question of whether it is possible to ground the succession of differential cognitions.

It is this question that propels Kant's move to distinguish between the *permanent* and the *transitory* in order to characterize the experience of change. Accordingly, while the *permanent* is associated with the qualities of substance, the transitory designates a "mere determination" of any object. Temporal relations become possible only in the domain of the permanent as "the *substratum* of the empirical representation of time itself" (214). The permanent is the "object itself, that is substance as phenomenon" (214). It cannot in its essence be affected by change, but only by appearances in time. This is the case insofar as alteration "presupposes one and the same subject as existing with two opposite determinations" (218). Change is (merely) the successive being and not-being of any phenomenon in relation to the permanence of substance.

Alteration can only be perceived by virtue of the permanent as a valence of the figure of substance—that which not only "remains and persists," but is also the site of all transitions and determinations (and existence as such). Ultimately, then, the permanent is "what alone makes possible the representation of the transition from one state to another" (217). It is, thus, the permanent against which temporal relations become intelligible within the manifold of appearance (214).[22] Determinations of changing appearances therefore depend on the figuration of the relatively permanent as a condition of inner and outer orientation.

Kant's identification of time as the a priori condition of inner experience sheds light on Freud's delimitation of the atemporal unconscious. This delimitation effectively idealizes the traces residing in the unconscious, thereby freeing them from the time-bound necessity of dispersing to "make room" for newer material. By virtue of this liberation, Freud implicitly ascribes the figurative continuity of metaphysical substance to the contents of the unconscious. Henceforth these contents assume their relative permanence, in contrast to the transitory excitations that pass through the pressured scope of the perceptual-conscious system.

It is noteworthy that Freud's division between the unconscious and the perceptual-conscious systems posits the coexistence of two realms wherein an event respectively persists and ceases to be simultaneously. Kant has taken pains to demonstrate that this kind of temporal simultaneity is "absurd," given his stipulation that succession is actually the alteration "of a substance which abides" (217–18). Kant writes: "If some of these substances could come into being and others cease to be, the one condition of the empirical unity of time would be removed. The appearances would flow in two parallel streams—which is absurd. There is only one time in which all different times must be located, not as coexistent but as in succession to one another" (217). This is a stipulation Freud finesses with his theory of memory traces that are alleged to persist in the unconscious without interfering in the work of the perceptual-conscious. For to suggest that the unconscious is timeless, is, in effect, to claim that memory traces abiding therein play the figurative role of the permanent as a mode of metaphysical substance in relation to the contents of the perceptual-conscious. In this respect, Freud effectively bypasses the principle of temporal noncontradiction upon which a transcendental "unity of apperceptions" (and a unified self-consciousness) might rest.

There are two permutations of Freud's functionally differentiated psychic economy. First, it spatializes the unconscious by converting it into a timeless repository for memory traces. Second, it raises the question as to whether these traces are themselves idealized pieces of substance that serve figuratively as the inner psychic equivalents of Kant's objects in "outer experience" that persist in space and thereby provide a relatively continuous backdrop for the recognition of change. This permutation suggests that the unconscious comprises an atemporal admixture of images. It remains to be seen whether such images might nevertheless retain the historicity of their respective contexts.[23]

In exploring the first permutation here, my reading of Freud's metaphysics in light of Kant implies that unconscious memory establishes a spatialized, substantial background against which changes in the external world are measured.[24] By extension, then, memory traces would assume the form of apperceptions upon (re)entering the perceptual-conscious wherein they also obtain the force of excitations. This "reactivation" of memory traces thus entails their conversion into mobile transitory contents. In short, memories emerging from the unconscious must lose their ideality when they become subject to the pressured and selective function of the perceptual-conscious system, which is vexed by the spatio-temporal flux of the external world. This is to suggest that fixated memories will be at least provisionally spatio-temporalized as they take on the disposition of perceptual phenomena. Of particular interest for psychoanalytic praxis is whether this spatio-temporalization permanently changes their content and libidinal charge if or when they "return" to (unconscious) storage.

A standard reading of Freud's etiology of neuroses suggests that the repressed is an anxiety-causing childhood experience, which establishes the libidinal precondition for the subsequent development of neuroses. In other words, libidinal fixation establishes a foundation in the past for a subject's neurotic future. The term *fixation* in this context implies a deterministic understanding of identity, according to which early childhood experiences produce a seemingly entrenched libidinal character that typically manifests itself as an anxious disposition. The aggravation of this anxious disposition by a distressing accident or situation mobilizes a defensive reaction, thus precipitating the onset of neurotic symptoms. Neurotic fixation is subsequently evinced through a subject's cathected misrecognition of memories, as the spurs of present anxiety and as fragments of an imaginary self that must be preserved against the flux of perception and the guilt or shame of perverse enjoyment. Neurotic subjects would then be defined by their tendency to idealize their memories when they grant them the stability of substance. In metaphysical terms, this is to construct libidinal fixation as the persisting substance of a neurotic disposition, which would then be activated by a traumatic event. Neurotic symptoms are henceforth to be read as resurgences of this "libidinal substance" located at the putative origins of repression.

I mention this account of the development of neurosis because it sheds light on the paradoxical character of Freud's recourse to a metaphysics of substance in *Beyond the Pleasure Principle*, where he theorizes the relationship between compulsive repetition and the libidinal economy. The success of the analytical encounter is, in part, measured by its efficacy in undoing a neurotic subject's narcissistic fixation on memories of the events that set into motion overdetermined processes of warding off and regulating anxieties. An analysand's investment in his or her neurosis is reflected in the "hardening" of these processes into a symptomatology, which is experienced as the "substance" of his or her being. This figuration of neurotic experience explains why the neurotic clings to his or her symptoms or, as Slavoj Žižek has argued, enjoys them. Yet on a logical level, such a figuration also falls prey to circular reasoning to the extent that it appears to confirm the priority of Freud's phylo- and ontogenetic narrative of the libidinal economy. In effect, the metapsychological figures and scientific references that serve to *represent* a neurotic's experience of his or her own neurosis naturalize the metaphysics of substance Freud employs to configure the economic and primal dimensions of psycho-physical life. The question remains as to whether a conceptual system dependent on the trope of substance belies a therapeutic commitment to defuse an autoerotic and ultimately masochistic fixation sustained by the narcissistic libido.

The implication for psychoanalytic praxis is that an analysand's ability to work through neurotic repression and fixation would depend on the possibility that an unconscious element, presumably atemporal, *can become an object of knowledge in time* by entering the realm of perceptual-consciousness. I would like to venture the claim that Freud's understanding of working through depends on this theoretical possibility. For if anxious memory were to retain its figurative character as a timeless substance impervious to change, then neither psychoanalytic therapy nor critical reflection would have any efficacy as processes that presumably bring about a decathexis from and corresponding integration of an overcharged ideation of an event, feeling, or belief for the neurotic or traumatically fixated subject.

To summarize, my analysis has touched on the phylogenetic and metaphysical permutations of substance in the context of Freud's speculations about the development of a divided psyche. In the first instance, vital substance is figured as the primordial origin of organic life as well as in the intertwined destinies of sex and death. In the second instance, Freud turns toward Kant to specify the timelessness of the contents of the unconscious in relation to the ephemeral quality of the perceptual-conscious. This move establishes the topographical and metaphysical conditions for the simultaneity of consciousness and repression. It also idealizes memory traces and other repressed elements by attributing to them the permanence of substance.

Ultimately, then, it is worth pointing out that substance also carries an ontological significance when it refers to the fundamental essence of a person or group's character. This usage attests to an investment in the ideal of a stable and unified identity, which, in societies that prize dependability, productivity, and efficiency, may obtain the status of a social norm. From a "post-metaphysical" perspective, Freud's recourse to the trope of substance might cast doubt on his conceptualizaton of the libidinal economy and, more generally, on the psychoanalytic account of the development of neurotic repression and fixation. Writing in the wake of the deconstruction of Western metaphysics, it is difficult to return to the ideal of substance without a certain degree of ironic distance. Yet critical suspicions regarding the ontological dimension of this ideal should not prevent us from recognizing its importance in the Freudian topography of the psyche. Freud is committed to establishing a scientific foundation for neurotic behavior. The phylogenetic and metaphysical trope of substance allows him to deploy the discourses of thermodynamics and biology in order to speculate on a corporeal and biochemical basis for psychic phenomena that seems consistent with Physicalist principles. It also provides him with a conceptual anchor for the component systems of the psychic apparatus. This is an apparatus that is split between the unconscious and the conscious systems with the preconscious as a variable border between them. It is also an apparatus that is overwrought with the very mechanisms that reproduce its ability to function as a thermodynamic economy. Psychoanalysis might be most effective when it counters an analysand's ontological investment in neurotic or traumatic substance with a different set of metaphors. But perhaps the radicality of psychoanalysis derives from its very circularity: from its power to assume such a metaphysics while simultaneously anticipating its death-driven destruction through the determinisms that define the neurotic subject as an object of psychoanalytic reflection.

Notes

I am grateful to Bettina Bergo and John Mowitt for their helpful comments on prior versions of this essay.

1. For a critical account of the history of this thesis in Freud's theory, see Jeffrey Moussaieff Masson's *The Assault on Truth: Freud's Suppression of the Seduction Theory* (New York: Pocket Books, 1984). See also *The Complete Letters of Sigmund Freud to Wilhelm Fliess 1887–1904*, trans. and ed. Jeffrey Moussaieff Masson (Cambridge: Harvard University Press, 1985), 264–66.

2. Freud provides a brief historical clarification of his revised understanding of the drives in a footnote appearing at the end of the sixth chapter of *Beyond the Pleasure Principle*. There he restates his finding that the narcissistic ego drives that he had earlier opposed to reproductive or object drives are also libidinal (i.e., sexual) in nature. This insight has led him to posit a "fresh" opposition between the libidinal (ego- and object-) drives and the "destructive" drives, an opposition that he translates into an antagonism between life drives (*Eros*) and death drives (*Thanatos*). Freud, *Beyond the Pleasure Principle*, SE XVII, 7–64; *Gesammelte Werke* XIII, 1–69.

3. Jean Laplanche, *Life and Death in Psychoanalysis*, trans. Jeffrey Mehlman (Baltimore: The Johns Hopkins University Press, 1970), 8; Laplanche's emphasis.

4. Jean Laplanche, *New Foundations for Psychoanalysis*, trans. David Macey (Oxford: Basil Blackwell, 1989).

5. Sigmund Freud, "The Libido Theory," SE XVIII, 255; "'Psychoanalyse' und 'Libidotheorie,'" *Gesammelte Werke* XIII, 229. Where necessary, I am substituting *drive* for *instinct*, which is the translation employed for *Trieb* throughout the SE.

6. Freud, "The Libido Theory," 255.

7. In "The Libido Theory," Freud suggests that sublimation might replace "sexual" objects with ostensibly "nonsexual" ones, which may, nevertheless, retain a libidinal charge. What is

crucial to both instances is how these objects remain embroiled in a fantasy about their contents, as well as the requirements for achieving satisfaction.

8. LaPlanche, *Life and Death*, 21.

9. Ibid., 18–20. Laplanche is attempting to redeem Freud's thought from the "errors" committed by theorists (such as M. Balint) who assert that sexuality has an object from the beginning. By emphasizing the abstract character of sexuality in Freud's writings, Laplanche effectively repudiates the idea that a fixation on certain objects is a "refinding" of a lost object (e.g., the lost breast of the mother); instead, he underscores the object's partiality as a metonym or metaphorical condensation of diffuse sexual tensions in search of an object.

In this respect, a broader definition of the source implies an abstraction of the drive, and this allows Laplanche to delineate a revised understanding of the libidinal object. This object is hereafter conceivable as a condensation or displacement of autoerotic stimulation deriving from the tension exerted by repressed instincts. Indeed, the implication is that the object will actually be constituted by the drive as a vehicle of residual instinctual energies that pressure the psyche to seek a locus of investiture and release. Sexual fantasies offer an obvious forum for this constitutive investiture, whereby an object is bestowed with its focal status. Significantly, Laplanche also identifies intense intellectual activity as a potential impetus for sexual stimulation. This identification anticipates a theory of objects of inquiry as sublimated and socially acceptable loca for the drives (21).

10. This observation pertains to Freud's mapping of the libidinal economy in "[Drives] and Their Vicissitudes," which is explicitly metapsychological to the extent that he breaks down the four components of the drive (impetus, aim, object, and source) as a configuration of psychic operations themselves figurative in character.

11. Laplanche writes that insofar as instincts are biological, the source, as Freud indicates, lies "outside the scope of psychology" (*Life and Death*, 13, citing Freud, "Instincts and Their Vicissitudes," in SE XIV, 123).

12. "*Ein Trieb wäre also ein dem belebten Organischen innewohnender Drang zur Wiederherstellung eines früheren Zustandes,* welchen dies Belebte unter dem Einflusse äußerer Störungskräfte aufgeben mußte, eine Art von organischer Elastizität, oder wenn man will, die Äußerung der Trägheit in organischen Leben" (*Jenseits des Lustprinzips*, 38, Freud's emphasis, GW XIII, 38).

13. Laplanche writes: "[T]he intervention of the life sciences in psychoanalysis is frequently invoked by Freud as decisive, notably in reference to the theory of drives, but the fact that that invocation most often refers to the speculative or poetic demons of biologism should give us pause" (*Life and Death*, 5).

14. Laplanche, *New Foundations*, 38. The Physicalist reference that constitutes the initial departure point for the mechanical, thermodynamic, and economic lines of speculation that intermingle in *Beyond the Pleasure Principle* is G. T. Fechner's *Einige Ideen zur Schöpfungs- und Entwicklungsgeschichte der Organismen* (1873; Tübingen: Edition Diskord, 1985).

15. LaPlanche, *New Foundations*, 38. It is as if Freud's key scientific references (and particularly to Fechner, whose work verged into vitalism, Wilhelm Fließ, A. Weismann, and Ewald Hering) seem to cull their major hypotheses from Goethe's *Elective Affinities* (1809), which, along with Schiller, Schopenhauer, and Plato, would have also served as a literary and philosophical source of inspiration for the metaphysical theses in *Beyond the Pleasure Principle*. Certainly Freud's speculations move in this direction when he cites Fließ (1906) on the completion of fixed periodizations of organic life that reveal the interdependency of "male" and "female"

modes of living substance. Freud brings the implications of these associations to bear on his reflection on the life and death drives in chapter 6 of *Beyond the Pleasure Principle* by extrapolating from A. Weismann's "morphological" theory of the mortal and immortal divisions of germ cells. Notably, such imagery anticipates Freud's reference, later in the same chapter, to Aristophanes' myth of sexual division from Plato's *Symposium* to suggest that when it came into being, living substance was torn apart into little particles that the sexual drives strive to rejoin.

16. Apart from A. Weismann's *Über die Dauer des Lebens* (1882), *Über Leben und Tod* (1884), and *Das Keimplasma* (1896), Freud also cites Hartmann (1906), Lipschütz (1914), Goette (1893), Woodruff, Doflein (1919), Hering, Maupas, and Calkins in this connection before turning to Barbara Low's concept of the Nirvana Principle (1920), which becomes the touchstone of his radical formulation of the death drive as the avatar of primal masochism.

17. For an incisive analysis of Freud's discussion of the single-celled organism and related concepts, see Judith Roof's "From Protista to DNA (and Back Again): Freud's Psychoanalysis of the Single-Celled Organism," in *Zoontologies: The Question of the Animal,* ed. Carey Wolfe (Minneapolis: University of Minnesota Press, 2003), 101–19.

18. Translation modified; *Jenseits des Lustprinzips,* 25.

19. Freud's emphasis; *Jenseits des Lustprinzips,* 26–27.

20. *Jenseits des Lustprinzips,* 27–28. In keeping with the German edition, I have removed the italicization of *conscious* in the phrase "conscious mental processes" in this passage.

21. Kant initially generalizes time as the condition of all experiences while restricting space to outer experiences. He subsequently recognizes that outer determinations are essential to an inner sense of identity and change; there is, in effect, a reciprocity between the temporal and the spatial, and between inner and outer determinations. He writes: "Not only are we unable to perceive any determination of time save through change in outer relations (motion) relatively to the permanent in space (for instance, the motion of the sun relatively to objects on the earth), we have nothing permanent on which, as intuition, we can base the concept of substance, save only *matter;* and even this permanence is not obtained from outer experience, but is presupposed *a priori* as a necessary condition of determination of time, and therefore also as a determination of inner sense in respect of [the determination of] our own existence through the existence of outer things. The consciousness of myself in the representation 'I' is not an intuition, but a merely *intellectual* representation of the spontaneity of a thinking subject. This 'I' has not, therefore, the least predicate of intuition, which as permanent, might serve as correlate for the determination of time in inner sense—in the manner in which, for instance, *impenetrability* serves in our *empirical* intuition of matter." Immanuel Kant, *Critique of Pure Reason,* trans. Norman Kemp Smith (New York: St. Martin's Press, 1965), 246–47.

22. In Kant's words, "Without the permanent there is therefore no time-relation."

23. I have found evidence for this second prospect in my analysis of the German reception of Steven Spielberg's *Schindler's List.* See Karyn Ball, "Remediated Memory in German Debates about Steven Spielberg's *Schindler's List,*" at www.kakanien.ac.at/beitr/fallstudie/kbal1.pdf.

24. My reading here draws on the implications of *Matter and Memory* (1908), where Henri Bergson argues that perceptions contingently reactivate "virtual" memories, which reciprocally attenuate the quality and force of perception (Henri Bergson, *Matter and Memory,* trans. Nancy Margaret Paul and W. Scott Palmer [1908; New York: Zone Books, 1991]).

22. Young Mr. Freud; or, On the Becoming of an Artist

FREUD'S VARIOUS PATHS TO THE DREAM BOOK, 1882–1899

Klaus Theweleit

Translated by Thomas Pepper with the help of an earlier version by Jason Peck

The starting material of this piece is stone—the different kinds of marble of which statues are made. Readers of the *T-Deutung*, as Avital Ronell has called it, will be familiar with this complex: Freud's wish to stand on a monument at the University of Vienna as something like "the Habsburg Kaiser." From his early youth on, Freud is convinced that the figure of a great explorer or inventor is hidden in his body, and that his life is aimed at the task of working this figure out. Let's say just like Elvis: his mother told him every day he would be King, the new Jimmy Rogers to come—until he *was*. Or Bob Dylan at seventeen, who had the certain feeling that he would be greater than Elvis. Andy Warhol, who saw himself on top of the art state of New York City—it took him fifteen years of hard work and then he was there. *Hochenergetiker:* bodies running on high energy. I used to write about quite a number of them: Warhol, Gottfried Benn, Ezra Pound . . . H.D. . . . Jean-Luc Godard . . . Freud . . . I still *am*.

T-Deutung: I love that little invention by Avital. It's more than just caprice; it expresses the feeling of a certain unfittingness of the term "interpretation." I have never accepted this translation of the German *Deutung* into the French and Anglo-Saxon spheres. "Interpretation" in German is reserved for the discourse on the poetic word: "*Man interpretiert Gedichte*": poems, novels, stories. Not even films—there you say "critique." And in the case of legal texts you say *Kommentar* or *Auslegung*, just as you do in the theological context. *Deutung, deuten,* is a word much more mysterious, a loaded word from the German Romantics: "*ich weiß nicht, was soll es be-deuten*" ("*das ich so traurig bin*") (I don't know what it should mean [that I'm so sad], Clemens von Brentano, or, ironically Heinrich Heine). Things have a *Bedeutung,* they have a *meaning*, a signification that goes far beyond any "interpretation." Interpretation has something arbitrary about it in German, even if it is done well. Traum*deutung* means more; it means "getting at the core," finding out about the very secrets, at least the secrets of your own individual life—and who or what could compare with *that?* So I'll stick with this *T-Deutung* vehicle as a new word of art, a new invention.

Just as *Traumdeutung*, in fact, has been understood as something like a work of art by many analysts, and still is. A very short while ago I came across a passage on this subject in Germany's most important psychoanalytic periodical, *Psyche.* There I read:

> As you all know, there is just a handful of rules you have to consider [when *deut*ing *T*s]. At first you have to give the dream a really big kick in its guts. Then I advise you to grab it, whirl it around, and throw it up high into the air, and then let it fall down to the ground, so that it will burst, sparkling with fire, into its single parts. If you don't dare to perform this piece of art, you will never be able to *deuten* a dream. *T-Deutung* is a violent business. To catch a hidden or latent thought, or at least to get a glimpse of it, you have to invest the same active, aggressive energy that was invested by the dreamer in order to repress just that thought. So . . .[1]

And then the *Deutung* of the *T* is begun by the author. This is not, as you might think, an aggressive, brutish analyst from the German backwoods. She is a civilized young lady from Zurich, even if she goes under the militant name of Judith Le Soldat. She has had her proper swim in the Lacanian seas as well. So we're back at the point of energy. *T-Deutung* is some high-energy work, dealing as it does with a certain aggressiveness on the part of the dreamer. High-energizer Freud, playing with explosives, and in the end leaving the scene under the self-given title of "conquistador" of this New World of *Traum*-violence, having started out as only a poor Jewish boy from the East. Thus I have made my choice to tell you this story of young Mr. Freud—or of younger Mr. Freud on his way to the "Dream Book," as he himself liked to call it—as a sort of bildungsroman of a marble-monument seeker on his way into the great Western world. For me the best way to convey an idea of what this *Traumbuch* is all about is to describe the tracks the book moves down—and this is the story of different kinds and pieces of marble.

In May 1895, in the eighth year of their correspondence, Dr. Sigmund Freud in Vienna and Dr. Wilhelm Fliess in Berlin were united, as Sigmund's letters to Wilhelm show, in a radical search for fame, fortune, and, ultimately, immortality. At this point it appeared that Dr. Fliess, the otolaryngologist from Berlin, was in the lead. Through his calculation of women's biorhythms on the basis of the menstrual cycle, he believed that he had found the way to determine a woman's fertile days with certainty. In May 1895 he informed Freud that he had solved "the problem of conception." Freud excitedly and unstintingly applauds his friend:

> Your news was enough to make me shout for joy. If you have really solved the problem of contraception, the only thing left for you to do is to make up your mind what

kind of marble you prefer. For me your discovery is a few months too late, but it may come in useful next year. In any case, I am burning with curiosity to hear more about it. (May 25, 1895)

By "next year" Freud means the period after the undesired pregnancy of his wife, Martha Bernays. It was the sixth time in nine years. The weak disposition of the "city woman" is a constant theme in Freud's letters; it refers—among other things—always to Martha's pregnancies. The Freuds would so much have loved to have an infallible remedy for this cyclic disease.

Sigmund himself was after something else in Vienna. He wanted to discover the cause behind the fin-de-siècle sickness that befell so many upper- and middle-class women, namely neurasthenia or hysteria. Neurologists had not been successful in finding any causes for this illness. Here medicine was confronted with such a mysterious aggregate of symptoms—headaches, dizziness, weakness, high blood pressure, loss of appetite, nervousness, irregular menstruation, cramps, as well as already known and newly discovered sexual disturbances—that a monument would be the smallest reward to be offered to this cultural hero, this wistfully awaited savior, who might solve the whole complex of hysteria and give women back to their work of procreation and social representation.

In the case of his friend, Freud is skeptical: "Your discovery. . . does credit to your name. You would be the strongest man; would hold the reins of sexuality in your hand; rule the people; you could achieve it all and prevent it all" (May 25, 1895). The slightly ironic tone is unmistakable. Freud doubted the validity of his friend's numbers game, even though he played it along with him for years.

For Freud, contraception was written in the stars. After the birth of their daughter, Anna, on December 3, 1895, the Freuds put a stop to procreation by means of simple sexual abstinence. Freud was in a dilemma. He, for whom sexuality "held the reins," was also a contemporary "nerve doctor," who was convinced that the contraceptive practice of coitus interruptus, "the only certain method," was psychically dangerous. He was not recommending it to his patients. Unwanted pregnancies would be preferable to the nervous illness resulting from "interruption." But the solution of the problem of conception would still have been as great an epoch-making event as the invention of psychoanalysis, which itself was still to come.

There is no single founding date of psychoanalysis. The anniversary texts of the speakers here at this conference cover the space of several years—just as we have seen with the parallel celebrations of the hundredth anniversary of the movies. Ilse Grubrich-Simitis, one of the experts most knowledgeable in the field of Freud's development, sees in Freud's and Breuer's *Studies in Hysteria* (1895) the *Urbuch*, the cornerstone of the experience of psychoanalysis. In it can be found "a quality of seeing and hearing unknown up until that point, the transformation of the doctor-patient relationship, the establishment of a new form of case presentation, and the development of the original form of psychoanalytic theory and technique."[2] This is certainly correct; but a necessary step beyond the *Studies* had yet to be taken, one that only Freud's Dream Book took. This is the step I attempt to retake here.

Die Traumdeutung was published in the autumn 1899 by the publisher Deuticke, of Vienna and Leipzig, and was relatively unnoticed. It took several years to sell those famous six hundred copies of the first run of the book. The story of its success starts only some years later, when Carl Gustav Jung, a young doctor at the Burghölzli, Bleuler's famous psychiatric hospital in Zurich, reads the book and decides to become Freud's follower.

Up until the *T-Deutung*, when "lightning struck," there were those common zigzag points along the way in Freud's life, which are so well known from the lives of many other inventors or conquistadors. The most important stations must be outlined—also to counter the impression that Freud's works, each on its own, can be taken as something like one in a series of individually canonical texts. Everything surrounding this inventor is in flux, is changing, and is still being constantly revised, even up until his sixty-fifth birthday. He is forty-three when the Dream Book is published. At that point he is just a lecturer in neuropathology, a freelance therapist, the father of six children—even if he has already seen quite a lot, that is to say he has had almost twenty years of different kinds of experience in the fields of neurology and psychiatry.

Albrecht Hirschmüller has given the most accurate account of Freud's first years after his time as a medical student.[3] Freud the neurologist stuck with physiology: "[H]is goal was to become a scientist, not a doctor. At this time he worked on the nervous system of river crabs."[4] His work in Brücke's institute of physiology, then in surgery, and subsequently in internal medecine, suffers from the fact that every single assistant professorship is occupied, and for a long time to come. No free place left for young Mr. Freud.[5] So in 1884 he goes to work as a psychiatrist at the Second Psychiatric Clinic of Vienna, directed by Theodor Meynert. This was Freud's first paid position. Forty-five reports on patients from Freud's hand survive in the archives. They are hardly distinguished, as Hirschmüller shows, from the reports of other physicians: "The anamneses first take into account the details of the cases given by the admitting physician; they are only secondarily based on the patients' own accounts."[6]

Along with his clinical work, Freud continues his experiments in Meynert's neuroanatomical laboratory. The abstract of the report on his minor inventions having to do with the process of dyeing histological specimens with Gold chloride (to give better contrast to the specimens) is translated into English.[7] But Freud did not expect in the least for his breakthrough to fame to come from this work in the laboratories and psychiatric clinics of Vienna.

There was a new medicine around, however, an alkaloid not yet studied, but which was yielding amazing results: cocaine. Freud took it himself, and quickly became euphoric in more than one way. Soon he tried the drug out on patients, prescribing this miraculous powder for all kinds of psychic weaknesses: hysteria, hypochondria, neurasthenia, asthma, melancholic disposition, inability to work, digestive trouble, and even psychically induced impotence. "[In] three cases, female melancholics," Freud writes, were able to "speak [once] again" by virtue of cocaine injections. And, together with Dr. Koller, a friend and specialist of eye diseases, Freud discovered cocaine's anaesthetic qualities for eye surgery. Freud's 1885 monograph on the coca plant caused a fury in Vienna. The Physiological Club congratulated the young researcher on this work, and Dr. Heuss, director of the eye clinic, believed that Freud's medical use of cocaine "had brought about a revolution."[8]

These adventures in research took place during Freud's four-year-long engagement to Martha Bernays, who was then living in Hamburg. She regularly received reports by letter. About his hopes for his work with cocaine Freud writes in a letter from April 21, 1885: "We don't need more than one lucky strike in the cocaine arena. It would guarantee us our household equipment, and we would be able to think about settling down."[9] Until then Martha's mother had not agreed to the marriage because of young Dr. Freud's lack of money, hence his inability to feed a family. If only one of those cocaine trials had worked. . . .

But Freud's further attempts at treating neuralgia and morphine addiction with cocaine failed, as did his similar experiments with diabetics. As Ernest Jones suggests, success with these patients would have meant "wealth and glory," marble and marriage. The lowest point occurred when Freud's close friend (and partial role model) Ernst Fleischl von Marxow, whom Freud had tried to heal of his morphine addiction by means of cocaine, died of a self-administered overdose. Freud's path to the monument via the means of cocaine ended in disaster, at least as far as *prescribed* medicine was concerned. Still, many authors read Freud's cocaine euphoria as a precondition for his later capacity for self-analysis and his ability to get into his own dreams so deeply—precisely in the sense of Jimi Hendrix's *Are You Experienced?* For such capacities presuppose a splitting of the self as a vehicle for self-exploration—something that may be enhanced through experimentation with drugs.

Here, albeit unintentionally, Freud had already dismissed the traditional doctor-patient relationship. He did not simply prescribe cocaine, but partook of it himself—and heavily. Nor did he discontinue this kind of work after the public disaster. The *self-experiment* would remain his distinct method of experience. The boundaries between doctor and patient would be remoted even further, to the point at which the doctor himself became the patient.[10]

At the time Freud's readings were in Darwin, Flaubert, Cervantes, and Dickens. In music—never Freud's special field—it was Bizet's *Carmen*. It is also at this time that he became interested in his own dreams, and, according to Jones and Hirschmüller, that he first started a dream journal, which he did on July 19, 1883.

These are also the years during which Freud also stayed for a while in Paris, studying at Charcot's Salpêtrière, with the help of a travel grant for which he was recommended by his superior, Meynert. Freud brought back to Vienna what would soon become his new obsession, his next big kick. He strongly positioned himself as Charcot's front man for using hypnosis treatment in Vienna. He wrote to Karl Koller: "Paris was a new beginning for me. I have found a new mentor, Charcot, just as I always imagined him; I have learned to observe clinical cases (as much as I have been able); and generally I have brought back a great amount of new and positive knowledge. The only bad thing is that I was stupid enough only to have money for five months."[11]

In his lectures, Charcot demonstrated that typical hysterical symptoms could be produced and removed by hypnotism, thus excluding primarily organic causes for this illness. Freud's translations of Charcot, as well as his lectures on the hypnotic method and "On Male Hysteria," which began in Vienna on October 15, 1885, caused a major falling out between Freud and the Viennese medical authorities. Hirschmüller writes: "All authors on Freud are united in their opinion that Freud's enthusiasm for Charcot's work reached missionary zeal, and that the Viennese professors were not only unimpressed, but considered it all quite inappropriate."[12] A lecture on aphasia followed, in which Freud argued against the localization of aphasia in distinguishable or discrete parts of the brain, thus exacerbating the confrontation with Meynert: "Within the course of less than a year, Freud thus came into conflict with three central tenets of Meynert's teachings. The points of dispute were caused by Freud's enthusiasm for hypnosis, his statements on male hysteria, and his anti-localization theory [of aphasia]."[13] Freud wrote to his fiancée on May 13, 1886: "So the battle with Vienna is in full swing!"[14] Little Napoleon, still in contact with his invisible marble ghosts. With the insulting decision to remove hysteria from the field of diseases reserved for certain members of European femininity, Freud made a further step in the direction of "becoming his own patient." Ten years later, he will discover himself as a special case of male hysteria.

The year 1887: At the time of this battle with Vienna's psychiatric authorities, an article by Freud appeared in Buchheim's *Ärtzliche Versicherungs-Diagnostik.* "In this astounding text, Freud discusses how to examine patients' nervous systems with respect to whether or not a life insurance company should accept or decline an application"—exactly the thing such companies try to work so hard at today with the help of the genetic code of potential clients. Hirschmüller comments thus on this neurologically rather sophisticated article: "Freud had completed his clinical education; finished his stay in Paris; and opened his own practice. It is obvious that he now possessed a clearly defined neurological diagnostic kit he could use whenever called for. In the earlier psychiatric anamneses of the Meynert period, nothing like this was visible."[15]

If we look at the time span during which Freud's development from a beginner in institutional psychiatry to an experienced neurological diagnostician takes place, namely from 1882 to 1885, we are surprised to find that these are also the years of Freud's cocaine experiments. As is so often the case with his biography, one gets the feeling of dealing with the lives of (at least) two different people. Only in his letters to his fiancée do all of these different strands come together. Many authors have come to recognize the diary-like function of these letters. Freud, with his fiancée off in the distance, brings his different lives together in the eyes of his bride to be, thus inventing the psychoanalytic technique in the letters to Martha Bernays. Fifteen years later, what will be called Freud's "self-analysis" in fact begins here as an experience between a loving couple, and as a procedure of self-splitting—a self-splitting that is not only an intra-psychic experience, but also a crucial fact of Freud's outer life or lives. Freud really lives in splits—in this technique between two and in this procedure of self-division—in order to arrive at a device for self-exploration, and one with durable results.[16]

After four years of this letter-life and nearly fifteen hundred letters to his fiancée—that makes about one letter every day, most of them still unpublished—the couple marries in 1886. Freud opens his practice the same year. And he is worried that it will not earn him a living in hostile Vienna. Furthermore, his stream of letters has lost its addressee, because Martha now lives with him. Now where will he send his letters, his stream of diary entries?

In 1887, in a lecture hall in Vienna, Freud and the otolaryngologist from Berlin, Dr. Wilhelm Fliess, meet for the first time and vehemently embrace each other. These two young Jewish doctors, both in their early thirties and convinced of their own extraordinary intellectual qualities, had no idea that the book that, twelve years later, would become the offspring of their life and of their correspondence as an intellectual couple, would eventually change twentieth-century thinking like no other. The two develop a productive friendship—love at first sight, so to speak. Their meeting makes a deep impression on Freud and engenders a letter with a "confession." To his new friend, Freud feels compelled to remark "in what sort of rank among men I put you"—the highest, of course.[17]

How does one prove to oneself and to a courted friend in a first letter that both are worthy of being included among the gods? In that one shows oneself to be incisive and well informed about the world—women, for example—in an especially interesting case: Freud hands over to Fliess a conclusion about Dr. A., a female physician whom both men know. This is the case the two men had spoken about: "her weak disposition," her "neurasthenic dizziness while moving," her so-called "vertige"—Freud uses the French word—a dizziness not, as Freud suggests here in this first letter, caused by neurosis. Rather she appeared to him as an actual "sufferer of simple vertigo," from a somewhat corporeal "post-diphtherial paralysis of the legs"; and perhaps one should also consider the possibility of "an infection of the spinal chord."

The passionate friendship and working relationship of Freud and Fliess in fact develops through a dialogue concerning Dr. A.'s *vertige*, her *Schwindel*, which, in German, means at once giddiness and swindle. This is the same constellation to be found seventy years later in Hitchcock's *Vertigo*. Scottie Ferguson and Gavin Elstir, the hidden male couple of the plot, click in to form the investigation machine that will kill Madeleine/Judy/Kim Novak.[18]

Freud and Fliess, the most important couple in the exploration of the psychical apparatus—theologically speaking, "the soul"—put their sniffers together over the case of a woman's vertigo. It is a marvelous ghost that guided Freud's hand in this very first letter to Wilhelm Fliess. Nowhere is the founding of psychoanalysis more accurately or revealingly documented than in this fifteen-year stream of letters. For us today, it is easily one of the books of another Hitchcockian concept, "the twentieth century."[19] Freud and Fliess are going strong in following this train, especially during the first ten years of their correspondence. More than ever do they expect their dreams of fame and fortune to be fulfilled through their discoveries regarding the bodies and the psyches of women. Marble: "the feminine stone."

But the temptations of the organic (or somatic) still continue, and they constantly resurface in Freud's attempts. The nasal operation performed by Fliess on one of Freud's patients, Emma Eckstein—and at Freud's request—is one of the last of these resurfacings. (Its horrible details can be read in Freud's letters to Fliess of March 1895.) For us, though, what is of interest is the reference to marble. On the basis of his alleged discovery of a connection between the vagina and the nose, Fliess was convinced that the irregular menstruation of hysterical patients could be brought under control by manipulations of the nasal region. On the grounds of his own discovery of the existence of a psychological mechanism of "symbolic substitution of the 'below' of the body for the 'above' of the body," Freud was convinced that Fliess's removal of swelling in the nose would have noticeable effects on Eckstein's menstruation. This would have been another path to the monument. But Fliess, just like Freud, failed to cure the patient. In fact, both of them avoided public scandal only through the benevolent silence of a professor friend, whose last-minute surgery saved Emma E.'s life. This attempt at marble did not come to a halt at the edge of the abyss; it already had one foot deeply *in* it.

The long recovery of Emma Eckstein corresponds with the publication of the *Studies on Hysteria* in May 1895. Again one notes with astonishment how, even in spite of this "*Urbuch* of psychoanalysis," Freud is still trying to find organic causes for hysteria. He experiments in both directions as part of two different male couples. While the book on hysteria (in collaboration with Josef Breuer) moved in the direction of "psychoanalysis," his work with Fliess remained firmly rooted within their sensational discoveries of "life rhythms," mathematical methods for the prevention of conception, and surgical procedures.

It is indeed remarkable that this splitting of Freud's research paths didn't lead him—or guide him—to something like more cautious formulations. In the *Studies on Hysteria* Freud claims that he has finally succeeded in finding the cause of female hysteria, namely that all hysterical patients suffered severe forms of sexual molestation as children, usually at the hands of a family member such as a father, uncle, or brother. In this work he presents these findings as the *caput nili*, the finally discovered source of the Nile, and himself as both the Stanley and Livingstone of neuropathology. Because of their friendship, Fliess was enthusiastic about Freud's publication; the public, however, remained distant. Even Breuer, Freud's coauthor, was not too happy with the *caput nili* business. He was not sure about the hundred-percent evidence Freud claimed in the matter. Modern authors, who think that the *real truth* of psychoanalysis lies buried here, like to blame Breuer as a coward—as is so often done with Freud himself. The social danger of Freud's theory is easily to be seen: if all cases of female hysteria were brought on by familial molestation, then bourgeois Vienna had far to go to clean itself up. Without a doubt Freud, by virtue of his theory, would have been able to fill his practice amply; but a reputation as a specialist in the healing of the abused daughters of the city's honorable men wouldn't get him a marble monument—more likely only a gravestone in the Jewish cemetery. So he did not trumpet his finding to the world, and later he would give it a status among other *sources* of the Nile. He had other reasons for this than just fear. We shall come to them shortly.

During the same year, another path to the heights of fame appeared. By virtue of experiments conceived to explain the emergence and function of human memory, the natural sciences were developing the thesis that there exist conductors in the brain, along which particles with varying electrical charges, called neurons (or, as it is written in the English Freud translations, neurones) move back and forth. These neurological paths resist sense data, or transfer them in varying degrees of intensity. Like a fanatic, Freud immersed himself in all the available literature, and plugged in the problem of the *resistance* of patients in the preanalytical cure. Within months, he attempted a complete electrophysiology of the brain. It was a radical theory in which he attempted to connect every psychic reaction with a measurable electrical or chemical process in the nervous system. And at the same time, he attempted the first formulation of a metapsychology in terms of a combination of natural science and his own findings in psychology.

Freud sent his text, the most ambitious he had yet written, to Fliess in Berlin in October 1895—this only five months after the *Studies,* with their famous technique of *chimney sweeping.* If Freud's letters had not fallen into the hands of Marie Bonaparte after Fliess's death, and if she had burned them, as Freud had demanded, we would not know anything about Freud's *Entwurf einer Psychologie,* the *Project for a Scientific Psychology.* But because the Princess, refusing Freud's demand, did not burn any of the letters, we can take note today, with astonishment and admiration, of Freud's attempt to define all psychic activity and its disturbances by means of neurophysiological processes. The invention of psychoanalysis, as we have come to know it, would have been superfluous if this approach had worked. One can only render justice to Freud if one realizes that contemporary neuropsychology is not really much more advanced today than it is in Freud's text, with the exception of an agglomeration of many details. The cure of psychological disturbances by means of measuring the energy of endopsychic systems and of prescribing medication is still a utopian project.

This was Freud's last attempt to achieve the status of a giant on the basis of work in human physiology. He broke off this work because he realized that it was so far ahead of its time. He might well have gained recognition as a genius in something like speculative neurophysiology—something a university professor could well afford, but which Freud could not.[20] What *he* had to do was to fill his practice and feed nine mouths.

If one begins to realize that all of these tracks are laid down in this same year of 1895, one gets a sense of just how many different and condensed conglomerations were cooking, moving around in Freud's head at the same time, each one more radical than the last. The *Studies in Hysteria* may indeed be the first significantly psychoanalytical book, but the psychoanalyst himself is still not yet born. Freud has his fingers in many pies [or dances at many weddings—"auf vielen Hochzeiten," as the German saying goes—Ed.], but the specific psychoanalytic space is not yet opened. Freud is on the way. The Dream of Irma's Injection, which he will present as the model dream in chapter 2 of the *T-Deutung*, is dreamt on July 24, 1895, right between the *Studies on Hysteria* and the *Project for a Scientific Psychology*. In her description of the cooperation between Breuer and Freud, Ilse Grubrich-Simitis stresses the ambiguity of this moment:

> That the desertion of the privileged position of the doctor aggrieves both researchers is quite obvious from their book. In Freud's case studies we can follow the gradual consolidation of the new method chronologically. For example, in the earliest phase of the treatment of Emmy von N., the whole body of the patient is still included in the therapy, for example by means of medicated painting of the anaesthetized leg, or through a total massage of the body and a regimen of food and drink. In his hypnotic suggestions, Freud does not even shy away from lies and tricks. Only in the conversations between the awakened patient and the doctor does there seem to be some free space secured for the reflection, appearance, and opposition of the patient.[21]

The really decisive change in all this occurs more than two years later, in September 1897. For years Freud had concerned himself with finding out what role *events in reality* had played in the instigation of psychic diseases, and thus with what had been *repressed* by the patient and hence might be *remembered* in therapy. Summing up his efforts, he comes to the cool conclusion: "I have not yet achieved the theoretical understanding of repression and of its role in therapy." And then he unfolds the full shape of these thoughts of taking stock in a letter of September 21, 1897: "The continual disappointment in my efforts to bring a single analysis to a real conclusion; the running away of people with whom for a period of time I had been most taken; the absence of the complete success on which I had counted. . . ." Thus he revises his *caput nili:* "And now I want to confide to you immediately the great secret that has been slowly dawning over me these last few months. I no longer believe in my *neurotica.*" By which he means: in sexual abuse as the regular etiological mechanism of hysteria.

Still in the same letter, Freud moves on to the core of the problem: "[T]he certain insight that there are no indications of reality in the unconscious, so that one cannot distinguish between truth and [a] fiction that has been cathected with affect." This is the official American translation of Freud's letters to Fliess, and I'm not quite happy with it. Freud writes: "daß es im Unbewußten ein Realitätszeichen nicht gibt." Here there is a new word, a new term; there is no *reality mark* in the unconscious.[22] The result—for the real history of the patient, for the moment of his or her actual traumatization—is thus: "that the unconscious never overcomes the resistance of the conscious. . . that even in the deepest stages of psychosis the unconscious memory does not break through, so that the secret of childhood experiences is not disclosed even in the most confused delirium."[23] As a fact of the unconscious, Freud admits that one never gets absolutely close to real history, that there is no sure way to find out what *really* happened to someone in the not-yet-conscious stages of early life, or even in later situations of traumatic experience. So there's no use and no necessity in trying to search for the bare bones of the *real facts.*

Freud's real stature shows up here in the force with which he throws out nearly all the central certainties he had relied on up to this point: after fifteen years of practice as a psycho-doctor, he concedes, he hadn't healed a single patient. After some ten grand attempts to achieve his monument, he is now isolated in Vienna, connected only with a single correspondent who shares his fantasies. He confesses to his co-fantasist: All of this is nothing yet, I don't have it yet. And yet he isn't depressed at all—quite the contrary: "I have more a feeling of victory than of defeat (which surely is not right)." (This is still the letter of September 21, 1897.) In other words, if this wasn't right, it wouldn't have made him happy in any future. It's a very clear-minded stance that Freud takes here; there is nothing of the usual complaints about his common headaches and heartaches of which these letters to Fliess speak on other days.

During these months of the second half of 1897 we see the rapid growth of what is later called Freud's self-analysis: I'm sick and I must use my own methods on myself, and first of all the method of *T-Deutung.* Freud finds out what his dreams tell him, something about the early stages of his life that *he* had repressed all the while: not the simple *truth* about his life, but rather things he had preferred to *not-know.* Something emerges out of his own unconscious in states of *vertige,* his own *Vertigo.* He communicates this to Fliess with some lines from Goethe:

> And certain lovely shadows reappear,
> Like an old half-forgotten myth,
> First love and friendship come therewith.[24]

And he continues:

> And also first fright and discord. Many a sad secret of life is here followed back to its roots; many a pride and a privilege are made aware of their humble origins. I find here once again all that I experienced with my patients as a third-person observer—there are days when I drag myself around, dejected because I have understood nothing of the dream, the phantasy, the mood of the day; and then again there are days when a flash of lightning illuminates the interrelations and lets me understand the past as a preparation for the present. (October 27, 1897)

Here the real moments of the birth of psychoanalysis are to be found: For the moment, the vision of the monument trades places with visions of "humble origins," first of all the fright and discord of his own life. Freud dives in and makes discoveries—but none medical. Much like his patients, he becomes a site for a restaging of his own lost stories and history. Earlier I referred to this as Freud's self-splitting or duplication—an impossible term to be sure, but I don't have a better one.

What happens here is the entrance of something like *art,* of the theatre stage, or even the film set, into the structure of what will become psychoanalysis. One must play and stage oneself: Thus, to find one's own "true story" is partly an act of performing. With the *Deutung* of dreams, literature makes a major entrance onto the scene of Freud's writings, as is already to be seen in the letters to Fliess: C. F. Meyer, Goethe, Shakespeare, Virgil, and finally, Sophocles. Not accidentally is all literature (become) a sort of daydream, a daydream realm dreamt on a bed of facts. With the opening of the psychoanalytic space in the Dream Book, medical experience, in the end, is replaced by the whole complex of literature, of *sounding out words.* The doctor's office turns into a stage for displaying one's self: as if at an audition, the patient is allowed to say whatever he or she wants because of being on this proscenium, on this experimental playground. This is Freud's final secret: he tried everything with the sciences of medicine, electrophysiology, chemistry, neurology—but to no avail. Too many fields remained uncharted and the results were not applicable. He tried to cure with drugs, but they were too dangerous, too uncontrollable, and, in the end, they killed. He attempted to cure patients by confronting them with their *real (hi)stories* (always molestation or rape), but in the long term this did not work, either: there was no lasting healing. And sometimes the realities came out as having been phantasied. You couldn't tell the phantasies from the real attacks, and—even more difficult—the imagined violations could be worse and harder to enter into than the real ones. He had tried to cure patients with the accuracy of numbers—cycles of the psyche, or menstruation cycles—and also with surgery based on such theories. So what? Hypnosis: attempting to cure through the control of the magnetism of a person's body. So what? Attempted more than once, and more than once the result was someone's arms around his neck. The problem of love in analysis will remain a problem, and there will be the technical writings. But that is for later.

What is important for now is that the setting has changed. As a result of these years, the patient and the doctor no longer sit across from each other, eye to eye; the doctor moves to a position behind the patient. Eye contact is avoided. Both parties sit oriented toward the same direction, facing the stage, the silver screen of the imaginary, upon which history, the present, and the future all run together—if anything runs at all. The secret: the absolutely deliberate intention to have replaced all medical procedures by the setting of *playing games.* The purported precision of medicine was not precise enough to bring about the hoped-for results to which it laid claim. But analysis as an art form can bring about *something like* a healing.

At the end of this process, Freud writes to Fliess: "As far as hysteria is concerned, I am at present completely disoriented" (March 15, 1898). Psychoanalysis is not born out of the chimney sweeping of hysterical women as this is described in the *Studies;* rather, it takes off from the vertigo Freud experienced within himself. Seventeen years later, this shift finds a wonderful formulation in the essay "Recollection, Repetition, and Working Through":

> The transference thus forms a kind of intermediary realm between illness and real life, through which the journey from the one to the other must be made. The new state of mind has absorbed all the features of the illness; it represents, however, an artificial illness which is at every point accessible to our interventions.[25]

An "artificial form of illness" is produced and treated in the intermediary realm of the transference. The entrance into this realm "between illness and life" is provided—and this is what Freud adds with the *Traumdeutung*—only by the dream, and by working on the dream with the technique of free association. Which means: by a body of narration that is not determined by something outside the analytic room, but which is produced in the session as something *art*-ificial.[26]

It is not before the *T-Deutung* that Freud first develops this awareness of the artistic space in analysis, that he perceives a *new reality zone* created just there. "*Von den intellektuellen Schönheit der Arbeit kann ich Dir eine Vorstellung nicht verschaffen*," writes Freud to Fliess concerning the *Deut*ing of his own dreams during self-analysis (March 10, 1897): "I cannot give you any idea of the intellectual beauty of the work." From then on, the envy felt by mainstream medicine focuses on this situation of the doctor as artist and on his or her co-production with the patient. The production begins the moment the patient encounters the artificial bed, the couch, immerses him- or herself in transference, and begins to play the part of him- or herself in this still-alien drama. Where else but in a dream does one appear to oneself in all kinds of possible or impossible configurations? The dream is the attempt at a permanent reinvention of the self. If this new self uncovers or appears to uncover something from childhood, or even from life inside the womb, this is a side effect. Or rather, it is Freud's way of turning the content of dreams into something writable and readable, the necessary attempt at transforming the dream's textuality into something like a novel.

What follows, if it is not the task of finding the real story behind traumata, and if it is not the goal of tracking down the original culprits—if it is not a matter of all of this? Entirely different abysses open up. The patient is as an adventurer in a virtual-reality chamber. Freud's first great step was the deemphasizing of organic causes. With this the medical scientist began his exit from the stage. With the ensuing removal of "what actually happened" from the space of the cure, the detective-like search lost its dominance. [27] After the exit of the medicine man, the policeman and the judge, too, left the analyst's office: They had still a home there as long as the analyst himself was on the trail of the real perpetrator. Freud was quit with this type of analysis on

September 21, 1897. On that day, at the end of a really stupendous letter to Fliess, he writes: "In this collapse of everything valuable, the psychological alone has remained untouched. The dream secures its place." And he adds: "It is a pity that one cannot make a living, for instance, by *deut*ing dreams." And where the illusions fall away, there remains the wise guy, the *eiron,* cracking jokes. Unburdened of his fifteen-year struggle to reach the top, he contented himself with a balloon, a game—and laughed. Then the balloon took him even higher.

Two years later, the Dream Book is there. Freud is both the rooster and the hen of this egg—a fact that is itself part of the very invention he has just made. His lifelong self-duplications will become more and more fruitful in this new setting, precisely insofar as each part of Freud will study the other. And this results in figures such as that of the *Nebenmensch,* of which Gérard Pommier writes, as well as in such figures as *Doppelgänger* and *revenants.* Since the structural similarity of dream images to images in art and literature had for such a long time been glinting in Freud's eye—until then a glint the *Deuter* himself did not yet know how to use in order to see—Freud takes precisely this mere glint of an eyebeam and converts it into a supporting pillar for the purpose of constructing the main hall of the analytic edifice. Certainly this had consequences for his way of representing *his own dreams* in his book. As we now have many more data concerning Freud's life than he himself ever assumed we might, it is easy for us to see where he wrote as a novelist, and not just as an accurate reporter of his dreams. He changed his dreams while writing them down; he combined dreams from different nights; he left out things about which he didn't want to speak—this is especially the case with the *Mustertraum,* the model "Dream of Irma's Injection." And yet, nothing would be more stupid than to blame Freud for this. *For precisely this is the very nature of the game.* I could well imagine that there is possibly not a single dream in the entire book that was dreamed exactly in the way in which it was written—even if such accuracy is conceivable in the first place. Freud himself made a very blunt remark about this to Fliess when the latter, reading the manuscript of the book, gave utterance to his fear that he might be recognized by readers in certain constellations of Freud's dreams, and begged his friend to take *some other* dream—please!—for the purpose of demonstrating or exemplifying a certain dream type. Freud answered him: "OK, dear Wilhelm, please tell me what you don't like, and I shall alter it. You know that I have the ability to make dreams to order for the next night" (September 6, 1898). This is the *artist* speaking.

Another revealing little utterance from the letters allows us a glimpse into Freud's own use of drugs in connection with his different phases of production. During these years, Freud confesses to Fliess that he has started to love wine, especially red wine, a liquor that had meant nothing to him before. This goes along with the fact that Freud had stopped treating his permanent nasal infections with a tincture of cocaine, a medication he had used for nearly a decade, along with friend Fliess: both were addicts, but without really knowing it. And now, at work on the Dream Book,

Freud the cocaine addict slowly turns to a milder use of red wine—you can even feel this while reading!

So, in the end, we count several Urbooks of psychoanalysis: first the *Studies on Hysteria,* then the *Traumdeutung*—but no less than these are his letters to Martha Bernays or to Fliess. What a quartet indeed!

For me it is rather impossible to really understand Freud's achievement with the *Traumdeutung* if one does not see the paths of his evolution from the preparation knife in the neuroanatomy lab to words as instruments for cutting up dreams. That is, certain symptoms cannot be cured by medicine, but rather what works is playing with verbal drugs. Furthermore, certain symptoms are only cured when the now so-called patient uses his or her own words in the healing process, thus turning this process into a working agreement, a therapeutic alliance, or *Arbeitsbündnis,* as German analysts like to call it. Finally, *cure* is not the right word; rather we should use *metamorphosis.* The patient changes into something of a different nature, untouched by the phantasia of eugenics of distressed philosophers, who burn with panic when driven to thinking about DNA and the threats of genetic personality construction.[28]

Since Freud, physicians—with rage and systematically—have denied or misjudged the character of psychoanalysis as an art form that lets the other use her or his own language to find his or her own special truths. Thus medical doctors think that they, too, can accomplish this little bit of chatting about problems—"good advice from your doctor"—and love having this on the list of things they can put on the bill. What they most likely overlook is that Freud postulated some rules for the patient's apparently unstructured chatter: he requested, first of all, that one remove from one's speech "every kind of order, syntax, logic, discipline, etiquette, or stylistic considerations as irrelevant, or even as disturbing."[29] That's precisely what physicians love: when their patients start with their discourse of pain in the context of a medical consultation.

D. W. Winnicott describes beautifully this newly and ever-to-be recreated artificial space in analysis. During a session, one of his patients (he was an engineer) had the feeling of rolling like a ball from the couch into the room, and without falling down. The room became something like a medium enveloping him; much as oil surrounds the ball in a ball bearing.[30] Winnicott found this medium of "grease" comparable to the mother's function in respect to holding the baby. What psychoanalysis means by transference and countertransference is something like the meeting of the bodies of the analyst and the analysand in a lubricated space, in which the parts of their bodies they "send" into this space can meet without touching. And thus there is an opportunity for growing into a new body, different from the one each of them carried around prior to this encounter: a third body, the real product of their common labor in "mutual transference."

Jürgen von Scheidt dedicates his study on Freud and cocaine to "the many young people who did not handle their own drug experimentation as well as Sigmund Freud handled his own cocaine euphoria." The tenor of this compassionate dedication may be applied to other fields of life experimentation. Generally one can assert that Freud handled his lifelong self-experimentations better than any other similarly interested explorer, and better than many similarly interested young people. This is one of his most significant trademarks. He masters drugs just as he masters the female patients who threaten to transform themselves into lovers. He also handles the dangerous self-experimentation with male friendships, and converts this experience into a ground of his productivity—thus he handles his own narcissistic transference. He handles his experimentation with marriage and with six children, as well as with two women in the household: Martha's sister Minna joins the family when her own fiancé dies young. He also handles the dangerous founding of an international movement. He copes with a new definition of woman—female analysts—by turning them into a community of daughters (under male leadership) in the *psychoanalytic state,* as Derrida loves to call it. And he handles the dynamite of his surroundings in the shapes of his various crown princes, from Jung to Ferenczi. Last but not least, his self-experimentation includes the progress of three different forms of writing: the philosophical, the narrative, and the technical-analytic. With his *Traumbuch,* surely he deserves the fame of having written the first book in the genre of the theory-novel.

In order not to get lost in the dangers of such self-experimentation, one needs the temperament of a conquistador, as Freud said on occasion.[31] In a similar vein, Arno Schmidt considered "the constitution of an ox" to be a necessary part of a being a good prose writer. Conquistadors have a particular kind of immortality. In reference to the burning of Freud's books on the order of Goebbels in 1933, A. R. Bodenheimer has a vision: "Freud's texts radiate bright and extremely hot flames. And then, when one looks at the smoke surrounding the ashes, one discovers the phoenix hovering high above, against all laws of nature, and against all prophecies of his demise."[32]

The ashes of the latest Freud burnings are still hot: anybody seen this bird starting up, somewhere? As an old man, Freud spoke of the great injury he had inflicted upon an enlightened humanity: that it wasn't the rational consciousness of mankind that was in control, the ego, with its reason, which was the head of the household, but rather this position of chief fell to the puzzling energy of the unconscious or to the sexual drives.

If I see things right, mankind has forgiven Freud for diagnosing this injurious nature, and has accepted his suggestions. No reasonable human being denies psychical processes such as the repression of basic perceptions and facts; no one doubts the dependence of one's actions on unconscious wishes. There is likewise no one who wouldn't speak of denial, projection, and of psychic resistances. The most ardent enemies of Freud use his concepts. No politician, scientist, or journalist could get along without them, and often without knowing that they are Freudian in the first place. Many of Freud's thoughts have become everyday, just as many parts of Marx's economic thinking have. Forgiveness through unrecognizability and integration: this is a somewhat bearable death. Probably only the physicians have not forgiven Freud's injury to their practice, in the form of the possibility of the dissolution of the difference between the patient and doctor, and the substitution, in place of "the right medicine" (a strong hierarchical device), of the right way of working together in an act of healing by artistic or creative play.

For me, the central thing in all of this is what I have referred to as the "third body." You can experience it in several arenas, especially in music, *electric* music, as well as in love—in all processes where a certain intermingling of bodies happens.

Amplified music: you meet the music and the music meets you, in a heavy encounter. Your body is in transference with the power of the waves beating up against your ear. Again, it's a sort of violent process. The bass works hard to tear the borders of your body down; but then you start to float and to mix in with the body of the music filling the room all over—and you're bathing in it, just like that engineer's metal balls in the oil of the bearings. Freud says that in analysis you learn *Probehandeln,* acting by trying out a part or a role, trying out new little steps in a newly achieved body in the shelter of the analyst's chamber. This body is built precisely out of the energy both analyst and patient put into that room. It belongs to both of them, and so I call it their third body. If everything goes well, the patient will connect it with his or her own body, and one day will take it away, out the door, as her or his own. You can do the same with the music you love most, or which you feel to have the strongest metamorphic power upon you. How this wonder works with two bodies in love I need not explain.

There is a strange thing about technical recordings, about records as items. They are sort-of *ready-mades* in Duchamp's sense, works of art that are themselves capable of being destroyed, but, at the same time, actually indestructible, untouchable, perfect, with the quality of being capable of being reborn. You always get them back again, they come back to you in another form: you use them, you leave them alone. You listen to them again after years and years and you make a strange discovery: they give something back to you that had not been there when you first heard them. They recorded your own *emotions* while they were playing. And now you hear and feel the emotions you had twenty years ago, and in a way more precisely than from any written record or from any way in which your so-called memory stored them in your mind. The recorded disk, with the music you loved on it, has stored them, saved them.

No kidding: this is not an exercise in mysticism, but rather something quite materialist. The *presence* of thoughts and emotions long gone, brought back by the disc, is a result of the body you built up between the music and yourself; and now the disc *is the memory* of this body, an outer memory, ghostly, but existing to an eminent degree. Here we touch on a whole range of phenomena that appear regularly in the interminglings of our bodies with different technical media.

Freud himself was on the way toward realizing things like this when he used the term "psychical *apparatus*" for the human soul, and when he gathered together his theoretical papers under the rubric of *"technische Schriften,"* "techn(olog)ical writings."[33]

Notes

[All references to the correspondence of Sigmund Freud and Wilhelm Fliess are to *Sigmund Freud. Briefe an Wilhelm Fließ 1887–1904,* complete edition, ed. Jeffrey Masson and Michael Schröter (Frankfurt am Main: Fischer, 1986), and are given according to the date of the letter. For the English we have consulted Sigmund Freud, *The Origins of Psychoanalysis: Letters to Wilhelm Fliess,* ed. Eric Mosbacher and trans. James Strachey (New York: Basic Books, 1954), which translation has been occasionally modified for reasons of technical accuracy or incompleteness.

Jason Peck produced a draft of a translation of an earlier version of this text for oral delivery. The reworking of that translation, as well as its expansion and editing into its current form, was done by Thomas Pepper in collaboration with the author. I wish to thank Klaus Theweleit and Monika Theweleit-Kubale for their indefatigable patience, good humor, and generosity in the preparation of this text.—Ed.]

1. Judith Le Soldat, "Der Strich des Apelles. Zwei homosexuelle Leidenschaften," *Psyche. Zeitschrift für Psychoanalyse und ihre Anwendungen* 54, no. 8 (August 2000), 752.

2. Ilse Grubrich-Simitis, "Urbuch der Psychoanalyse: Die 'Studien zur Hysterie,'" *Psyche* 12 (1995): 1115–55.

3. Albrecht Hirschmüller, *Freuds Begegnung mit der Psychiatrie. Von der Hirnmythologie zur Neurosenlehre* (Tübingen: Edition Diskord, 1991).

4. See Sigmund Freud, "Über den Bau der Nervenfasern und Nervenzellen beim Flußkrebs," *Sitzungsbericht der Akademie der Wissenschaft Wien* (Math.-Naturwiss. Kl.), 3 Abteilung, Band 85 (1882): 9–46.

5. Hirschmüller, *Freuds Begegnung,* 118.

6. Ibid., 141, 208.

7. Freud, "A New Histological Method for the Study of Nerve-Tracts in the Brain and Spinal Chord," *Brain* 7 (1884): 86–88.

8. Jürgen von Scheidt, *Freud und das Kokain. Die Selbstversuche Freuds als Anstoß zur "Traumdeutung"* (Munich: Kindler, 1973), 13-18.

9. Freud, *Brautbriefe. Briefe an Martha Bernays aus den Jahren 1882–1886,* ed. Ernst L. Freud (Frankfurt am Main: Fischer, 1960).

10. Only Freudian officialdom has had a problem with this notion, as Jürgen von Scheidt observes: "Isn't it strange that the idea that cocaine might have helped Freud to find the entrance to his own unconscious, and might even have played a crucial role in his self-analysis, occurred neither to Jones nor to the other Freud biographers?" (Scheidt, *Freud und das Kokain,* 13).

11. Hirschmüller, *Freuds Begegnung,* 130.

12. Ibid., 213.

13. Ibid., 213ff.

14. Freud, *Brautbriefe,* 225. Still to follow was the major public discussion concerning hypnosis in Vienna in 1889, in conjunction with the Paris Congress on Hypnosis (August 8–12, 1889). Freud stood in opposition to Meynert and to his school, which accepted *only* organic reasons or major problems in nutrition as the causes of neurological and psychical diseases. As Meynert was publicly considered to be the absolute authority in Vienna in this field, Freud thus broke not only with his former teacher and boss, but with the head of a medical racket.

15. Ibid., 155ff.

16. The course of medical publications had never stopped; besides the book on aphasia, there was also an essay on poliomyelitis, as well as various articles written for dictionaries.

17. See Freud's letter to Fliess of November 24, 1887.

18. The first edition of Freud's letters to Fliess was published in 1950, right in the middle of Hitchcock's most ardent psychoanalytic phase. I am quite sure the filmmaker knew of the *vertige* in Freud's opening letter and made it into the title of *Vertigo* in 1955–56. [And what, indeed, are we to say about the *Madeleine?* In the context of the co-occurrence of the names *Madeleine* and *Elstir* there is only one possible reference: Proust.—Ed.]

19. [This is, of course, the name of the train from New York to Chicago on which Cary Grant meets Eva Marie Saint in *North by Northwest.*—Ed.]

20. For a just evaluation of this text, see Cordelia Schmidt-Hellerau, "Geburt der Meta-psychologie: Der 'Entwurf einer Psychologie,'" *Psyche* 12 (1995): 1156–95. Schmidt-Hellerau finds the *Project* to be a "theoretical document of astounding modernity and contemporane-ity," and to be "Freud's ambitious attempt to overcome the schism of body and soul, the split between neurophysiology and psychology" (1156).

21. Grubrich-Simitis, "Urbuch," 1120.

22. [Of many alternatives—reality sign, reality criterion, etc.—we prefer *reality mark* as a parallel to the notion of an *irony mark* in Rousseau's *Essay on the Origin of Languages.*—Ed.]

23. Sigmund Freud, *Briefe an Wilhelm Fliess 1887–1904*, ed. Jeffrey Moussaieff Masson, German edition by Michael Schröter (Frankfurt am Main: Fischer, 2d ed. 1999), 283–84. We have slightly modifed the translation to be found in *The Complete Letters of Sigmund Freud to Wilhelm Fliess 1887–1909*, Jeffrey Moussaieff Masson, ed. and trans (Cambridge: Harvard University Press, 1985), 264–65.

24. "Und manche liebe Schatten steigen auf;/Gleich einer alten, halbverklungenen Sage,/Kommt erste Lieb' und Freundschaft mit herauf." These are lines 10–12 of the "Dedica-tion" to *Faust*. Thirty-three years later, in 1930, Freud will cite the same lines in the Goethe House in Frankfurt am Main as an expression of gratitude for the Goethe Prize awarded to him there: "words we could repeat about any of our analyses," he says.

25. "Erinnern, Wiederholen, Durcharbeiten," in *Zeitschrift für Psychoanalyse* 2 (1914), now reprinted in GW X, 135.

26. [Playing on the German adjective *künstlich*, meaning *artificial*, from *Kunst*, art.—Ed.]

27. ["(W)ie es eigentlich geschehen ist": Ranke's formula for what the historian's work should depict.—Ed.]

28. With such phantasies from Schloss Elmau, Peter Sloterdijk reveals himself as part of the company of those who can't withstand the temptation of being God for fifteen minutes. See his "Regeln für den Menschenpark," in *Die Zeit* 38 (September 19, 1999).

29. Peter Gay sums up this point in his *Freud. Eine Biographie für unsere Zeit* (Frankfurt am Main: Fischer, 1989), 337.

30. See D. W. Winnicott, "Withdrawal and Regression," in *Through Paediatrics to Psycho-Analysis* (New York: Brunner/Mazel, 1992 [1958]), 255–61.

31. For example, see his letter to Fliess of January 2, 1900. In his letter of July 5, 1900, he wonders whether any of the "undiscovered provinces of the soul" will ever be named after him.

32. See "Einen Freud suchen fürs dritte Jahrtausend," in *Freuds Gegenwärtigkeit. Zwölf Essays*, ed. A. R. Bodenheimer (Stuttgart: Reclam, 1989), 7.

33. The freewheeling, ninety-six-year-old Zurich analyst, Paul Parin, considers the ques-tion as to "whether the techniques of psychoanalysis belong to art or to science" in what is one of the most productive investigations for the future of the business. See his preface to Johannes Reichmayr, *Spurensuche in der Geschichte der Psychoanalyse* (Frankfurt am Main: Nexus, 1990), 8.

23. Such Stuff As Dreams Are Made Of

FREUD, LIFE, AND LITERATURE

Mary Lydon

A Disturbance of
Memory at the Podium

TO MARY LYDON IN MEMORIAM

John Mowitt

Thank you very much, John, and I have an impulse before I begin to remember a late dear friend of ours who is always associated for me with the University of Minnesota, who is George Bauer, who is professor of French here for a number of years. [Pause, exhale.]

The title of my presentation is "Such Stuff As Dreams Are Made Of: Freud, Life, and Literature."

With these words Professor Mary Lydon began her opening remarks, remarks that marked the formal beginning of the conference from which all but one of the chapters in this book were selected. It is fitting to place them here, at the end of this volume, not merely to remember their original function, but because the loss to which the author of these remarks points—the death of a colleague—has now, alas, been visited on her. Mary Lydon died on April 29, 2001, just seven months after the words above were pronounced and recorded.

In my introduction of her I made whimsical reference to the telephone conversation Mary and I had had during which I extended the invitation to speak at our conference. Specifically, I recalled that in broaching the matter of style or genre (the opening plenary was to be somewhat less formal, less elaborate in its argument than the others), I had told Mary that we (the organizers) were looking for something "serious, but not deadly." We giggled, recognizing in this lame spoonerism the very texture of our friendship, a friendship forged in the language games enabled if not authorized by what she was to refer to in her talk as "the French Freud." Mary replied by invoking that friendship: "John, you know me, you know the kind of thing I can do." The deal was, as is said, sealed. Now, of course, I wish that the thing I knew Mary could do included overcoming the disease that had been and was haunting her. In this I am surely not alone.

Now again I am struck by the painful fact that I was the one to call up the unspoken and now tragic theme of our exchange: "serious, but not deadly." As if anticipating what it could only fail to ward off, this phrase, this lame bit of wit, doubtless put in motion the chain of allusions that culminated in the blunt acknowledgment of Mary's passing printed in the journal of the Modern Language Association. At least so it seems to a survivor, especially one who mourns, as Freud might have predicted, by attributing to himself, in the mode of guilt, the very power his mourning belies. After learning of her death I understood immediately why there was no "final version" of her paper, but also why my distress over her not having shared her suffering with me during the conference was at once defensive and narcissistic. In responding to her impulse to "dedicate" her praise of Freud, life, and literature to George Bauer, and to do so as an expression of gratitude to her Minnesota sponsors, she, or her "impulse," was telling me more than I could hear. The "third ear," like Hegel's owl, picks things up only after the fact.

Those familiar with our respective careers know that Mary joined the faculty at Wisconsin several years after my departure. We did not study together. This did not stop me, however, from clipping a wonderful color photograph of Mary from the Wisconsin alumni magazine. It marked her assumption of the Pickard-Bascom Chair in French Studies, and instead of tediously capturing her at the lectern or posed in front of the bookcases in her office, it depicted her seated, tan skirt, white blouse, back propped against one of the surviving Dutch elms dotting the hills around Van Hise Hall, surrounded by students. If I mention this it is not primarily because I longed to number among those touched directly by her teaching, or because, as I look down again at the clipping now, I imagine my phantom in the field falling in the range of her readings. I mention the clipping because it is a photograph, and because one of my favorite essays of Mary's, "Amplification: Barthes, Freud, and Paranoia" (1989), is one in which she taught me to hear things in images, a lesson that quietly orients my own teaching and research in unfathomable ways. Is it a coincidence that this essay also renders coincidence a methodological principle of literary criticism in the wake of psychoanalysis? Is it a coincidence that what "falls together" in this essay is the click of a camera, the snap of a compact, and the withdrawal, the death, of the maternal image? I suppose not. After all, what is the rhetorical function of the expression "mere coincidence" if not, somewhere between English and French, to silhouette the enabling necessity at work within coincidence itself. Mary, ever suspicious of the adage *nomen est omen*, could not but resist the suggestion.

But what necessity is thus asserting itself in this image? To be sure it is not in the photograph, it is in my grasp, the very one now wrinkling and thus hastening the demise of the clipping. It is in the coincidence of my distracted attention, attention that in "Amplification" is presented as the way to get one's head around the navel wherein psychoanalysis and the work of literary criticism knot. Mary's opening remarks went on to explore precisely this point by tracking the legible opacity of the dreams staged in Beckett's *Waiting for Godot*. More than a reiteration of Shoshana Felman's figure of "implication" as a way to dream-weave psychoanalysis and literature, Mary's reading put what Felman had opened, what she had inaugurated, on a different footing. The old and still vibrant sectarianisms—those between clinicians and critics, theorists and historians, etc.—all seemed to slacken faced with the faceless *chora* where meanings are forged, given shape, and bent to task in the hands of readers and analysts alike. Mary put, as it were, the opening in the open. This site of exposure and encounter is one where the death invented by Freud, the glitch in the drive, passes through every crowd. Now I understand the anxiousness with which I attended Mary's opening remarks. She brought us to the anxious opening into which psychoanalysis and literature hurl themselves with seemingly endless abandon. This gift— "the kind of thing I can do"—I thank her for. Regardless of what I say here, I did not know how soon she would follow. I do know, however, that I will not be alone in missing her terribly.

I have an impulse before I begin to remember a late, dear friend of ours, who is always associated for me with the University of Minnesota, who is George Bauer, who was a professor of French for a great number of years.

"TELLING ONE'S DREAMS"

The topic of this conference, "The Dreams of Interpretation/*The Interpretation of Dreams*," is enough to set one dreaming—about dreams, one's own and others, about Freud's theory of dreams and the dream of psychoanalytic theory, what Shoshana Felman calls "the on-going psychoanalytic dream of understanding," about the dream of the conference, about what I dream of doing in this introductory talk, which as I embark on it seems fraught with risk. For no less than dream interpretation, dreaming and especially telling one's dreams have consequences, a point Samuel Beckett emphasizes in *Waiting for Godot*. Three times in the course of the play, Estragon, who claims to have been a poet once, manages temporarily to opt out of his intolerable situation by falling asleep. Vladimir, his companion in misfortune, rouses him twice, unable to bear the loneliness of remaining awake beside his friend's sleeping body. On the third occasion, Estragon is awakened by a nightmare. Each time on waking, Estragon tries, starts to tell Vladimir his dream, and each time Vladimir stops him, twice violently. The first of these scenes, which occurs early on in the play, goes like this:

> ESTRAGON: Let's stop talking for a minute. Do you mind?
> VLADIMIR: *(feebly)* All right. *(Estragon sits down on the mound. Vladimir paces agitatedly to and fro, halting from time to time to gaze into the distance off. Estragon falls asleep. Vladimir halts finally before Estragon.)* Gogo! . . . Gogo! . . . GOGO!
> *Estragon wakes with a start.*

> ESTRAGON: *(restored to the horror of his situation)* I was asleep! *(Despairingly.)* Why will you never let me sleep?
>
> VLADIMIR: I felt lonely.
>
> ESTRAGON: I had a dream.
>
> VLADIMIR: Don't tell me!
>
> ESTRAGON: I dreamt that—
>
> VLADIMIR: DON'T TELL ME!
>
> ESTRAGON: *(gesture towards the universe)* This one is enough for you? *(Silence.)* It's not nice of you, Didi. Who am I to tell my private nightmares to if I can't tell them to you?
>
> VLADIMIR: Let them remain private. You know I can't bear that.
>
> ESTRAGON: *(coldly)* There are times when I wonder if it wouldn't be better for us to part.[1]

Obviously Estragon's hurt reaction is a precise counterpart of the romantic wish so often expressed in popular song that the loved one share our dreams. Later, in Act II, Vladimir, in an outburst of love that momentarily supersedes his fear of being alone, touchingly encourages Estragon to sleep, even singing him a lullaby though he does so amusingly (such is the conflict he feels) in a loud voice so that Estragon is obliged to plead, "Not so loud!" "Estragon sleeps," Beckett continues:

> VLADIMIR: [...]
>
> (Vladimir gets up softly, takes off his coat, and lays it across Estragon's shoulders, then starts walking up and down, swinging his arms to keep himself warm. Estragon wakes with a start, jumps up, casts about wildly. Vladimir runs to him, puts his arms around him.) There . . . there . . . Didi is there . . . Don't be afraid.
>
> ESTRAGON: Ah!
>
> VLADIMIR: There . . . there . . . it's all over.
>
> ESTRAGON: I was falling—
>
> VLADIMIR: It's all over, it's all over.
>
> ESTRAGON: I was on top of a—
>
> VLADIMIR: Don't tell me! Come, we'll walk it off. (445–46)

Finally, as the play nears its end, Estragon falls asleep for the third time, leaving Vladimir to see the now blind Pozzo and mute Lucky off the stage. Once they're gone, Vladimir goes toward Estragon, contemplates him a moment, then shakes him awake.

> ESTRAGON: *(wild gestures, incoherent words. Finally.)* Why will you never let me sleep?
>
> VLADIMIR: I felt lonely.
>
> ESTRAGON: I was dreaming I was happy.
>
> VLADIMIR: That passed the time.
>
> ESTRAGON: I was dreaming that—
>
> VLADIMIR: *(violently)* Don't tell me! (470)

There would be a lot to say about the haunting progression from the simple statement "I had a dream . . ." through the nightmarish "I was falling. . ." to the regretful "I was dreaming I was happy." But what is noteworthy in the present context is that the topic that interests Beckett in these scenes interests him enough to make him want to repeat them: the desire to sleep or to go on sleeping, the escape that sleep provides, the acute loneliness of the individual, the impulse to tell one's dreams on waking—these are all topics that interested Freud as well. And this leads me to wonder what Freud would have made of the repeated representations of sleeping, dreaming, and being awakened in Beckett's text; how Freud would have interpreted the dream that is *Waiting for Godot* in which precisely the telling of dreams is proscribed. For not only is the content of Estragon's dreams never revealed, but the blank left by its repression is most tellingly repeated, creating a *mise-en-abîme* of the play itself, where, as Vivian Mercier wittily and acutely observed, "Nothing happens, twice." Registering the implications of that quip and recalling the opening lines of the play, "rien à faire," nothing to be done, I wonder parenthetically how Beckett and *Waiting for Godot* could have escaped Lacan's attention. Perhaps for the same reason that Derrida has willfully avoided writing anything on Beckett to date, that is to say his awareness of the extent to which Beckett's work uncannily anticipates and hence usurps any possible theorizing about it. But what can we make of Vladimir's adamant, indeed violent, refusal to hear his friend's dreams? "Let them remain private," he says harshly, "You know I can't bear that." One might speculate that the repeated refusal could be a belated expression of Beckett's ambivalence vis-à-vis his analysis with W. R. Bion, in which presumably the author, too, had been induced to tell his own dreams. But whether or not that is the case, one thing at least is clear. We are here today because Freud could bear to hear people's dreams, which he actively encouraged people to put into words. It is clear that for Freud and for the poet and dreamer Estragon, the universe of waking life was precisely not enough. That it is not enough for any of us is perhaps one of Freud's most pregnant lessons—perhaps what Beckett wanted to convey, however negatively. Estragon's question is, after all, greeted by silence.

FREUD AS DREAMER

Not only could Freud bear to listen to other people's dreams, he could bear to confront his own dreams of anxiety and failure about psychoanalysis, the practice he was trying to theorize and establish at the turn of the last century via *The Interpretation of Dreams*. This is particularly evident in his dream of July 23–24, 1895, the Dream of Irma's Injection, which has been so brilliantly analyzed by Shoshana Felman.[2] It seems appropriate, at the beginning of this conference, to spend a little time both on this specimen dream (as Freud himself called it) and on Felman's illuminating interpretation of it. It is Felman, by the way, who proposes "practice" as the mediating term between art and science, thus allowing a re-description of psychoanalysis. After pursuing a detailed and highly nuanced reading of the dream from the perspective of a second-stage feminism, which would view Freud neither as an unmitigated villain, as first stage American feminists tended to do, nor as an unadulterated hero, as Juliet Mitchell, in reaction to this position, did in her *Psychoanalysis and Feminism,* Felman opts instead for acknowledging Freud as simply what she calls a male genius, with all the insight and blindness that this term implies.[3] Emphasizing that the Irma dream is the dream from which psychoanalysis proceeds, Felman skillfully traces the threads in Freud's text, relating the central theoretical notion of the navel of the dream, which emerges fully fledged only toward the end of *The Interpretation of Dreams,* to the knot of female figures there: Irma, her more intelligent, ostensibly more compliant friend (Freud's wife)—in this specimen dream where the navel first surfaces—most interestingly in a footnote. Might not Freud's footnotes be the place where his unconscious is most overtly active? Then, by linking the Irma dream to Freud's controversial lecture on femininity, Felman is able to lead her reader gradually and skillfully to the conclusion:

> The question of the woman and the woman as a question, the question precisely that femininity raises is bound to remain unsolved and unresolved in psychoanalytic theory to the extent precisely that it is the very navel of psychoanalysis, a nodal point of significant resistance. Irma had been resistant as you recall, to Freud's "male" solution.[4]

The question of woman, then, is a nodal point in the text of the ongoing psychoanalytic dream of understanding. It would be impossible in the time I dispose of here to do justice to Felman's subtle structural reading of Freud's text, in which, rather than attempting reductively to outsmart Freud in his own psychoanalysis, to psychoanalyze the Irma dream and use it against Freud in a demystifying manner (these are Felman's terms) as it has become fashionable to do, she proposes rather "to learn more from Freud himself by turning to him not as a theoretician, but as a dreamer and as an interpreter of his own dream" (74).

To learn more from Freud himself, neither as hero or villain, but rather as male genius and as a dreamer, I cannot think of a better rubric under which to pursue the ongoing psychoanalytic dream of understanding, which is what I take to be the object, the wish, the dream of this conference. And to the degree that this is the case, if we follow Felman, the question of the woman and woman as question: this nodal point of significant resistance in the pursuit of that dream must concern us, too. But how do we learn from Freud, or for that matter from anyone else? If we are to believe Adam Phillips, we do it by a process that is similar to the dream work as Freud described it, that is, by the operations of condensation, displacement, secondary revision, and considerations of representability. Significantly, however, as Jean-François Lyotard has demonstrated, the dream-work does not think, it transforms. Thus, when Phillips likens learning to the dream-work, he means that the student consciously and unconsciously makes something of her own out of what is being taught and finds the bits she can use, the bits that make personal sense.

This is why the question I posed earlier was: "What would Freud make of Beckett's play, *Waiting for Godot?*" This transformation, this making something of our own out of material presented to us, is what generates and sustains interest, Phillips claims; and interest is what interests Phillips a great deal and is what keeps us alive. Beginning with the sexual theories of children, which fascinated Freud, this kind of transformation produces theory and produces art. This is the insight derived from Freud that Phillips explores so interestingly in his book *The Beast in the Nursery,* which speaks subtly *sotto voce* throughout this paper.[5]

How does one make something of one's own out of Freud, out of psychoanalytic theory? It sounds like an ambitious, even grandiose project. But this is precisely what happened, I believe thirty or so years ago, with the startling emergence of what Jeffrey Mehlman, in a famous number of *Yale French Studies,* called "French Freud," an invention that has all the vividness and mischievousness of childish language. What currency does French Freud have today? I wonder whether it still has either the expression or the transformation it represented in the academic study of literature in the United States in the 1970s. Perhaps this is one of the things we will find out. But I suspect the loss of interest—not only in French Freud, but in psychoanalysis—which makes this conference so welcome and so unexpected has to do with the backlash of hostility against the spectacle of adults (and academics at that!) having so much fun with what suddenly became known as theory, an activity that, in retrospect, seems to be related to the sexual theories of children in ways that have yet to be explained. Freud wrote of what he called the sexual theories of children that they have one curious characteristic: although they go astray in a grotesque fashion, each one of them contains a fragment of real truth. And in this they are analogous to the attempts of adults, which are looked at as strokes of genius at solving the problems of the universe, which are too hard for human comprehension.

The phrase "French Freud" seemed to suggest a going-astray in a grotesque fashion. This indeed was part of the excitement and the incitement it offered, though it also gave rise to a certain amount of nonsense. While the elaborate coherence of any theory can produce, or degenerate into, nonsense at any time, it holds a fragment of real truth: to wit, that knowledge, whether for the adult or the child, is sexually inspired, just like the dream-work. This might not have been evident in Jeffrey Mehlman's introductory statement in *Yale French Studies* 48, where, emphasizing the importance of translation in the rereading of Freud that was embarked upon there, Mehlman writes:

> Our effort at translation is an attempt at working through in the analytic sense, a textual reality, which the American reader will no doubt be reluctant to assimilate. If we dedicate this issue to that task, it is partly out of a sense that the recent French reading of Freud has strategic value, for any future articulation of American thought,

a permissible simplification with that far-ranging ill-defined speculative enterprise which has flourished in France in the last twenty years and come to be associated with the word structuralism. The texts presented thus wage their interpretative battle on grounds in which America has an elaborate investment.[6]

This is elegant, sober, academic language. But the interest obliquely suggested by the final word, "investment," points to French Freud, to the bad joke that evokes the unconscious and the vivid mischievous language games of children. The French Freud experience, I would suggest today, and as I am encouraged in doing by my reading of Phillips, is equally related to what Winnicott calls the second stage of learning, where, instead of the compliance, the identification that marks the first stage, each student makes something of his or her own out of it all, finds something in the bits that he can use in that personal sense. Phillips writes:

> The student finds herself being unwittingly drawn to specific bits of the subject being taught—whatever the emphasis of the teacher happens to be—which she will then, more or less secretly (even to herself), transform into something strange. If she did this while she was asleep, we would call it a dream. If she does it while she was awake, it will be called a misunderstanding, a delusion, or an original contribution to the subject.[7]

To those who espoused it, whom it interested, French Freud allowed theory to be felt as "real"—that is a phrase of Winnicott's—rather than as "irritating and maddening" (that is also Winnicott's phrase: he is talking about psychology)— as it appeared to those unable or unwilling to pass from the compliance and identification of the first stage of learning (competence as a kind of imitation), to the second stage of transformation; that is, from a person who knows things to being the child who continues to ask questions. No wonder French Freud and all it stands for, dream-work and pleasure, couldn't be allowed to go on. All too soon after it had become axiomatic, those of us who were its practitioners or its apprentices, whom it vitally interested, for whom "we are such stuff as dreams are made of"—we were obliged to acknowledge that "our revels now are ended," as Prospero also said in the same speech. "Don't tell me!" became the response to our desire to tell our dreams.

I will leave you, then, with two questions: First, can those of us who study literature regenerate, refind our pleasure in that activity at this conference? And second, can this conference rekindle our interest in dreams and in psychoanalysis, so that we can again put it to work in our reading and declare? The days to come will tell.

NOTES

1. Samuel Beckett, *Waiting for Godot,* in Beckett, *I Can't Go On, I'll Go On: A Samuel Beckett Reader* (New York: Grove Press, 1976), 378–79.

2. A discussion of the Irma dream first appears in Shoshana Felman's "Postal Survival, or the Question of the Navel," *The Lesson of Paul de Man,* special issue of *Yale French Studies* 68: 49–72. Felman's work on the Irma dream is amplified in *What Does a Woman Want?* (Baltimore: The Johns Hopkins University Press, 1993).

3. Juliet Mitchell, *Psychoanalysis and Feminism* (New York: Pantheon Books, 1974).

4. Felman, *What Does a Woman Want?* 120.

5. Adam Phillips, *The Beast in the Nursery* (London: Faber, 1998).

6. Jeffrey Mehlman, "French Freud," *Yale French Studies* 48 (1972): 9.

7. Phillips, *Beast in the Nursery,* 56.

Contributors

Willy Apollon is a practicing psychoanalyst. Since the early 1970s, he has worked to introduce Lacanian theory in Québec; he has written frequently on issues fundamental to the practice and theory of psychoanalysis, from questions of psychoanalytic training, the ethics of analytic action, and the logic of psychoanalytic treatment, to the psychoanalytic treatment of the feminine, the pervert, and psychoses. He is a founding member and a past president of Gifric, as well as director of its center for research and training, and he is the consulting psychoanalyst and director of training of the staff at the Center for Psychoanalytic Treatment of Young Psychotic Adults. He has a doctorate in philosophy from the Sorbonne in Paris, and he is on the editorial board of the journal *Savoir.*

Karyn Ball is associate professor of English and film studies at the University of Alberta, Edmonton. She is the editor of *Traumatizing Theory: The Cultural Politics of Affect in and beyond Psychoanalysis,* as well as a special issue of *Cultural Critique* ("Trauma and Its Cultural Aftereffects") and an issue of *Parallax* ("Visceral Reason"). Her essays on critical theory, cultural studies, and the Holocaust have been published in *Cultural Critique, Research in Political Economy, Women in German Yearbook,* and *differences.* Her current project reflects on figurations of melancholy in recent cultural theory.

Raymond Bellour is director of research at the Centre National de la Recherche Scientifique (CNRS) in Paris. His publications include *Jean-Luc Godard: Sound-Image, 1974–1992, The Analysis of Film,* and other books on literature and cinema. With Serge Daney, he launched *Trafic,* a journal of cinema.

Judith Feher-Gurewich practices psychoanalysis in Cambridge, Massachusetts. She is the publisher of Other Press and has written numerous articles on psychoanalysis and the social sciences.

Patricia Gherovici is an analyst in private practice in Philadelphia. She is director of the Philadelphia Lacan Study Group and Seminar and a supervising analyst at Après-Coup, New York. She is author of *The Puerto Rican Syndrome*, which was awarded the 2004 Gradiva Prize of the National Association for the Advancement of Psychoanalysis and the 2004 Boyer Prize of the Society for Psychological Anthropology of the American Anthropological Association.

Jonathan Kahana teaches in the Department of Cinema Studies at New York University. His writing has been published in *Social Text, Afterimage, Film Quarterly,* and *Camera Obscura.* He is writing a book on the public spheres of American documentary cinema.

A. Kiarina Kordela is associate professor in the Department of German at Macalester College. She is the author of *$urplus (Spinoza; Lacan)* and of several essays that have been published in *Cultural Critique, Parallax, Rethinking Marxism,* and *MLS.*

Pablo Kovalovsky, a physician and psychoanalyst, was born in Buenos Aires. He was president of the first Lacanian association in Latin America, the Escuela Freudiana de Buenos Aires, and he has published extensively in psychoanalytic journals in Argentina, Uruguay, Brazil, and the United States. He is editor and director of the psychoanalytic journal *Clínica de Borde.*

Jean Laplanche is a theorist and psychoanalyst. He is best known for his work on psychosexual development and Freud's seduction theory, and he has written many books on psychoanalytic theory. For many years he owned and operated the Château de Pommard winery in Burgundy, France.

Catherine Liu is author of *Copying Machines: Taking Notes for the Automaton* (Minnesota, 2000) and of the novel *Oriental Girls Desire Romance.* She is associate professor of film and media studies, and visual studies and comparative literature, at the University of California, Irvine. She held a Fulbright teaching fellowship at Tainan National University of the Arts in Taiwan and is completing a book on mimesis, critical thinking, and cultural studies.

Mary Lydon was Pickard-Bascom Professor of French at the University of Wisconsin, Madison. Her studies of twentieth-century French literature focused on psychoanalytic, feminist, and poststructuralist theory, and she is author of *Skirting the Issue: Essays in Literary Theory* and *Perpetuum Mobile: A Study of the Novels and Aesthetics of Michel Butor.* She was a member of the Samuel Beckett Society and editor of *The Beckett Circle.* She died in 2001.

Laura Marcus is professor of English at the University of Sussex. Her publications include *Auto/biographical Discourses: Theory, Criticism, Practice, Virginia Woolf*, and, as editor, *Sigmund Freud's "The Interpretation of Dreams": New Interdisciplinary Essays* and (with Peter Nicholls) *The Cambridge History of Twentieth-Century English Literature*. She is completing a book on cinema, literature, and modernity.

Andrew McNamara teaches art history and theory at Queensland University of Technology, Brisbane, Australia. He coedited *Medium Cool* (with Peter Krapp) and *Modernism and Australia: Documents on Art, Design, and Architecture 1917–1967* (with Ann Stephen and Philip Goad).

John Mowitt is professor of English, cultural studies, and comparative literature at the University of Minnesota. He has written numerous books on culture, theory, and politics, most recently *Re-Takes: Postcoloniality and Foreign Film Languages* (Minnesota, 2005). He is coeditor of the journal *Cultural Critique*.

Claire Nahon works as a psychoanalyst in Paris. Her Ph.D. thesis from the University Paris VII—Denis Diderot is on the subject of trans-sexuality. She is the author of several articles and the editor of an issue of the French journal *Cliniques méditerranéennes*, "La trans-sexualité: défiguration, déformation, déchirement."

Yün Peng is a Ph.D. candidate in comparative literature at the University of Minnesota. Her dissertation concerns the culture and literature of the 1980s in China.

Thomas Pepper is a thinking language worker in the Department of Cultural Studies and Comparative Literature at the University of Minnesota.

Gérard Pommier is a psychoanalyst in Paris and a professor at Nantes University. He is author of *How New Sciences Are Proving Psychoanalysis* and *Erotic Anger: A User's Manual* (Minnesota, 2001).

Jean-Michel Rabaté is the Vartan Gregorian Professor in the Humanities at the University of Pennsylvania. He has authored or edited thirty books on modernist authors, psychoanalysis, and literary theory, including *James Joyce and the Politics of Egoism*, *The Future of Theory*, and *The Cambridge Companion to Lacan*.

Laurence A. Rickels is author of *The Vampire Lectures, The Case of California*, and the three-volume *Nazi Psychoanalysis*, as well as editor of *Acting Out in Groups*, all published by the University of Minnesota Press. He teaches at the University of California, Santa Barbara, Art Center College of Design in Pasadena, and at the European Graduate School in Saas Fee, Switzerland.

Avital Ronell has chaired the German department at New York University, where she taught an annual course with Jacques Derrida and directs Trauma and Violence Transdisciplinary Studies with Shireen Patell and Judith Alpert. She was also the Humanities Council Distinguished Visitor at Princeton University. Her most recent book is *The Test Drive*, and she appears in several videos and films, including *Derrida*.

Elke Siegel is assistant professor of German at New York University. She is author of a book on Robert Walser's micrograms and of *Entfernte Freunde*, a study on friendship in Nietzsche, Freud, and Kafka. Her next project examines the diary as a literary interface between experience, writing, and everyday life, with an emphasis on contemporary diary projects.

Jakki Spicer received her Ph.D. in cultural studies and comparative literature at the University of Minnesota. Her writing has been published in *Criticism: A Quarterly for Literature and the Arts*.

Rei Terada is professor of comparative literature at the University of California, Irvine. She is author of *Feeling in Theory: Emotion after the "Death of the Subject."* Her essays on critical theory have appeared recently in *Common Knowledge, ELH,* and *Studies in Romanticism*.

Klaus Theweleit, a long-time associate of the Department of Sociology at the University of Freiburg-im-Breisgau, is professor of theory at the Academy of Arts in Karlsruhe, Germany. His publications include the two volumes of *Male Fantasies* (Minnesota, 1987 and 1989), *Object Choice: All You Need Is Love,* the three volumes of *Das Buch der Könige* (The Book of Kings), and *Der Pocahontas-Komplex* (The Pocahontas Complex), as well as numerous works on music, politics, literature, and the visual arts. With other musicians, he recorded the CD *BST.*

Paul Verhaeghe is senior full professor and chair of the Department of Psychoanalysis at the University of Ghent, Belgium. He is author of *Does the Woman Exist? From Freud's Hysteric to Lacan's Feminine, Love in a Time of Loneliness: Three Essays on Drive and Desire, Beyond Gender: From Subject to Drive,* and *On Being Normal and Other Disorders.*

Silke-Maria Weineck, associate professor of German studies at the University of Michigan, is writing a book on fatherhood that explores paternity as the ambivalent master metaphor of legitimate power, drawing on literary, political, theoretical, legal, and biological discourses at historical crisis points. She is author of *The Abyss Above: Philosophy and Poetic Madness in Plato, Hölderlin, and Nietzsche,* and she has published on Plato, Hölderlin, Shelley, Kleist, Nietzsche, Freud, and Celan.

Index

displacement. *See Interpretation of Dreams, The*

Doane, Mary Anne, 266, 267, 277

Dora. *See* Freud, Sigmund, patients of: Dora

Dostoyevsky, Fyodor, xviii, xviii, 55–70; *The Brothers Karamazov*, 67–68; *The Idiot*, 59–70

Double, The (Rank), 203–4

Dream Analysis (Sharpe), 205

dreams: and awakenings, 221; as "capitalist" to the unconscious, 20, 186; and the Cartesian cogito, 18; of children, 6, 25, 135; and cinema, 197–98, 205, 219–22; the cipher method of interpretation, 288–89; clarity of, 239–42; clarity vs. distinctness, 235–36; and the constitution of knowledge, 23; of the death of a loved one, 97; and desire, 7, 16; differences in intensity of, 235–48; and the dissolution of inner and outer world, 227; and the ego, 17–18, 34, 229; and ethics, 3–10, 11–21, 35–36; and forgetting of, 181, 193; functions of, 136, 186, 228; future orientation of, 292; and historical context, 51; intelligibility of, 235–48; interpretation of, 24, 123, 177–94; and intersubjectivity, xvii, 50; and language, 178, 236, 241–48; and memory, 15, 181, 206, 243–46; narration of, 28, 30, 33–34, 37, 177–94; the narrative of, 8, 24, 27, 246; of the neurotic, 290; of newborns, 6; nightmares, 7, 138, 232; and the occult, 183–84; political elements of, 46, 47; and reality, 216–18; and relation to mental illness, 159; and relation to waking life, 238; and repression, 7, 240; and Satan, 76; and the signifier, 24; the space and time of, 222; and the symbolic method of interpretation, 288, 292; and telepathy, 184; transitional states between sleep and dreams, 206, 209–12; and trimethylamin, 162, 236–37; vivacity of, 237–9; the *Vorbild* of, 159, 163–64; and the unconscious, xvi, 29, 34, 35, 36, 135–36, 177, 193, 246, 310–11. *See also* Freud, Sigmund, dreams of

drive *(Trieb)*, the, xx, 19, 137–38, 140, 321–33; and death, 80; the death drive, 6, 10, 26–28, 31, 32, 65, 80, 81, 93, 142, 306–7, 326; the

genesis of, 188; *Geschlectstriebe*, 163; and instinct, 324; and orality, 175; and the Q-factor, 137; and self-preservation, 163; sexual and nonsexual, 321

ego, xix, 18; as bodily projection, 206; and borderline personality disorder, 165; and dreams, 17–18, 34, 229; and "father-identification," 66; Hartmann's conception of, vs. that of Freud, 165–67; imaginary structure of, 228; and Lacan, 19; and language, 89; and the mirror stage, 48, 52, 166; and repression of the drives, 322; subservience to unconscious, 352

"Ego and the Id, The" (Freud), 206

Ellis, Havelock, 199

Ellroy, James: *Clandestine*, 293–95

epilepsy, 57–68

erotomania, 34

ethics, xv, xvii, 3, 5, 58–59, 67–68; and clinical practice, 29, 31, 36; contrasted to morals, 3; and dreams, 3–10,11–21, 35–36; and Lacan, xvii, 150; and masochism, 58; and overdetermination, 4–5, 11–12, 18; and politics, 58; and repression, 4; and transference, 30, 32, 34–35, 37; and the unconscious, xvii, 3–4, 10

Eudemian Ethics (Aristotle), 106

expiation, 209–10

Fanon, Frantz, 270–80; attitude toward homosexuality, 277; *Black Skin, White Masks*, 270, 275; and colonialism, 272; death of, 278–79; difference between the gaze and ordinary vision, 270; on the Oedipus complex and the black male, 271; theory of the "look," 272, 277

father, the, xvi, 9, 65, 66, 67; and addiction, 65; and ambivalence, 5, 65; analyst as counter-father, 113n36; and Christianity, 78; death of, 97; and God, 107–8; idealization of, xiv; identification with, 9–10; and immortality, 99–102, 106, 124; and Lacan, 107; pre-Oedipal, 75, 79; and Satan, 77, 85–86; and sexual difference, 79; and the Wolf Man, 79